Philosophical Anarchism and Political Obligation

CONTEMPORARY ANARCHIST STUDIES

A series edited by
Laurence Davis, *University College Cork, Ireland*
Uri Gordon, *Loughborough University, UK*
Nathan Jun, *Midwestern State University, USA*
Alex Prichard, *Exeter University, UK*

Contemporary Anarchist Studies promotes the study of anarchism as
a framework for understanding and acting on the most pressing
problems of our times. The series publishes cutting-edge, socially engaged
scholarship from around the world—bridging theory and practice,
academic rigor and the insights of contemporary activism.

The topical scope of the series encompasses anarchist history and
theory broadly construed; individual anarchist thinkers; anarchist informed
analysis of current issues and institutions; and anarchist or
anarchist-inspired movements and practices. Contributions informed
by anti-capitalist, feminist, ecological, indigenous, and non-Western or
global South anarchist perspectives are particularly welcome. So, too,
are manuscripts that promise to illuminate the relationships between the
personal and the political aspects of transformative social change, local
and global problems, and anarchism and other movements and ideologies.
Above all, we wish to publish books that will help activist scholars and
scholar activists think about how to challenge and build real alternatives
to existing structures of oppression and injustice.

Philosophical Anarchism and Political Obligation

Magda Egoumenides

B L O O M S B U R Y

NEW YORK · LONDON · NEW DELHI · SYDNEY

Bloomsbury Academic
An imprint of Bloomsbury Publishing Inc

1385 Broadway
New York
NY 10018
USA

50 Bedford Square
London
WC1B 3DP
UK

www.bloomsbury.com

Bloomsbury is a registered trade mark of Bloomsbury Publishing Plc

First published 2014

© Magda Egoumenides, 2014

Library of Congress Cataloging-in-Publication Data
Egoumenides, Magda.
Philosophical anarchism and political obligation / by Magda Egoumenides.
pages cm. – (Contemporary anarchist studies)
Includes bibliographical references and index.
ISBN 978-1-4411-9357-5 (hardback) – ISBN 978-1-4411-4411-9 (paperback) –
ISBN 978-1-4411-2445-6 (ePub) – ISBN 978-1-4411-5182-7 (ePDF) 1. Political obligation.
2. Legitimacy of governments. 3. Authority. 4. State, The.
5. Anarchism–Philosophy. I. Title.
JC329.5.E46 2014
320.01–dc23
2014002159

ISBN: HB: 978-1-4411-9357-5
PB: 978-1-4411-4411-9
ePub: 978-1-4411-2445-6
ePDF: 978-1-4411-5182-7

Typeset by Integra Software Services Pvt. Ltd.
Printed and bound in the United States of America

For my beloved parents

The true exile is never *at home.*
Paul McLaughlin, Anarchism and Authority:
A Philosophical Introduction to Classical Anarchism *(Farnham:*
Ashgate, 2007), 78.

The state is a condition, a certain relationship among
human beings, a mode of behaviour between men;
we destroy it by constructing other relationships, by behaving
differently toward one another.

Gustav Landauer, "Schwache Stattsmänner, Schwacheres Volk!"
Der Sozialist, *June, 1910.*

CONTENTS

PREFACE

In this study I define and defend critical philosophical anarchism, showing it to be superior to alternative approaches to the problem of the justification of political institutions. In particular, I lay out and examine the critical philosophical anarchist approach to the problem of political obligation, contrasting this approach with traditional treatments of the problem. The anarchist stance within the contemporary debate on political obligation has been dismissed too easily. I advance a clearer statement of the critical philosophical anarchist position than those currently available and demonstrate the continued value of adopting an anarchist perspective on the problem of political authority.

This study has nine chapters. In the Introduction, I set out my argument and the anarchist position I want to defend. The first chapter presents the problem of political obligation, the main aspects of this central problem and the main argument for the solution that I develop in the following chapters. Chapter 2 provides an analysis and restatement of anarchist arguments against consent and contract theories of political obligation. Chapter 3 offers considerations against a natural duty theory of political obligation. Chapter 4 addresses a reciprocity-based theory of political obligation, to wit, the principle of fairness as formulated by Hart and Rawls. The fifth chapter presents John Horton's distinctive theory in an effort to demonstrate its value in the debate. Chapter 6 illustrates in general the distinctive contribution of critical philosophical anarchism to the problem of political authority, completing the argument set out in the Introduction and Chapter 1 and developed in the preceding critical chapters on the different defenses of political obligation. In Chapter 7 I connect the perspective of critical philosophical anarchism on the main tasks and aims of political anarchism with a more comprehensive anarchist political theory and approach to society. In the conclusion I tie together my argument for critical philosophical anarchism as developed over the course of the study.

ACKNOWLEDGMENTS

This study is the result of a series of arguments about and discussions on the issue of political authority. I am indebted to those who inspired my thinking and helped me formulate the ideas presented. They are too many to mention.

I would like to thank the series editors of Contemporary Anarchist Studies, especially Dr Alex Prichard and Assistant Professor Nathan Jun, and the team in Bloomsbury, especially Ally Jane Grossan and Kaitlin Fontana, for giving me the wonderful opportunity to write this book and having it published, as well as Rajakumari Ganessin for her help in the process. I would like to express my gratitude to my friends and ex- PhD supervisors Professor Véronique Munoz-Dardé and Professor Jonathan Wolff for their continual advice, encouragement, and devotion. Furthermore, I would like to thank Professor Christopher Schabel for his support.

I am grateful to my parents for their endless love and support.

I would like to thank Professor Vassos Karageorghis, my mentor, for his constant support and influence on me; and Dr Meropi Tsimili, who has been a mother, a teacher, and a real friend to me.

Special thanks to my dear cousins Penelope and Matthew Papapetrou, George and Michael Christodoulides, as well as my dear friends Raj Sehgal, James Wilson, Saladin Meckled-Garcia, Ian Hulse, Isabella Muzio, Sara Santa-Clara, Tawny Gray, Sharon Shatil, Alex Voorhoeve, Andreas Onoufriou, Rena Choplarou, Giorgos Stogias, Lena Ioannou, Maria Michael Constantina Zanou, Maria Polychronopoulou, Maria Rammata, Miltos Karkazis, Manos Farmakis, Marius Nabal, Melina Argyriou, Katerina Mansfield, Nancy Thomaidou Agamemnon Zakos, and Paris Papagiorgis for providing the intellectual, moral, and emotional background that enabled this work and for their continued belief in me.

Introduction

According to Anarchism, relations of domination are immoral. The coercion and exploitation of one individual by another is unjustified, as is the control of the individual by a collective, such as the state. The values of freedom and equality are paramount. A strand of anarchism expresses these positions within the philosophical debate on political obligation, and this has a distinct impact on our approach to political institutions.

Anarchism is *"scepticism towards authority."*[1] Its unifying position is that not all forms of authority are justified and we should be skeptical about any acceptance of them prior to their satisfactory justification. One form of authority that anarchists consider unjustified is the political authority of the state.[2] Opposition to the state's *right to rule*, although a non-definitive anarchist concern, is common to all forms of anarchism and its proponents, despite the variety and division among them. The rejection of the state's right to rule relates to the stronger anarchist challenge to its *right to exist*. This challenge is the upshot of political anarchism, which maintains that the state must be *resisted* as an *evil* and a new social form must emerge that succeeds the state and constitutes an improvement on societies organized around the state. Thus, in order to pave the way for a complete evaluation of anarchism, including the project of political anarchism, it is helpful to examine first the principled rejection of political authority that philosophical anarchism proposes and to detail the positive views, if any, that it expresses. My strategy throughout this study will be to examine this challenge as formulated within the debate on political obligation.

In this introduction, I briefly describe four basic forms of anarchism by way of a preface in order to clarify the theoretical perspective of critical philosophical anarchism that I defend, placing it in the context of the current debate on anarchism. Then I discuss the main parts of my argument and a number of underlying ideas that help us assess the general contribution of philosophical anarchism to the problem of political authority.

The variety of anarchisms: Defining critical philosophical anarchism within the current debate on anarchism

I begin with the discussion of *different forms of anarchism*. There are many lines of anarchism, which divide the tradition in different ways. One division is that between gradualist and revolutionary anarchism, which refers to the path toward change that anarchists advocate. Another division is between pacifist and terrorist anarchism, drawn according to the revolutionary methods that anarchists adopt (whether they use peaceful means, like social reconstruction, or violence, like some forms of propaganda by deed, respectively). These divisions refer mostly to political anarchism, however, and the main logic of any such division remains the same: it concerns primarily the revolutionary methods and the form of economic organization that each school proposes.[3] Generally, there is a huge debate around the forms of anarchism and some conclude in favor of an "anarchism without adjectives." My focus is on the position that each form of anarchism adopts with regard to the two fundamental problems concerning the state: its right to exist and its right to rule. For the purposes of my argument, I want to distinguish between political anarchism and philosophical anarchism. While the second one refers to a very specific debate in philosophy, which I examine here, the first one refers to practically everything else. The first one can be further divided into individualist and communal (or social) anarchism and the second one into positive (a priori) and negative (a posteriori) anarchism. As a result, we have four main forms of anarchism. These categorizations serve mostly as clarifications of the main tendencies involved in the anarchist approach to the fundamental issue of political authority. The taxonomy is not exhaustive and the overlaps are important. Political anarchists can be philosophical and vice versa and, in the end, outside the specific debate over political obligation, the distinguishing characteristic of political anarchism is that it is also practical. The discussion below consists of a brief description of each form of anarchism in order to arrive at a basic account of the anarchist position that I discuss throughout this study.

Political Anarchism is primarily devoted to the task of demolishing the state. It sees this task as an immediate implication of the rejection of political authority. But this form of anarchism also views the state as a very bad form of social organization, a reason for opposition in addition to its belief that the state's existence and authority remain unjustified. Correspondingly, this critique of the state is premised on a vision of social life without political institutions. *Philosophical Anarchism*, on the other hand, concentrates on the critique of political authority and does not necessarily require the abolition of the state. This latter characteristic is reflected in the fact that negative philosophical anarchism is compatible with "a wide range of alternative political outlooks,"[4] as will become clear below. Many anarchists are both philosophical and political, but a philosophical anarchist may remain nonpolitical.

Political Individualist Anarchism is marked by its emphasis on a central aspect of anarchism: the commitment to individual autonomy, or freedom,[5] as a primary value. It promotes the idea that each individual has an "inviolable sphere of action" with absolute sovereignty.[6] It views social relationships as interactions among independent beings, able to lead their lives abstracted from their social environment and its impacts.[7] This leads individualist anarchists to indicate the importance of voluntariness in any relation to, and interaction with, others and to attack political obligation on the grounds that states are not based on voluntary relations. They thus see them as coercive, exploitative, and evil.

Political Communal (or Social)[8] *Anarchism* has roots in socialism, but it nonetheless differs from other socialist ideologies, especially in their devotion to politically centralized forms of organization and control (if not always as ends, at least as means toward an ideal society).[9] Communal anarchism stresses "the social character of human life": the value of community, mutuality, free cooperation, and, in the general case, social arrangements of a reciprocal character.[10] Its proponents have devoted themselves to developing visions of society that involve a series of cooperative enterprises in every aspect of social life (economic, cultural, educational, etc.)[11] and that are offered as alternatives to views of society that include the state as an essential element. These visions are accompanied by the (anarchist) rejection of coercive schemes and are based on reasonably optimistic views of human nature[12] and accounts of morality.

Moving to *Philosophical Anarchism*, I begin with some terminological points in order to arrive at the view I want to defend. Horton distinguishes between *positive* and *negative* philosophical anarchism.[13] Positive anarchism is the stronger, since it provides an explanation for the moral impossibility of the state and thus of political obligation. Negative anarchism is weaker, for it relies merely on "justification by default": the failure of all attempts to provide supportive accounts of political obligation is taken to be reason enough for denying the existence of such an obligation, even though no "positive" analysis of why such attempts are bound to fail is provided.[14] These terms correspond to a certain extent to Simmons's notions of "*a priori*" and "*a posteriori*" anarchism. A priori anarchism states that the impossibility of legitimacy is inherent in the nature of the state, that some essential feature of the state makes it impossible for it to be legitimate. For Robert Paul Wolff, for example, state authority is necessarily incompatible with individual autonomy. In general, a priori philosophical anarchists are motivated by prior commitments—e.g., to voluntarism, to egalitarianism, or to communalism—that, on their view, the state contradicts fundamentally.[15] In contrast, the claim of a posteriori anarchism that "all existing states are illegitimate" is based mainly on empirical observations of actual states, rather than on an argument that there is some inconsistency, or incoherence, in the *possibility* of a legitimate state, although this form of anarchism is pessimistic about this possibility.[16] This is a central reason why a posteriori anarchism does not necessarily lead to political anarchism, why its project is presented as mainly one of theoretical criticism and of enlightenment, and why it leaves room, in many cases, for obedience to particular laws and for the justification of particular obligations on the part of different individuals.

In this study I focus on the negative side of philosophical anarchism, intending to evaluate its contribution to the debate on political authority. For this, I adopt an alternative terminology, using it to structure the debate. I focus on what I call "*critical philosophical anarchism*,"[17] defining it through a combination of the features of the definitions just explained (those of Horton and Simmons above) that I find the most characteristic of the anarchist position that is to be assessed. From negative philosophical anarchism I keep the characteristic that it is a theoretical view, grounded in criticisms of the failures of accounts of political obligation. Yet I do not deny that this view's criticisms are determined by a prior analysis of what is involved in an adequate justification. From a posteriori philosophical anarchism, I take this: Simmons argues that a posteriori anarchism is not based merely on justification by default, but that it is rooted "either in an ideal of legitimacy (which existing states can be shown not to exemplify) or in some account of what an acceptably complete positive attempt [to justify political obligation] would look like."[18] This feature works as a normative horizon for evaluating theoretical defenses of political obligation: a prior standard in reference to which a posteriori anarchism derives its negative conclusions about political obligation and political institutions. These conclusions stem from the failures of the defenses of political obligation and from what these failures reflect about reality.

Given the above two features, I define "critical philosophical anarchism" as the view that examines the best candidates for moral theories of political obligation and derives *from their failure*, as a constructive conclusion of its own, the result that there is no general political obligation and that in this respect political institutions remain unjustified. Operative in this approach is a prior standard of theoretical criticism merged with *some idea of what an ideal legitimate society should be like*. The main input of this standard is to stress what political societies must *not* be like in order to be considered legitimate. Critical philosophical anarchism considers all existing states to be illegitimate insofar as they fail to meet this ideal, especially the demand for non-domination. In this it is in line with political anarchism. In the end, the position of critical philosophical anarchism is a mix of philosophical and political anarchism.

My aim is to examine this anarchist position closely as it figures within the debate on political obligation, in order to demonstrate that it offers something valuable to the perspective we have toward political institutions and our relation to them, and to determine this contribution. I stress both its critical perspective and its ideal of legitimacy, because I see them as defining features of this position, incorporating the elements that are of essential value in the arguments of philosophical anarchism against political obligation.

These parameters are envisaged as compatible with certain valuable features of social anarchism. In fact, this compatibility is not limited to social, or communal, anarchism. It is, to my mind, necessary in any anarchist vision that displays two features of communal anarchism, namely, on the one hand, its recognition of the social dimension of human beings and, on the other, its idea of free social relationships and decentralized, cooperative forms of social order along with attention to matters of economic equality and distribution. Such perspectives are found in contemporary writings of anarchist conviction, such as Murray Bookchin's "Libertarian Municipalism," Alan Carter's "Towards a Green Political Theory,"[19] Samuel Clark's *Living Without Domination: The Possibility of an Anarchist Utopia*,[20] Benjamin Franks's *Rebel Alliances: The Means and Ends of Contemporary British Anarchisms*,[21] Uri Gordon's *Anarchy Alive*, and Peter Marshall's "Human Nature and Anarchism." The essentially social character of human life is reflected both in anarchist proposals for free social relationships and in the claims regarding the defects of relations of domination. These claims have important implications for defenses of the state in light of its coercive character and its underlying corruption.[22] Communal anarchism contains a positive project, namely the establishment of human cooperative relations free of both domination and exploitation. But its relation to coercion appears unclear and problematic, because it seems to re-introduce coercive structures, tactics, and attitudes in its visions of social reconstruction.[23] The most demanding project of anarchist theory would consist of a combination of the communal anarchist ideal with the attack on coercion reflected in the exacting perspective and standard of legitimacy that critical philosophical anarchism defines. This study will therefore attempt to prepare the way for this combination. In particular, I will aim at understanding what the implied perspective of philosophical anarchism is and at indicating how it might be applied to the positive horizon of political social anarchism.[24]

The anarchist enters the debate on political obligation with a concern about freedom, which is immediately related to its attack on domination and dominative authority. He concentrates on the importance for individuals to be self-governed, to be able to have a say on and determine the main aspects of their own lives. But how can this be compatible with external constraints? The respect for self-government and the rejection of constraints are characteristic anarchist tenets, each of which might take, and at times has taken, priority over the other within the anarchist tradition. Still, an anarchist can insist on the priority of freedom and criticize political institutions without any prior rejection of constraints in general. The anarchist is sensitive to the fact that most *political* constraints create problems for self-determination. It is with this realization that the critical philosophical anarchist criticizes the way traditional defenses of political institutions work. What he wants to point out is that, if these defenses start with a different perspective on political institutions, one that involves centrally the task of requiring and showing a positive relation between institutions and self-determination, they will address more successfully the difficulties that they face in their efforts to justify political reality. The debate, and with it our relation to the state, can then develop in a different light, which will provide more fruitful ways of assessing political institutions. These are the significant features of the position of critical philosophical anarchism, features that it is the task of this study to explain and defend.

Before moving on to present the argument and the underlying ideas of this work, I would like to refer briefly to certain categories of anarchist thought that continue to form the debate within the anarchist arena today and to which critical philosophical anarchism might be related in some significant way. This will help situate this latter form of anarchism within the current debate on anarchism, preparing the way for the more general current anarchist concerns that will be discussed in Chapter 7 and in the conclusion of the book.

The first category is *New Anarchism*, as it is rooted in Errico Malatesta's thought[25] and appears today in the work of Noam Chomsky.[26] Based on Bakuninian ideas and Kropotkinian orthodoxy, Malatesta's critique of mainstream anarchism marked the transition from classical to new anarchism. Although greatly influenced by those major anarchist thinkers, Malatesta moved from their preoccupation with big ideas, their intellectual reverence for Marx, and their excessive revolutionary optimism (and the dogmatism related to it) to a more practical outlook that was pragmatically engaged with the realization of a just society.[27] Despite criticisms that this activism encouraged intellectual incoherence and simplicity, new anarchists made theoretical advances and their thought prefigured the New Left and its reorientation toward social analysis and cultural critique. Emma Goldman's anarcho-feminism is a characteristic example.[28] At present, Noam Chomsky is the most representative contemporary new anarchist. He has not developed a general theory of anarchism and he sees anarchism more as a historically developed trend, sharing Malatesta's suspicion of the creation of big theoretical systems. Yet he has contributed to anarchism a sharp social and political criticism, with his analysis of the role of propaganda in determining the opinion of people regarding economic issues, international relations, and war affairs. Above all, Chomsky has developed a profound critique of the propaganda of the media as a method of social control in "open" societies, which indicates the influence of power and wealth on the way Western media handle information and specifies the various relevant determining factors.[29]

Chomsky offers a parallel at the practical level to the thorough criticism that, as argued here, critical philosophical anarchism offers at the theoretical level. The latter can be compatible also with the concerns of genuine forms of individualist anarchism, such as that of Marx Stirner[30] and of our contemporary Herbert Read,[31] who refers to the priority of the aesthetic development of the individual, of a creative individuality free of all forms of social oppression. Furthermore, critical philosophical anarchism can be inspired by postmodern anarchism, as it appears in the work of Todd May and Saul Newman, in its focus on social critique and change rather than just political or economic.[32]

In my opinion, however, critical philosophical anarchism's compatibility with social anarchism and its concerns with the social and political implications of its criticism of obligation can better be seen in its connection with another category of contemporary anarchist thought: the *neo-classical eco-anarchism* as it appears in the work of Murray Bookchin and of Alan Carter. Critical philosophical anarchists can develop their own micropolitics of power. It is nevertheless important to examine the relation of this kind of anarchism to the most promising contemporary implementations of anarchist visions and practices rooted in the concern with free and equal social relationships found in social anarchism, to carry its principles even further to meet present demands and correct past prejudices. Bookchin's theory is promising to this end. I will examine a significant part of it in Chapter 7 and relate it to David Pepper's discussion of anarchist practices. Since this theory also has its shortcomings, however, and because in this study the focus is on the contribution of critical philosophical anarchism, I will evaluate it with reference to this anarchist perspective. I will apply the critical philosophical anarchist test of legitimacy to Bookchin's account. I will complete my discussion with an examination of certain ideas found in the contemporary work on existing anarchist structures, tactics, and practices advanced by Samuel Clark,[33] Benjamin Franks,[34] and Uri Gordon,[35] which renders a wider picture of contemporary anarchist utopianism.

The main parts and underlying ideas of my argument

In the rest of this introduction, I present the main parts of my argument and the considerations that underlie my program.

My aim is to provide a theoretical defense of critical philosophical anarchism. My argument is that *the main perspective and ideas of critical philosophical anarchism can be appealing to anybody*, whether they are anarchists or not. I myself am not a self-proclaimed anarchist. Nevertheless, my opinion is that the critical philosophical anarchist position on political obligation is correct and that the virtues of this view make an examination and acknowledgment of its contribution worthwhile.

Critical philosophical anarchism has been criticized as mere skepticism: as a purely negative view, it works as a denial of positive defenses of political institutions without offering an alternative positive proposition of its own.[36]

Without denying its theoretical function (which I retain and stress in my definition of critical philosophical anarchism), one of my main concerns is to argue that this view involves something more positive than it first appears to do: I aim to show that the arguments of critical philosophical anarchism express *a prior perspective*. This perspective is characteristically anarchist in its motivating concerns and its proposals, one that is also indispensable for theorists of political obligation and necessary for the evaluation of institutions more generally. A closer analysis of anarchist arguments against defenses of political obligation is the first step toward my objective. The four conditions for theories of political obligation that the anarchist employs in his arguments, which I will present in the next chapter (the section "The conditions of political obligation"), play a central role within this analysis for understanding the anarchist perspective. These formal requirements define characteristic features of the political nature of the obligations to be examined. In fact, taken *together* these conditions *express* this political nature itself, that is, the particularistic, coercive, centralist, permanent, and exclusive character of the institutions to which these obligations relate. This nature is defined by "the theses on the political," which will also be presented in Chapter 1 (the section "The two main aspects of the problem of political obligation"). In my effort to explain the anarchist perspective, I use this point to make explicit how "the conditions of political obligation," being difficult to dispense with, become useful vehicles for very valuable yet neglected elements of the anarchist position, that their formality nevertheless leads to wide-ranging moral conclusions. In part, the examination of anarchist criticisms of political obligation serves to establish (the role of) these conditions as definitive of the link between the political and the moral feature of the problem of political obligation (which will also be analyzed in the section "The two main aspects of the problem of political obligation" of Chapter 1). I employ this point to demonstrate the value of the philosophical anarchist perspective. The crux of my argument is that the anarchist perspective involves an insight that everyone needs to share. It indicates that the lack of a special relationship that characterizes political institutions (which exists when the conditions of political obligation are satisfied) raises a fundamental question as to whether they can exist and function at all.

The anarchist *ideal of legitimacy*, as part of the definition of critical philosophical anarchism (see the section "The variety of anarchisms. Defining critical philosophical anarchism within the current debate on anarchism" above), is another aspect of this anarchist view that I attempt to evaluate, which will play a central role in my argument for its positive contribution. Philosophical anarchists defend voluntarist, communitarian, egalitarian, and ecological visions of the ideal society.[37] Because these visions are not dominating models of society, they serve as indications of the proper relations that institutions must have in order to be legitimate and justified in the eyes of human beings. Characteristically, these ideals are also in constant interaction with the social visions of political anarchism. The fact that such ideals underlie the arguments of critical philosophical anarchism provides another factor explaining the positive character of this form of anarchism. Both the anarchist social visions and the anarchist attacks on the state aspire to a better understanding of human nature and society and to an assessment of human actions, relations, and achievements that is compatible with the most commonly shared moral values. I endorse the claim that anarchists are concerned with *"the quality of relations between people,"* namely with defending and realizing within society direct and many-sided relations, characterized by reciprocity and equal authority and participation.[38] This is a ground that can be shared by many anti-authoritarian and nonauthoritarian theorists,[39] with or without anarchist convictions. Furthermore, the arguments that bring the defenders of the state and anarchists into conflict refer to issues of an explicitly social character.[40] The positive horizon defined by political communal (or social) anarchism provides a suitable background for addressing these concerns. I want to argue, however, that this horizon is compatible with and in fact already incorporated within the challenge of critical philosophical anarchism. Political social anarchists oppose the state not only because of its illegitimacy, but also because of its essentially dominative, coercive, corruptive, and therefore *evil* character. But this characterization of the state as evil is not an essential element of philosophical anarchism, although it may play a part in certain philosophical anarchist views. It is necessary to combine a diagnostic of what goes wrong in domination and coercion, as expressed in philosophical anarchist views, with an explicit prescriptive horizon of harmonious social relations. The required link might be found in a theoretical account that includes a properly articulated ideal of legitimacy that will set a standard, elements of which must be met by any vision of society. I want to argue that we would all, on reflection, probably agree with the anarchist on the question of the values needed to defend obligation and institutions. In examining different theories of political obligation in their dialogue with the anarchist perspective, I will approach them with respect to different instances of the anarchist ideal of legitimacy. A related central aim is to carry the role of the ideal of legitimacy further: I will examine how, more generally, it can make the task of the justification of political institutions harder. I will consider how the debate as defined by the anarchist and its results for political obligation might affect further defenses of constraints even within a background presupposing that we need, and remain with, political institutions. The extension of the role of the anarchist ideal of legitimacy in this study is an analysis of the anarchist perspective's effect on any justification of constraints. More precisely, the ideal standards, in the light of the failure to justify political obligation, help further evaluations of institutions by imposing the relevant moral criteria as principled conditions on existing and newly arising forms of domination. It will be proved that voluntariness, justice, fairness, and association cannot ground political obligation, but they can determine the value of political institutions more generally. Thus the anarchist contribution to the political debate will be estimated both with regard to what it offers to the debate on political obligation itself and with respect to the implications of the results of this debate for more general evaluations of political institutions. In these functions, the ideal of legitimacy and the anarchist criticisms become two expressions of one comprehensive view.

This view states primarily that legitimacy is *exigent* because it is difficult to see how political institutions can meet the requirements of the moral forms of the standard of legitimacy. The conditions of political obligation become themselves reflections of the relation between the two expressions of the anarchist view, the criticism that it advances and the ideal of legitimacy that it offers. As I claimed above, these conditions reflect the political nature of obligation and help in determining the positive character of the anarchist conclusions against political obligation. This is parallel to the function of the ideal of legitimacy as a standard for moral relations that institutions, with their political character, fail to meet. This standard is merged with a theoretical account of what an acceptably complete defense of political obligation must include, which may be identified as a successful combination of the four formal conditions with the different moral bases of political obligation.[41] Thus one could say that the elements of the debate on political obligation as provided by anarchism and its ideal of legitimacy become alternative expressions of a unique outlook. If the anarchist conclusions about political obligation are correct, both the four conditions that constrain accounts of political obligation and the ideals reflecting proper social relations that states fail to meet indicate something about the political that every theorist must attend to—and they provide the way for doing so. The defenders of political institutions *assume what they should seek to prove*: they focus on the merits of political institutions and attempt to derive political obligation from them. Instead, they should address the prior question about what institutions demand of us and whether these demands are justified. Political institutions cease to be viewed as lovable, and they need to be tested *continually* on the basis of *the problems* they create.

The category of *transactional evaluations* of institutions, which will be introduced in the section "Quality-based and interaction-based evaluations of political institutions" of Chapter 1, is also relevant to the combinations presently suggested. In the following chapters, it will become clear that the anarchist ideals of legitimacy reflect the relations that would be involved in a society that met transactional evaluations. Moreover, the anarchist's prior idea of an acceptably complete positive attempt to justify political obligation would successfully combine the four formal conditions with a moral principle, a combination that is no more than a theoretical reflection, defining the anarchist criticisms, of the application of proper social relations. In terms of the traditional defenses of the state, the different versions of the ideal preserve the demand that any defense of that kind should make clear that the four conditions of political obligation are satisfied. Thus transactional evaluations, the ideal of legitimacy, and an account of a comprehensive theory of political obligation may be seen as three different expressions of a perspective already underlying the anarchist challenge. Together these features comprise the anarchist position that I aim to explain and defend.

Critical philosophical anarchism is mainly engaged in what Miller calls the "*subversive campaign*" of philosophical anarchism.[42] As Simmons highlights, it encourages a substantial revision of our conception of ordinary political life.[43] More specifically, it questions a common-sense conception of the relationship between governments and their citizens in terms of political obligation. While philosophical anarchists accept the traditional understanding of political obligation as a special relationship with our own governments, they deny its existence. This entails the rejection of a general moral attitude toward the state and the adoption of a critical stance from which the propriety of obedience to the law is assessed on a case-by-case basis.[44] Raz, who also denies the existence of general political obligation, proposes another possible attitude, namely "respect for law," which can apply in the absence of such an obligation, and he supports a possible special relationship between institutions and those who adopt that attitude.[45] For philosophical anarchists, such as Simmons, however, even the anarchist denial of a special political relationship and an insistence on a critical stance will not result in widespread disobedience. Indeed, Simmons claims that our political lives will not change radically at the practical level.[46] Horton makes a crucial point with regard to the last claim. He argues that change in our ordinary thinking about "political relations," i.e., that which construes such relations in terms of political obligations, will have "*radical*" effects on the way we usually talk about our relation to our governments as ours and, through this, on our "political relationships" and lives.[47] Thus, he conceives the challenge of philosophical anarchism as a dangerously radical one: it is "the subversion of political relationships through undermining the shared understandings which are constitutive of such relationships."[48] That is why Horton wants to undermine philosophical anarchism. I disagree with Horton's attempt and, following Simmons, I also reject the claim that a shift in our conception of our political relationships will entail widespread disobedience and chaos. The reason for this is that we have to work with existing institutions and build the new in the shell of the old. Yet I agree with Horton that such a shift can affect radically our political relationships and lives. In my opinion, philosophical anarchism both requires drastic revision in our thinking about political relations and entails radical change in our political lives. However, I see this as a positive effect of the anarchist perspective.

This claim leads to a final point. The anarchist criticisms and ideal of legitimacy explain *the link between philosophical and political anarchism*: they remind us that the enduring deficiency of the state is a position that is initially shared by both forms of anarchism, and the moral criteria of philosophical anarchism are intended to be inherent in the society that political anarchism seeks to create. A demonstration of the compatibility of political anarchist social visions with the perspective and ideals of legitimacy of critical philosophical anarchism establishes a continuity within the anarchist ideology. Such a demonstration is necessary as a test on both sides of anarchism. It would provide the required combination of a diagnostic of what goes wrong with coercion with an explicit positive horizon of non-dominative harmonious social relations. I will make an attempt at this combination in the final chapters of this study.

I proceed, then, as follows: in Chapter 1 I present the overall aim and structure of my argument in this book. More precisely, the role of the first chapter is to present in more detail the problem of political obligation and the main arguments that will be developed in the following chapters. Then, in Chapters 2–5, I provide an examination of the arguments for political obligation as scrutinized from the perspective of critical philosophical anarchism. This task must be completed in order to understand the anarchist criticism. In Chapter 2 I will examine the anarchist criticisms of voluntarist theories of political obligation. In Chapter 3 the object of criticism will be a justice-based theory. Chapter 4 will look at the anarchist dialogue with a reciprocity-based theory, to wit, the principle of fairness as formulated by Hart and by Rawls. Chapter 5 will present Horton's theory of associative obligations, mainly as a valuable view within the debate rather than as a complete theory of political obligation. The main strategy in these chapters is to extract from anarchist arguments valid claims that will form the basis of my analysis of the anarchist contribution. The focus of this strategy will be the perspective and ideal as well as the arguments about self-government, proper relations, and political constraints that characterize critical philosophical anarchism. I will then move in Chapter 6 to a direct defense of the distinctive contribution of critical philosophical anarchism as derived from the debate on political obligation. I will analyze the character and claims of the special perspective involved in the anarchist position, examining the role of this perspective and of the ideal of legitimacy in improving accounts of the justification of constraints more generally. In Chapter 7, I will examine the tasks of political anarchism in the light of the contribution of critical philosophical anarchism. In the conclusion I will provide an overview of the anarchist contribution as defended in this study.

Notes

1   Paul McLaughlin, *Anarchism and Authority: A Philosophical Introduction to Classical Anarchism* (Farnham: Ashgate, 2007), esp. Chapter 2, 29–36.

2   Although "'anti-statism' does not define anarchism," because anarchists challenge authoritative relations other than, within, and alongside the state (McLaughlin, *Anarchism and Authority*, 97), the anarchist challenge involves opposition to the authority of *the state*, which focuses on the state's special characteristics as "a specific form of government," namely its being a "*sovereign*," "*compulsory*," "*monopolistic*," and "*distinct* body" (see David Miller, *Anarchism* [London: Dent, 1984], 5). But anarchism's opposition to the state reflects its more general opposition to political authority and the institutionalized coercion that characterizes it (for these, see Miller, *Anarchism*, 5, and my characterization of the "political" below), although not necessarily to a looser sense of political society as a form of social organization. So, in its core, anarchism objects to the authority of all political phenomena, institutions, and practices that involve institutionalized coercion. In the rest of this study I will use the term "state" interchangeably with "political institutions" (or "political constraints") and "institutionalized coercion" (or "institutionalized domination") to designate the object of the anarchist opposition to political authority. For political authority and the state, see also McLaughlin, *Anarchism and Authority*, 74–80. For discussion of the state in relation to its "specific organs" (such as the police, bureaucracy, the law, and the army) and especially of the five factors of governmental action in modern states (giant-sized central administration, coordination of big business, technological dominance, eroded bureaucracy, and war), see April Carter, *The Political Theory of Anarchism* (London: Routledge and Kegan Paul, 1971), Chapter 2; the section "Anarchist approaches to concrete dilemmas" of Chapter 7 and Conclusion of this book. See also a relevant discussion of "enforcement" by Uri Gordon, *Anarchy Alive: Anti-Authoritarian Politics from Practice to Theory* (London: Pluto Press, 2008), 67–69: the features of enforcement that make it an objectionable form of coercion are also features of the institutionalized coercion of the state. On these lines, capitalism is a central form of domination that anarchists object to.

3   For these, see George Woodcock, *Anarchism: A History of Libertarian Ideas and Movements* (Harmondsworth: Penguin, 1975), 19; McLaughlin, *Anarchism and Authority*, 2.

4   John Horton, *Political Obligation* (London: Macmillan, 1992, revised 2nd edition in 2010), 132.

5   In the sense that each individual has a capacity and right to be "self-legislating" (Robert Paul Wolff, *In Defense of Anarchism* [London and New York: Harper and Row, 1970], 14), to make and act on his/her own decisions—as long as these do "not violate the similar rights of others" (Horton, *Political Obligation*, 115) and "avoid causing dramatic social harm" (Alan John Simmons, *On the Edge of Anarchy* [Princeton: Princeton University Press, 1993], 267). At a basic level, freedom can be conceived as the ability to make choices on various issues of one's life under circumstances

of the lack of coercion of any kind, adequate knowledge, and unimpaired capacity for rational deliberation. Anarchists construe freedom in striking opposition to domination and coercion. In individualist anarchism, absence of coercion is seen primarily as the lack of interference in a private sphere of individual life. For a unique individualist anarchist view of freedom and its replacement with what is meant by "ownness," see Max Stirner, *The Ego and Its Own*, ed. David Leopold (Cambridge: Cambridge University Press, 1995), 145–146 and 154. See also Crispin Sartwell, *Against the State: An Introduction to Anarchist Political Theory* (Albany: State University of New York Press, 2008), esp. Chapter 5, for a certain sort of individualist anarchism. More generally, anarchism is committed to the ideal of self-determination understood best as self-development under conditions of proper social relationships, where subordination of some to others is replaced with mutual respect, equal active participation, and common flourishing. Here the absence of subordination and coercion becomes a matter of the denial of domination that engages with aspects more comprehensive than the negative demands of individualist anarchism.

6   Miller, *Anarchism*, 30.

7   "Self-made" and "self-sufficient"; see Horton, *Political Obligation*, 116–117.

8   Throughout this study, I will use the terms "communal anarchism" and "social anarchism" interchangeably.

9   See, for example, the split between Marx and Bakunin: James Joll, *The Anarchists* (London: Methuen, 1964), Chapter 4; McLaughlin, *Anarchism and Authority*, 158.

10   For these notions, see Miller, *Anarchism*, chapters 4 and 12; Horton, *Political Obligation*, 119–120.

11   For example, Petr Alekseevich Kropotkin, *The Conquest of Bread and Other Writings*, ed. Shatz Marshall (Cambridge: Cambridge University Press, 1995 [reprint of 1913 revised edition]); Petr Alekseevich Kropotkin, *Fields, Factories and Workshops Tomorrow* (London: George Allen and Unwin, 1974); Petr Alekseevich Kropotkin, *Mutual Aid: A Factor of Evolution* (Boston: Extending Horizons Books, 1955); Murray Bookchin, *Toward an Ecological Society* (Montreal: Black Rose Books, 1980); Murray Bookchin, "Libertarian Municipalism," in *The Murray Bookchin Reader*, ed. Janet Biehl (London and Washington: Cassell, 1997), 172–196.

12   For an approach to the notion of human nature, its use in the anarchist tradition, and its role in the anarchist theory, see Peter Marshall, "Human Nature and Anarchism," in *For Anarchism: History, Theory, and Practice*, ed. David Goodway (London and New York: Routledge, 1989), 127–149. His proposal of abandoning the idea of human nature as a "fixed essence" (Marshall, "Human Nature and Anarchism," 138) and of viewing the human species in an evolutionary way, taking into account the continual interaction of many aspects in it and their capacity for "self-regulation" within open possibilities (Marshall, "Human Nature and Anarchism," 139–144), expresses a view of human nature that is compatible with the position of this study. On similar lines, but even more compatible with our position and more radical, is the view of the self as a "kernel of nothingness" serving as a canvas for constant recreation, developed in the theory of the idiosyncratic classical

anarchist Max Stirner and adopted and expanded by poststructuralist thinkers such as Michel Foucault and the anarchist Saul Newman; see Stirner *The Ego and Its Own*; Michel Foucault, *Discipline and Punish: The Birth of Prison*, trans. Alan Sheridan (London: Penguin, 1991); Michel Foucault, "The Ethics of the Concern of the Self as a Practice of Freedom," in idem, *The Essential Works of Foucault 1954–1984*, Volume 1: *Ethics. Subjectivity and Truth*, ed. Paul Rabinow, trans. Robert Harley (London: Penguin, 2002); Saul Newman, *The Politics of Postanarchism* (Edinburgh: Edinburgh University Press, 2011). I will discuss this view later in the study.

13   Horton, *Political Obligation*, 124.

14   Horton, *Political Obligation*, 124.

15   Wolff, *In Defense of Anarchism*; Alan John Simmons, "Philosophical Anarchism," in *For and Against the State: New Philosophical Readings*, ed. John T. Sanders and Jan Naveson (Lanham, MD: Rowman and Littlefield, 1996), 20–21. For more on R. P. Wolff's conceptual argument against the state, see Rex Martin, "Anarchism and Scepticism," in *Anarchism*, ed. James Roland Pennock and John William Chapman (New York: New York University Press, 1978), 116–117, 121, 126–127.

16   Simmons, "Philosophical Anarchism," 21. For this and other distinctions applying to philosophical anarchism, see "Philosophical Anarchism," 19–39. See also Chapter 1.

17   Gans coins this term for the anarchist position that he explains as "the denial of the duty to obey the law which is based on a rejection of its grounds" (Chaim Gans, *Philosophical Anarchism and Political Disobedience* [Cambridge: Cambridge University Press, 1992], 2). But the sense in which I use it in this study is different from his—more comprehensive, technical, and specific. I give my own definition in the next paragraph.

18   Simmons, "Philosophical Anarchism," 36, n. 9.

19   In *The Politics of Nature*, ed. Andrew Dobson and Paul Lucardie (London and New York: Routledge, 1993), 39–62.

20   Aldershot: Ashgate, 2007.

21   Edinburgh: AK Press, 2006.

22   For issues that highlight the independence of "state actors," see Alan Carter, "Outline of an Anarchist Theory of History," in *For Anarchism. History, Theory, and Practice*, ed. David Goodway (London and New York: Routledge, 1989); Carter, "Towards a Green Political Theory," esp. 51, n. 12; Alan Carter, "The Nation-State and Underdevelopment," *Third World Quarterly* 16 (1995): 595–618.

23   Horton, *Political Obligation*, 122–123.

24   For a development of these points, see Chapters 6 and 7.

25   See Errico Malatesta, *Anarchy*, trans. Vernon Richards (London: Freedom Press, 1984), and Errico Malatesta, *Errico Malatesta: His Life and Ideas*, ed. Vernon Richards (London: Freedom Press, 1965).

26   Noam Chomsky, *For Reasons of State* (London: Fontana, 1973); Noam Chomsky and Edward S. Herman, *Manufacturing Consent: The Political Economy of the Mass Media* (New York: Pantheon Books, 1988); Robert F. Barsky, *Noam Chomsky: A Life of Dissent* (Cambridge: MIT Press, 1997); Peter Wilkin, *Noam Chomsky: On Power, Knowledge and Human*

Nature (New York: Saint Martin's Press, 1997); Noam Chomsky, *The New Military Humanism: Lessons from Kosovo* (London: Pluto Press, 1999); James McGilvray, ed., *The Cambridge Companion to Chomsky* (Cambridge: Cambridge University Press, 2005).

27 McLaughlin, *Anarchism and Authority*, 160–161.

28 Emma Goldman, *Anarchism and Other Essays* (New York: Dover, 1969).

29 Characteristically so: see the "Propaganda Problem," in Chomsky and Herman, *Manufacturing Consent*.

30 Stirner, *The Ego and Its Own*.

31 Herbert Read, *The Philosophy of Anarchism* (London: Freedom Press, 1940); Herbert Read, *Anarchy and Order: Essays in Politics* (London: Souvenir Press, 1974).

32 See Todd May, *The Political Philosophy of Poststructuralist Anarchism* (Pennsylvania: Pennsylvania State University Press, 1994), and Newman, *The Politics of Postanarchism*, respectively. There is discussion of their ideas later in this book.

33 Clark, *Living Without Domination*.

34 Franks, *Rebel Alliances*.

35 Gordon, *Anarchy Alive*.

36 For example, Jonathan Wolff, "Anarchism and Skepticism," in *For and Against the State*, ed. John T. Sanders and Jan Narveson (Lanham, MD: Rowman and Littlefield, 1996), 99–118. This criticism is anticipated by the usual understanding of critical anarchism as a view relying merely on justification by default (see the presentation of negative anarchism above).

37 On such ideals, see Simmons, "Philosophical Anarchism," 19–21; Alan John Simmons, "Justification and Legitimacy," *Ethics* 109 (1999): 769–770.

38 Michael Taylor, *Community, Anarchy and Liberty* (Cambridge: Cambridge University Press, 1982), 3 (emphasis mine). See also Joseph Raz, "Introduction," in *Authority*, ed. Joseph Raz (Oxford: Basil Blackwell, 1990), 16–17.

39 McLaughlin is right to stress that anarchism is *nonauthoritarianism* rather than an anti-authoritarian view, since it does not reject authority and every form of it as such: McLaughlin, *Anarchism and Authority*, 28–29 and 33–36.

40 A good example is provided by the argument from public goods. This argument focuses on the importance of coordinating activities in order to secure the production and distribution of goods vital for a decent life, and it reveals conflicting intuitions—those of anarchists, on the one hand, and those of their opponents, on the other. For this issue, see, e.g., Mancur Olson, *The Logic of Collective Action: Public Goods and the Theory of Groups* (Cambridge, MA: Harvard University Press, 1965); John T. Sanders, "The State of Statelessness," in *For and Against the State: New Philosophical Readings*, ed. John T. Sanders and Jan Narveson (Maryland: Rowman and Littlefield, 1996), 266–271, Chapter 4 here.

41 This anarchist understanding of "an acceptably complete positive attempt" to defend political obligation involves also two narrow criteria of success: that the accounts are "accurate," namely that they offer plausible principles of obligation in "their most defensible form and appl[y] them correctly," and that they are "complete," namely that they "identify as bound all and only

those who are so bound" (Alan John Simmons, *Moral Principles and Political Obligations* [Princeton: Princeton University Press, 1979], 55–56). In his criticism of accounts of political obligation, the anarchist first recommends the most plausible ones, then tries to render them accurate, and then asks whether they are complete in meeting the four conditions of political obligation (Simmons, *Moral Principles and Political Obligations*). Thus the anarchist participates in the development of defensible theories of political obligation and the anarchist conclusions against political obligation are derived on the basis of distinctive criteria of success when applied to defensible theories. This already shows the approach of critical philosophical anarchism to be much more than a justification by default (see Simmons, "Philosophical Anarchism," 36, n. 9).

42 Miller, *Anarchism*, 18 (emphasis mine).
43 For example, in Simmons, *Moral Principles and Political Obligations*, 200; Alan John Simmons, "The Anarchist Position: A Reply to Klosko and Senor," *Philosophy and Public Affairs* 16 (1987): 279; Simmons, *On the Edge of Anarchy*, 263; Simmons, "Philosophical Anarchism," 29.
44 For example, Simmons, *On the Edge of Anarchy*, 269; Simmons, "Philosophical Anarchism," 31.
45 Joseph Raz, *The Authority of Law* (Oxford: Oxford University Press, 1979), 94–99 and 104–105; Joseph Raz, *The Morality of Freedom* (Oxford: Oxford University Press, 1986), Chapter 13.
46 Simmons, "The Anarchist Position," 275–279; Simmons, *On the Edge of Anarchy*, 261–269; Simmons, "Philosophical Anarchism," 31–32.
47 Horton, *Political Obligation*, 135–136.
48 Horton, *Political Obligation*, 135.

1
What the problem is

In this chapter I set out the central problem and argument developed in this study. For this I focus on three theorists, each of whom relates in a significant way to the position of critical philosophical anarchism. I discuss Rousseau as a traditional theorist whose view is a basic inspiration for the anarchist approach to political institutions. Joseph Raz's theory is analyzed as a view largely compatible with critical philosophical anarchism. I use it to illustrate how accounts of state authority motivated by the anarchist perspective can be understood and improved. Finally, I discuss Simmons as a representative critical philosophical anarchist, from whose approach, however, I depart, criticizing it on central points in my defense of critical philosophical anarchism.

The problem of political obligation

The correlativity thesis

The problem of the existence and justification of political obligation is usually taken to be identical to the problem of the justification of political authority, which involves the establishment of the state's (claim to the) right to rule. This right is most often seen as the logical correlate of an obligation to obey: when we assert the state's right to rule, we *automatically* recognize that citizens have a political obligation to the state.[1] Alternatively, this correlativity of right and obligation can be conceived as a normative doctrine: if we have one, we *should* have the other. On this view, political obligation is understood as either a normative condition for or a normative consequence of political authority, although not identical to it.[2] Theorists are divided concerning whether to accept correlativity in any of the above senses.[3] To the extent that political authority is understood as a complex right to exclusively and coercively make regulations, impose duties, and demand compliance (i.e., command and be obeyed, or, more inclusively, *issue directives*[4] and have them followed), then it is properly taken as correlative to a complex set of obligations constituting a general obligation to comply, i.e., political obligation.[5] In this study I take this correlativity as one central sense of legitimacy, whether in its logical or in its normative form. Since normative correlativity already involves substantive considerations about the nature of political authority and our relation to it, however, it is sufficient to focus on the normative form of correlativity for us to keep in mind that it is in the nature of the state's claim-right to rule to generate obligations to it.

The two main aspects of the problem of political obligation

Thus the problem of political obligation is primarily the problem of finding a special justification for the various obligations imposed on citizens by their political institutions, which are correlative to a complex right of those institutions to rule those citizens. Theorists like Horton seem to be correct that this problem in fact involves a range of questions and that, in addition to the *question of justification*, the issues of the *author* and of the *scope* of political obligations are also central. This study concentrates on the question of justification, which, as Horton rightly points out, is presupposed by the other two and in general "has been taken to be the kernel of the philosophical problem of political obligation."[6] It is with regard to the question "why should we obey political authority?" that I evaluate the anarchist position. The traditional philosophical discussion of political authority concerns attempts to account for *de jure* political authority, that is, authority that *has* the right to rule—or is exercised in accordance with a certain set of principles or rules—rather than for *de facto* political authority, namely one that *claims* to have this right and has this claim *acknowledged* by its subjects.[7] Because no state has the right to rule, the anarchist demands the moral justification or, in other words, the legitimacy of *de facto* authority. This problem has also been identified as that of *state legitimacy* morally understood. I use "state legitimacy" interchangeably with "state authority" and "political obligation."[8]

Political obligation has traditionally been regarded as that notion through which we must understand a *special relationship* between individuals and the political institutions of their country of residence. There are two main features of the nature of the problem of political obligation:

(a) *The state, the law, and political institutions in general have a special character and status.* This is described by four theses.[9] *The sources thesis*: political institutions take their own validity from within the political/legal structure, from legally defined criteria and standards. *The particularity thesis*: citizens are taken to have a special relationship with their own government as it itself determines the conditions of membership within its territory. This means that political institutions have a particular constituency to which they apply and any justification of political obligation should provide a basis for obeying one's own particular government with its own criteria for membership.[10] *The coercion thesis*: institutional requirements may be backed by coercion. The state is sovereign and monopolistic in the sense that it determines the rights and duties of its citizens in an authoritarian, permanent, and exclusionary way. With respect to this function, legal sanction, or coercion, is its primary means. *The independence premise*: an account of political obligation should include criteria that show the independent nature of the "political" (as this nature is reflected in the elements of the three previous theses), and it is by appeal to this essentially political nature of institutions that political obligation should be justified. That is, the special commitment that such an obligation is supposed to express needs to be shown to be necessarily connected to its *political nature*. I will be referring to these four premises as "the theses on the political."

(b) *The commands of political authorities are directed at the behavior of individuals in the public domain*. This means that such commands have a direct effect not only on the beliefs of individuals, but also on their actions (such directives guide their practical reasoning and behavior). In this way they are reasons for action—*normative requirements*, those with the power to direct action—in the same way as moral or prudential reasons. More importantly, for those who accept and discuss the problem of political obligation, political obligations are understood to be *moral* in character.[11] They are the defining terms of a special moral relationship between citizens and their polity, a concomitant of the latter's status as a normative power, that is, of its claim to a moral right to impose directives on its citizens. Yet the most convincing reason for requiring a moral ground is that it provides the most appropriate way of *filtering* political requirements in order to decide which of them can properly be attributed the status of obligations. Thus it works as a criterion for distinguishing requirements that can be accepted as valid laws from requirements that are unacceptable. When, for example, individuals are presented with laws against bodily harm and laws discriminating against a specific group of people (such as immigrants), they need to be able to assert the acceptability of the former and exclude the latter by reference to a stable testing ground. Since institutions have a considerable effect on our lives, such filtering is necessary and valuable, because it demands that institutions need to be sufficiently motivated in doing so: there have to be convincing reasons in favor of their interference. A moral ground provides the strongest basis for normative requirements, creating a distance from our institutions that is beneficial to a critical assessment of their function and quality. These points express the second important aspect of the issue of political obligation as traditionally understood: a justification of political obligation must involve the provision of *moral grounds* for supporting political institutions, if political obligation is to be acceptable.

Together (a) and (b) say that an adequate justification of political obligation involves the *recognition of the legitimacy of political authority qua political, on the basis of moral reasons*. Following philosophical anarchists, I see as inevitable the need to defend the existence of special obligations in the political domain with *moral* principles and arguments. This is so mainly because of the direct and dominant role that political institutions, with their requirements and present practices, play in our social lives and because they claim the right to do so. The demands of political institutions affect primarily individual self-determination and social equality, which gives rise to a constant requirement to put limits on these institutions and conditions on how they do so, rooted in individual life and morality. As the anarchist reminds us, domination and coercion can never be desirable in themselves, without proper motivation. They are always a defect, needing to be counterbalanced by merits that are sufficiently strong to qualify the agencies that incorporate them. The very fact that obligations are requirements, which involve a "pressure to perform," makes explicit the tie between obligation, domination, and coercion, thus pressing the demand for proper justification.[12] These points relate to the other central feature in the traditional understanding of the debate over political obligation: the appeal to a moral reason as a ground of the political *qua political*. To appeal occasionally (or even frequently) to moral reasons as justifications for compliance with particular laws does not constitute a moral recognition of the authority of the law.[13]

Quality-based and interaction-based evaluations of political institutions

Two central elements of the evaluation of states that are found in discussions of political obligation are *quality* and *specific interaction*. The former involves general positive qualities or accomplishments of institutions (such as justice and the supply of important goods), and it is a commonplace in moral arguments for their existence. The latter refers to "morally significant features of the specific histories of interaction between individual persons and their polities" (components such as actually giving one's consent).[14] Judgments about the *nature* of political institutions, the qualities that might make them morally acceptable, provide a basic condition that institutions must satisfy, and in this respect they affect judgments about political obligation.[15] Some of the theories of political obligation employ them more centrally, as grounds of that question. But the general moral relationship based on the nature of a state overall differs from the particular moral relationship that is the focus of the problem of political obligation. It will be part of the argument of this study to see whether the one can ground the other and, in general, to assess the role of institutional qualities in justifying political obligation. This study follows a classical perspective in seeing the problem of political obligation as concerned with grounding a special bond between individual and government through understanding "the *relationship* or *transaction* which could create" such a bond.[16] This study also stresses the fact that political obligation is a special bond between a *particular* government and each *particular* citizen. Having such a particularized character, political obligation seems more likely to derive from very specific relationships, characterized by the actual and particular features of direct transaction, and it is doubtful that these can be captured by more generally described connections between states and subjects.[17] Thus, political obligation appears more relevant to the category of transactional evaluation, which Simmons considers to be the proper one for assessing the question of political obligation.

These are some preliminary points that will play an important role for the main argument of this study and will be further clarified in the course of its development. Whether or not justification and legitimacy are separate dimensions of the evaluation of institutions and whether or not justification in terms of institutional qualities (or of generic evaluation) is directed primarily at the existence of the state, anarchism challenges political institutions with regard to both existence and obligation. This study concentrates on its position with regard to the particular relationship of political obligation. Nevertheless, one of my main objectives is to show how the critical philosophical anarchist perspective makes the problem of political obligation central for a broader evaluation of political institutions, thus ultimately a challenge to their very existence.

The conditions of political obligation

The four theses that define the political nature of obligation and the demand for a moral ground are accompanied by certain formal conditions that have traditionally been used to determine theories of political obligation and that are pressed by anarchists. In the next few pages I will clarify which of these conditions remain operative and introduce their role within the debate on political obligation.

Theories of political obligation, which attempt to justify morally a specially political kind of requirement, are constrained by four formal conditions: *particularity*, *generality*, *bindingness*, and *content-independence*. I call them "the conditions of political obligation." These conditions appear as merely formal requirements, which a theorist of political obligation might find reasons to dispense with, against the anarchist standpoint. But one task of this study is to make explicit how their role is indispensable in the debate on political obligation and how these conditions characterize the anarchist perspective, ultimately helping decide the anarchist contribution within this debate. This study is aimed at confirming that they are justifiably offered as determinants of the link required between the political nature of obligation and its second aspect, that of moral justification.

The particularity thesis, which defines a central part of the nature of the political, itself provides a first condition on how to attempt to assign moral weight to the bond of political obligation, namely that we show the moral significance of citizens being bound to *their own* states. Being coherently in the nature of political institutions to address their requirements to a specific constituency, *particularity* is a natural and inevitable condition within the debate. Two other general assumptions of a justification of political obligation involve the demand of "universality," namely that moral justification applies to all subjects with regard to all laws, and the demand of "singularity in ground," namely that all obligations are based on one and the same moral reason.[18] Both of these assumptions have been questioned:[19] the first because of the possibility and appropriateness of excluding some people from having political obligations; the second because of the possibility and appropriateness of appealing to more than one reason to explain different individuals' obligations to obey the same law and to explain the same individual's obligation to different laws. Several theorists are content with seeing reasons for political obligation as *prima facie* reasons, with appealing to a plurality of grounds, and with establishing political obligation for many of the citizens but not for all.[20] Even philosophical anarchists such as Simmons recognize that universality and singularity are not necessarily features of political obligation.[21] Thus, I do not adopt these two conditions as appropriate constraints on accounts of political obligation.

Nevertheless, what should be drawn from the above considerations is the recognition that, in order to justify political obligation, a sufficient amount of *generality* is necessary. This is not because of the worry that is claimed to have generated the demand for the universal application of political obligation, namely, that without political obligations certain people will become a threat to those who obey.[22] Beyond this worry, I insist on generality and on the other three conditions of political obligation proposed by philosophical anarchists[23] because they provide an appropriate (and perhaps the most suitable) way of ascribing to the traditional understanding of the problem of political obligation the significance that, I argue in this project, it has. Generality also corresponds to the centralized and monopolistic character of political institutions. Finally, it captures a central characteristic of the anarchist approach to accounts of political obligation, namely that we should be interested "in describing all moral requirements which bind citizens to their political communities."[24] Klosko (1987) and other defenders of the state recognize the necessity of generality, and it is in fact this aspect that has created the most difficulties for them. As I will argue, all accounts of political obligation proposed so far fail to justify political obligation for *most* of the people. Thus, the justification of a general political obligation has not yet been given.

The other two conditions that work as proper formal constraints on accounts of political obligation become very explicit in the last facet of the problem to which I want to draw attention, namely our understanding of the character of the notion of political obligation. A good example is Raz's proposal. Political obligation "is a general obligation applying to...all the laws on all occasions to which they apply."[25] It is not an "incidental reason."[26] It is a reason to obey the law *because it is the law*, that is, "to obey the law *as it requires to be obeyed*."[27] It involves the acceptance of the directives of the law not only for their content, but also for the conditions or criteria by which they may be overridden. The law is not absolute, but the considerations under which it is defeated should be recognized by the law itself. Such considerations might be strong moral reasons that override the obligation to obey the law, but one's acting according to them irrespective of any recognition of their application by the law itself constitutes a violation of the law. Thus, although the application of the law does not imply that reasons other than those recognized by the law are less important, the law is "exclusionary" and "its rules and rulings are authoritative."[28] It is in the very nature of the law and it is its raison d'être that it functions as a conclusion of practical reason, already excluding certain considerations; this is what the law is. Only by understanding that political obligation is the obligation to obey the law because it is the law can we avoid losing sight of the demand that any suggested justification should be a ground for exactly this kind of requirement. Given this understanding of political obligation, it is possible to recognize that what anarchists deny is a *general obligation to obey political institutions as they require to be obeyed.*[29] These considerations are represented in the following chapters by the terms "*content-independence*" and "*bindingness*," which designate the last two conditions of political obligation.[30]

The upshot of the above discussion is that it makes obvious that the four conditions of political obligation already provide defining features of the political nature of such obligations, which is a central aspect of the debate.[31]

In sum, the problem of political obligation concerns fundamentally (a) an *ethical* relationship between people and the political community of which they are members, that is, one involving *moral grounds* for a special relationship to our polities. These grounds are strong, but neither absolute nor exhaustive. This issue is also (b) *political* in the sense that membership in a polity is characterized by the special features of the political as defined by the theses on the political and as reflected in the conditions of political obligation. The arguments to be examined in the main part of the study are approached on the basis of accepting the debate over political obligation in these terms.

The paradox of authority

We live in a world dominated by political institutions. We find our lives ruled and controlled by them. We mostly take this situation for granted. How did we arrive at such a state of affairs? And is this how things should be? In many other areas of our lives we feel that things should be under our own control. We think that it is important to be able to decide and make choices for ourselves. We consider it important that we be free to act within a background of various options and free to pursue the best options for ourselves in life. We do not want other people to tell us what to do and to take control over what concerns us. So why in the case of the state do we take rule for granted? Even within the state, the desire for self-government survives in the form of dissatisfaction, when there comes a point that political interference feels unbearable. Why, then, do we so readily accept political power? Should we do so?

We can attempt to answer the philosophical question of the justification of authority by answering first the question of its genesis: why did centralized power arise? And how? And why does it continue to exist now? A good explanation for *how* this happened is the *hybrid* approach defended by Michael Taylor.[32] This view focuses on the development of gross inequality and the weakening of community, asserting that these are both the concomitants and the consequences of state formation. More specifically, state formation has two bases, the first being the emergence of leadership in acephalous[33] primitive societies. Leadership was enhanced by the provision of services to the members of the community through the arbitration of a system of redistribution. The existence of threatening conditions, such as ecological pressures and external enemies, facilitated this development by leading to the need for the concentration of power that made the arbitration of redistribution of goods possible. The second basis for the formation of states was the need to inhibit fission, that is, to prevent the continual division of large groups into small, self-sustaining ones. This happened due to the threatening circumstances mentioned above, which, by their nature, tended to promote the coherence of a group. This coherence led in turn to the weakening of community, since fission helped people to live in the decentralized and self-sufficient way that community requires. In other words, state formation is explained as follows: when there is surplus of goods, redistribution creates efficiency and the leader's capacity to discharge it makes his authority acceptable. Also, geographical circumscription and the threat of enemies make people leave small communities and concentrate under the protection of a beneficial, and thus already accepted, leadership within an enriched, growing community. This in turn leads to the concentration of force and to political specialization. The latter is the hallmark of the state and involves the inequality of power, or political inequality. In addition, the specialization and exchange of goods, which effective production and redistribution under a centralized leadership involve, lead to economic inequality, which functions in favor of the rulers and is thus maintained by them. So inequality is both the concomitant and the consequence of state formation, being "the *integrative* role of the emerging central power" that led to this formation.[34]

This explanation of how the state arose is, however, more important for what it says about *why* the state was created. This opens the way to addressing our central concern with *why it seems justifiable*. The answer lies in the integrative role of the emerging central power, because this entails that the leadership was *beneficial to the people*, good at providing them with services, and thus *voluntarily accepted* by them.[35] This is a good reason for wanting the state: it is justified as long as it is *at the service* of those who are ruled, as long as, that is, the state serves as an instrument for the individuals who make up the societies it governs. Having been created for their own good, it can be seen, for this reason, as *their choice*, which means that political power is compatible with the capacity of, and desire for, self-government. Even better, it is a good way for individuals to preserve and enhance this capacity. Traditional, state-of-nature based defenses of political authority make exactly this argument, and their case for the existence of the state seems strong. Paradoxically, however, this entails that *we decided to be ruled because we do not want to be ruled*.

The appearance of this paradox is the starting point in this study for examining the anarchist position and its approach to the problem of authority. The paradox reflects the idea that the best way to justify rule to individuals who can be, and have the right to be, self-ruled, and who thus find constraints undesirable, is to show that this rule is their own decision, that government is the result of self-government in the sense that *we* put constraints on ourselves. A *decision* to be constrained seems to be the most promising and comprehensive account of political constraints. What is required is to demonstrate how this can happen. The preceding explanation of the origins of the state suggests an answer, but we need to determine whether this is what actually happens. Indeed, as we will see, the paradox in fact is not a paradox.

Nevertheless, its seemingly paradoxical character helps reveal an error in the defenses of political institutions. The problem lies in that showing the state to be good for us does not amount to showing that we accept it voluntarily. The state's being good can be a reason for our voluntary acceptance, but the two are not identical. Unless it is our own actual appreciation of the beneficial character of the state that leads us to accept the state, the state cannot be seen to be the result of self-government, namely the result of the participation, decision, and control of those who want to survive and live together freely. One could say that "being in our benefit" makes it a reason *for us* to want the state, and that a reason for us is our own reason and thus our own choice. But we still need to prove that the state is beneficial on the basis of reasons that actually are for us and thus that it can be, or is, our choice. The error of the state defenders lies in the fact that, in demonstrating the merits of the state, they also thought that they had demonstrated its legitimate authority. But something that is potentially a benefit for a number of individuals is not so, unless it is based on their informed choice. In addition, something that was a benefit for some in the past is not necessarily a benefit for those concerned at present. For the latter to be the case, it needs to be actually a benefit at present and to be seen as such by those whom it concerns.

The defenders of the state (those who adopted the theories that will be examined in the following chapters, for example, social contract theories of political obligation)[36] committed themselves to a correct starting point when they attempted to defend the state on the basis of self-government. But this involves a continual assertion of choice. Instead, they provided reasons for seeing institutions as desirable and thus deserving of acceptance, reasons that could motivate choice, but that are not themselves choice. They also thought that such reasons can be given once and for all, which ignores the continual need for the expression of choice. An argument for the benefits of political institutions could defend their existence, but not their authority. Nor could it defend their existence once and for all. Nevertheless, the defenders of the state thought that their argument did exactly this. The result is that, in addition to showing that the state is necessary for providing order and safety, they started out facing the state as a good in itself and as an entity over and above individuals, with independent existence. This might be described as a romanticized view of the state. This view may be what lies at the bottom of our unreflective acceptance of the state as an inevitable reality and what makes us forget its defects and our initial dislike of constraints. It has not yet been proven that constraints are beneficial for us as constraints we choose *ourselves* to impose on ourselves and on one another. Showing constraints to be self-imposed is the only way to demonstrate that the state exists for the sake of those it constrains and not at their expense.

The philosophical anarchist presses this point within the debate on political authority. In order to explain this position better, I want to illustrate the above argument about the seeming paradox. An effective argument for the state is based on the point that autonomy is extremely important and that, for the state to be justified, it needs to be shown to protect it. But, the argument goes, for this the state need not be autonomously chosen.[37] People make mistakes in their choices, and the right kind of choice cannot be derived from the universal consent of actual individuals. Rather there are concerns that are primary for us, good reasons that apply to us, whether or not we are able to see them. When the agents of the state are sensible enough to find and serve these reasons, then we are better off if we let them do so. We should make sure that a state serves good reasons that apply to us, whether or not we can actually choose them. In this way we have our capacity to be autonomous protected and enhanced, through a good government built on such reasons. So a good government is justified because it protects autonomy, but it is not the case that we choose it autonomously.

This is a good starting point for approaching our relationship to the state. It asserts the value of autonomy without facing the difficulties arising when we try to defend it through individual consent.[38] It also clarifies why the protection of important benefits is essential for our self-government, even if we do not actually choose them.

The anarchist will eventually concede that this argument can be a basis for defending the state. In order for the defender to make proper use of this perspective, however, he needs first to see the point of the insistence on choice that the critical philosophical anarchist maintains. The anarchist claims that for the state to be legitimate, it needs to be shown to have been chosen. He finds a point in a perspective that argues that a good government is good *because we choose it*; it is *our choice* that makes it so that it protects us. This idea implies that we are self-governed *through* the state: rather than claiming that the state is justified because it allows us to be self-governed and enhances this capacity, the argument holds that the state can be justified only if it is a way through which we govern ourselves. The difference between the two approaches is that, while the defender sees autonomy to be respected because it is protected and served through a good government, whether or not we choose that government, the anarchist claims that autonomy is respected only if we choose the state such that it becomes positively a way through which we govern ourselves: the state is good because we choose it and because it becomes a way through which we choose.

This difference is important, because each view has a different criterion of justification. For the one view, the respect for autonomy that government is expected to show consists in finding and serving what is right; freedom is realized through the realization of good reasons. For the other view, autonomy is shown to be respected by government only if government becomes itself a way through which we exercise autonomy, and maybe the best way. This distinction is crucial also because it points out a confusion that needs to be avoided in evaluations of the state. The romanticized view of the state exhibits this confusion: it emerges from an illegitimate move from unjustified identification and vacillates between one criterion and the other. It sees the service of good reasons on the part of the state as a way in which the state *makes* us autonomous, instead of just *allowing* us to be autonomous at best. It identifies rightness, or merit, with individual authorization. It is this assumption that leads defenders to see the state as an independent good in itself, as inherently connected with and as expressing the value of persons and of the interaction among them.

As a new alternative, the critical philosophical anarchist accepts the approach that focuses on good reasons with regard to some justifications of the state, and yet insists on the value of choice for the purpose of political relations. Anarchism returns to choice in a way different from that of the second approach discussed above and with a criterion that becomes less problematic: it reminds us that it is important that through the state we *remain* free, rather than become free. What is the importance of such an insistence on choice?

At the beginning of this section it was pointed out that in many areas of our lives we care most about being self-governed and about preserving this capacity and right for ourselves, because it is the only secure way we can survive and flourish. We do not want our lives to depend on others. The defenders of the state follow this natural way of thinking when they begin to show that the state is at our service. The idea then is generated that the state can be justified because it is created for the sake of, and on the basis of, our very capacity to be self-ruled. Yet now a paradox also seems to be generated: we create a condition in which we are ruled by others in order to remain self-ruled. That is, we do exactly what we do not want to do in order to secure what we want the most. As indicated above, the paradox is not really a paradox, but its seemingly paradoxical nature helps reveal the confusion in the defenders' argument. It is not a paradox because, in order to be self-ruled in some ways, we need both ourselves and others to be constrained in some other ways. Most importantly, however, it is not a paradox because it is a consistent and reasonable idea that, in order to be self-ruled, we need to be self-constrained: it is possible and sensible that self-imposed constraints constitute appropriate conditions for individuals to enhance their capacity for choice. When, for example, one decides to quit smoking because it is better for one's health, one puts a constraint on oneself not to smoke again. This constraint enhances one's freedom by helping one to apply the decision with which one chooses to rule one's life in this respect. If the state is a way for us to be self-constrained, then it can serve as a way for us to be self-ruled. The impression of a paradox arises from the fact that it is in the nature of the state that some rule others, and so the state is offered as a way of our becoming self-ruled that involves being ruled by others.

Dissolving the paradox: Rousseau as a paradigm of state justification

There is a way through which the seeming paradox is dissolved, and it lies in Rousseau's intuition that the state is justified only as a way of our being governed by ourselves. As Rousseau states in his *The Social Contract*: "The problem [of political justification] is to find a form of association which will defend and protect with the whole common force the person and goods of each associate, and in which each, *while uniting himself with all, may still obey himself alone, and remain as free as before*."[39] To create such a civil society, individuals must unite under an agreement the conditions of which are unanimously accepted and with the intention to hold each other to those conditions. As Arthur Ripstein puts it, "Rousseau's claim is that a community consists in a group of people in agreement both about the conditions of their interaction and their intention to hold and be held by each other to that agreement."[40] By becoming a member of a community created by such an agreement, each individual identifies with the *general will*, which is the united will of all self-legislated citizens expressing the choice applied within political society. Thus in order to be free, the citizen always needs to hold to the general will, "to will impartially with all the others."[41] So if he disobeys this will, others have the right, based on their mutual agreement, to *coerce him to be free*: "[W]hoever refuses to obey the general will shall be compelled to do so by the whole body. This means nothing less than that he will be *forced to be free*."[42] "Coercion is legitimate on grounds of freedom because the agent has *chosen* to be coerced."[43] The idea defended here is that having others decide for us and serve us with regard to some matters is not a denial of freedom or choice, if the nature of their decisions and the content of their choices represent our own choice: we are the legislators, thus the creators of the ways we are to be constrained, thus self-constrained, and thus free. In order for the defenders of political institutions to preserve this argument, however, they need to attend to it properly as the only way of defending the state in terms of self-government. They need to attend to the proof and preservation of this kind of choice.

As established in the previous section, there is a difference between seeing something as justified because it is rightly discovered to causally promote our autonomy and seeing it as justified because it constitutes a consequence of our autonomy. The anarchist insists on the need for the latter, which captures Rousseau's idea of self-government, to make the argument for the state a defense based on the idea of freedom through self-constraint. But the defenders of the state do not stay consistent in their use of this argument. By focusing on benefits of the state that make it good for us, they gradually change the initial argument from choice into an argument for the protection of choice through benefits. They are right to see the fact that the state provides safety as a strong reason to support it, but in the end they also believe that this makes the state a good in itself. Thus their defenses end up saying that we are ruled by others in order to be self-ruled. That their view allows the defense of the state to be rendered paradoxical is an indication of the mistake the defenders make in the process. The problem is reflected in the failure of accounts of political obligation that the anarchist stresses.[44]

There is, however, a way of correcting the state defenders' error. By staying clear and insisting on the form that Rousseau gave to state-defense, we might come to realize that at one level it is unachievable for the state. Then we may legitimately move to the other argument—still in the light of the importance of choice indicated by the argument that we cannot achieve in a direct form—which gives an alternative view of legitimacy in terms of autonomy, although clearly not choice-based. We can then pay attention to its specific implications for the state.

If, with Raz, we try to determine what we can tell about how the state works and focus on its protecting our capacity for autonomy through its service of good reasons, we need to see what direction such a defense takes. It cannot prove political obligation, nor can it justify the state once and for all. Rather it can concede the continual instability of the state and concentrate, as most important, on the attempt to justify the reasons why they are subjected to *individuals themselves*, not through actual choice, but through reasonable testing and evaluation in the light of the lack of such a choice. (This is facilitated, for example, by the enforcement of law through transparent and accountable mechanisms, which, at some level, is an expression of continuing choice.) This is a demanding approach, yet one that is consistent as a recognition of the value of choice, not departing from the initial argument about choice in a destructive way. The two arguments come together through a fair compromise: we assert the value of choice, while realizing that we cannot base the state directly on choice; in the light of this impossibility, we insist on the importance of finding acceptable ways of justifying reasons to the individuals subjected, making the defense of the state in terms of goodness a recognition of self-government. The idea of basing government on ethical concerns that we all share arises as the prominent task of justification for the defenders to pursue.

Raz's theory as an illustration

Raz's position helps illustrate the preceding discussion. I will use it as a representative example to show how we can better understand and improve the views on the state offered by those motivated by the anarchist position.

Starting from the central anarchist intuition that there is some puzzlement with the idea that "one person has the right to rule another," i.e., that the right to rule is deeply disturbing as a notion,[45] Joseph Raz sees this puzzlement as rooted in the fact that authority involves a "dimension of subjugation" that is distinctive of it, namely it involves duties that are "deliberately imposed by one human being on another with the aim of subjecting that other to a duty."[46] Hence, he sees the anarchist complaint to be ultimately about "the problem of subjugation," that is, of the *subjection of one person to another*,[47] where unequal dependence is the main aim, and this is facilitated by giving dependence a specific form. In essence this "is a problem of the relations between one person and another," which, as I will illustrate throughout this study, concerns the anarchist most and remains vivid with regard to political authority.[48] Importantly so, it signifies the central role of domination within political authority, of "*the capacity of one party to exercise control over another party*."[49] The anarchist worries further about the fact that domination and hierarchy are definitive aspects of authority at the expense of freedom and equality, encouraging other harmful social phenomena such as exploitation and coercion.[50] Thus, Raz's account helps us illustrate how the concern with the creation of problematic relations between people, as it appears in subjugation, or domination, lies at the heart of the anarchist skepticism about authority. This study also aims to demonstrate that it takes on special significance in the criticism of political obligation.

Given this problem, one should at least concede the idea that "no unlimited authority can be legitimate" and thus that "[w]e need a doctrine of limited government, i.e. of the principled limitations on the possible scope of governmental authority."[51] As we will see later in this chapter, this requirement is not a demand simply and primarily to limit the scope of authority as much as possible. Rather, it is a demand to find reasons and principles that determine the nature and functions of authority in a manner that makes it justifiable to all reasonable, adult individuals subject to it. The suggestion I will develop, to apply an ideal of legitimacy to further justifications of constraints in view of the results of the debate on political obligation, sets such a background as a primary condition. Although the concern with limited authority is a liberal demand and anarchism is defined by a prior concern with whether authority can ever be morally legitimate, once this concern is properly recognized, further evaluations of constraints can function within this background. Moreover, the defenses provided by various contemporary political theorists, such as Rawls and Dworkin, may be seen to work within these boundaries, in fact to work adequately only within them. Within this framework, Raz's reply to the anarchist challenge is that "[t]he basis of legitimacy is relative success in getting people to conform to right reason."[52]

To explain: Raz's defense of "practical authority," that is, "authority with power to require action,"[53] involves three main normative theses.[54] These work within the background of his general approach to the analysis of authority, which includes the idea that authority necessarily entails obligations to obey.[55] It also involves the claim that the indispensable feature of authority is "surrender of judgment," which is not taken to mean that obedience erases personal deliberation, but rather that it is not conditional on personal examination of the thing prescribed. When individuals follow authoritative prescriptions, they do so on the understanding that, whatever their opinion is about the thing prescribed, after they have acknowledged the authority they are expected to follow its directions as given.[56] Finally it involves an account of the nature of authoritative instructions as "dependent" and "preemptive" reasons for action, namely reasons meant to *reflect* the balance of reasons on which they depend, instead of being added to them, and reasons meant to *replace* the original reasons on which they depend, while not having absolute supremacy.[57]

Accordingly, Raz's first thesis is the *dependence thesis*, concerning "the general character of the considerations which should guide the actions of authorities,"[58] which is the position that authorities should act on dependent reasons in order to achieve an ideal exercise of authority.[59] That is, "*[a]ll authoritative requirements should be based, in the main, on reasons which already independently apply to the subjects of the directives and are relevant to their action in the circumstances covered by the directive.*"[60] The second thesis, the *normal justification thesis*, which "concerns the type of argument required to justify a claim that a certain authority is legitimate,"[61] is the position that for authority to be justified it should be shown to be the best way for individuals to conform to reasons that apply to them, reasons to which they themselves are committed.[62] This thesis maintains that

> the normal and primary way to establish that a person should be acknowledged to have authority over another person involves showing that the alleged subject is likely better to comply with reasons which apply to him (other than the alleged authoritative directives) if he accepts the directives of the alleged authority as authoritatively binding and tries to follow them, rather than by trying to follow the reasons which apply to him directly.[63]

This is the crux of Raz's defense of authority. Together, the dependence and the normal justification theses "articulate the service conception of the function of authorities, that is, the view that their role and primary normal function is to serve the governed."[64] This leads to the third normative thesis that Raz adopts, the *preemption thesis*, which "concerns the way the existence of a binding authoritative directive affects the reasoning of the subjects of the authority."[65] On this position, such requirements preempt the reasons they are intended to serve: when they guide action, they replace their underlying justifying reasons.[66] The thesis claims that "[t]he fact that an authority requires performance of an action is a reason for its performance which is not to be added to all other relevant reasons when assessing what to do, but should exclude and take the place of some of them."[67] The resulting idea is that, because authoritative reasons should, in order for authorities to be justified, be dependent on already existing underlying reasons, authorities "should have the right to replace people's judgments on the merits of the case."[68]

Let me note here that the contractualist approach to authority, which will concern us extensively in this study, adopts the service conception of Raz and the ideas reflected in the two theses that compose it. According to this approach, authority can be justified on the basis of reasons that represent, apply to, and are the best for the individuals subjected. Yet this approach departs from Raz's third thesis. In contractualism the central idea is that, in the case of practical justifications such as those concerning political authority, the relevant reasons have to be explicitly justifiable to those they concern. Thus in the social world it is important that individuals actually *see* the reasons that apply to them. Practical reason differs from theoretical reason, and in the case of the former individual judgment can never really be replaced. This is because in theoretical reason the point is to find the truth as it applies irrespective of individual opinion (as is the case with axioms in mathematics), whereas in practical reason the truth is determined on the basis of individual evaluation and interaction itself. As we will see in the main part of the study, this position leads the contractualist to a distinctive method of justification that gives a special role to choice and is of great importance for the debate on political authority.

In contrast, within the context of his own theory as described above, Raz sees "theoretical" authorities, referring to "authority for believing in certain propositions," to be more likely to have the same structure as practical authorities and to be supported in the same way by his dependence thesis.[69] Yet there is crucial difference between theoretical and practical authority. To start with, the former is *nonexecutive*, while the latter is exactly "the right of A to *issue practical directives* and the correlative duty of B to follow them or to obey them."[70] It is crucial to note that Raz relates his account strongly with the idea of theoretical authority when he focuses on authority in terms both of "its expertise (or that of policy-making advisers)" and, more importantly, of its "ability to secure social coordination."[71] This assimilation seems to sit well with his normal justification thesis and the service conception as well as with further general ideas that motivate his view, ideas that I will discuss in my criticism below. It is also consistent with the anarchist attitude toward authority, a skepticism that does not reject forms of authority such as parental authority or the authority of the teacher and that demonstrates a complex attitude toward theoretical authority.[72] But it also brings to the fore the concept of "*an* authority" with its special characteristics.[73] More precisely, this notion of authority maintains that deference to someone as authority is based on his special knowledge and the presupposition that others are debarred from such knowledge. The idea of authority here puts "the person prior to the system," the latter concerning established procedures for creating authority, which are prior according to the idea of "*in* authority."[74] The concept of "*an* authority" also focuses on special capacities and the quality of one's decisions as what sets one apart from others, irrespective of whether they accept that person or not, and as what makes one person an intermediary between the world and the rest of us, who adds something to it for us to take—it centers on *differential access*.[75] This notion of authority also presupposes a kind of inequality, namely personal differences (unequal capacities) and a hierarchy prior to the authority relationship on which that relationship is based.[76] Given the involvement of these features in the idea of theoretical authority, its use within Raz's account must be approached carefully. I will explain how in the following paragraphs.

Finally, Raz sees his account as making the surrender of judgment, characteristic of authority relations, compatible with keeping one's moral responsibility.[77] He situates his position in relation to the liberal theorizing on authority, explaining that the liberals focus on the Rawlsian "duty to support and uphold just institutions" as a proper way of justifying limited government, while his own account is offered as an attempt to answer the prior question of an "understanding of which institutions are just"—or, to be "setting the question in a certain way[, o]ne has a duty to uphold and support authorities if they meet the conditions of the service conception."[78] Raz's account also becomes a basis for the attitude of "respect for law" (it is actually what grounds its application, meaning, and validity), which he sees as an acceptable expression of the morally desirable sense of identification with our societies and thus one that binds to the authorities of their societies those who adopt it.[79]

Given the preceding analysis, we can now examine how central aspects of Raz's view bear on our argument.

Raz's normal justification thesis respects the anarchist idea that authorities, if they are to exist, can exist justifiably only if they are shown to be *for* the people and not vice versa. The service conception already claimed this. The position reflected in the combination of all his theses, that it is only on the basis of the independent reasons determining the moral responsibility of people that relations of authority can be accepted, corresponds to the anarchist perspective on justification. In the debate on political obligation, anarchism establishes a demand for justification that has been neglected, a demand activating an ideal of legitimacy as a constant test for any account of constraints. This throws new light on Raz's account. He offers his account as explaining which institutions are just. Although anarchism begins with the prior question of legitimacy rather than justice, as far as institutional evaluation is concerned we can see Raz's approach as functioning within the background of justification established by the anarchist: his theses set the terms for the moral acceptability of constraints. We can also read his claim that the dependence thesis articulates a condition for the legitimate exercise of authority in the language of the anarchist ideal of legitimacy: only institutions that serve generally acceptable moral values are justifiable. This correlation will be understood when we will see how the anarchist ideal of legitimacy arises.

It is also important that Raz recognizes that "a complete justification of authority has to do more than provide valid reasons for its acceptance," as is the case with the normal justification thesis.[80] Such an account "also has to establish that there are no reasons against its acceptance which defeat the reasons for the authority," namely that the justifiable ways in which it functions are not accompanied by aspects that defeat their acceptability. For example, an important reason against its acceptance would concern "the intrinsic desirability of people conducting their lives by their own lights."[81] This recognition fits the fundamental anarchist idea that our approach to political institutions needs to start from a prior consideration of the undesirability of constraints, of the need to consider both the defects of political institutions and their merits, rather than focusing only on the latter, which, as I will argue, helps reformulate the debate. The focus on people's initiative, a strong motivating reason for such an outlook, expresses the very anarchist concern with freedom and the importance of creating a background of appropriate relations among them that enables people to control their lives meaningfully. In the light of these considerations, Raz's justification thesis qualifies as one that functions properly within the background of justifications of limited authority as determined by the anarchist ideal. The whole account of Raz, then, is thoroughly characterized by the anarchist perspective and the way that perspective determines our approach to political institutions. Each of the specific elements of this account acquires a clear meaning and position within the framework established by the anarchist as one settling the tasks of political theory and action.

In order for this account to work properly, however, there are certain aspects that should be approached with caution. The considerations shown in the previous paragraphs to be recognized by Raz can apply to his view, provided that it satisfies certain conditions. Although the idea that the justification of political authority lies in its being an efficient vehicle of the reasons of individuals as moral agents is intuitive, its real force within political reality lies in making sure that authority is actually and continually proven to be such a vehicle. We need methods for applying the ideals of legitimacy that ensure that people understand their reasons, that they see how those reasons apply to them, understand authorities to serve them properly, and also feel capable of overthrowing them the moment they cease to do so. The view that authority may do well in helping us satisfy reasons that apply to us is valuable when used in the critical spirit that the anarchist encourages with regard to political obligation, and which extends to every evaluation of constraints, rather than in a spirit of confidence that leaves authority unquestioned in these respects. In the end, the relation of the anarchist position to accounts of limited authority is a natural consequence of the central anarchist tenet that it is extremely difficult to legitimize political institutions.

Against this background, the idea of "an authority" is not helpful. The critical outlook that we need to adopt and apply with regard to political institutions contrasts with this conception. The concern with proper relations between individuals and with a sincere exercise of moral responsibility and control over their affairs, which makes active participation indispensable, opposes a view of expertise based on exclusion and differentiation. Rejecting the idea cultivated throughout history that there are areas of exclusion and groups of agents who can entirely and constantly decide for the rest, with its resulting differentiation among people and the subordination of some to others, is what motivates the anarchist challenge in the first place. The notion of "an authority" encourages that idea and raises expertise to the level of an exceptional capacity and a higher goal. Its connotations with differential access obscure the crucial understanding of social life as a practice that concerns us all equally and for which we are all qualified. When we accept that the anarchist challenge expresses a legitimate and valuable concern, we cannot attempt to meet it by applying such elements that it itself falsifies.

Raz's view constitutes a representative way of how to account for claims of authority within the framework of justification defended by the anarchist, but his understanding of authority must not contain the connotations indicated above. To avoid this it is important not to identify practical authority with theoretical authority. In practical reason it is not enough to find and follow the right answer. Rather it is crucial that we participate in formulating and applying such answers to ourselves. Individuals must be able to *see* as justifiable to them the reasons that authorities served. This is the impulse involved in the contractualist rejection of Raz's preemption thesis and in the anarchist insistence on the role of choice. Ultimately, Raz's theory facilitates and should be interpreted to account for the idea that political institutions can be an authority because they are based on an authority that we all constitute. The anarchist forces on us the task of ensuring in every case and at every level that authorities qualify as ways of discharging our social responsibilities and goals. This makes justification a hard process. We should remember that in fact the anarchist critical impulse rejects the surrender of private judgment and endeavors to confine it to the largest possible extent when it is inevitable that we live with authorities, of which this aspect is a central characteristic. Making this feature as compatible as possible with the basic inalienable capacity of freedom and with the kind of social relations that it requires characterizes the demand for justification established by the anarchist. This makes it a central concern of this demand that the surrender of judgment, whenever it occurs, genuinely reflects an aspect of *our* authority. Thus the idea of expertise, if used at all, must be seen as a difficult exercise rather than a prior ideal—something for political institutions to be actually and continually proven to qualify as and to become, by approximating to the ideals of legitimacy in the way the task of justification demands. It itself becomes an issue of constant evaluation that concerns all of us.

In the end, the above remarks redirect us to the real issue of political legitimacy, which is *the moral justification of practical authority*, of the authority to issue practical directives and have them obeyed. The form of authority that anarchists find morally suspect and is discussed here is *a dominative social power that is binding and content-independent, necessarily involving recognition and submission by its subjects, which uses coercion even if it is not defined by it.*[82]

The argument for critical philosophical anarchism

In the rest of this chapter, I outline the main argument developed in this study in defense of critical philosophical anarchism. This argument takes two directions. On the one hand, it examines how critical philosophical anarchism helps improve our perspective on the state by presenting an alternative to the dominant positions concerning it (the section "An alternative to prominent positions on the state"). On the other, it focuses on a way of understanding critical philosophical anarchism that departs from, and improves on, the perspective of its theoretical defenders (the section "Improving the way critical philosophical anarchists see their position. Simmons's theory as an illustration").

An alternative to prominent positions on the state

The aim of this study is to demonstrate the positive character and contribution of critical philosophical anarchism, an anarchist view that argues that there is no adequate defense of political obligation and concludes that in this sense the state is illegitimate. This position helps us understand that the reasons on the basis of which we set out initially to justify the state are correct. Indeed, they are exactly those motivating the anarchist in the first place. But the method the defenders of political institutions seek for satisfying these reasons is wrong. The anarchist reminds us of and focuses on what it leaves behind. In fact, anarchism involves a perspective that we can all share. Anarchism is the only perspective that holds consistently the view that we want to be self-governed and that the only way to be so within the state is to prove it to be a self-imposed constraint. An analysis of the dialogue between the philosophical anarchist and the defender within the debate on political obligation is critical for this purpose and will be the central part of this study. Its result will be that we have no political obligations. The anarchist, I will argue, can treat this as a demonstration that we do not have a comprehensive argument for such a special relationship to the state, and as a good reason explaining why we cannot have such an argument. This, in turn, will open the way toward seeing a higher challenge to the enterprise of justification as a whole: maybe we chose the wrong argument altogether. Does this lead to the conclusion that there is no way to ground the legitimacy of the state? In terms of political obligation, there is probably no way. The state offers no additional ethical concern over and above the ones that we can share with one another. Self-government and equality cannot be expressed by consent within the state.

Yet there is a way of looking at the state that may be helpful. We can bracket the question of political obligation—take into account its results, but leave aside any effort to change them—and concentrate on something else: ethical reasons that we share are expressive of equal, autonomous, and active participation, and we should try to prove the state to be based on these. It can be legitimate in terms of not violating such ethical concerns and of being compatible with them. We can see the state as an association that we create for goods that, we find, ordinary associations do not provide. We are social beings. Yet our societies are the result of *our* collection and interaction. The state is not something mysterious, an entity over and above us that raises special demands. Once we say, as the traditional defenders have, that the state frees us, we adopt a romanticizing view. Instead, we need to remember that the state is not a good in itself, that it does not have an independent existence and value of its own. We need to see that the dominant defenses of the state have gone too far in attempting to identify beneficial order as a source of choice. Constraints are always constraints, and their being good for us does not change that. The real challenge is to see whether the political world in which we find ourselves living and which we might not want to abandon is one that deserves to continue to exist, on the basis of reasons that apply to us. This sense of legitimacy is our aim.

Political anarchism says the state is an evil. Naturally, on this basis, it rejects any effort to justify authoritative and coercive institutions, their existence and legitimacy, and our obligation to them. Critical philosophical anarchism does not reject the state in such an absolute way. (Note that strong philosophical anarchism such as the view of Robert Paul Wolff is more directly connected to the strong demands of political anarchists, but this is not the view I examine.) What critical philosophical anarchism does is reject the legitimacy of existing political institutions, by proving that there is no adequate moral defense of political obligation, given its idea of what a legitimate state would be like. It also stresses the distinction between different kinds of evaluations of political institutions. In the face of these characteristics, critical philosophical anarchism has been criticized as a purely negative view, one that is skeptical of any positive effort of justification without providing its own alternative solutions to social problems. I disagree with this criticism. Although much of the argument of this study is an attempt to show dissatisfaction with the defenders of the state, I do so by addressing positively the fundamental question about the very existence of political institutions, which these defenders neglect.

There are two prominent, opposing positions on the state that are defended, and they seem to be the main options available. On the one hand, the defenders of the state focus on the fact that it can provide necessary peace and order. From this they move further to declare the state an end in itself, having an independent ethical status of its own and, for some, being over and above individuals. We are urged to believe that we should have the state as a matter of moral necessity. On the other hand, the second position starts from the idea that we are rational adults who do not need the state to tell us what to do. Its advocates are motivated by an opposition to extended state interference, even for reasons of welfare. They even aim at rolling the state back, creating as minimal a state as possible, one that employs just the army and the police to protect individual property. The first, which was mentioned earlier in this chapter, is the romanticizing approach to the state, a kind of idealism. This approach obscures the fact that the state is created by individuals and is a collection of people who come together in a particular way for their own good. The second is the (Right) libertarian position, which focuses on undermining the state and limiting its role to practices that can elicit individual consent. It nonetheless sees autonomy only as the independent interest of self-contained individuals and understands human relations only in terms of negative rights and duties, neglecting thus the sociability and interdependence of human beings and tending to endorse great inequalities. But are these the only defensible options we have? Should we either consider the state as an imperative moral ideal or try to reduce it as much as possible?

The argument of this study is that there is a third option that has been neglected by these two perspectives: the position offered by the critical philosophical anarchist. This anarchism agrees with the libertarian that we are self-ruled and we do not need the state to decide for us. From this, it points out the mistake of romanticizing the state. The anarchist criticism of political obligation reinforces the claim that the state should be seen as a means for our ends as morally developed (adult) agents, that it exists to serve us and has no ethical value over and above us. But seeing this, the solution is not to create a minimal state or eliminate the state altogether. Philosophical anarchism offers a perspective from which we can be entirely distrustful of the state while at the same time accepting a full welfare state. This means that the existence of the state does not replace our critical assessment of it, but, at the same time, when it exists, it is better that it cover more areas of social need rather than fewer. Otherwise its functions are characterized by self-generated and unjustified domination, exploitation, and coercion. In this light, the anarchist ideal of legitimacy stresses that our focus should be on *quality*, rather than quantity: on the legitimacy of the character that state authority takes when exercised. This is the most reasonable position for us to adopt while living in the state. As a result of this position, the anarchist stands with the friend of the state in that we should help out and offer our positive participation while living in it.

Improving the way critical philosophical anarchists see their position: Simmons's theory as an illustration

According to the preceding argument, prominent positions on the state are unsatisfactory. But the view that philosophical anarchists themselves have about their position is also unsatisfactory. This part of my argument is necessary for a demonstration of any positive contribution on the part of critical philosophical anarchism. Although a discussion of Simmons is not the aim of this study, I will examine his position as representative of the literature on philosophical anarchism that I find incomplete. Simmons misses nothing of the main characteristics of critical philosophical anarchism defined in the introduction and analyzed so far. Indeed, these are the features on which I base my account. My aim is to detect and defend something about them that has been neglected.

Simmons's theory

Critical philosophical anarchism is involved in a "subversive campaign."[83] That campaign aims to demonstrate, through criticism of the state, that the nonexistence of a general political obligation affects broadly our thinking and acting in the public domain. By leading us to the conclusion that there is no general political obligation, the anarchist criticism "removes any presumption in favor of obedience," and with this it "force[s] us to view the position of man in political society in a different way."[84] It forces us to cease to think and act on the assumption that there is a morally binding special political relationship and to approach cases of obedience and disobedience on the basis of independent moral grounds. It invites us to distinguish moral reasons for action from grounds related to a distinctively political status and their political formalization, calling on us to accommodate ourselves to a careful weighing of the various moral considerations that are at issue in social situations. We need then to cultivate within the political structure the way we think about political institutions. We should begin to consider instances of illegality under a different light. In everyday life, we ought to appeal to particular laws as long as they overlap with morality and to recognize that many of them are arbitrary (for example, policies interfering with private conduct that is harmless to others, like the criminalization of drugs). In this way, we may gradually get used to depending less on authority in most of the practices and interactions of our social life.

The critical outlook that the anarchist project forces upon us involves a more difficult way of discharging our social responsibilities. It suggests "that we be more thoughtful about and more sensitive to the particular moral issues in our lives."[85] We are reminded that we owe it both to ourselves and to others *qua persons* to take a responsibility for our social lives that goes beyond blind obedience, that the latter would be unacceptable even if we had political obligation, and that "citizenship does not free a man from the burdens of moral reasoning."[86] Because in practice we are used to acting as if the directives of political authorities are beyond question, despite the fact that we now recognize that all relationships of authority need justification, "[i]t is this widespread habit of compliance that the philosophical anarchist is trying to subvert."[87]

Correspondingly, the anarchist perspective and its accompanying ideals of legitimacy insist on the evaluative role of a set of generally acceptable moral standards, thus functioning as a principled reflection on the seriousness and the implications of an attempt to justify political authority. In this, the anarchist position becomes a suitable standpoint for the political theorist and for the wider population to adopt in order to conceive and apply adequately political ideals in an attempt to construct proper forms of social organization. It thus constitutes a strong basis for a deeper understanding and improved conception of our social relationships and lives. On the whole, as philosophical anarchists themselves claim, the anarchist skepticism challenges social order "from within," it forces us to reassess the moral status and significance of social order, and it "makes a difference to the nature of social relations."[88]

Nevertheless, critical philosophical anarchists also claim that the widespread adoption of such an attitude does not challenge the existence of political institutions or lead necessarily to a significant change in our existing social reality at the practical level. These positions relate to a list of arguments that these anarchists employ against the accusation that their position leads to an extreme and invariable radicalism and entails disorder.[89] As Simmons claims, the view that there is no political obligation does "not entail that disorder or revolution is justified."[90] He advances his claim mainly on the basis of three lines of argument: first, that to be a correct position, critical philosophical anarchism should also be "weak" and adopt a "balance-of-reasons" approach concerning the weight of "judgments of state illegitimacy."[91] Second, that there are various classes of moral reasons that individuals may have for complying with the law, even in the absence of political obligations.[92] Third, that political obligation is only one aspect of the justification of political institutions, and the kind of evaluation properly involved in it does not replace the kinds of evaluation involved in other justifications of them.[93] These arguments interact with each other.

According to the first argument, philosophical anarchism should be seen as giving to its conclusion against state legitimacy a "minimum content," namely that "the subjects of illegitimate states have no political obligations."[94] This conclusion does not extend to a claim that either these subjects or people generally have an obligation to oppose and eliminate the state, although defenders of weak anarchism may hold such a view on independent grounds. Thus the anarchist conclusion of the debate on political obligation "does not translate into any immediate requirement of opposition to illegitimate states."[95] In addition, the judgment that there is no political obligation is not held to provide final reasons for action, which outweigh all other moral considerations, but rather to present the relevant rights and obligations within a "balance-of-reasons" approach, to be examined in view of other good reasons.[96] On balance there may be good moral reasons for not opposing the state, even if it is illegitimate.

Accordingly, as Simmons's second argument goes, there are three classes of such reasons. One such class includes moral duties to others as persons, such as duties not to harm others, which cover acts that are *malum in se*, and "wrongs of coordination."[97] The latter are not wrong in themselves, but they become morally forbidden within contexts that make them harmful (e.g., when we endanger others by driving on the left in a society where the common practice is to drive on the right).[98] In cases where political institutions prohibit these kinds of wrongs, their laws overlap with morality and thus citizens are morally required to obey them. Also, if persons have a natural right to enforce these duties on others, then governments themselves (as "sets of persons") must have the same natural right, even if the absence of political obligation deprives them of a civil right. In this case coercion arises as part of a nonpolitical context and is not seen to be an exclusive function of government as such.[99] Furthermore, we have a "natural duty of justice" to support institutions that exhibit certain qualities, such as benevolence or the promotion of happiness.[100] Such merits relate to "dimensions of 'justice'" that might counterbalance a government's "coercion without right," thus constituting grounds that provide governmental action with justification even where it functions without right.[101] Finally, there are weighty moral reasons for acting that do not have the status of duties but play a role in determining our judgments about action, for example when we would inconvenience others or disturb their plans when disobeying just because we are entitled to disobey.[102] Thus, Simmons concludes, the lack of political obligation does not entail that the state's right to command and be obeyed disappears in every particular case, nor that illegitimate states always act without justification in particular instances, nor further that we have a conclusive right to disrupt their functioning and oppose their laws.[103] All the reasons just discussed limit instances of disobedience and encourage support, even though the proof of no general political obligation shows that there are areas where the state is not entitled to require our support. Governmental action for preventing harmless private conduct, laws enforcing conduct that serves the protection of the state, and those imposing payments that finance government operations constitute examples of the latter.[104]

These considerations bring us to Simmons's third argument.[105] Simmons claims (a) that political obligation concerns only one area of justification of political institutions, namely their right to rule and its correlative obligations, and (b) that this needs to be assessed in terms of a particular relationship created on the basis of significant elements of specific interaction between governments and each of their citizens. My study attempts to bring to light the importance of such transactional evaluations for the problem of political obligation and the anarchist position. For one thing, they help avoid the derivation of political obligation from evaluations of political institutions that might cover for different claims about justification. For Simmons, the distinction between different areas of justification itself is of great importance. As he argues, the state may be defended for having a right to exist, which refers to a kind of justification other than state legitimacy (qua obligation) and which can be used to support the state independently of and despite the conclusions concerning its legitimacy. In this context, considerations about the general virtues of institutions play a primary role, generating the ones referred to as generic evaluations. I will argue that such evaluations can be seen to play a role within the problem of political obligation, but not to be primary and sufficient to generate this special political relationship. Given the implications of the problem of political obligation for further justifications of institutions that the anarchist criticism stresses, I will also show how these evaluations can be reintroduced in the political debate and be useful.

At this point, considerations about the general qualities and accomplishments of institutions can be seen as the elements that justify the general moral duties to comply with political institutions discussed in the preceding paragraphs. In the hands of the anarchist theorist, and against Horton's claim, they become reasons for showing that the anarchist perspective does not dictate widespread disobedience, retaining its critical value within a context that carefully separates various moral assessments and allows evaluation to take multiple directions and create various avenues of support. Significantly, critical philosophical anarchists can use these reasons to distinguish good from bad governments, contrary to the accusation that their view implies that all illegitimate states are morally equal and should be treated in the same way.[106] Another "dimension[..] of evaluation" that is distinguished in this context is that states may sometimes "*act with justification*," i.e., have some of their particular actions or policies justified on moral grounds, even when they lack the justification to exist and the legitimacy to rule: for example, a thoroughly inegalitarian government is justified in prohibiting murder even though it neither is virtuous to merit support nor has a right to issue directions and use coercion to back them up.[107] The separation of at least three dimensions of evaluation of political institutions corresponds to the different classes of moral reasons for complying with them, functioning according to the rationale of "weak" anarchism and of a "balance-of-reasons" approach. The combination of these aspects allows for great flexibility in the political debate. Thus certain critical philosophical anarchists think this combination characterizes the anarchist perspective, offering it in defense of their claim that their view does not have dramatically counterintuitive implications.

However, I think that we need to examine the resulting anarchist position more carefully. Simmons is right to claim that the anarchist conclusion about political obligation provides reasons for action that can be overridden in light of other serious moral considerations. I also concede that the lack of political obligation does not directly challenge the existence of institutions, given the independent function of generic evaluations of them and the indispensable moral force of such evaluations. Moreover, I find the idea that philosophical anarchism does not entail widespread disobedience and chaos a legitimate conclusion of these arguments, compatible with my support of the positive contribution of critical philosophical anarchism. The title of Simmons's book *On the Edge of Anarchy* has the positive meaning that this is exactly where we should be, that anarchism is not something we have to escape, that the edge of anarchy is not the verge of chaos—and it is on this idea that his work concludes. Nevertheless, I find this conclusion compatible with a radicalism that is central to the contribution of philosophical anarchism, a radicalism that Simmons's line of argument seems to neglect. The distinctive role of the anarchist is not to distinguish good from bad governments, nor to merely put limits on political institutions. Its edge lies somewhere else, and this is what I argue below.

To support my view, I begin with an estimation of specific claims made by Simmons in relation to the preceding account. Then I will follow this estimation with an account of my broader departure from his position.

Specific arguments against Simmons

Simmons closes his book *On the Edge of Anarchy* with an account of the wrongs done to us by illegitimate yet benevolent states, given the nonexistence of any special political obligation, deriving his Lockean anarchist conclusions about the position individuals should take with regard to this phenomenon.[108] At one point he confirms that "most of us in the 'free world' are in Lockean terms just persons in the state of nature (*simpliciter*), subjected by our governments to a variety of (usually) relatively minor, but *frighteningly regular, wrongful acts and policies*."[109] This explains why "[g]ood governments might merit our support, but *they are not entitled to require it* (without our free consent)."[110] Later he suggests that certain

> moral facts [that oblige us independently of any special legal requirement to obey, facts as those discussed above], plus considerations of simple prudence (i.e., our interest in avoiding legal punishment), seem to dictate that moderately good governments, *which violate our rights only in ways such governments typically do, ought not to be resisted in ways*

that threaten to destroy them or to replace them with distinctly inferior alternatives.[111]

He then concludes that, "[i]n the world of illegitimate states that will continue, moral persons must cast off their childhood lessons in good citizenship, and proceed *by selectively supporting or opposing their governments' actions and policies solely according to the particular moral standing of each governmental move.*"[112] Simmons offers these points as representative of the critical philosophical anarchist position, which comes out of the debate on political obligation with the message that we should adopt a more skeptical attitude toward existing governments—an attitude, however, that does not involve rejecting them altogether, but focuses rather on the quality of their particular functions.

Yet Simmons is missing something. First, his account of our moral obligations is determined by his advocacy of Locke's philosophy, which is not a view that someone, including an anarchist, has to be committed to. Even if his idea of moral responsibilities is an acceptable one, however, the problem with his approach still remains. With his first claim cited above, he dismisses as minor wrongs done to us by governments that are, nevertheless, *frighteningly regular*. He then supplements this claim with his further suggestion that good governments that *violate our rights in ways that such governments typically do* should not be dangerously resisted. But these statements constitute a very incomplete representation of the anarchist criticism that preceded them and its results. Indeed, this is obvious in the very form they take: how can a politically informed and active person, or just a reasonable one, let alone an anarchist, consider as minor violations acts and policies that are at the expense of the individuals concerned in a frighteningly regular manner? What is the habit of compliance if not such an untroubled acceptance of continual violations? How can a critical approach to political institutions accept their violations as those typically committed by such institutions? Is this not an unquestioning concession to the existing status quo rather than a challenge to it, as misguided as the romanticizing view of the state? Simmons's relevant appeal to prudence and to the dangers of possible destruction of good illegitimate governments and their replacement by inferior alternatives is a concession concealed by an air of political realism, rather than a reasonable pragmatic realization. Furthermore, these claims contradict the concluding demand for a critical and selective approach to governments, based on the quality of their particular policies. This attitude involves much more reflection and scrutiny, as well as abstraction from existing determinations, than a tendency from the very beginning to make concessions to them involves.

On the whole, in dismissing the importance of certain facts about governments that the anarchist view brings to the fore, Simmons commits philosophical anarchism to a view much less radical than really entailed by the anarchist perspective. To be sure, to believe that for specific instances minor violations of rights are better than major ones, and also that it is not bad to accept minor violations of rights, is reasonable. But when these views are used as indications of an approach to the very problem with authority, they render an account that is incomplete and misguiding. The problem is that from such a perspective they seem to suggest that it is fine if our relations to the state are declining a bit and that the whole issue is to establish a minimal state. Simmons's statements lead him to this approach.

A more general departure from Simmons's approach

My following arguments for the significance of the question of obligation, for a departure of the anarchist view from supporting the minimal state, and for the role of the anarchist ideal of legitimacy are meant to demonstrate where my approach differs fundamentally from Simmons's and where I find his approach to be more generally inadequate.

The Significance of the Question of Political Obligation. When the anarchist says that we cannot ground the state on voluntariness, justice, reciprocity, and association, he reveals a gap in the justifications of the state. This is his message derived from the debate on political obligation: we do not participate in creating and managing the state and there are no ethical concerns that arise distinctively from it as such. This makes the state illegitimate in terms of political obligation, although it is not a positive proof of its illegitimacy in general: we have no special ethical relationship to the state, although for it to be illegitimate, or wholly unjustified, we need to show that it does something wrong. Thus, Simmons thinks that this conclusion is perfectly compatible with keeping the state. It encourages a critical outlook toward it and an independent approach to our obligations to others, perspectives that nevertheless continue to be expressed within a framework widely determined by the state: the state can have the right to impose specific duties, it should be supported when it serves ethical duties, and it can very well continue to exist in a justified manner (when it is a good rather than a bad government). This view stresses the importance of differences between various ways to evaluate political institutions: in terms of their existence, in terms of their legitimacy qua obligation, and in terms of specific obligations that these institutions might be justified to impose even when they are neither justified nor obligatory. It also asserts that political obligation is just one criterion of evaluation. It is the latter claim that I challenge in my approach to critical philosophical anarchism. This study accepts that the difference between kinds of evaluation of the state matters, and so, in this light, the state can exist even when there is no political obligation. Yet although the separation between different kinds of evaluation is central to the anarchist perspective, its value does not lie in permitting different kinds of justification to proceed independently of one another. It rather lies in helping us see the force of the considerations provided for and against political institutions in each case by drawing attention to the elements that characterize primarily each of these considerations, according to the issue we want to examine. For example, it reminds us to look for morally significant features of specific interaction as the elements relevant for generating the particular relationship characteristic of the problem of political obligation, instead of trying to derive argumentative force from general qualities of institutions, which play a secondary role in creating such a relationship. This does not mean that the different avenues for the justification of political institutions do not affect each other considerably.

The result of the anarchist criticism is not that political obligation is just one evaluation among others with no distinctive effect on the justification of the state. I argue instead that, by showing the state to provide no distinctive ethical concerns, to be based on no special relationship of political obligation, the anarchist uncovers a very serious gap: lacking political obligation is a defect in the very nature of the state. How can political institutions relate to their subjects if they lack political obligation? And how can they function and be distinguished from their alternatives if they lack such a relationship? That is, how can they be (considered as) permanent and exclusive if they have no right to command and be obeyed? These questions lead to more general doubts about political institutions. They make us examine their very nature and discover defects that have been neglected. The coercion that makes political institutions efficient is also *a problem*, and this needs to be addressed. It is at this point that the romanticized view of state-order starts to look out of place. In this way, the challenge to political obligation is not just a restricted and harmless criticism of the state, but a viewpoint from which the state is seen as a defect (even if not as totally evil) and *something difficult to justify*.

Political obligation cannot be derived simply from arguments for the existence of political institutions, for the latter might survive the debate on political obligation. Nevertheless, as I will also explain, the character of institutions is a relevant and important condition for finally validating the right to rule,[113] while the considerations and results of the debate on political obligation crucially affect further defenses of political constraints. The particular and actual relationships required for political obligation to exist are not indispensable elements for deciding the moral value of institutions more generally, but the absence of such an obligation constitutes a serious gap in their status. The different view of our position in society that the anarchist subversive campaign creates with the removal of the presumption in favor of political obligation constitutes a serious change for social life in the presence of political institutions. But further, the absence of this central relationship that characterizes their status as political raises doubts about the very plausibility of their validity, function, and viability.

Even more importantly, the difficulty with proving political obligation that the anarchist criticism reveals redirects the debate to the deeper concerns that need to determine our approach to political institutions. I argue that the anarchist position on the problem of political obligation brings back a more fundamental question that underlies every approach to political institutions. The perspective that every theorist needs to adopt is one characterized by the question *whether political institutions should exist at all*. The anarchist indication that political obligation cannot be established by appeal to the general merits of institutions, the basis required for it making it a matter of continual justification, leads to a wider consideration about whether appeal to general virtues is enough to motivate constraints and whether it motivates them once and for all. The argument of this study stresses that for such evaluations to be effective they need to apply within the background set by the fundamental question that the anarchist brings to the fore and that such a question makes the demand for justification constant. This clarifies the complexity of avenues toward a defense of political institutions, indicating what the proper way of using their merits to support them is and how difficult this may be. Subsequently, in the light of the debate on political obligation and its results as effected by the anarchist criticism, every attempt at justification is reformulated and the task of justification becomes harder.

This way, we can claim that *indirectly* the justification of political obligation has a significant effect on other dimensions of the justification of political institutions and thus on their overall justification. Ultimately, the outlook of every theorist and every person is determined by the demand that, rather than considering the merits of political institutions on the basis of an assumption that we need them and desire them, we start to ask whether we should need them at all, appealing to their merits in the light of this question. This is the anarchist perspective. Moreover, the way it is activated within the debate on political obligation makes that problem, if not decisive for the content of other kinds of defense, still totally decisive for their structure and force—decisive in the way it leads to a proper reformulation of the considerations applying to them and a correspondingly different estimation of their input. The skeptical approach and a careful weighing of the independent moral grounds that bear on action in different political circumstances that the philosophical anarchist recommends should be seen in this light.

On the whole, we can see a parallel between the position that the anarchist establishes within the debate on political obligation and the one advanced more generally with regard to political institutions. The removal of a presumption in favor of obedience involved in the subversive campaign of philosophical anarchism corresponds to a removal, through the fundamental question that the anarchist perspective raises, of a presumption in favor of the existence of political institutions. The fundamental concern becomes the very possibility of political obligation, or the very possibility of political institutions. The subversive campaign of philosophical anarchism within the debate on political obligation also necessitates a different outlook on our position in political society, which corresponds to a different outlook with regard to the status and stability of political institutions. Again, through the fundamental question that the anarchist criticism brings to the fore and the demand for justification that this raises, their existence is not taken for granted, their desirability becoming a matter of constant justification.

So although the anarchist position does not privilege one specific avenue of justification to the detriment of all other avenues, it nevertheless reintroduces an approach that constitutes a unified challenge to every avenue at the deepest level. Even if not obvious to its advocates, the perspective of critical philosophical anarchism carries with it and remains faithful to the classical position of anarchism that there is *nothing lovable* about external constraints and that *the state remains a problem*. It is in this respect that philosophical anarchism remains thoroughly radical. The claims that it challenges social order from within[114] and that it helps us press for the respect of self-government and equality within social life[115] should be seen in this new light. Correspondingly, by making the demand for justification harder,[116] the anarchist position does not render the various expressions of the critical approach it recommends[117] vehicles of an immediate and radical change. It surely renders them, though, more obviously representative of a serious challenge to actual societies and more effective as indications of active citizenship. More precisely, the demand to show in every instance that the existing political constraints respect the values they are held to help secure creates a central role in the political debate for the task assigned to individuals: to think carefully about the relevant moral reasons for support or rejection. In this sense, critical philosophical anarchism has a much stronger link with the political anarchist criticism of the state as an evil than first thought. Horton is right to claim that the challenge to political obligation can change much in our political lives, since a central part of our view of the political world is shown to be a myth. In the end we have moral reasons to be more independent in our reasoning about social behavior and also to develop nonpolitical forms of solutions to social problems, or, at least, to understand their intuitiveness. Yet this view does not adopt the political anarchist demand for the removal of the state, not as the initial and primary anarchist goal anyway. But then, what does it help change?

The anarchist does not provide a broad criticism concerning different variables, which would have no strong overall impact. Rather, the anarchist criticism reflects a unified demand for justification that affects our perspective on political institutions. And it is not the case, as some philosophical anarchists claim, that the anarchist position within the debate on political obligation and the attitude it recommends will not change much in practical terms. On the contrary, this position and attitude reflect a significant implication of the anarchist outlook with regard to real institutions and our lives in relation to them: a gradual but stable effort to make substantial, *actual* changes. By rendering a principled support of the nature of state authority problematic, the anarchist position invigorates the debate on political obligation; it presses for the exercise of our critical powers; it allows the construction of improved accounts of the authority of the state and of more satisfactory political arrangements, imposing more demanding criteria on wider evaluations of constraints; it also paints a picture of the political that stimulates an innovative conception of our political relationships and that inspires more informed views about the role of public institutions. These aspects suggest substantial changes to our conception of the political and to our political lives, which might neither be based on an instant reconstruction through revolution nor be a desperate expression of our dissatisfaction with authority and the present character of public life.

Anarchism becomes a reminder that we should now recognize and apply what we are more qualified and seem in fact to recognize, to wit, that all relations of authority are in need of justification and that the proper approach to political authority is one that regards its scope as limited on the basis of considerations of quality. This is the way the anarchist critique helps remove the habit of compliance. More importantly, the anarchist position remains consistent. Its fundamental concern is still not to establish limits on political domination. It rather remains the claim that domination is always problematic. All this involves a proposal that is as radical as it is valuable: it testifies that anarchism suggests and remains the continual source of a move toward *a fundamental reconstruction of our social relationships and lives.* The possibility of such a reconstruction is still to be proven and its realization is necessarily gradual. Yet it remains a desirable end and an alternative worthy of taking its place in our moral and political history.

Departing from the Minimal State. But, how does the anarchist perspective and its accompanying ideal of legitimacy *differ* from already existing views for and against political institutions?

The anarchist message is that we do not have a comprehensive argument for political obligation and that there are good reasons why we cannot have such an argument. This is a way of *understanding* the gap in justification instead of trying to fill it: it prepares a perspective for, rather than a ground for, obligation. Beginning from the gap created from the absence of political obligation, critical philosophical anarchism suggests that we leave aside the attempt to answer the question of obligation, that political obligation concerns an everlasting effort of justification that is not susceptible to a final resolution. Indeed, the anarchist skepticism is not about providing such a justification for the state. Rather it is about bracketing the question of obligation and concentrates on something else, which is nevertheless motivated by the difficulty of this question. Instead of attacking the existence of the state and trying to roll it back, the critical philosophical anarchist claims that, whether we love it or not, when we have it, the state is not a matter of magnitude, or quantity, but rather of *quality*. To be critical toward the state in the way that the philosophical anarchist suggests means to see whether it matches ethical concerns that we need, whether, that is, as it exists, it is acceptable in view of justifiable claims we have toward one another. I call this "the quality thesis" on the state.

Such an approach departs both from romanticizing accounts of the state and from those against the welfare state. With regard to the latter, it is important to see how the anarchist approach differs from defenses of the minimal state. In contrast with what Simmons's account suggests, for the critical philosophical anarchist there is no way of filling the gap that the lack of voluntary participation creates by diminishing the tasks of the state to the minimal. A state that does not support education and healthcare and does not provide distribution and general protection, but merely polices property, is more unjustifiable than a full state. Such a state is even further from a condition of liberty without inequality that all forms of anarchism desire: instead of being an establishment that protects individuals without undermining their equal right to self-government and participation, it gives liberty to the few, whose interests it protects and perpetuates, at the expense of the many, who remain unsatisfied and unequal. It cultivates division and conflict by supporting a society where competition and social discrimination thrive. Thus, in fact it is very far from what is supposed to be the primary function of the state, for which it is claimed to deserve justification in the first place, namely to serve its citizens.

The Anarchist Ideal of Legitimacy. This guides the perspective on the state that the anarchist adopts. In its different forms, this ideal represents what a society characterized by appropriate relations between persons would be like. And because the state is not such a society, i.e., it is not the ideal, as the anarchist criticism of political obligation shows, what it can do instead is approximate it—to prove in every instance that its functions are compatible with the moral criteria of the ideal. This does not mean that it proves to have political obligation, but rather that, in the absence of it, this is the only way of ensuring active participation, not in the making of the state, but in the process of evaluating its functions and in being able to restrict it to what it can justifiably demand from us.

This is what results from the evaluation in terms of political obligation and what makes that evaluation more important than Simmons thinks, not merely one among other evaluations that is moderate and limited, but rather the basis for a substantive transformation of our view of the state. It shows that the state has gone too far and is taking too much from us, that it offends self-government, equality, and proper relations in the name of a good that it is not. But instead of either overthrowing it or trying to fill the (unbridgeable) gap of justification that its defenders have attempted, we can become those who determine in a justifiable way where and how it should stop: when its functions are of a character that is justifiable to us and not at our expense, when by protecting through coercion it does not overdo the latter at the expense of the former. The perspective that the philosophical anarchist offers shows us a way of being entirely distrustful of the state while at the same time accepting the welfare state. This view does not depart from my claim that critical philosophical anarchism is still linked with political anarchism: at every instance there is the possibility of becoming dissatisfied with the state in terms of the ideal of legitimacy, and this endangers its existence. In light of the results of the debate on political obligation that the anarchist brings to the fore, the undesirability of illegitimate constraints becomes categorical. And the ideal of legitimacy becomes a constant guardian against abuses of the state, not by providing a form of consent, but by testing continually the quality of state functions. The anarchist thus reminds us that the dissatisfaction and lack of patience that we feel toward the state in times of crisis should be the characteristic attitude and the starting point for us to view our social responsibilities. This is the way for the state to be an instrument at our service, compatible with individual self-government and equal positive participation.

Conclusion

We therefore have to be committed neither to an inevitable acceptance of the state nor to a complete rejection of it. The anarchist approach offers an option that has been neglected and that is *the most reasonable* one: we can stay within the state and participate in advancing the social aims it is meant to serve, and yet always keep an eye on the way its dominative tendencies and its coercion might overstep its initial task.

But having adopted this view, the philosophical anarchist has further to answer the question of how we fulfill our obligations to others without the state within a background where the state exists. How do we do without the state apparatus in a situation where we do not have perfect abundance? That is, how do we manage independently of the state to coordinate and cooperate toward an effective and fair satisfaction of our needs in a world where goods are not abundantly available? This is a legitimate question to ask the anarchist who does not insist on removing the state and yet finds its defects in terms of illegitimacy to be a good reason for independence from it. He has to answer this question in order to prove that he remains an anarchist and can convince others of the merits of his position. I will deal with this issue in the seventh chapter of the study.

In the remainder of the book, I elaborate on the arguments presented in this chapter: I examine in detail how the anarchist raises the problem about political institutions and how the distinctive contribution of critical philosophical anarchism works. In the following four chapters I examine the anarchist position within the debate on political obligation in order to demonstrate that it is correct. In the final two chapters and conclusion, and in view of the implications of the debate on political obligation, I demonstrate the value of critical philosophical anarchism pertaining to the problem of political authority as it arises from that debate.

Notes

1   The "doctrine of 'logical correlativity' ": Simmons, *Moral Principles and Political Obligations*, 58 and 195–197; Simmons, "Philosophical Anarchism," 21 and 36, n.11.

2   This means that either authority or obligation is already independently justified and becomes the ground of the other, and that it reflects "a substantive ... thesis about the state, namely that it is properly the instrument of its citizens' aims" (Leslie Green, *The Authority of the State* [Oxford: Clarendon Press, 1988], 236).

3   Defenders of political obligation and philosophical anarchists usually adopt correlativity; for example, Simmons, *Moral Principles and Political Obligations*; Simmons, "Justification and Legitimacy"; Green, *The Authority of the State*; Raz, *The Authority of Law*; Raz, "Introduction"; Joseph Raz, "Authority and Justification," in *Authority*, ed. Joseph Raz (Oxford: Basil Blackwell, 1990), 115–141; Gertrude Elizabeth Margaret Anscombe, "On the Source of the Authority of the State," in *Authority*, ed. Joseph Raz (Oxford: Basil Blackwell, 1990), 142–173; Horton, *Political Obligation*; McLaughlin, *Anarchism and Authority*. This perspective might be explained to a significant extent by the fact that these theorists conceive political authority, or the right to rule, as something more than mere permission to coerce. For example, "What we really have in mind is a right to make laws and regulations, to judge and to punish for failing to conform to certain standards, or to order some redress for the victims of such violations, as well as a right to command" (Raz, "Introduction," 2); and "Political authority has coercive powers, but its authority extends beyond its use of those powers. It appeals to people's recognition of their moral and civic duties, while being ready, in many or even most cases, to use coercion if the appeal fails" (Raz, "Introduction," 15); also, "Authority on the part of those who give orders and make regulations is: a right to be obeyed. We may say, more amply: authority is a regular right to be obeyed in a domain of decision" (Anscombe, "On the Source of the Authority," 144). Characteristically, defenders of non-correlativity conceive authority as mere liability or permission to coerce, which is justifiably distinct from, and does not necessarily entail, a duty to obey, that is, political obligation (see David Daiches Raphael, *Problems of Political Philosophy* [London: Macmillan, 1976]; Robert Ladenson, "In Defense of a Hobbesian Conception of Law," in *Authority*, ed. John Raz [Oxford: Basil Blackwell, 1990], 32–55); Christopher Heath Wellman, "Liberalism, Samaritanism and Political Legitimacy," in *Philosophy and Public Affairs* 25 [1996]: 211–237).

For a useful discussion of objections to logical and to normative correlativity, see Green, *The Authority of the State*, 234–240.

4   "Directives" is a wider term, more suitable than "command" to cover all cases of authoritative utterance (for this, see McLaughlin, *Anarchism and Authority*, 54).

5   This description is closer to the Lockean account of the right to rule. But it is meant to capture the elements of conceptions such as those presented in note 3 above to be given by defenders of correlativity.

6   Horton, *Political Obligation*, 12–13.

7   For this distinction, see, e.g., Wolff, *In Defense of Anarchism*, 2; Simmons, *Moral Principles and Political Obligations*, 41–42, 196, and 206; Simmons, "Justification and Legitimacy," 746–751; Raz, *The Morality of Freedom*, 18–19; Raz, "Introduction," 3; McLaughlin, *Anarchism and Authority*, 59. In relation to these points, see the discussion of the moral feature of the nature of the problem of political obligation below.

8   But this use of legitimacy should not be confused with other, proper yet different, uses of the notion. For state legitimacy and an insistence on the clarification of the different uses of the notion, see Simmons, "Justification and Legitimacy," 746–751. For example, within contemporary contractualism the focus is on deciding the *content* of legitimacy (or of justice), on examining what demands political institutions should satisfy in order to be legitimate (or, otherwise, on formulating legitimate principles for institutions), a question different from an explicit defense of their right to exist and their right to rule (e.g., John Rawls, *A Theory of Justice* [Oxford: Oxford University Press, 1971]; Thomas Michael Scanlon, "Contractualism and Utilitarianism," in *Utilitarianism and Beyond*, ed. Amartya Sen and Bernard Arthur Owen Williams [Cambridge: Cambridge University Press, 1982]), 103–128. Simmons sees the contractualist approach as a special conception of "justification" of the state and opposes its being drawn together with the question of "state legitimacy," which corresponds to the problem of political obligation, namely of legitimacy as the right to rule (Simmons, "Justification and Legitimacy," 758–769). He himself conceives the *justification of the state* as the question concerning *which institutions, if any, have the right to exist* and takes it to be separate from the question of *state legitimacy* as one about *justification of the right to rule* (Simmons, "Justification and Legitimacy," 739–751). For other senses of legitimacy, see Simmons, *Moral Principles and Political Obligations*, 40–44 and 197. For nonnormative accounts of political legitimacy, see Max Weber, *The Theory of Social and Economic Organization* (London: William Hodge, 1947); Rodney Barker, *Political Legitimacy and the State* (Oxford: Clarendon Press, 1990).

9   For these theses, see Saladin Meckled-Garcia, *Membership, Obligation and Legitimacy: An Expressivist Account* (Unpublished PhD dissertation, University College London, 1998), 14–18.

10   "The particularity requirement": Simmons, *Moral Principles and Political Obligations*, 31–35; Green, *The Authority of the State*, 227–228.

11   See, e.g., Raz, *The Authority of Law*, 244; Horton, *Political Obligation*, 13–15.

12   Simmons, *Moral Principles and Political Obligations*, 7.

WHAT THE PROBLEM IS

13   For the meaning of such a recognition, in comparison with other kinds of reliance on moral reasons, see Miller, *Anarchism*, 16–18, and Raz's view discussed below.

14   Simmons, "Justification and Legitimacy," 764. These elements ground Simmons's distinction between "*generic*" and "*transactional* evaluations" (Simmons, "Justification and Legitimacy"). In this study I also apply, in relation to the first kind of evaluation, the term "institutional morality," which is drawn from an analogous distinction between "theories of institutional morality" and "theories of emergence" (Meckled-Garcia, *Membership, Obligation and Legitimacy*, Chapter 2). Schmidtz makes a distinction similar to Simmons's, between "teleological" and "emergent" justifications (David Schmidtz, "Justifying the State," in *For and Against the State: New Philosophical Readings*, ed. John T. Sanders and Jan Narveson (Lanham, MD: Rowman and Littlefield, 1996), 81–97; Simmons, "Philosophical Anarchism"). But I find his account less satisfactory.

15   Quality is the factor that Simmons ties to the question of justification as he understands it, which is considered to precede arguments for political obligation (Simmons, "Justification and Legitimacy"). The basic idea here is that we cannot morally bind ourselves to immoral institutions.

16   Simmons, *Moral Principles and Political Obligations*, 4 (emphasis mine).

17   In relation to these points, see on the "particularity requirement" (Simmons, *Moral Principles and Political Obligations*, 31–35) and the discussion of "the political" above. The arguments of the following chapters will help decide the force of these considerations.

18   Jonathan Wolff, "Pluralistic Models of Political Obligation," *Philosophica* 56 (1995): 10.

19   For this, see Simmons, *Moral Principles and Political Obligations*, 35–37. Particularly for arguments against "universality," see Green, *The Authority of the State*, 240–247.

20   Gans, *Philosophical Anarchism*; Wolff, "Pluralistic Models of Political Obligation."

21   Simmons, *Moral Principles and Political Obligations*, 35–37. And yet Simmons and other anarchists have been criticized for posing "particularly rigorous and demanding standards of moral justification" of the state (Horton, *Political Obligation*, 134).

22   For an expression of this worry, see Wolff, "Pluralistic Models of Political Obligation," 27.

23   Namely, "particularity" as reflected in the particularity thesis above, "bindingness" and "content-independence" (for these two, see the next paragraph).

24   Simmons, *Moral Principles and Political Obligations*, 37. For his support of generality, see Simmons, *Moral Principles and Political Obligations*, 55–56.

25   Raz, *The Morality of Freedom*, 234.

26   Raz, *The Morality of Freedom*, 234.

27   Raz, *The Morality of Freedom*, 236. I agree with Simmons that political obligation is not only the obligation to obey the law but involves much more, such as the duties of citizenship, which involve supporting political institutions in other ways, for example, by participating in the defense

of one's country (Simmons, *Moral Principles and Political Obligations*, 5). This point is suggested also by the analysis of correlativity at the beginning of this chapter. For a similar position, see also John Horton, "Peter Winch and Political Authority," *Philosophical Investigations* 28 (2005): 235–252; John Horton, "In Defence of Associative Political Obligations: Part Two," *Political Studies* 55 (2007): 15. Yet in the present paragraph I use Raz's discussion to make a different point about the character of political obligation and I adopt his terminology only as part of that discussion.

28   Raz, *The Morality of Freedom*, 236–237.
29   Green, *The Authority of the State*, 225–226.
30   The recognition of these features as characteristic of political obligation is not incompatible with the claim that political obligations are not "all things considered" reasons for action (Simmons, *Moral Principles and Political Obligations*, 7–11). They are also reflected in the special nature of the "political" as defined in the four theses presented above. Similar considerations about the character of political obligation are echoed in Friedman's analysis of the notion of authority (Richard B. Friedman, "On the Concept of Authority in Political Philosophy," in *Authority*, ed. John Raz [Oxford: Basil Blackwell, 1990], 56–91). See also Herbert Lionel Adolphus Hart, "Commands and Authoritative Legal Reasons," in *Authority*, ed. John Raz (Oxford: Basil Blackwell, 1990), 92–114.
31   Another way of rejecting universality and singularity of ground as conditions of political obligation is observing that neither of the two has a direct and relevant connection with the features that make the requirements of political institutions political. That is, neither of them is necessary for the permanent, authoritative, monopolistic, and coercive character of political institutions.
32   For the analysis of the origins of the state that follows, see Taylor, *Community, Anarchy and Liberty*, section 3.3.
33   "Acephalous," or "acephalos" in Greek, means "without a head" (<a- (without) + "cephali" (head)). Here it means without a formal leader.
34   Taylor, *Community, Anarchy and Liberty*, 133.
35   Taylor, *Community, Anarchy and Liberty*, 133–134.
36   When I refer to "defenders of the state," I mean all those theorists who defended accounts of political obligation that reflect the approach I criticize in this study from the perspective of anarchism. Such theorists range from traditional political philosophers, such as Hobbes, to contemporary theorists, such as George Klosko. But their approach might be adopted by any theorist or individual. So, the argument presented here and developed in the rest of the study concerns the accounts that I discuss in the following chapters and addresses whoever might adopt them as views on justified authority, rather than a specific and complete list of theorists.
37   See Raz, *The Authority of Law*; Raz, "Authority and Justification"; Raz, "Introduction." This argument constitutes Raz's theory of the state, which is explored in the works just cited and is analyzed below in this chapter (in the section "Raz's theory as an illustration").
38   For these difficulties, see Chapter 2.

39 Jean-Jacques Rousseau, "On Social Contract or Principles of Political Right," in *The Social Contract: Bound with, Discourses*, ed. George Douglas Howard Cole, John Henry Brumfitt, and John C. Hall (London: Everyman, 1973), book 1, Chapter 6 (emphasis mine).

40 Arthur Ripstein, "The General Will," in *The Social Contract Theorists: Critical Essays on Hobbes, Locke and Rousseau*, ed. Christopher W. Morris (Lanham, MD: Rowman and Littlefield, 1999), 224.

41 Ripstein, "The General Will," 231.

42 Rousseau, "On Social Contract," Chapter 7 (emphasis mine).

43 Ripstein, "The General Will," 231.

44 And it is telling of something the anarchist observes and indicates with worry: that, by nature, the state involves subjugation in the disagreeable sense of some ruling others with the intention to subject them, which creates inappropriate relations among individuals and is concomitant to domination. See the discussion of Raz in the section "Raz's theory as an illustration" below.

45 Raz, "Introduction," 3–4.

46 Raz, "Introduction," 16–17.

47 Raz, "Introduction," 16–17.

48 Raz, "Introduction," 16–17.

49 McLaughlin, *Anarchism and Authority*, 47.

50 For a useful account of domination and exploitation in relation to authority and the prior role of domination in this regard, see McLaughlin, *Anarchism and Authority*, 47–53. See also Green's and McLaughlin's view that authority is problematic and potent: Green, *The Authority of the State*, and McLaughlin, *Anarchism and Authority*, 37, respectively.

51 Raz, "Introduction," 12.

52 Raz, "Introduction," 13.

53 Raz, "Authority and Justification," 115.

54 For the following account, see Raz, "Authority and Justification."

55 This is because the justified use of force would not be authority unless it included an appeal to compliance, which is meaningful only if there are things to comply to. In short, legitimate authority is usually exercised by giving directives and issuing instructions. It is much more than use of coercive threats; it *imposes duties and confers rights* and thus involves an obligation to obey (Raz, "Authority and Justification," 115–118; see this in contrast with Ladenson's view of authority as merely permission to use coercion, all discussed above, in the section "The problem of political obligation"; see also McLaughlin, *Anarchism and Authority*, 54–60).

56 Raz, "Authority and Justification," 118–122. For this idea, see also Friedman, "On the Concept": the first distinctive feature of authority is "surrender of private judgment," which means that with regard both to conduct and to belief, an individual who accepts authority recognizes that someone else's prescription is to be followed simply because it comes from one "acknowledged by him as entitled to rule," that that person is entitled to decide for him or her in certain specified areas without any need for persuasion through further argument whenever a relevant issue arises (Friedman, "On the Concept," 63–68). The second distinctive feature of authority, which is relevant to the present discussion, is the "mark" of

authority, namely the need to provide the sign or credential of authority through "some public way of identifying the person whose utterances are to be taken as authoritative," which regards "the recognition and acceptance of certain *criteria* for designating who is to possess this kind of influence" (Friedman, "On the Concept," 68–71, emphasis mine). It is also important that we concentrate on the *source* of authority, the source of the special sort of reason for action that authority is meant to denote, rather than its content (Friedman, "On the Concept," 60–61), and that we find this on *the person* and his or her *status* (Friedman, "On the Concept," 65–67). For similar points, especially his reference to "peremptory reasons," see Hart, "Commands and Authoritative Legal Reasons," 100–101.

57 Raz, "Authority and Justification," 121.
58 Raz, "Authority and Justification," 115.
59 Raz, "Authority and Justification," 122–129.
60 Raz, "Authority and Justification," 125. Yet, while they reflect reasons that apply to the subjects of authority, authoritative reasons still "make a difference to what [the] subjects ought to do" (Raz, "Authority and Justification," 126).
61 Raz, "Authority and Justification," 115.
62 Raz, "Authority and Justification," 129–133.
63 Raz, "Authority and Justification," 129.
64 Raz, "Authority and Justification," 131, emphases mine.
65 Raz, "Authority and Justification," 115.
66 Raz, "Authority and Justification," 133–137.
67 Raz, "Authority and Justification," 124.
68 Raz, "Authority and Justification," 135.
69 See, for example, Raz, "Authority and Justification."
70 See McLaughlin, *Anarchism and Authority*, 67 (emphasis mine).
71 Raz, "Introduction," 6.
72 For relevant and very clarifying accounts of theoretical authority and the anarchist position on it, see Richard T. De George, *The Nature and Limits of Authority* (Lawrence: University Press of Kansas, 1985), 33–45; McLaughlin, *Anarchism and Authority*, 63–67.
73 For the following analysis of this idea, see Friedman, "On the Concept," 74–85 (emphasis mine).
74 Friedman, "On the Concept," 77–80 (emphasis mine).
75 Friedman, "On the Concept," 75 and 80–81.
76 Friedman, "On the Concept," 82–85. A second condition, which however does not concern us primarily here, is that the knowledge available to the person of authority should be "in principle available—at least to some humans," i.e., that there exists an "'epistemological' framework," a "class of things capable to be known," this involving the second-order "belief that the mind of man can have contact with the reality on which [the relevant] authority speaks" (Friedman, "On the Concept," 83).
77 Raz, "Authority and Justification," 139.
78 Raz, "Authority and Justification," 138.
79 See Raz, *The Morality of Freedom*, Chapter 13; Raz, *The Authority of Law*, 94–99.
80 Raz, "Authority and Justification," 132.

81 Raz, "Authority and Justification," 132–133.
82 For a comprehensive account of all these features of authority, see McLaughlin, *Anarchism and Authority*, 54–60, 74–80.
83 Miller, *Anarchism*, 18. See last pages of the Introduction of this book. For representative bibliography, applying to the rest of this paragraph, see Wolff, *In Defense of Anarchism*, 11 and 18–19; M.B.E. Smith, "Is There a Prima Facie Obligation to Obey the Law?" *Yale Law Journal* 82 (1973): 969–973; Simmons, *Moral Principles and Political Obligations*, Chapter 8; Simmons, "The Anarchist Position," 275–279, and Simmons, *On the Edge of Anarchy*, 263–269; Green, *The Authority of the State*, 254–255.
84 Simmons, *Moral Principles and Political Obligations*, 200.
85 Simmons, *On the Edge of Anarchy*, 269.
86 Simmons, *Moral Principles and Political Obligations*, 200.
87 Miller, *Anarchism*, 18.
88 Green, *The Authority of the State*, 254–255.
89 For such accusations, see Thomas D. Senor, "What If There Are No Political Obligations? A Reply to A. J. Simmons," *Philosophy and Public Affairs* 16 (1987): 260–268; Horton, *Political Obligation*, 135–136; George Klosko, "Political Obligation and the Natural Duties of Justice," *Philosophy and Public Affairs* 23 (1994): 269–270.
90 Simmons, *Moral Principles and Political Obligations*, 200.
91 Simmons, "Philosophical Anarchism," 23–27.
92 Simmons, *Moral Principles and Political Obligations*, Chapter 8; Simmons, "The Anarchist Position," 275–279; Simmons, *On the Edge of Anarchy*, 261–269; Simmons, "Philosophical Anarchism," 28–32.
93 Simmons, *Moral Principles and Political Obligations*, Chapter 8; Simmons, "Philosophical Anarchism," 26–27; Simmons, "Justification and Legitimacy."
94 Simmons, "Philosophical Anarchism," 22.
95 Simmons, "Philosophical Anarchism," 23. This feature is also usually seen to be what differentiates philosophical anarchism from political anarchism.
96 Simmons, "Philosophical Anarchism," 23–25.
97 Simmons, "The Anarchist Position," 276.
98 Simmons, "The Anarchist Position," 276, Simmons, *On the Edge of Anarchy*, 262.
99 Simmons, "The Anarchist Position," 276. On the whole, the arguments of this paragraph can be understood better within the context of Lockean political philosophy and its account of natural rights and duties, to which Simmons adheres (Simmons, "The Anarchist Position," 276, Simmons, *On the Edge of Anarchy*, esp. Section 8.4). The present argument in particular derives from Locke's doctrine of the natural right to punish (John Locke, *Two Treatises of Government*, ed. Peter Laslett [Cambridge: Cambridge University Press, 1988], Second Treatise, Section 13).
100 Simmons, "The Anarchist Position," 277.
101 Simmons, "The Anarchist Position," 277–278.
102 Simmons, "The Anarchist Position," 278.
103 Simmons, "Philosophical Anarchism," 24–25.
104 Simmons, *On the Edge of Anarchy*, 264–268.

105 For the following presentation of this argument, see Simmons, "Justification and Legitimacy."

106 See Simmons, *Moral Principles and Political Obligations*, 196–199; Simmons, *On the Edge of Anarchy*, 260–269; Simmons, "Philosophical Anarchism," 26–27.

107 Simmons, "Justification and Legitimacy," 770 (emphasis mine).

108 Simmons, *On the Edge of Anarchy*, 264–269.

109 Simmons, *On the Edge of Anarchy*, 266 (emphasis mine).

110 Simmons, *On the Edge of Anarchy*, 265 (emphasis mine).

111 Simmons, *On the Edge of Anarchy*, 268 (emphasis mine).

112 Simmons, *On the Edge of Anarchy*, 269 (emphasis mine).

113 It is not likely that morally unacceptable (e.g., extremely bad) governments would allow their right to rule to be valid even if the required specific transactions could apply to them. As will be shown throughout this study, quality is still relevant in the debate on political obligation.

114 Green, *The Authority of the State*, 254–255.

115 In the criticism of Raz above, I stressed the importance of voluntary choice in securing freedom and equality within political society. In the hands of anarchism, the force of consent is expressed in a negative form: we could not possibly agree on having a state; if we were given the possibility to agree on it, we would not (for more on anarchism and consent, see Chapter 2). But I agree with Raz that it is wrong to believe that political societies can become voluntary associations. Simmons is wrong to believe this (see Simmons, *On the Edge of Anarchy*, 268). It is because they cannot become such associations that the anarchist opposes them and sees them as destructive to proper relations. In light of this problem, we need to find another way of asserting self-government, equality, and legitimacy within political societies. The anarchist perspective and ideal of legitimacy work in this direction.

116 See Chapter 6, especially my explanation for the way the anarchist perspective makes the demand for justification continual and of the role of the anarchist ideal of legitimacy in further justifications of constraints.

117 For example,

> Even if we find that we can seldom justify or forbear the consequences of disobedience or substantial opposition, we can at least lobby for the elimination of those laws that interfere with harmless choices, impose needless regimentation of behavior and lifestyle, limit personal liberty without securing important social benefits…. [We can ask] questions about the moral merits or defects of the individual laws, actions, or policies of our governments. (Simmons, *On the Edge of Anarchy*, 269)

2
The limits of voluntarism

Social Contract and Consent theories are the most familiar and, perhaps, attractive accounts of political obligation. Such accounts center on a *voluntarist interpretation* of political obligation, which places a premium on the free decisions and choices of individuals. For this reason, they are discussed here under the title "Voluntarism." However, as will be seen in this chapter, these theories differ in the degree to which they deserve this characterization in virtue of the kinds of decisions and choices that they require of individuals in order to justify political obligation.

Voluntarism, or the belief in the normative significance of the choices, decisions, or agreement of individuals, is highly valued by both anarchists and many defenders of political institutions. Even oppressive rulers take care to claim that their rule is compatible with the will of their subjects. Contractualists have placed consent at the center of their defense of political authority. What is appealing about consent? *Why* does agreement matter?

Consider the following example: a woman tells her partner that some time ago she made a big decision about their relationship, which involves certain new conditions and which she thought would be the best for both of them. She did not say anything to her partner, because she thought that if they continued to live as they did and she carried out this decision for both of them without him knowing, he could continue his plans and would have the matter sorted out for him without being frustrated. Thus, her behavior has been overall good for him. The man gets very upset. His main complaint is that, however beneficial her attitude may have been for him, he still wanted to know about something so important that affected him and to be able to have a say on it, to participate in the solution of the problem, to think, decide, and agree by himself. The complaint of the man seems justified. What is appealing about it? There is a basic form of freedom that we cherish the most. We care a lot about living our own life, about being able to make our own decisions concerning who to be, how to live, and what to value and achieve. We feel that there is a big difference between letting others impose constraints on us and deciding about the matter ourselves. That we can and do decide to put constraints on ourselves changes significantly their status and application. Although it is believed that there are ways other than consent through which freedom can be realized, the aim of this chapter is to show how consent remains a primary route to this end, despite its failure to ground political obligation. For this, an understanding of the basic freedom at issue is necessary, and I will attempt to provide it in this chapter.

This chapter is constructed on the basis of two underlying leading considerations:

(a) The questions to be addressed *differ in character*. Questions such as "What are the proper signs of consent?" or "Is consent possible?" are factual in character, although with significant normative implications. They concern primarily the realization and proper applications of consent. Questions such as "What are the conditions for regarding consent valid?" or "Is consent valid even when given?" are directly normative ones. They are asked in an attempt to establish the normative relevance and significance of consent in order for it to be used as a basis for social relations and practices. It will become obvious that different contractualist arguments address different questions or sets of questions—some addressing all of them, others only some of them. This will affect the role each contractualist view plays in the present endeavor.

(b) There are distinct kinds of consent. The main distinction is between *actual* (explicit or tacit) and *hypothetical* consent. Further, hypothetical consent itself takes different forms. All these forms of consent appear already in the work of traditional contractualists such as Hobbes, Locke, Rousseau, and Kant and are almost commonplace among contemporary political theorists. Some forms of consent more naturally give rise to coherent voluntarist theories.

Versions of contractualism also differ from one another. For example, while in Locke's theory of the social contract we find versions of actual consent (both explicit and tacit)[1], others are closer to hypothetical-consent views. Thus, as I will argue later in this chapter, Hobbes's contractualism is based on a hypothetical-consent argument. My arguments with respect to Rawls, in Chapter 3, show that his appeal both to concerns of rationality (of a Hobbesian character) and to concerns of fairness (of a Rousseauian-Kantian character) is reflected in his adoption of a hypothetical-contract view. Most importantly, it will become obvious that the rationale of actual consent differs from the rationale of hypothetical consent.

Thus there are different types of contractualist reasoning: the voluntarist accounts to be examined here *differ in nature* and the distinctions between them reflect the *different difficulties* that these theories face with respect to the *same* general problem, that is, the problem of proving the possibility of agreement or of some other morally acceptable way of reflecting voluntary engagement, as an expression of an ample characterization of why and how agreement matters. Therefore, my criticisms will not be directed toward the theory of any particular philosopher, but rather will be developed in light of these variations. These criticisms are the first step toward a defense of the critical philosophical anarchist position within the debate on political obligation.

An anarchist criticism of voluntarist theories of political obligation

The historical roots[2] of voluntarism and its characteristic individualist account of persons as free and equal rational beings explain the centrality within voluntarism of the notion of "obligation" and its source in the voluntary undertakings of individuals. The focus of the present study is this *centrality* itself. That is to say, it is the insistence on the importance of developing a voluntarist account of political obligation consistent with the active dimension of obligations—in contrast to the passivity of obedience—that I will examine.

As explained in Chapter 1, all theories of political obligation should provide a *moral ground* for a special kind of obligation, namely the *political*. For this, their moral ground should meet the conditions of political obligation, that is, "generality," "particularity," "bindingness," and "content-independence." Generality requires political obligation to apply to *most* of the individuals in a society governed by the state. Particularity requires individuals to be obligated to the *particular* government of their *own* country of residence. Bindingness and content-independence mean that the law is authoritative as such and is to be obeyed *in the way it requires to be obeyed*. Together these four conditions express the distinctive nature of "the political." Voluntarist theories attempt to meet these conditions by appeal to the voluntary undertakings of individuals. They should thus show that this type of act is both possible and of a sort that is appropriate to their demands. This kind of endeavor has created the most fundamental difficulties for these theories: both contract and consent theories are criticized for their failure to provide, in a suitably generalized form, an actual and effective analogue in the political sphere of the type of commitment they take to be a necessary and sufficient ground of the obligations in question.

The arguments to follow show that *the possibility of agreement* is ungrounded: either consent is not given or it is given in a way that perverts its voluntarist and intentional nature. This constitutes the central problem for voluntarism. For its core element fails if it is not shown to be extensively realizable and in a way that preserves the core intuition of the theory—that is, the desirability of meaningful individual authorization. The problem of agreement involves both factual questions, concerning the existence of consent, and normative ones, regarding its validity and bindingness—each kind affecting voluntarism in a particular way.

Actual consent

I begin with theories based on *actual* consent. These include views based on the notion of "explicit" consent and those based on the notion of "tacit" consent. In what follows each view is discussed in turn.

The existence of actual consent would directly reflect the required act of commitment in the political world. It finds its most promising definition in terms of *explicit* consent. Voluntarist theories of political obligation would establish their success if they could demonstrate conclusively the possibility of a widespread form of explicit consent. I take such a consent to be either "historical," namely the original consent of the first members of a political organization, or "personal," namely the consent given by each citizen individually.[3] Explicit consent, so defined, would satisfy the basic conditions of free choice and commitment. These conditions are as follows: that there is an intentional and voluntary decision and choice over the content (and, hence, implications) of the commitment in question, under circumstances of unimpaired knowledge and rationality; that all this is also communicated as an object of public assessment.[4] The following considerations display the difficulties with establishing the possibility of explicit consent, first, in a historical and, second, in a personal form.

The obvious problem with any account that may appeal to an "original" consent is that it has hardly been a historical reality: the historical evidence in support is rare, and there is no convincing reason to accept its possibility around the world. It is also doubtful whether primitive, pre-social individuals would be able or willing to create this consent. Still, even if consent had once existed, it would later constantly require the consent of future generations. This requirement generates two worries: first, the problem of agreement,[5] reflected in the risk of refusal of the next generations to undertake the required commitment; second, the question whether the form of self-assumed duty constituted by such a commitment can be accepted as the right form of voluntary undertaking. Political consent provides only one understanding of "self-assumed obligation"—namely, as the "authorization" of someone else's acting on one's own behalf, as the acceptance of "an already existing relationship of obligation"—and probably not the most appropriate one for capturing this notion.[6] This understanding defines a passive acceptance of a relationship determined and characterized by someone else and hence of whatever he or she authorizes. And it differs from the conception of self-assumed obligation as "the free creation of a [new] relationship."[7] This latter conception involves a relationship initiated by individuals themselves and determined in content by their own autonomous judgments. It is the conception exemplified in the practice of promising and, in fact, it is the model of what would make the case for voluntarism in the political sphere. The political correlate of this notion is the objective of a consistent voluntarism, and it is this that voluntarism cannot provide. When the voluntarist character of the notion of consent is thus questioned, its implementation by further generations becomes even more controversial: apart from the difficulty with acquiring their agreement, the character of this agreement itself becomes problematic. On the whole, historical consent has more of a rhetorical function. All consent and its value are based rather on personal consent.

In the case of personal consent, the impossibility of its general realization, which is in fact determinative of the difficulty of establishing historical consent, is more obvious. Almost none of us has ever given such consent, and we rarely have the opportunity today to give it to the governments of the societies we inhabit. The conditions of living of the populations of democratic governments, the size of modern cities, and other external circumstances make it impossible for their citizens to commit themselves individually. Ethnic, class, and gender differences and the discriminations accompanying them, along with the controversial status of voting as a proper implementation of personal consent on a large scale,[8] are also substantial obstacles to this possibility, especially because they affect the very validity of personal consent. Moreover, the way even the most familiar sorts of democratic governments are organized makes it difficult to compare them to voluntary associations, the nature of which would render practices similar to promising possible.[9] Importantly so, such schemes have little relevance to the structure and characteristics that make our societies political. The large-scaled, centralized, hierarchical, monopolistic, and coercive character of the political societies does not provide a background where close and directly informed relationships can flourish, and this character in fact generates the social difficulties just stated.[10] This is observed by various theorists, whether they are anarchists or not. An additional observation is that there are many people—anarchists and others—who do *not want* to consent to the authority of their governments, and thus would never give their personal consent even where possible. Finally, the content of agreement itself becomes questionable, since appeal to explicit personal consent involves the absurd demand that we consent to laws that we do not know and to those that will be made in the future.[11] All these obstacles become more difficult in the light of an aspiration to understand personal consent to involve the appropriate form of self-assumed obligation distinguished in the previous paragraph, namely as the free creation and determination of a new relationship.

The above considerations represent prominent philosophical anarchist criticisms of the voluntarists' appeal to explicit consent. They can all be summarized in the following assertion of Simmons: "[E]xpress consent is not a suitably general ground for political obligation. The paucity of express consentors is painfully apparent. Most of us have never been faced with a situation where express consent to a government's authority was even appropriate, let alone actually performed such an act."[12] This assertion reflects a failure to combine generality with particularity within a voluntarist account of political obligation. The element that voluntarism offers is, in its proper form, a very suitable instance of what would explain a relationship with our *own* government in terms of its own criteria, thus meeting (where it is actually given) the particularity condition of political obligation. But it fails to remain so to a sufficiently general extent, as the generality condition requires.

Tacit consent

The aforementioned difficulties with explicit consent contribute to the considerable appeal to voluntarists of the notion of *tacit* consent. Given the way it is used by the theories in question, my suggestion is that tacit consent is a hypothesized form of commitment meant to acquire, through an appropriate interpretation, the actual substance required to make it relevant to, and effective within, a voluntarist theory of political obligation.

The importance of tacit consent lies in the fact that a proper instance of tacit consent is not significantly different from explicit consent. The former differs from the latter in "the special mode of its expression": it is either "silent and inactive" or legitimately inferred from certain actions construed as "signs of consent."[13] The problem then becomes one of discovering and establishing the proper instances of tacit consent, by proving the possibility and actuality of the legitimate modes of its expression, either in terms of *silence* or in terms of *legitimate inference*.

In the case of silence, there are certain conditions to be met in addition to the ones placed on explicit consent (for the latter, see the section "Actual consent"). These further conditions include the demand for a precise definition of the time during which one can decide whether to consent or not and of the reactions that may be taken as indications of consent (for example, remaining present during the time of decision-making). These clarify the terms in which the communication desired can be achieved. There is also the demand that reasonable means be used for the indication of consent and that the consequences of dissent not be too severe (for example, that no complicated physical acts are required to express consent and that no dismal punishment threatens potential dissenters). These latter conditions are extremely important for the validity of consent, since complicated procedures and alternative choices with undesirable effects limit or even cancel the availability of options, which is what makes consent free.[14]

Only passive attitudes meeting these conditions form instances of tacit consent. Relying on these conditions, however, provides no more than a basis for a case-by-case estimation. Such a procedure qualifies only for settlements at an empirical level, depends largely on contingencies, and is sometimes very complex and impractical. Thus, it complicates the establishment of a valid act of authorization, because it does not represent a general normative guide of a theory of tacit consent in the political sphere.

In the case of legitimate inference, appeal to which is the most usual method of defending tacit consent, the need is for the specification of certain acts correctly regarded as implying consent. There is disagreement over the extent to which we should decide which acts qualify as signs of consent on the basis of "conventional criteria," namely conventional means for members of a society to commonly invoke as determinative of whether certain words or gestures are signs of consent (for example, whether a nod in a marriage ceremony is a way of saying "I do").[15] But the main issue here is normative. It affects whether the kinds of acts usually invoked do entail consent. Indeed, it is these very acts that, as the anarchists point out, do *not* seem to satisfy the conditions of validity given above—especially the basic normative conditions of knowledge, intentionality, and choice. They are interpreted by the theorist in defiance of the normative demands and obligate persons in absence of their own permission.[16]

The failure of consent theorists to provide proper instances of tacit consent and to establish their validity, in order then to show their general application in existing polities, is demonstrated by the following discussion of three kinds of acts traditionally construed as signs of consent.

The first is residence. Appealing to residence creates perhaps the clearest ground for doubts. Hume criticizes this effectively in his famous argument from "Of the Original Contract." There he compares remaining in one's own country with the situation of "a man ... remaining in a vessel ... [within which] he was carried on board while asleep, and must leap into the ocean, and perish, the moment he leaves her."[17] This comparison describes residence when emigration as the corresponding alternative is both extremely difficult and painful (think of conditions in contemporary nation-states, let alone the varying financial and other material as well as psychological circumstances of different citizens). Thus, it shows that residence alone cannot be counted as consent, since it does not present itself against a real alternative that would make it a free choice.[18] This should not be taken to mean that the impossibility of dissent makes it impossible to consent, but rather that intentional consent through residence cannot be assumed.

In response, it has been objected that emigration is not an unacceptable choice forced upon us, unless the only attitude available under residence is the acceptance of the authority of the state.[19] But survival within a state does not necessarily require acknowledgment of its authority. Indeed, these observations might free residence from being a kind of invalidating duress. The salient point here, however, is that they confirm rather than oppose its inappropriateness as a sign of consent to authority. Whether bearable or not, residence still cannot necessarily be assumed as evidence of such consent. And, in the end, the real force of Hume's argument can be seen to lie in its revealing this point: even if valid intentional consent remains possible under residence, we cannot infer that residence is a voluntary decision, nor can we infer simply from residence a voluntary decision to acknowledge the state. Still, we may have underestimated Hume's position if we link it too closely to residence. For he is making a more general point that is crucial for discussions of political authority. I will return to this view in the end of my discussion of tacit consent.

At this point, we can see that consent theory is deprived of an element that would guarantee a high level of generality in a properly particularized way. Generality and particularity are two of the main conditions that theories of political obligation have to satisfy together. Tacit consent in the form of residence would, if it were shown to be a valid sort of authorization, commit a large part of the population to their own particular government and thus provide a satisfactory moral justification of the obligations suitable to its political nature. But residence is far from a validating acquiescence to political authority.

The second kind of action construed as a sign of consent is the acceptance of benefits provided by the government of one's own country. This appeal is found in Locke's *Second Treatise of Government*. Such benefits usually have the status of public goods, namely goods that may be reasonably regarded as valuable to (almost) everyone and that are "non-excludable" and "non-rival" in nature. Non-excludable goods are those that, once produced, cannot be enjoyed by some members of a society without being enjoyed by all the others. Goods are non-rival if the extent and the way they are enjoyed by an individual do not affect the utility enjoyed by others.[20] Acceptance of such benefits does not constitute a clear sign of consent, however, but at best a "consent-implying" act, namely, an act that commits morally to the same performance that would be required on the basis of consent, but that would not normally be taken as an attempt to consent—nor would its agent normally be taken to have intended to consent.[21] It is an act better described and justified on the basis of the principle of fairness, which will be discussed in Chapter 4. Although, as I will argue in that chapter, an adequate interpretation of that principle has to be voluntarist, its nature is still different from consent. The acceptance of benefits is deprived of a directly consensual character. It is also vulnerable to the objections to the principle of fairness as a ground of political obligation.

The third candidate is voting. Voting can be taken as explicit (or express), rather than tacit consent, given that it is an act expressing commitment to specified aspects of a constitution. But here it is understood as the authorization of specific governments that might be taken as a sign of consent to political authority, and in this respect its function is of a less overt kind.

Plamenatz[22] and others appeal to democratic elections as a proper indication of consent to the authority of the state. Nevertheless, reliance on voting involves at least three difficulties. First, the background conditions for qualifying elections as free seem to be properly met only in direct participatory democracies, namely, where there is direct, equal, and extensive participation in political decision-making. Even in such polities, mixed motivations in voting complicate the issue of consent, i.e., the presence of both self-interest and a concern for the common good as functional motivating bases of decision-making. For example, on which of these two grounds does consent count? And how do we understand which motivation operates each time? However, the point here is that, even if direct democracy offered the most suitable background for legitimate consent, it is not the kind of constitution found within any current democratic society.[23] Second, the contemporary expression of liberal ideals by representative democracies is defective. Voting for representatives is the kind of authorization that was referred to in the above discussion on explicit consent as a questionable paradigm of self-assumed obligation. It is in fact a promise to obey the directives of the representatives, an attitude reflecting more conformity to, rather than willing and active approval of, those directives. Pragmatically speaking, moreover, the social differences (class and gender) and circumstances present in contemporary democracies do not allow for an informed and deliberate choice of rulers at a general and equal level. Third, and in the face of the second criticism just made, there are (at least) two points that suggest the failure to meet the generality condition of political obligation as understood and applied in the debate.

Point one is that voting is not always an accurate gauge of freely expressed preferences. There are people who vote in response to continual moral intimidation by social leaders in different social areas (such as schools, the church, and the media).[24] Can their consent be regarded as real? Many people even abstain from voting or cast invalid votes, while the choices of many others are defeated in the elections. Can these persons be regarded as voluntary supporters of the elected government? The former surely are not, and the latter are only if they themselves confirm the result as their second-best preference. This also shows that a possible appeal to the consent of the majority as binding for all invokes a form of consent that is redundant to personal consent and thus open to all the problems that the latter has been shown to involve.[25]

The second and most important point I want to make is that, even if voting were sufficiently general, it would not necessarily imply recognition of the authority of the state. It could express a choice of good over bad governments, consistently made even by an anarchist, and other instances of decisions concerned with who shall rule, but not bearing on questions of the justification of authority.[26] Given the alternatives available, any individual can vote on specific aspects of a constitution without at the same time expressing his or her opinion on the general question of its foundation. On the other hand, even if through voting citizens legitimated government, this would still not authorize every one of its significant acts and thus would not establish a permanent actual obligation to it. All these points show additionally how voting defeats the particularity condition of political obligation. On the whole, voting takes place within already existing institutions, when the existence of the state is taken as a given. It cannot thus be taken as the basis of an obligation to the state.

Given these arguments, it should be clear now that appeal to tacit consent is not as promising as it appears to be initially. Silence needs careful detection and interpretation, and a legitimate inference rarely obtains. Tacit consent fails to exemplify the kind of act that could be seen as the voluntary undertaking of political obligations at a sufficient level of generality. This is the fundamental complaint that anarchists raise against voluntarists.

Here is where we can return to the important, additional insight that Hume provides in his discussion of the social contract.[27] Hume explains the distance between philosophical appeals to an original contract as the basis of political authority and the actual relation between individuals and the governments of their societies. He stresses the effects on the acquiescence on the part of individuals of force, necessity, and habit, and his criticism of residence examined above is an aspect of this demonstration. But the crux of his argument is that the constraints of political authority have a special nature. We can escape constraints of a different nature, but political constraints are *inescapable*. This distinctiveness of political norms requires a distinctive perspective on them and a distinctive way to think about whether they are constraining. We cannot derive the best political norms through abstraction. The motivations for allegiance to existing societies are too complicated for an ideal appeal to consent to provide a proper explanation and basis for it. We have to provide a justificatory basis for political norms that accounts for and at the same time overcomes the actual inclinations of individuals and the conditions of social life and their complexities. We have to attend to their special nature and find a proper way of assessing them in view of that nature. If we insist on the language of consent, in the case of residence, for example, it can justifiably be asked: Where are the alternatives given to each individual? Why do individuals have to live with the constraints imposed on them without ever having given their free consent? How can they escape them without losing too much that is important?

This is to a large extent the essence of the anarchist perspective. Anarchists remind us that the political nature of institutions and of the obligations attached to them demands a special kind of justification. The moral reasons provided in their support might account for the acceptability of certain aspects of them. But they need first and foremost to apply as a recognition that the coercive and inescapable nature of political institutions puts particular constraints on what is going to count as legitimate justification. We might be advised to support political institutions, but why is this an overriding obligation the violation of which should be punished? How is it that a dominant, permanent, and coercion-based determination of social relations is ever justifiable? For Hume, consent theories cannot give the answer. For the anarchist, this need for a proper assessment of the nature of the political draws attention to the significance of choice, the character and role of which must be shown to be much stronger than that of the acts involved in tacit consent. For this, hypothetical consent seems a more promising approach.

Hypothetical consent

Thus, the next candidate for grounding political obligation in voluntarist terms is *hypothetical* consent. This has received considerable attention from contemporary theorists,[28] and an influential improvement of its Kantian roots is found in Rawls's *A Theory of Justice* (1971). However, it has taken a form that departs from voluntarism. As explained at the beginning of the section "An anarchist criticism of voluntarist theories of political obligation," in the context of the present discussion on political obligation, voluntarism is understood in its most literal and direct form, namely as theories appealing to the unimpaired, *actual* decisions, choices, and actions of individuals. The discussion on hypothetical consent introduces another dimension to voluntarism. It will also clarify the extent to which this form of consent belongs to voluntarism as understood so far, or if it properly extends voluntarism to purely incorporate a different sense, and whether this is useful for the debate on political obligation.[29]

We can see this if we bear in mind an important distinction between two forms of hypothetical consent and the roles of their different rationales. I will argue that there are two ways of understanding hypothetical consent, neither of which grounds political obligation. On the first understanding, which falls more clearly under voluntarism, consent is offered as a device of reasoning that helps us understand our actual disposition toward the authority of political institutions. On the second understanding, hypothetical consent becomes a moral route representing the conclusions of unimpaired and impartial reasoning. I will show that the first way of understanding hypothetical consent is the more problematic of the two, and that the second, which is the one usually involved in theories of political obligation, is irrelevant to direct voluntarism.

It is important for voluntarist accounts to preserve a link between the ground of political obligation they provide and the quality of the institutions to which it is owed. Even if some form of actual consent were successfully given, it would have to be given to institutions that exhibit some morally relevant merits in order to be valid.[30] I suggested in the section "Quality-based and interaction-based evaluations of political institutions" in Chapter 1 that both quality and specific interaction are relevant aspects of institutional evaluation within the debate on political obligation. In the discussion of consent so far, given that my focus is on actual consent, I have developed elements of transactional evaluation (i.e., features of specific interaction). At this point of the discussion, I reintroduce the idea that quality, or institutional morality, is relevant to any account of political obligation and thus should be examined in relation to the accounts analyzed here, namely voluntarism. The discussion of hypothetical consent will provide the first steps for understanding and deciding the proper role of quality-based considerations in the debate.

In the context of the discussion of actual consent, an effective solution to the problem would be for the theories under scrutiny to incorporate institutional morality in an exhibition of a suitable instance of voluntary undertaking: an act involving actual choice that is also reasonable would likely provide the required link. As explained above, however, these theories fail to provide such an instance of voluntary commitment, and the link with quality remains a related unsolved problem. This fact eliminates the possibility of success for voluntarism on the basis of the most promising route. Thus, the attention of its defenders has been reoriented toward *hypothetical* consent. In this context, there is an initial concern with institutional quality: the demand that the arrangements to which people consent should be to an acceptable extent reasonable and fair gives rise to the idea that this could be achieved "by characterising the circumstances of voluntary agreement in such a way that indisputably irrational, unreasonable, or unfair agreements [would] not meet the conditions for voluntary consent."[31] A representative example of an attempt at such a characterization is given by the description of the "state of nature" provided by traditional contractualists.[32] The discussion below shows how the endeavor fails to combine voluntarism with a hypothetical-consent view of political obligation.

The point of hypothetical consent is to show what it would be fair, reasonable, and rational for people to agree to within appropriately characterized circumstances. This signifies a departure from direct voluntarism, since it makes the *actual* consent of individuals irrelevant: the question here is not whether they have actually consented, but whether they *ought to* consent. The hypothetical consent becomes a theoretical device used to represent the conclusions that reason would yield, whenever unimpaired and consistently exercised.

The first form of hypothetical consent that I want to discuss, however, both utilizes this device and might allow voluntarism. It involves an understanding of hypothetical consent that aspires to actuality. According to this form of consent, although we may be unwilling to agree to something under the present circumstances, we *would* in many cases have consented to it under circumstances of unbiased reasoning. Such circumstances obtain when we are ready to adopt the course of action that is derived from rational and reasonable deliberation, not influenced by our knowledge of information concerning what is beneficial to our personal interests or by our feelings about the persons involved in the relevant case. In this way hypothetical consent claims to retain the character of voluntarism, since it shows that reason leads us to the conclusion that we would *in fact* consent, and thus to the realization that we *do* consent, in many cases. Even though our reasoning does most of the job here, the last court of appeal lies in the existence of a disposition in us to personally consent. Unfortunately, this form of consent falls prey, even if in a counterfactual way, to problems similar to those that affect the notion of personal consent and its function within voluntarism, which were discussed in the section "Actual consent." Most pressingly in this case, the validity of our disposition to consent depends largely on the circumstances within which such a consent works. Its existence and function do not generate obligations unless the circumstances are such that the conditions of the validity of consent survive the relevant thought-experiment, i.e., that the disposition for actual choice applies naturally under them. Thus, with regard to most of us, it is very difficult to prove what we really think in each case about the relevant functions of the political institutions of our country of residence and to demonstrate that our conclusions represent a valid choice. Once again, the required satisfaction of both the generality and the particularity conditions of political obligation is not achieved.

It follows that the *possibility of agreement* collapses once more. These considerations show that the attempt, under this first form, to combine voluntarism with the rationale of hypothetical consent, so as to justify political obligation on this basis, is problematic. For this reason, a different form of hypothetical consent is usually involved in accounts of political obligation.

This second form of consent provides the most representative implementation of the essence of hypothetical consent as described at the beginning of our discussion. It is this form that constitutes a device used to clarify the demands of Reason. It concentrates exclusively on what a rational, reasonable, and unbiased person is in the position to recognize as indisputably reasonable and fair; that is, it provides a theory of *good reasons*. In this way, consent becomes irrelevant. Voluntarism as represented in forms of actual consent is absent in this hypothetical account. On the other hand, if the fundamental intuition of voluntarism is modified via the rationale of hypothetical consent, such a rationalistic voluntarism seems to be invoked within a theoretical background where it plays no role. Hypothetical consent cannot be located within the voluntarist effort to prove the actuality of agreement. One could of course argue that, if a question such as "can I will that..." *reveals* moral aspects that were not visible, then surely voluntarism *has played* a fundamental role in deciding the possibility of agreement. Although I agree with this, my claim is that it has no role to play for *actual* obligation. Whether or not it is accepted as a proper expression of the essence of voluntarism, the rationalism of hypothetical consent is still distinct from the concern with actuality invoked in straight voluntarist accounts.[33]

The theorist then has to choose between an approach that commits him to a proof of actual, valid choice—which so far has been shown to be unsuccessful—and one that provides a phenomenology of how we might feel about our duties through reasonable reflection—which is important for explaining and affecting choice, but does not actually prove its existence and application.

One important point to derive from these considerations is that hypothetical consent—which is not, as explained, of an actual voluntary nature—might have its ultimate source either in "teleological" or in "deontological" accounts of "good reasons" for political obligation.[34] Teleological accounts are those focusing on final ends as the criteria of the morality of actions and institutions. Deontological accounts are those focusing on the quality of actions and institutions themselves—the intentions and the procedures on which they are based—as the morally relevant criteria. Its success thus depends on the success of either of these theories, although, as I will proceed to argue in Chapters 3 and 4, neither is, in fact, successful. My discussion of an improved understanding of contractualism below anticipates these difficulties: it generates doubts as to whether hypothetical consent should be used to ground political obligation in the first place.

The conclusion of the examination of hypothetical consent in the light of the anarchist criticism is indicative of the continued failure of voluntarism to establish the possibility of agreement. The first application of hypothetical consent remains bound to the failures of its individualist roots. It faces all the problems present in actual consent accounts of political obligation, among which is the problem that it cannot keep voluntarism in line with the concern about the quality of institutions. The second and most accurate application of it, on the other hand, provides a route toward a promising account of political obligation, accommodating concerns about the quality of institutions, but, in doing so, it departs from direct voluntarism. Its plausibility and success are thus independent of the present discussion.

Raz on consent

At this point, I turn to consider Raz's views on the validity of consent, as set out in his book *The Morality of Freedom* (1986). My discussion of Raz forms a natural bridge between the preceding examination of consent and the following criticism of contractualism.

Raz examines instrumental and noninstrumental justifications of consent as a ground of authority and considers the extent of its validity in each case. The conclusion he derives from his reference to instrumental justifications is that,

on instrumental grounds [namely, considerations regarding the benefits either of consent itself or of being able to consent], consent can only be held binding if it is so qualified that its effect is *almost entirely confined to reinforcing independently existing obligations to obey* ... But it cannot be used as a way of endowing anyone with authority where that person had none.[35]

This assertion is founded on the recognition that, while consent might be used to facilitate the establishment of authority where there are independent good reasons for so doing, its unqualified and unlimited use is more likely to lead to bad and undesirable consequences,[36] which defeat its initially valuable role. Raz's remarks are on par with the preceding arguments, which show that consent does not constitute a generally applied actual basis for political obligation and that, in its failure to represent choice on this matter, it needs to be established in other ways in order to ground political authority. They prepare us for the forthcoming examination (later in this chapter and in the following two chapters) of attempts to derive a general political obligation from (hypothetical) consent as a theory of good reasons and of the limitations of these attempts.[37] The discussion of the social contract below will confirm these conclusions.

Social contract theories

Appealing to *The Social Contract* is the most popular way of developing a consent-based theory. Thus, it is vulnerable to all the preceding criticisms, regardless of its precise formulation. Therefore, the role of the following discussion on contractualism is merely to provide some additional considerations that throw more light on the anarchist attack on voluntarism. The objective is to confirm that, when subjected to anarchist scrutiny, the centrality of free individual undertakings within the voluntarist account of political obligation either commits the theory to an ongoing attempt to solve the problem of agreement or is transformed in a way that compromises the theory's primary appeal to such undertakings.

The classical contract theorists Hobbes and Locke were haunted by the problem of *the possibility of agreement*, since its resolution was the decisive move for establishing their theories. This problem remains crucial and perhaps insoluble for contemporary contractualists as well, even though it is misleadingly circumvented by the appeal to hypothetical contract.[38] The use of tacit consent and of the hypothetical contract created, for the most part, either a fictional actuality of agreement or the mistaken impression that from the detection of desirable characteristics of the state we can assume, without further proof, the possibility and existence of agreement.

The above considerations simply restate that for contractualists the problem remains vivid.[39] Both Hobbes and Locke used the social contract to describe an initial undesirable pre-social order and to explain the constitution of civil society through a contractual agreement of individuals as a rational escape from that order. In Hobbes, however, the state of nature involves a social characterization (life without security), while in Locke it is primarily a moral characterization: it represents the moral condition of individuals who have no political obligations.[40] Also, in Hobbes the two stages toward the establishment of authority are simultaneous: at the same time that the parties agree to create a political society, they directly give authority to the Sovereign through an individual, noncontractual transference of their rights to it. With Locke's theory, on the other hand, it becomes clear that the move from the creation of civil society to the recognition of authority is a distinct one, and it is this move that involves the (actual) consent from which political obligations arise and which is of great importance for contractualism. The creation of civil society itself is the first necessary and important act and the legitimate escape from the state of nature for Locke, and it is the result only of an actual and *unanimous* original contract between all those individuals who wish to create it. The transference of political authority from civil society to government (through majority rule) is legitimate only on the basis of an initially created membership of this kind, involving a trust based on actual, individual consent.[41] Locke's theory is a paradigm of an actual contract account of political obligation. It thus insists on the importance of actual consent as a way of declaring the value of choice. Nevertheless, without losing its value, actual consent still renders the theory vulnerable to the problem of agreement that, as shown in the preceding discussion, such a form of consent generates for political obligation.

The way the problem of agreement shows up in Hobbes's theory is characteristic.[42] In Hobbes, the impossibility of agreement takes the form of a paradox: the very impossibility of agreement constitutes a central reason for requiring agreement.[43] The combination of this paradox with the Hobbesian instrumental notion of rationality—namely, of the reasoning of individuals as one based on rational self-interest, on the protection and promotion of their private situation—has brought Hobbes's theory to the fore of social choice and rational choice theory. These theories are mainly concerned with rendering individual choices compatible with collective ones and with the connected problems of cooperation and the coordination of decisions and actions in the social sphere. Hobbes's description of, and contractualist solution to, the "state of nature" has acquired a dominant transformation through these theories. The problem of agreement has been depicted as the game-theoretical situation called the "Prisoner's Dilemma."[44] This is the story of (any) two (or more) prisoners who have each to choose whether to betray one another and make a deal with the authorities in circumstances where they do not know what the other party will do. If the one betrays and the other does not, the former will suffer a smaller sentence and the latter a bigger one. If they both betray, they will both get a bigger punishment. If the two cooperate by not betraying each other, they will both get the initial deal with the authorities, which is a better deal collectively, but not as good as each would get individually if the other did not betray. No prisoner knows what the other will choose; and the deal resulting from cooperation is the best collectively, but not the best individually. The Prisoner's Dilemma, however, differs from problems of pure coordination (in its most ordinary sense) in that it is primarily a problem of the impossibility of cooperation (due to an unwillingness based on the individuals' rationality of self-interest, since it is in their personal interest to behave badly). It is not one of practical obstacles to achieving the best application of cooperation, which ordinary coordination is about. (This is based not so much on rational unwillingness, but on the lack of knowledge of their situation on the part of the individuals involved or on their doubts about the knowledge of the rest of the participants and thus about the possibility of the morally best outcome).[45] In using this game, the point for contractualists is to show that the state is a preferable solution to a situation where self-interested rational individuals are led to continual deception, due to uncertainty about the other individuals' behavior, which deprives them all of the advantages of cooperation. The state is seen as the guarantor of agreement and advocated as the most effective provider of essential goods.

Irrespective of the related dispute between anarchists and defenders of the state about the best social order for achieving these tasks,[46] the theme is interesting because of the two issues that underlie it. These issues highlight the failure of voluntarism to ground political obligation on actual free agreement.

First, the paradox of agreement remains insoluble. On the one hand, the state seems to *presuppose morality,* since individuals unable to keep their promises would not be able to keep the contract to create government. On the other, the state is created *because* without it agreement is impossible. In the first case, the state becomes unnecessary, since agreement can be enforced by morality. In Raz's words, if we obey due to independent moral reasons, agreement as a further reason for obeying becomes derivative and is rather a part of and confirmation of primary reasons for obligation than its basis itself. In the second case, the crucial question is created for contractualism of how to prove the possibility of consent to the government itself by individuals who are unable to keep their agreements. Given that only the government can play the role of "an enforcing agent" in the first place, there seems to be no satisfactory response to this question.[47] Both Hobbes and Locke saw the contract to hold only between individuals; they did not extend it to hold between individuals and the state.[48] The state, thus, became the only enforcer and guarantor of contract, in the case of Hobbes, an absolute sovereign not itself bound by any contract.[49] Yet this does not solve the paradox, since it creates an infinite regress starting from a guarantor of the very accomplishment by the state itself of the role ascribed to it by the contract. But then that guarantor needs a guarantor, and so on.[50]

Again, one could say, following Raz, that in the absence of morality there is no guarantee of and no validity in the enforcement of any agent.

The preceding considerations suggest that, for contractualists, the paradox of agreement is inescapable. They support Antony de Jasay's claim that the contractualist argument "is either self-contradictory (contract can remedy the impossibility of contract) or circular (cooperation requires contract which requires cooperation)."[51]

In fairness to social contract theory, however, I believe we can see ways out of this dilemma. As far as the (second above) argument about the impossibility of the state is concerned, Hobbes himself does not believe in absolute egoism: his individuals care for self-preservation, but this does not exclude their ability for limited altruism, which leaves room for some sympathy for others and for compassion. These features might still be a basis for a basic agreement to create and preserve a common guarantor, even if not for keeping agreements without him. What remains to be proved is whether we would agree to such a guarantor. Also, in his defense of the state, Hobbes sees in the sovereign the universality that can guide individuals out of their egoistic tendencies, although it is on this that anarchists and defenders of the state disagree. Most importantly, there is something further to be said against the argument that the state is unnecessary if morality exists. Even if individuals are moral, the state might still be needed for settling quite important problems: for judging what the demands of morality are and how to coordinate. For this, a hypothetical contract might be an indispensable device. It may be used as a route for finding out what the specific way of addressing interaction is. If, according to Raz's position, agreement can be valuable in reinforcing independently existing reasons for obedience, then its role in a hypothetical form in explaining what it is that we have reason to do and how we might get to know it is very valuable. This seems to be the strongest point of social contract theory, and I will develop it as part of an improved understanding of the social contract that I will attempt in the section "A defense of hypothetical contractualism" below. However, having such a role, the social contract device provides a very useful explanation for how we might understand our duties to others, but not a basis of the enforcement of these duties. In other words, it might provide a good diagnostic of the reasons we have for explaining the state, but not a proof of our support of it.

The second issue that arises for contract theorists in the present discussion is that concentration on the advantages to be achieved by the creation of the state reveals misdirected concern. The contractualist argument is transformed from one concerning the actual possibility of agreement into one about the merits of the state. The story about the social contract becomes a strategy used to confirm the merits of certain forms of government. In the case of Hobbes, it becomes an argument in favor of the state as an independent factor that *would* or *could* (or even, *can*) gain our agreement on the basis of its qualities. Agreement, possible or not, has no bearing on the success of this argument.[52] The theoretical basis of the latter ceases to be voluntarist. The link with the self-assumed commitment taken by voluntarists to establish a special relationship between individuals and their governments disappears, and the whole discussion is transformed into a debate concerning the accomplishments and desirability of institutions.

A central problem underlying the above issues is that the plausibility of the contractualists' conception of circumstances that make dominant and coercive (and even absolute) interference desirable is based on the presumption of the necessity of domination and coercion. In turn, this is rooted in our experience of the societies in which we find ourselves. As I indicated in the previous chapters and in dealing with Hume's argument earlier in the discussion of tacit consent, domination and coercion are not desirable in themselves: they cannot be presupposed as inescapable, nor established without proper justification. More crucially, insistence on the role of coercion as a motivation for compliance seeks to found the authority of governments on the wrong ground. As I claimed in the previous chapters, coercion is, indeed, a feature of the political. It is not its only feature, however, nor its most definitive, and it cannot on its own create binding requirements.[53] As many critics insist, laws might be obeyed on the basis of prudential fear of legal sanctions. However, this does not reveal recognition of the law's authority, that is, of political obligation. There is a difference between explaining the role of coercion in social interaction where institutions are already established, for which the above arguments from the social contract might be helpful, and connecting coercion to grounds for further justification without adequately defending it in the first place.

Even if the state-of-nature argument for the state established a need for institutions, such a justification would require constant reinforcement. The contractualist depiction of institutional merits might provide a first motive for creating political institutions. But this does not exclude alternative possibilities and it does not preempt the argument that autonomy and equality might be prior to certain merits and difficult to sacrifice. For this reason, the state-of-nature argument cannot be final and does not in itself lead to the justification of political obligation. The contractualist failure to prove consent-based agreement reflects a discontinuity between quality-based arguments for the existence of the state and arguments for the actual creation of political obligation through morally relevant interaction.[54] Through contractualism we can understand that, although we might have reasons to consider the state a good thing to exist—for example, due to its ability to protect us—this does not establish a special relation of rights and obligations between political institutions and ourselves as the individuals who live in the territories where these institutions exist. There is a big difference between considering the state to be good and having an actual moral relation of duty to it, and neither of these aspects can be derived from the other. This point is also central for deciding the role of quality in the debate on political obligation.

The above discussion of contractualism reveals the strength of the anarchist attack on voluntarism. The considerations adumbrated show that the problem of agreement remains insoluble. Its resolution by appeal to the services of the state is an illegitimate move, one that survives only outside the boundaries of voluntarism and has further defects of its own as an argument for political authority. In this, they are representative examples of the strength of the anarchists' strategy, which is to show that the free commitment of individuals, which voluntarism considers to be its strongest weapon, actually leads to its downfall, due to the inability of voluntarists to realize this requirement and give true expression to its demands.

A defense of hypothetical contractualism

There is, however, a better and stronger claim in favor of the idea that hypothetical contractualism might provide legitimate support for a voluntarist theory of political obligation. On this basis, hypothetical consent, precisely because it is a theory of good reasons, can be consistently incorporated within voluntarism and can perhaps facilitate a solution to the central problem of the theory.

This claim makes use of a further argument for political obligation, found in Hobbes, that was not mentioned above. According to this argument, the citizen is bound by the law exactly because he is *the author* of this law.[55] He *makes* the law and he is, therefore, contradicting his own will if he later denies its authority over him. By consenting to authorize a ruler, the individual never alienates his will, but he still lends his will's authority to him for the purpose of being bound by his directives.[56] This "argument about the citizen"[57] aspires to provide *a moral route* toward an understanding of what can be a subject of agreement in a way that stresses the centrality of the role of individual power, that is, of the freedom every individual has to make the decisions concerning his life on his own. This centrality is very much the focus of voluntarism.

According to this argument, the crux of contractualism is that you *lend* your individual power, but you still *retain* it. Yet it is this idea that creates continual instability in the theory, since the problem arises whether we can keep our power while lending it in such a way as to be bound by it. This problem is reflected, here, in the contradiction between the argument about the citizen and the "argument about the sovereign,"[58] which Hobbes also adopts. According to this argument, the sovereign is *never* bound by the law, strikingly, for the *same* reason for which the citizen *is* bound, namely because he is the author of the law. This argument expresses the idea that, if it is the autonomous will of the individual that makes the law binding, then his decision to make it can be *changed at will*. And the significance of this claim does not lie in Hobbes's supposition that we are never bound to what we can change. Rather, it lies in the thought that, even if we are bound by a law as long as we do not change it, "the very fact that [we] can change it diminishes the significance of the fact that [we] are bound by it."[59] The possibility of change undermines the bindingness that the creation of authority by contract is meant to guarantee.

This worry is given precise expression in the problem of agreement, which haunts contractualism. Its solution requires establishing the argument about the citizen while devaluing the argument about the sovereign, at the same time without undermining their common appeal to autonomy. It requires the establishment of the former in a way that the bindingness derived from the power of the will of the individual does not deprive him of this power. Thus, the problem of instability, or agreement, that contractualism faces necessitates a satisfactory moral explanation of the form that *the change of will* must take. Such an explanation is necessary if the will of the individual is to play, in a stable manner, the role that voluntarism attributes to it with regard to the problem of political obligation.

In this context, perhaps the most suitable manifestation of the crux of voluntarism as expressed in contractualism—i.e., that "you lend your power but you still retain it"—is provided by a purely hypothetical contract, or a device that is no contract at all. This is perhaps the most promising route toward a solution to the problem of instability created for voluntarism by the lack of literal agreement. The hypothetical contract, or consent, seems to provide the most representative form of voluntarism. As explained earlier (in the section "Hypothetical consent"), it is a theoretical device used to direct our reasoning to the conclusions it would lead us to whenever unimpaired, that is, to the conclusions we would reach when impartially deliberating on the basis of acceptable moral convictions. These are convictions such as those represented in Rawls's "original position," which constitute our considered judgments about fair conditions on agreement and proper restrictions on reasons for principles.[60] These elements of the contractualist device make it special as a way of combining morality with rationality that provides the bindingness of our will—or so I argue below.

The conclusions derived are good in themselves. They are good either in virtue of their content, or "in virtue of [their] internal structure," their "form," or their "*functional* arrangement."[61] Their moral input can be shown by means other than a contract. They can be construed in a theory either as moral directives to which we might be committed unconditionally in a Kantian manner,[62] or as commitments not necessarily moral in nature but still important to our personal identity and integrity.[63] So construed, they can play the role of reasons for action (i.e., good reasons). Their moral validity is by itself important for creating the stability that helps contractualism. But the irrationality of breaking these requirements, necessary in order to marry bindingness with autonomy as required within voluntarism, can be shown only by the hypothetical contract. This device shows that a deeper aspect of the authority of such reasons lies in that they are the *commands* of our *reflective* will: "It is not the bare fact that it would be a good idea to perform a certain action that obligates us to perform it. It is the fact that [*though reflection*] we *command ourselves* to do what we find it would be a good idea to do."[64] Our most considered judgments are the stipulations of our reasonable point of view. Having been extracted from our impartial and most considered judgments, these reasons can be seen as the directives of the will of a rational being that, at the same time, bind that being.

In other words, our most considered judgments are reflected in the premises that guide individuals in the course of their choice and that represent their reasonableness. Individuals face a common (social) problem and they have to take into consideration, and deliberate on the basis of, the responses of others. Through the hypothetical contract, they reason from the same premises and reach the same solution to that problem. The acceptable solution is the one they all agree to, because the guiding idea is that there is no breaking point in the procedure: agreement is the only way forward. The results of these judgments are the binding directives of the will of rational beings, because, as Korsgaard explains, they pass the test of "reflective endorsement."[65] Good reasons are thus the principles expressive of "the conceptions of ourselves that are the most important to us," the violation of which would mean that we contradict our best reason, lose our "practical identity."[66] It can now be legitimately claimed, in support of the argument from the citizen, that the authority of such reasons is "beyond question" because it is "the authority of [our] own mind and will" *as a legislator.*[67] Another explanation lies in Rousseau's words: "[T]here is a difference between incurring an obligation to yourself and incurring one to a whole of which you form a part."[68] The reasonableness of our considered judgments, reflected in the reasons (moral principles) we share, constitutes an "entity," or will, that is a whole of which we are a part, and as such it is binding on us in a way that we would not be bound if we placed obligations on ourselves irrespective of this reflective capacity. We thus follow the directives of a will that cannot be changed according to personal inclinations (and cannot thus be destabilized by them). Also, it remains an important aspect of the contractualist framework that, in endeavors to assert the validity of either side, moral principles and considered judgments stand in mutual support.[69]

Used in this way, as a method of making transparent to us the demands of reason, the hypothetical contract offers an expression of *a moral route of conception* of what can be, or *ought to* be, a subject of agreement, as *the essence* of contractualism. This is the crux of the rationalistic tradition of Voluntarism, which is largely inspired by Rousseau's idea of the "general will" in *The Social Contract* (1762) and newly developed by contemporary contractualists.[70] The element of voluntarism in this outlook lies in a focus on reasonableness (through an insistence on understanding and agreement) and in individualism: principles are legitimate only when accepted by individuals, i.e., as results of their capacity for self-governance (as expressed morally). The central idea is that individuals have the willingness to modify their reasons on the basis of a shared moral ground, one that others would not reasonably reject. This perspective gives a new direction to the role of the social contract in relation to political institutions. According to this understanding, the idea of reasonable agreement as the subject-matter of contractualism functions as a heuristic device for the formulation of legitimate moral principles that might then be applied to existing political institutions and determine their acceptability. The aim is neither to establish the existence of political institutions nor to prove a general political obligation. It is rather to find and justify legitimate principles.[71]

In this manner, contractualism becomes a primary expression of self-governance. The hypothetical contract represents a process through which individuals can see their reason work, forming the conditions that govern their lives by substantial reference to themselves. They come to understand their responsibilities and duties in the light of this framework. They get involved in a kind of reasoning that helps them see how they can be guided by impositions they themselves decide, which are suitable to determine their life and which represent their will and sense of their conditions. It is a process that improves their self-understanding and at the same time combines it with a comprehension of the moral terms that should characterize their personal and social relations. They thus evolve as moral agents, who realize themselves by putting constraints on themselves. Hypothetical consent provides *a phenomenology of how individuals can be ruled by themselves*, representing a route through which they come to identify with important aspects of their life and social world, even when they do not actually give their consent.

However, this approach does not remove the problem of agreement being the focus of the present criticism of voluntarism with regard to political obligation. It only preserves a hope for proving political obligation from a different direction through the rationale of the hypothetical contract. As argued above, such a contract is irrelevant to voluntarist attempts to explain political obligation in terms of actual agreement and to establish the plausibility of voluntarism as applied to this obligation on that basis. It rather anticipates a theory of good reasons for political obligation. It offers a route toward understanding what the proper basis of our duties and relations might be, rather than a direct basis for duties and relationships themselves. The stability of individual will that rationalistic voluntarism offers is the main indication of the value of a phenomenology of how we might feel obligated, which the theory provides. As such it is morally important, but only theoretical. In departing from actual voluntarism, it does not secure the kind of actual interaction that the relationship of political obligation, I argue, requires, an actuality demanded by the very nature of this relationship as reflected in the four conditions of political obligation applied in the debate.[72]

As I explained above, while analyzing the crux of the rationalistic tradition of voluntarism, the hypothetical reasonable contract is a form of reasoning to be applied when we examine the legitimacy of the activities of political institutions from within and apart from an establishment of their bindingness. It concerns the *content* of legitimacy (or of justice), the provision of sound principles of legitimacy in the light of which institutions, as an unavoidable reality, must be assessed. In the hands of theorists such as Scanlon, this form of contractualism does not see its role as arguing for actual obligations. Actual obligation could result only in the (improbable) case of the absolute coincidence between actual institutions and ideal principles, that is, if existing institutions were a perfect application of the principles of legitimacy, so that individuals could affirm those principles by obeying the institutions constantly. These points prepare the way for reevaluating the attempt of those contractualists who use the hypothetical contract to ground political obligation: their very approach within the debate is misguided. This lies mostly in the discontinuity between quality and actual obligation indicated in the preceding discussion of contractualism (see the section "Social contract theories"). And it remains to be examined in the following chapters whether any theory of good reasons could ground actual obligation.

Dismissing the conceptual argument for political obligation

At this point, let me preface the general conclusions of this chapter with some brief comments on a different approach to the problem of political obligation. This approach might at first seem to provide an alternative solution to this problem and to eliminate the difficulties examined so far. However, a closer inspection reveals that it is not part of this debate. My aim here is to dismiss it as an obstacle to a proper speculation of the issues in question.[73]

This alternative approach is known as "the conceptual argument."[74] It adopts an internal viewpoint with regard to the problem of political obligation, in order to deny its very existence and meaning. It advocates an internal, logical relationship between the state, or political authority, and political obligation, on the basis of which it attributes the requirement for a general justification of political obligation to a conceptual confusion: the very concept of authority is claimed to be inseparable from political obligation and thus to preempt any need for the independent justification of the latter.[75]

This is not the correlativity thesis explained in Chapter 1, which concerns understanding the notion of political obligation. The conceptual argument represents a normative outlook on the problem of political obligation as a whole, a position about the very point of asking the question of such an obligation, which has normative implications. In addition, the conceptual argument considers political obligation as playing a constitutive role in our understanding of ourselves as members of a polity.[76] In this way, it dispenses with the problem of finding a moral filter for separating unacceptable from acceptable political requirements. They are already moralized by our membership in a particular polity.

Admittedly, such an approach could undermine the whole debate over political obligation, since it entails that the moral aspect of the problem of this obligation, and all the criticism of the state deriving from it, has no meaning.[77] But, in my opinion, accepting this approach has two negative effects. First, it sacrifices the connection of the notion of obligation with the self-assumed undertakings expressive of individual autonomy. Second, and, more importantly, it circumvents, instead of addressing, the motivations that give rise to worries about the problem.

The first worry reflects the following significant point: even though moral obligations are not necessarily and exclusively connected with voluntariness—for example, duties to aid and parental obligations are not self-assumed[78]—the concept of "obligation" itself involves the *active role* of individuals conceived as free and equal persons able to make substantial judgments and decisions, not only in the private, but also in the public domain.[79] It reflects the effective initiation of action that the voluntarist insistence on the importance of individual will requires.[80] This perspective is characteristic of liberal political theory. Nevertheless, it can be adopted by any view of social relationships that rejects theories of "divine authority" and of "natural subordination," namely those claiming that authority is founded on divine right and granted by God and those maintaining that it is a result and reflection of the natural inequality between human beings.[81] In other words, it can be adopted by any view that, in general, dismisses theories involving a hierarchical and inegalitarian understanding of the positions of and relations between individuals within society. That obligation embodies this perspective is what brings it into conflict with obedience or mere subordination.

The second worry derives from a more significant point, a central one from the perspective of the current inquiry. With this point I close my discussion of the conceptual account, satisfied that its failure has been established. I mentioned in the section "The two main aspects of the problem of political obligation" in Chapter 1 that the use of morality as a way of *filtering* political requirements serves the very motivations that relate to the worries that give rise to the problem of political obligation. These motivations are basically found in a concern to avoid the unlimited and unqualified imposition upon us of political requirements and the hardships of not obeying them, and in the resulting doubts about the very idea of being subjected in this way. If we accept the conceptual argument, we disregard these motivations and we are deprived of any representation of the reflective dispositions that enable us to create, from time to time, an autonomous critical distance from the political world we inhabit. The problem that the conceptual argument denies illuminates an aspect of ourselves as reflective social beings. Thus, by rejecting this argument, and, in doing so, accepting the problem of political obligation, we continue to assert the expression of ourselves as autonomous, reflective beings and to react against a blind subordination to existing authorities.[82]

The implications of the anarchist criticism of consent

The general conclusion derived from this chapter is that it is the very *centrality of the voluntary undertakings* within contract and consent theories that leads to their failure as accounts of political obligation. The essential feature of these theories cannot be combined with the basic conditions involved in a proper justification of political obligation—more precisely, it cannot meet the generality condition in conjunction with the other three, namely particularity, bindingness, and content-independence—and so it cannot found a satisfactory account of that notion.

This, to be sure, has already been recognized in the relevant literature as the upshot of the anarchist criticism of voluntarism. My aim in this chapter has only been to provide a careful elaboration of the anarchist criticism, in order to make clearer the roots and the development of its conclusion and to establish its soundness. However, my aim in doing so is not limited to providing such a clarification. It also lies in establishing the *implications* of the success of the anarchist criticism. It is these implications that will concern me in this section.

The lesson that should be learned from the anarchist criticism of voluntarism is that neither the value of voluntariness nor the conditions of a valid justification of authority should be dispensed with. The failure of voluntarism indicates the defective character of the state and connects this to its involuntary establishment. The very term "institutionalized coercion" designates the function of political institutions as distinct bodies that concentrate and monopolize the determination of the rights and obligations of individuals, using force in order to back up this determination. The absence of voluntariness for political obligation indicates the dominant and coercive character of the state. That this absence reflects a failure to meet the four conditions of political obligation indicates that it is the *"political"* character of obligation (or of the state)—namely, its permanent, coercive, binding, and exclusive (i.e., its dominant) nature—that cannot be combined with voluntariness to create a proper instance of a suitably particularized and sufficiently general moral relationship.[83]

It follows that voluntarism provides a significant element to be used as a test for forms of social order. Even if not unanimously accepted as the primary or necessary condition for them, *the free commitment of individuals* constitutes a desirable feature for such forms to incorporate. An insistence on the centrality of voluntary undertaking would guarantee, and enrich our view of, the value of any social organization to the extent that such an organization is compatible with it. A strong reason for this is the compatibility of this feature with, and expression within social life of, the value of *freedom*, or *autonomy*. This claim holds under any of the three ways in which autonomy might be construed: (1) as a property of persons conceived as "ideal moral legislators" capable of an impartial ascription and review of moral principles; (2) as a right each of us possesses to arrive at decisions about certain aspects of our life without interference from others; (3) as "self-governance," involving the conscious understanding of the components of whatever problem should arise, as well as moral integrity.[84]

Taylor's analysis of "pure negative freedom" and of "autonomy" provides a further clarification of these dimensions of freedom: according to the former, a person "is unfree if, and only if, his doing of any action is rendered impossible by the action of another individual," while the latter involves that

> the individual must have the capacities and inclination for subjecting his values and beliefs, norms and principles to critical scrutiny, he must be able to make out of this critical process a coherent set of values, beliefs, etc., and he must be able to choose or to create (with the cooperation of others) an appropriate role or character with which he identifies.[85]

These conceptions of freedom, especially that of autonomy, are compatible with the critical philosophical anarchist approach. In its most complete expressions, this approach involves an understanding of freedom that is even more inclusive and captures better the picture rendered by the above conceptions. Such an understanding can be expressed amply by the idea of "free individuality," which can be identified as the sort of scrutinized and rounded life conduct reflected in a combination of self-legislation with self-realization and the kind of self-expression and self-development involved in it.[86] I take this ideal to be effectively captured by Karl Marx's notion of "human emancipation" as the liberation of our humanity from all material obstacles and all the suppressing dualities that curtail the free development of human capacities, experiences, and activity in the world, a liberation effected within social activity and interaction and transcending mere "political emancipation."[87]

Yet a basic understanding of freedom might suffice to motivate the central concern with it that characterizes anarchism and the inevitability of such a concern for all human beings. Such an understanding can be found in Rousseau's theory. According to Rousseau, freedom involves an immediate sense of responsibility and the capacity to control our own decisions, and it is something that we care about as much as we care about our self-preservation. It is *that basic capacity through which we can protect the fundamental elements of our being.*[88] On the whole, it constitutes part of ourselves, and renouncing it would be to be deprived of any guarantee of the protection of anything essential to us and thus to renounce our own nature. More importantly, this understanding stresses the *compatibility of autonomy with equality* as well as the indispensability of the latter and its necessity for both freedom and society on the whole. Together these two values open the way for revealing and satisfying the underlying fundamental *anarchist demand for proper relations between people.* I discuss the importance of this connection in the following paragraphs, and I attempt to render a complete account of it throughout this study.

The above-mentioned compatibility of freedom with equality leads us to stress a principle that constitutes a main guideline of this book and goes beyond the arguments of Chapters 1 and 2, which neighbor the concept of liberal freedom. It is the principle of *equal-liberty* proposed by the poststructuralist anarchist thinker Saul Newman.[89] This is "the idea that liberty and equality are inextricably linked, that one cannot be had without the other."[90] They both belong to the category of emancipation, they mutually resonate, and they are situated in a collective context. Equality does not come secondary to liberty, as usually happens under the liberal reading; the demand for it goes beyond the formal equality of rights and there is no tension between the two, no separation and conflict between individuals as passive recipients within society. Liberty is collective, as is its realization, being shared instead of diminished and being "only imaginable in the context of the liberty of all," and accompanied also by social and economic equality.[91] The principle of equal-liberty is an "open-ended horizon that allows for endless permutations and elaborations."[92] Moreover, it is closer to anarchist political ethics: transcending the socialist as well as the liberal tradition, it entails that liberty and equality cannot be implemented within the state, and it interrogates all forms of domination and hierarchy. This perspective relates to a certain conception of the self inspired by the anarchist philosopher Max Stirner and by Michel Foucault as well as by the latter's understanding of power. For Stirner, the ego is "a kernel of nothingness out of which different expressions of the self can arise."[93] The humanist notion of the essence, on which classical anarchism relied, and along with it the ideas of rationality and morality, are alienating because they are abstract illusions to which individuals are required to conform.[94] Essence bears no meaningful relation to the human subject and no effective ground for political action. The individual can act freely only under this realization, and in the end freedom is the possibility and ability to recreate ourselves as we choose.[95] This parallels Stirner's view that society is based on a world of contingency, a void, rather than an essence reflecting rational scientific objectivity.[96] Similarly, for Foucault, the "essential self" of the liberal individual is an effect of relations of power.[97] Personal liberation is a matter far more complicated, which demands the awareness of and resistance to far greater subjections, a questioning of the power that knowledge itself and with it many other discourses and identities bear. Power exists in all social relationships, and the interaction between the state and society is much closer than imagined by the classical anarchist critique. Power relations are extremely complex and pervasive. Yet we can try to establish those that are more flexible and less dominating, to avoid the forms of power that involve domination.[98] In the end, freedom and resistance to power are a matter of micropolitics, of activity that starts with transforming power at an everyday micro-level and from there expands at every level. Foucault proposes the "ethics of the care of the self," which constitute ethical strategies constructed by the subject him- or herself as ways of relating to and recreating ourselves that also affect our relations with others, an ongoing ethical practice and interrogation, a series of "practices of freedom."[99] At the political level, this striving for freedom and struggle against domination becomes, for Foucault, "a hyper- and pessimistic activism," a continual questioning of practices and institutions, a constant awareness and exposing of the dangers of the multiple dominations and exclusions involved in current social arrangements.[100] In the words of Stirner, it becomes a matter of insurrection as a way "to arrange ourselves" against both external and internalized domination.[101]

Returning to the subject matter of this chapter, and given the reasons just stated about the importance of choice, the problem is that our societies do not facilitate the exercise in the political sphere of a practice analogous to promising as exercised at a more private level. To a large extent, however, this has been encouraged by the prevailing view of the political as a centralized and coercive form of social order. Perhaps it would help to consider more pluralistic representations of it, having the form of free social relationships of a cooperative character, as constructed on a small scale. We can find such an orientation among the main anarchist proposals,[102] and it is compatible with the normative core of voluntarism. It also facilitates a reconciliation of our private and public lives and a barrier against any radical separation of these two domains.[103]

Nevertheless, the crux of the present insistence on voluntariness lies in the following point: freedom may be respected in ways much less strict than explicit voluntary commitment, and alternative views of the political might properly accommodate a looser sense of self-assumed choice. The aim of the present discussion is not to insist exclusively on contractualist instances of voluntary commitment.[104] It is rather to introduce the element that makes voluntariness, either in a strict or in a looser sense,[105] important and that will prove central to the rest of this study for the problem that I examine: that is, the idea that individuals' self-determination and equal, active, effective participation should be preserved as the central characteristics of social relationships. This element remains the constant concern of the anarchist challenge. It reflects the anarchist claim that certain authoritarian attitudes undermine the status of persons as free and equal and the kinds of interaction that are suitable to them.

As argued in the preceding discussion of hypothetical consent, it is important for human beings to see fundamental aspects of their lives as being under their control, "up to them." Self-governance seems indispensable, at least when understood as the capacity to rule one's own self and life. This can be characterized as the ability to understand, decide, and determine the elements concerning the most important aspects of one's personality and life and to understand the features of situations that affect it significantly in order to control them. Fundamentally it is a basic capacity to continually secure and determine one's own survival and moral world, which is freedom in its most basic form.[106] Human beings cannot live without it. It secures survival through the exercise of reason as it distinctively characterizes human beings. This does involve constraints, but they are constraints that one puts on oneself. What is required is not being ruled by another, which might concern both not being subjected to others' interests and will and, most importantly, not standing in an unequal relation (of power) to others that generates the possibility of dependence and subjection and undermines one's status. Domination in any of these forms stands against freedom, as it stands against equality. Thus self-governance and equal status and participation, which pertain to the preservation of proper relations between people, stand together as the most valuable features of the kind of social life suitable to human beings. Voluntarism remains a valuable expression of this idea. We will see in Chapter 4 a different way of stressing it.

At the same time, the conditions of generality, particularity, content-independence, and bindingness can hardly be dismissed as inappropriate or demanding. Far from being confined to an anarchist conception of legitimacy, they are reflections of the political nature of the obligations examined in this study and they are accepted by many theorists, with different and even opposing convictions, as a reasonable and suitable test. Their formality does not undermine the strength of the normative implications that these conditions create in combination with the moral ground of political obligation discussed in the present chapter.

These considerations lead to a final thought. In the previous chapters I referred to an *ideal of legitimacy*, which is part of critical philosophical anarchism as a complete philosophical position. Some of the critical force of this form of anarchism has been demonstrated by the preceding arguments. In the same manner, the ideal of legitimacy that will be provided as a positive contribution of critical philosophical anarchism finds its initial elements in the considerations incorporated in the present chapter. The proposal is that the central feature of voluntarism, while being the cause of the failure of this theory *as a defense of the authority of the state*, nevertheless qualifies as *a feature that could characterize centrally the interpersonal relations of a society that constituted an ideal of legitimacy*. That is, attempts to ground political authority on voluntariness have failed, yet the value of choice remains and a pattern of voluntarist social relations provides a guiding model of a legitimate society. Present polities aspire to, but fail to exemplify, such an ideal.

Some critical, philosophical anarchists begin from such a voluntarist picture of societies in developing their arguments against the state.[107] The anarchist arguments examined in this chapter, along with the insistence on the conditions of political obligation that they involve, become an indication of the prior anarchist consideration that the voluntarist kind of specific interaction that existing institutions fail to involve is a valuable feature of a morally acceptable social life. Thus, voluntariness is at the same time *a desirable element for the construction of what would be an acceptably complete theoretical attempt to justify political obligation* and a central characteristic of what would be a *legitimate society*. To reiterate, the combination of the four conditions of political obligation with this moral criterion becomes a first instance of what a positive account of political obligation would be like. This combination also reflects at the theoretical level what at the social level would be the basis of proper social relationships, namely the application of a morally significant feature of specific interaction as the central characteristic of the relationship of government—in the present case, the actual consent or choice of each individual. Without dismissing quality, this picture of what would be a successful voluntarism incorporates "transactional evaluation" as the appropriate test of political obligation.[108]

I will therefore regard voluntariness as a useful criterion to be taken into account, along with the traditional conditions of validity, in a theory of political obligation, and I will argue in Chapter 6 how it can be important for further evaluations of institutionalized domination.

To conclude, the criticisms analyzed in the present chapter have confirmed the importance of voluntariness as a condition to be respected and reflected in an ideal of political legitimacy. This condition, when used for the purposes of theories of general political obligation (or of the authority of the state), leads to their failure and, in this, motivates a different outlook to social relations and to what is to be regarded as a legitimate form of political organization. Its role as involved in the anarchist criticisms becomes a first indication of a positive and comprehensive outlook reflected in the anarchist perspective. Most importantly, it expresses the skeptical, nonauthoritarian impulse that anarchism contains, the idea that there is always a legitimate complaint against the sacrifice of individual self-determination and of equal status and the relations of equal participation that determine the quality of human interaction.

Notes

1   In his appeal to "tacit consent," Locke aspires to promote it to actuality. As we will see in the discussion of this notion of consent below, he considers the acts that he calls "signs of consent" to be legitimate inferences of consent, having the status of genuine consent. More generally, and as we will see in the relevant subsection, tacit consent is in fact a form of actual consent, only of a subtler nature.

2   There is an extensive literature concerning the prominence of voluntarist theories of the state during the seventeenth century and its connection with the ideological and economic consequences of the Reformation and the rise of Capitalism. See, for example, Quentin Skinner, *The Foundations of Modern Political Thought* (Cambridge: Cambridge University Press, 1978). Also, these are the theories that helped define the Liberal Democratic form of society (for example, see Carole Pateman, *The Problem of Political Obligation: A Critique of Liberal Theory*, 2nd edition [Oxford: Polity Press 1985], Chapter 1).

3   This is a distinction used by Simmons, *Moral Principles and Political Obligations*, 60–61 and 71–74.

4   For these conditions, see Rousseau, "On Social Contract"; Simmons, *Moral Principles and Political Obligations*, 77; Pateman, *The Problem of Political Obligation*, 13; Horton, *Political Obligation*, 28. The central idea is, in Raz's words, that "the core notion of voluntary obligations is the knowing undertaking of an obligation" (Raz, *The Authority of Law*, 95).

5   This problem is realized by traditional contractualists, not only in their recognition of the difficulty of establishing the original contract, but also in their appeal to future consent as a necessary stage following the initial contract, since it would be a proper form of authorization.

6   See Pateman, *The Problem of Political Obligation*, 21. It could be contested that this understanding is better described under the notion of "consensus" rather than "consent." For example, Green is in agreement with P. H. Partridge when he refers to the latter's refusal to join other theorists in an uncritical consideration of a "permission given deliberately in advance, with or without subsequent approval of the permitted action," and various other examples of "political and social conforming behaviour," as original examples of consent (Green, *The Authority of the State*, 159). However, what matters here is that the "permission" of future generations to which contractualists appeal is properly represented only by the contested understanding of self-assumed

obligation; and we can submit without contradiction to the idea that this is better captured by the notion of consensus.

7 Pateman, *The Problem of Political Obligation*, 21.
8 The place of voting and of "majority consent" in the theories in question will be considered in the discussion of tacit consent below. Voting is otherwise characterized as a form of express consent (see Paul McLaughlin, *Anarchism and Authority: A Philosophical Introduction to Classical Anarchism*. Farnham: Ashgate, 2007, 89–90). Here, following Simmons, I use the notion of express consent interchangeably with that of explicit consent.
9 For such schemes, see the section "Fairness, political obligation, and the idea of societies as 'Schemes of Social Cooperation' " in Chapter 4.
10 For more on the relationships involved in voluntary associations, see Chapter 4.
11 For this, see William Godwin, *An Enquiry Concerning Political Justice and Its Influence on General Virtue and Happiness* (London: G.G.J and Robinson, 1793), 1: 146–147.
12 Simmons, *Moral Principles and Political Obligations*, 79.
13 Simmons, *Moral Principles and Political Obligations*, 80.
14 For five conditions such as the ones discussed in this paragraph, see Simmons, *Moral Principles and Political Obligations*, 80–83.
15 See, e.g., Green, *The Authority of the State*, 166–173.
16 For such a criticism, see Pateman, *The Problem of Political Obligation*, 16.
17 David Hume, "Of the Original Contract," in *Hume: Political Essays*, ed. Knud Haakonssen (Cambridge: Cambridge University Press, 1994), 193.
18 Green, *The Authority of the State*, 174. For similar points on tacit consent and residence in Locke and on the status of tacit consent in general, see David A. Lloyd Thomas, *Locke on Government* (London and New York: Routledge, 1995), 38–40. Also see Horton, *Political Obligation*, 34; Jonathan Wolff, *Political Philosophy: An Introduction* (Oxford: Oxford University Press, 1996), 46–48; McLaughlin, *Anarchism and Authority*, 90.
19 Green, *The Authority of the State*, 175.
20 For a definition of public goods similar to the one I give here, see Howard H. Harriott, "Games, Anarchy, and the Nonnecessity of the State," in *For and Against the State: New Philosophical Readings*, ed. John T. Sanders and Jan Narveson (Lanham, MD: Rowman and Littlefield, 1996), 120. For a more extended discussion of, and bibliography on, public goods, see Chapter 4.
21 This point has been argued decisively in Simmons, *Moral Principles and Political Obligations*, 88–95.
22 John Petrov Plamenatz, *Consent, Freedom and Political Obligation* (Oxford: Oxford University Press, 1968), 170. Although, in fairness to Plamenatz, we can take his theory on the whole to be an attempt to account for aspects that should create more or less conditions of political obligation rather than arguing that voting expresses consent. More precisely, his claim can be taken to be that a society that allows voting is more legitimate than one that does not. Nevertheless, my following points on the relation between voting and consent still hold.
23 For this observation, see, e.g., Horton, *Political Obligation*, 37, and Wolff, *Political Philosophy*, 45.

24 For this point, see McLaughlin, *Anarchism and Authority*, 90.
25 For this, see also Horton, *Political Obligation*, 39–40.
26 For this point, see also Horton, *Political Obligation*, 38.
27 Hume, "Of the Original Contract."
28 For example: Hanna Pitkin, "Obligation and Consent," in *Philosophy, Politics and Society, Forth Series*, ed. Peter Laslett, Walter Garrison Runciman, and Quentin Skinner (Oxford: Basil Blackwell, 1972); Ronald M. Dworkin, "The Original Position," in *Reading Rawls: Critical Studies on Rawls*, ed. Norman Daniels (Oxford: Basil Blackwell, 1975), 16–52; David Zimmerman, "The Force of Hypothetical Commitment," *Ethics* 93 (1983): 467–483; Jean Hampton, *Hobbes and the Social Contract Tradition* (Cambridge: Cambridge University Press, 1986); Thomas J. Lewis, "On Using the Concept of Hypothetical Consent," *Canadian Journal of Political Science* 22 (1989): 793–808. For an influential contemporary theory of the hypothetical contract outside the debate on political obligation, see Scanlon, "Contractualism and Utilitarianism"; Thomas Michael Scanlon, *What We Owe to Each Other* (Cambridge, MA and London: The Belknap Press of Harvard University Press, 1998).
29 For a relevant distinction between the two different trends claiming to be proper identifications of voluntarism, namely the voluntaristic and the rationalistic, see Jeremy Waldron, *Liberal Rights: Collected Papers, 1981–1991* (Cambridge and New York: Cambridge University Press, 1993), 51–57; Simmons, "Justification and Legitimacy," 760–769.
30 Simmons, "Justification and Legitimacy," n. 18.
31 Horton, *Political Obligation*, 82.
32 Thomas Hobbes, *Leviathan*, ed. Crawford Brough MacPherson (Harmondsworth: Penguin, 1968); Locke, *Two Treatises of Government*, and Rousseau, "On Social Contract."
33 Being such, it remains a question whether it can ever be a direct basis of political obligation. For more clarifications, see my discussion of a stronger claim in favor of contractualism and hypothetical consent in the section "A defense of hypothetical contractualism."
34 Horton, *Political Obligation*, 88.
35 Raz, *The Morality of Freedom*, 90 (emphasis mine).
36 Such bad consequences may be the unjustified serving of personal interests; such undesirable ones may be unpredictable misfortunes as effects of the shortcomings of human knowledge.
37 Raz's discussion refers mainly to actual consent. It is developed within the context of his own theory of political authority, which is based on the idea that state authority is justified only when it is proven to be the best way for individuals to realize the independent reasons that apply to them. As explained in the section "Raz's theory as an illustration" in Chapter 1, his theory consists in a combination of three theses that express this idea, namely the "normal-justification," the "preemptive," and the "dependence thesis" (e.g., Raz, "Authority and Justification"). Yet, the role of consent in such a theory applies also to the relation of hypothetical consent to good reasons examined here, even though the rationale of the latter differs from that of actual consent.

38 This is the case only with regard to contractualist theories of political obligation. Those contractualists who offer their theories as accounts of principles for already existing institutions do not offer direct replies to the debate on political obligation and their arguments should be examined in a different light. Characteristic examples are the theories of Rawls and Scanlon. I return to this difference within contractualism throughout the study.

39 As De Jasay puts it, for social contract theories "the problem of keeping promises is crucial and indispensable" (Anthony De Jasay, "Self-Contradictory Contractarianism," in *For and Against the State: New Philosophical Readings*, ed. John T. Sanders and Jan Narveson [Lanham, MD: Rowman and Littlefield, 1996], 140).

40 Alan John Simmons, "Locke's State of Nature," in *The Social Contract Theorists: Critical Essays on Hobbes, Locke and Rousseau*, ed. Christopher W. Morris (Lanham, MD: Rowman and Littlefield, 1999), 97–120. This difference supports the idea that Locke's theory of political obligation remains more clearly one of actual consent: that instead of deriving political obligation from a state-of-nature hypothetical-consent argument, as Hobbes does, he rather uses the latter as a way of depicting the merits of political institutions as well as the moral condition of nonpolitical individuals, but without deriving an alteration of that moral condition from those merits. Also one could see the state-of-nature arguments of contractualists as separate justifications of the existence of the state rather than as arguments for political obligation, whether or not they tried to derive the one from the other (see Simmons, "Justification and Legitimacy": his distinction between justification and legitimacy; see my Chapter 1, the section "The two main aspects of the problem of political obligation," n. 8).

41 Locke, *Two Treatises of Government*, book II, 96, 99, 171, 243. Furthermore, those individuals who want to join a civil society after its first creation may do so by consenting to the terms of the original contract and thus explicitly giving their own trust to government (Locke, *Two Treatises of Government*, 89). For useful discussions of the two-stage creation of authority and the role of individuals' actual consent in this in Locke, see Lloyd Thomas, *Locke*, 11–56; Simmons, "Locke's State of Nature"; Alan John Simmons, "Political Consent," in *The Social Contract Theorists: Critical Essays on Hobbes, Locke and Rousseau*, ed. Christopher W. Morris (New York and Oxford: Rowman and Littlefield, 1999), 121–141.

42 I concentrate here on *Leviathan* (Hobbes, *Leviathan*).

43 See, e.g., De Jasay, "Self-Contradictory Contractarianism," 142. The same paradox holds for Locke: see Jean Hampton, *Political Philosophy* (Boulder: Westview Press, 1997), 64.

44 The name was given by Albert W. Tucker in the 1950s. The game was invented by Merrill Flood and Melvin Dresher. For representative literature, see, e.g., Merrill Meeks Flood, "Some Experimental Games," *Management Science* 5 (1958): 5–26; David Gauthier, *Morals by Agreement* (Oxford: Clarendon Press, 1986); Hampton, *Hobbes*, chapters 2 and 3, and Hampton, *Political Philosophy*, 41–49; Sanders, "The State of Statelessness," 261–265; Harriott, "Games, Anarchy, and the Nonnecessity of the State," esp. 121–125. Against

the dominant tradition, one might not read Hobbes through the Prisoner's Dilemma. The Hobbesian contract might be seen as a contract for self-preservation, not self-interest. But my argument concentrates on the dominant reading of Hobbes's theory. It suffices to say that the results of the anarchist criticism remain the same under either reading.

45 For this difference between the two, see, e.g., Raz, "Introduction," 6–11.
46 The anarchists' arguments concerning this dispute are part of more *positive* proposals for alternative social orders and are a valuable extension of the direct anarchist contribution to the debate on political obligation. These arguments make use of the Prisoner's Dilemma and of discussions of public goods. See, for example, Olson, *The Logic of Collective Action*; Robert Axelrod, *The Emergence of Cooperation* (New York: Basic Books, 1984); Michael Taylor, *Anarchy and Cooperation* (London: John Wiley and Son, 1976); Taylor, *Community Anarchy and Liberty*; Michael Taylor, *The Possibility of Cooperation* (Cambridge: Cambridge University Press, 1987); Green, *The Authority of the State*, 138–144; Sanders, "The State of Statelessness," 261–271. See also Chapters 4 and 7 of this study.
47 See De Jasay, "Self-Contradictory Contractarianism," 146.
48 It is important, however, to stress that Hobbes claims that the sovereign is finally and independently authorized *by each individual in particular*, but not through a contract. See Hobbes, *Leviathan*, 87, 221, 265.
49 In addition, in this authority ascribed to it by the contract made between the citizens, the sovereign is free to change the law at will. For this, see Gerald Allan Cohen, "Reason, Humanity and the Moral Law," in *The Sources of Normativity*, ed. Christine Marion Korsgaard (Cambridge: Cambridge University Press, 1996), 167–170, based on Hobbes, *Leviathan*, 313, 367.
50 See De Jasay, "Self-Contradictory Contractarianism," 146.
51 De Jasay, "Self-Contradictory Contractarianism," 158.
52 Although agreement as used on the basis of the rationale of hypothetical consent still has an important role to play. See the discussion of hypothetical contract in the next section.
53 On these, see Green, *The Authority of the State*, 151–152; McLaughlin, *Anarchism and Authority*, Chapter 2.
54 For such a discontinuity, see Simmons, "Justification and Legitimacy."
55 On this, see Hobbes, *Leviathan*, 221, 265. My discussion here has profited from the analysis of this and the following argument of Hobbes's found in Cohen, "Reason, Humanity and the Moral Law."
56 For a powerful argument in defense of the claim that, even in Hobbes's insistence on absolute authority, what is implied cannot, in the end, be alienation, but only lending to "an agency," see Hampton, *Hobbes*; Hampton, *Political Philosophy*, 49–52.
57 For this terminology, along with "the argument about the sovereign," see Cohen, "Reason, Humanity and the Moral Law," 169.
58 Cohen, "Reason, Humanity and the Moral Law," 170.
59 Cohen, "Reason, Humanity and the Moral Law."
60 See Rawls, *A Theory of Justice*, 146–147 and Section 24; John Rawls, "Justice as Fairness: Political not Metaphysical," in *John Rawls: Collected Papers*, ed. Samuel Richard Freedman (Cambridge, MA: Harvard University

Press: 1999), 399–403; John Rawls, *Justice as Fairness: A Restatement*, ed. Erin Kelly (Cambridge: Harvard University Press, 2001), 14–18 and 80–134. For this hypothetical-contract device and its main features, such as those mentioned here, see my Chapter 3.

61   Christine Marion Korsgaard, "The Authority of Reflection," in *The Sources of Normativity*, ed. idem. (Cambridge: Cambridge University Press, 1996), 107–108.

62   Kant's formalism establishes the authority of morality by disconnecting it from the contingencies relevant to human nature, e.g., from the problem of social conflict, and by making its laws universally prescriptive imperatives. See Immanuel Kant, *Groundwork of the Metaphysics of Morals*, ed. Mary Gregor (Cambridge: Cambridge University Press, 1998); Immanuel Kant, *Critique of Practical Reason*, ed. Mary Gregor (Cambridge: Cambridge University Press, 1999); Immanuel Kant, *The Metaphysics of Morals*, ed. Mary Gregor (Cambridge: Cambridge University Press, 2001).

63   The affirmation of non-moral commitments might deprive the strictly moral from the superiority usually attached to it, as concerning demands that represent impartiality and that override commitments attached to particular persons, perspectives, and lifestyles. Also, such commitments are rooted in human nature and the social effects on it. In this way, they might seem to create again the problem of instability, since human nature and society facilitate a *change of will* that undermines the "law-like" status that would make them binding requirements (Cohen, "Reason, Humanity and the Moral Law," 174–177). Still, the centrality of non-moral commitments in an individual's life and sense of identity can give them the role of valid and overriding requirements for this individual. Bernard Williams is characteristically devoted, as a philosopher, to a defense of such commitments and of the centrality of personal integrity in our lives and concerns about the ethical (see, for example "A Critique of Utilitarianism," in *Utilitarianism: For and Against*, ed. Sir Bernard Arthur Owen Williams and John Jamieson Carswell Smart, [Cambridge: Cambridge University Press, 1973, 75–150], esp. Chapter 5, 108–118). And yet, there is a very natural though more subtle connection between normativity, morality, and non-moral reasons for action, involved in the present use of the hypothetical contract, as explained below in the text, and emphasized in the work of contemporary contractualists (Scanlon, "Contractualism and Utilitarianism"; Scanlon, *What We Owe to Each Other*). This connection is based on the idea that individuals express their autonomy in a moral capacity. They have to be motivated by a willingness to justify their reasons (of whatever kind) to others, to try and modify them according to what a "reasonable" person would accept, and to reach agreement (the "reasonable" is a central idea of contractualism: Rawls, *A Theory of Justice*; John Rawls, *Political Liberalism* [New York: Columbia University Press, 1993]; John Rawls, "Justice as Fairness," in *John Rawls: Collected Papers*, ed. Samuel Richard Freedman, [Cambridge, MA, London: Harvard University Press, 1999, 47–72]; John Rawls, "Kantian Constructivism in Moral Theory," in *John Rawls: Collected Papers*, ed. Samuel Richard Freedman, [Cambridge, MA, London: Harvard University Press, 1999, 303–358]; Rawls, "Justice as Fairness: Political not Metaphysical," 388–414;

Rawls, *Justice as Fairness*; Scanlon, *What We Owe to Each Other*; Simmons, "Justification and Legitimacy," 764–767). This is where morality and its binding force lies, which is central to the present discussion (this rationale is basically Rousseauian, but it also involves and carries further the idea of the autonomous motivation accorded to individuals by Kant). For more on this central idea of contractualism, see below in the main text.

64 Korsgaard, *The Sources of Normativity*, 104–105.
65 Korsgaard, *The Sources of Normativity*, 104–105, lecture 3.
66 Korsgaard, *The Sources of Normativity*, 100–102.
67 Korsgaard, *The Sources of Normativity*, 104.
68 Rousseau, "On Social Contract," book 1, Chapter 7.
69 See on "reflective equilibrium," e.g., Rawls, *A Theory of Justice*, 19–21, 46–53, and 578–586; Rawls, *Justice as Fairness*, 29–31, 66–72, 134, and 136.
70 Especially: Rawls, *A Theory of Justice*; Rawls, "Justice as Fairness"; Rawls, "Justice as Fairness: Political not Metaphysical"; Rawls, *Justice as Fairness*; Scanlon, "Contractualism and Utilitarianism"; Scanlon, *What We Owe to Each Other*.
71 Or, as McLaughlin rightly explains (and criticizes), their focus is the content of justice and not the fundamental question of the possibility of legitimate political authority: see McLaughlin, *Anarchism and Authority*, 95–96.
72 For these, see especially my Chapters 1 and 6.
73 This is not only with regard to voluntarism, but also as far as the other theories criticized in this study are concerned.
74 See Pateman, *The Problem of Political Obligation*, esp. 104–105 and 132; Horton, *Political Obligation*, 137–145 and 170.
75 See Horton, *Political Obligation*, 138.
76 Thomas McPherson, *Political Obligation* (London: Routledge and Kegal Paul, 1967), 64.
77 For this aspect, see the section "The two main aspects of the problem of political obligation" in Chapter 1.
78 See Horton, *Political Obligation*, 43 and 144.
79 See Pateman, *The Problem of Political Obligation*, 13–14.
80 See also the beginning of my discussion of arguments regarding theories of consent in the section "An anarchist criticism of voluntarist theories of political obligation."
81 For a paradigmatic examination of such theories, see Hampton, *Political Philosophy*, chapters 2 and 3.
82 Hypothetical contractualism, in being a route of reflective deliberation, asserts this aspect of ourselves and, in this way, it has at least a *negative* impact with regard to political obligation: if we can show that we would not possibly have agreed to some conditions, probably we *should not*.
83 For a useful account of the basic features of "the state," see Miller, *Anarchism*, 5. As explained in note 2 of the introduction, I use the state interchangeably with "institutionalized coercion." For a basic definition of the notion of coercion and a useful analysis of other instances of the notion of "power," see Taylor, *Community, Anarchy and Liberty*, 13–25; for these as well as the crucial notion of "domination," see McLaughlin, *Anarchism and Authority*, chapters 2 and 3.

84   For these three senses of autonomy, see Thomas E. Hill, *Autonomy and Self-respect* (Cambridge: Cambridge University Press, 1991), 43–51.

85   See Taylor, *Community, Anarchy and Liberty*, 142 and 160, respectively.

86   For a relevant analysis, see Jürgen Habermas, "Human Rights and Popular Sovereignty: The Liberal and Republican Versions," *Ratio Juris* 7 (1994): Section I.

87   Karl Marx, "On the Jewish Question," in *Karl Marx: Selected Writings*, ed. David McLellan (Oxford: Oxford University Press, 1977), 57; Karl Marx, "Economic and Political Manuscripts," in *Karl Marx: Selected Writings*, ed. David McLellan (Oxford: Oxford University Press, 1977), 92.

88   See, e.g., Rousseau, "On Social Contract," book 1, Chapter 6.

89   See Newman, *The Politics of Postanarchism*, 6, 17, 20–24, 32–34, 39–40, 46, 69, 144, 179–181.

90   Newman, *The Politics of Postanarchism*, 20.

91   Newman, *The Politics of Postanarchism*, 22.

92   Newman, *The Politics of Postanarchism*, 23.

93   Newman, *The Politics of Postanarchism*, 146, 60. See Stirner, *The Ego and its Own*.

94   Stirner, *The Ego and its Own*, 43.

95   Stirner, *The Ego and its Own*, 150.

96   Stirner, *The Ego and its Own*, 40. For this view against the tendency of classical anarchists, rooted in the essentialism and the scientific rationalism of the Enlightenment, to explain human nature and society in terms of natural law and rational order, see Newman, *The Politics of Postanarchism*, 149–151.

97   Foucault, *Discipline and Punish*.

98   Foucault, "The Ethics of the Concern of the Self as a Practice of Freedom," idem; "The Subject and Power," in idem, *The Essential Works of Foucault 1954–1984, Volume 3: Power*, ed. James Faubion, trans. Robert Harley (London: Penguin, 2002), 280–290.

99   Foucault, "The Ethics of the Concern of the Self as a Practice of Freedom," 282–283.

100 Foucault, "On the Genealogy of Ethics: An Overview of Work in Progress," in idem, *The Essential Works of Foucault 1954–1984, Volume 1: Ethics. Subjectivity and Truth*. Edited by Paul Rabinow. Translated by Robert Harley. London: Penguin, 2002.

101 Stirner, *The Ego and its Own*, 279–280.

102 See, e.g., pieces from the original work of the classical anarchists Proudhon, Bakunin, and Kropotkin, such as Pierre-Joseph Proudhon, *General Idea of the Revolution in the Nineteenth Century*, trans. John Beverly Robinson (London: Freedom Press, 1923); Mikhail Aleksandrovich Bakunin, "Power Corrupts the Best," in idem, *Marxism, Freedom, and the State*, ed. Kenneth Joseph Kenafick (London: Freedom Press, 1950); Mikhail Aleksandrovich Bakunin, *Statism and Anarchy*, ed. Shatz S. Marshall (Cambridge: Cambridge University Press, 2005); Petr Alekseevich Kropotkin, *Kropotkin's Revolutionary Pamphlets*, ed. Roger Nash Baldwin (New York: Dover, 1970); Kropotkin, *Mutual Aid*. See also Joll, *The Anarchists*.

103 For a criticism of this separation, see Pateman, *The Problem of Political Obligation*, e.g., 129–133.

104   Although, due to its very nature, for a justification of the political as we
       know it, it is more likely that this element will be necessary. For more
       clarification, see my Chapter 4, the section "Fairness, political obligation,
       and the idea of societies as 'Schemes of Social Cooperation,' " on the relation
       between existing polities and the idea of schemes of social cooperation.
105   For a looser but equally worthy and demanding sense of voluntariness,
       Graham's explanation of the way traditional anarchists understood it is
       characteristic:

> Implicit in the idea of free agreement is some notion of self-assumed
> obligation, but it is a concept of obligation which is not connected to any
> concept of equivalent exchange. Through the process of free agreement
> individuals publicly commit themselves to future courses of conduct
> voluntarily chosen by them. The underlying model of obligation then is
> no longer contract, but promising.... Kropotkin could argue that the
> free agreements in an anarchist communist society would not have to be
> enforced because these agreements would not be contracts of equivalent
> exchange. Rather, they would be *the public expression of free choice*
> *between persons whose relationships are characterized by co-operation*
> *and mutual aid* instead of the manoeuvring for competitive advantage
> found in capitalist society

> (Robert Graham, "The Role of Contract in Anarchist Ideology," in *For*
> *Anarchism. History, Theory, and Practice*, ed. David Goodway [London and
> New York: Routledge, 1989], 165; emphasis mine). This idea of voluntariness
> is centrally supported by the main lessons of this study. Chapter 4 provides
> another instance of a weaker implementation of voluntariness, which also
> preserves its core.

106   See Rousseau's view as introduced and adopted above in the text, which
       explains also why freedom is not alienable. See also Stirner's view of the self
       and its relation to the principle of equal-liberty as discussed above.
107   See, e.g., Simmons, *Moral Principles and Political Obligations*; Simmons,
       "Philosophical Anarchism"; Simmons, "Justification and Legitimacy."
108   See: Simmons, "Justification and Legitimacy"; my Chapter 1, section
       "Quality-based and interaction-based evaluations of political institutions."

3

An anarchist critique of the Rawlsian idea of a natural duty of justice[1]

In this chapter I focus on the anarchist criticism of a deontological theory of *good reasons* for political obligation. More precisely, I criticize attempts to ground political obligation on a Rawlsian conception of natural duty. This criticism is not aimed at Rawls's theory, but rather at the appeal to his natural duty of justice as a basis for a general obligation to obey the state. The reason for concentrating on this form of natural duty is that the dominance of Rawls's *Theory of Justice* in political philosophy has placed his notion of the "natural duty of justice" at the focus of the debate on political obligation. Nevertheless, while for Rawls this idea and other "principles that apply to individuals"[2] are an essential part of his theory, the establishment of a general political obligation on its basis is not central to this theory, nor does it directly determine its success. Thus, in this chapter, I address the following criticism only to whoever might want to adopt the Rawlsian notion of natural duty as the foundation of an, allegedly, adequate theory of political obligation; I do not claim that Rawls himself is committed to such an endeavor.[3]

There are, however, connections between the basic elements of Rawls's theory as a whole and his notion of natural duty. These links preclude the development of a theory of political obligation in terms of the latter in complete abstraction from the former. This becomes clear, for example, in the argument from particularity which is analyzed in the sections "The argument arising from particularity" and "Rawls and particularity." In this argument, reference to a central part of Rawls's theory is necessary if one is to clarify the force of the criticism of natural duty suggested by the particularity condition. Thus, in the following section, I provide a brief presentation of the basic elements of Rawls's theory as they relate to his formulation of natural duty.

Rawls's theory and the natural duty of justice

Rawls's *Theory of Justice* is a paradigm of contemporary contractualism. It makes use of an individualist account of rationality similarly at work in Hobbes's contract theory of political obligation. More centrally, it aspires to capture considerations of fairness, as a theory "which generalizes and carries to a higher level of abstraction the familiar theory of the social contract as found...in Locke, Rousseau, and Kant."[4] That is to say, Rawls advances a theory that draws on the social contract tradition in order to clarify the concept of justice as fairness, where contract takes the form of hypothetical agreement the object of which is the first principles of justice.[5]

In its formulation, Rawls's theory draws significantly on Kant's contractualism. Rawls himself claims affiliation with Kant in certain fundamental structural features and elements of his theory, such as the distinction between the Reasonable and the Rational, the priority of right, the role of the conception of the person as free and equal, and its accordance with Kant's notion of autonomy.[6] These aspects of Rawls's theory are indicative of its character as an example of a contemporary development of the social contract. In such a development the idea of conceiving the hypothetical contract as a moral route for deciding the content of morality, justice, and/or legitimacy and the role of reasonableness in this are central.[7]

The theory of justice Rawls proposes consists mainly in, first, a methodological framework that includes his device of the "original position,"[8] and, second, a view about the content of justice as captured in his two principles of justice.[9] These two parts to his theory constitute Rawls's liberal proposal as a basis for a just political organization.

In this chapter I concentrate on a discussion of Rawls's *original position* and its relation to the problem of political obligation. This contractualist framework provides the formulation of good reasons in the manner of a hypothetical-contract argument. Thus conceived, the contract is a conceptual device that helps to show how the idea of fair agreement, which Rawls adopts for explaining how to specify the terms of social cooperation, justifies the principles of political justice that constitute those terms.[10] For the agreement to be "fair and supported by the best reasons,"[11] this hypothetical contract device is characterized by various stipulations regarding our reasoning on how to situate the parties participating in the agreement and on what restrictions to make with regard to the knowledge and reasons they have or lack. Thus the political principles are supported by an agreement that is worked out deductively, rather than a historical and actual covenant. It is an agreement that represents reasonable considerations under due reflection. The original position is "a theoretical structure" used to represent "the fixed points of our considered convictions" about social justice.[12] According to Rawls, it "serves as a mediating idea by which all our considered convictions, whatever their level of generality—whether they concern fair conditions for situating the parties, or reasonable constraints on reasons, or first principles and precepts, or judgments about particular institutions and actions—can be brought to bear on one another."[13] In other words, it is a device of representation that "models our convictions" about "fair conditions of agreement" on political principles and about "acceptable restrictions on reasons" we give for these principles.[14] As such it is proposed as a proper philosophical basis for evaluating, or choosing, principles for political institutions and principles for individuals. It is these so-called principles for individuals that include the natural duty of justice.[15]

From the perspective of the debate on political obligation, Rawls's main account[16] is found in his discussion of "natural duties," which "apply to us without regard to our voluntary acts."[17] The points Rawls makes about his interpretation of "natural rights" provide an important step toward a better understanding of what he means by the notion of "natural duty."[18] He connects the term "natural" with the attributes that are ascertained by natural reason as naturally belonging to *persons*, independently of social and legal conventions, and that are given *special weight*. He also uses the term to distinguish the rights and duties identified by his *Theory of Justice* from those defined by law and custom. I take it that the two features connected with the "natural" here are central to the Rawlsian definition of natural duties.

According to his main account, "the natural duty of justice" is defined as "the duty...to support and to comply with *just* institutions that exist and *apply to us* [and which] also constrains us to further just arrangements not yet established, at least when this can be done without too much cost to ourselves."[19] The arguments below are developed around this definition of natural duty as a theory of political obligation, and, more precisely, around its first part. The idea here is that, if the basic structure of society is just, or reasonably just,[20] then we all have a natural duty to do our part in supporting and promoting the existing scheme independently of any voluntary commitment on our part. The basis for obligation is justice, not voluntary acquisition.

The argument of this chapter draws the limited conclusion that an alternative in terms of good reasons for political obligation fails as much as consent to justify this obligation: the natural duty of justice does not qualify as a ground of political obligation. Yet this argument reveals implications for our evaluation of political institutions that have not been derived before. The consideration of Rawls in relation to the anarchist criticism from particularity illuminates these implications and what they show about the role that the anarchist position plays in understanding our relation to political institutions. The Rawlsian account of our duty to obey raises an interesting problem. It brings to the fore a focus on good reasons as a basis of political obligation. Such a focus departs from voluntariness as affirmed by the anarchist criticism in the previous chapter. In being a theory of hypothetical consent, however, the Rawlsian account of natural duty still preserves a significant appeal to self-governance. In both these aspects, it helps the argument developed in this study by providing further insight into what the role of institutional qualities is in justifying political authority and into how this relates to the role of specific interaction. Most importantly, it brings to the fore the fundamental anarchist positions about the value of consent and the problematic character of political constraints.

An anarchist criticism of the natural duty of justice

The anarchist criticism in this section may be separated into two interrelated parts: first, arguments against taking the *justice* of the institutions as a reason for obedience and, second, arguments about the relation of the Rawlsian natural duty to the *particularity condition* of political obligation. I will deal with each in turn.

Against the justice of political institutions as a ground of political obligation

Appealing to the *just nature* of political institutions as the basis of political obligation is what makes theories of natural duty such as Rawls's theories of institutional morality. By definition, such theories focus on the moral qualities of institutions in order to establish political obligations. Namely, they concentrate on the character of political institutions: on their general moral virtues (such as justice) and their moral accomplishments for their subjects as a whole (such as the promotion of social happiness), rather than on any elements of specific interaction between them and individuals (such as the giving of consent).[21] But can the justice of an organization ground a general obligation to obey the law?

The problems that stand in the way of such a conception of our political duties arise from the consideration that just or good legal systems might provide grounds for obeying their laws and for distinguishing them from bad systems and yet not create political obligation. In what follows I will argue that the sufficiency of justice as a ground of political obligation is questionable.

Raz's discussion facilitates the anarchist criticism at this point. As he has indicated, the substantial functions of the law, which are reflected in two main "legal techniques," can be evaluated by appeal to certain general reasons for action that underlie those techniques—reasons that nevertheless do not suffice to establish general political obligations.[22] The first technique provides legal sanctions as useful prudential reasons for obedience, in such a way as to support the respect of valuable moral duties, whether negative duties, like the avoidance of harm, or positive duties, like the provision of aid. The second technique provides "publicly ascertainable standards" that help to guide the social behavior of officials and the active contribution of citizens for the preservation of "worthwhile forms of social co-operation," insofar as these officials and citizens accept the independent moral reasons that underlie the standards in question.[23]

These connections might show how general moral reasons, and in our case the fundamental duty of justice, might explain the moral acceptability of certain political functions, but they do not generate any special relation of political obligation. The prudential grounds that constitute the first technique might be appropriate ways of securing valuable moral duties. My argument, however, is that it cannot be taken for granted that they are the only ways of doing so and in virtue of their political character: individuals' sense of duty and of their responsibility to others might themselves provide stable motivations for respecting these duties, without the need of centralized, permanent, exclusive, and compulsory constraining measures. But, more importantly, if such duties have a real moral value, then it is on the force of this value that we should concentrate as the direct reason for support and see what kind of justification this provides. That the reasons for support lie in the value of these primary duties might make various, political or nonpolitical, ways of administering them morally acceptable, but it does not define the necessity of any specifically political means of enforcement and of a specifically political obligation. The natural duty of justice is more clearly emphasized by the reasons underlying the second technique that represents functions of the law. Yet the observations concerning the first technique provide the foundation for an estimation of the role of the standards provided by the second technique. The prudential grounds of the first technique that support the moral duties underlying it stand in interaction with the standards that affirm the reasons underlying the second technique and should be compatible with them in the way they both characterize the system. Their role is relevant to the present focus on natural duty as a moral reason and primary ground of political obligation. In general, prudential grounds provide additional motivational support for moral reasons.

Crucially, in the case of the second technique, it is part of the character of political institutions that legal sanctions play a central role in sustaining moral reasons. But my objection here is that there is no necessary principled and empirical connection between this political character and the sustaining of moral values within society. On this basis, my objection in the case of the standards provided by the second legal technique is that the reasons underlying that technique are *moral reasons* for action that work independently of the existence of any political requirement on action.[24] It is the force of the morality of these reasons and their acceptance by those whose behavior they are to determine that generate obligations. The morality that makes these reasons strong and acceptable bases of action does not derive from the political character of their enforcement, nor does it exclusively authorize political techniques even when such reasons are facilitated by them. Thus it deprives these reasons from being grounds of a specially political obligation. Pertaining to such moral reasons, the natural duty of justice neither indispensably requires publicly ascertainable standards of the kind imposed by the state nor defines a duty special to them.

Nevertheless, one might appeal to the existence and value of good laws on which the character of a political system is founded, or by which it is expressed, as a reason for supporting any further laws that contribute to the preservation of the good ones. Thus appeal to the value of good laws as a reason requiring general obedience for this system to be respected. This is an appeal to the moral "argument from setting a bad example."[25] It is the argument that known disobedience to certain (even bad) laws on the part of some individuals will badly affect other individuals' conformity to good laws or to a good legal system as a whole. Therefore only general obedience to any law can preserve and thus respect good laws. Raz seems right that this argument is inadequate as a ground of general political obligation. Disobedience is undetected in many cases and, more important, it does not always set a bad example encouraging offenses against good laws. In fact disobedience to bad laws could encourage the improvement of a system and enforce conformity. The known violation of good laws can also invite disapproval on the part of those individuals who engage in a reflective assessment of their value. Individuals can support good laws on the basis of their own evaluation, without the need for a general requirement of obedience to affect their reasoning and behavior. These observations indicate that the argument from bad example lacks generality. That is, it simply does not apply to various cases of legally evaluable actions that must be shown to be such by a theory of political obligation. The relevance of this criticism to the natural duty of justice lies in that the argument from bad example can apply to *just* laws, since they are a paradigm of goodness that might be expressive of a system. The qualified argument falls prey to a similar objection: disobedience does not provide a bad example generalized enough to hurt a just system and thus violate the requirement of the natural duty. It follows that the natural duty of justice fails, in a similar manner, to combine the duty to support just institutions with the generality condition of political obligation.[26]

The above remarks suggest that the just character of an institution does not provide a *sufficient* ground for political obligation. The arguments from justice just examined fail to conjoin it with the essentially political character of this obligation. The conclusion reached so far finds expression in John Simmons's statement that, while morality means that "just institutions are the sort that ought to be promoted (for a variety of reasons), ... it is this fact alone that is expressed by a duty of justice."[27] Thus, "the mere justice of an institution ... is insufficient to derive a moral requirement to comply with and do one's part in that institution."[28] In other words, although justice is a necessary precondition for grounding political obligation, it is insufficient as a ground of such an obligation.

Jeremy Waldron gives an explanation of how the demands of justice involved in the natural duty account should be understood that might facilitate an effective reply to the preceding objection.[29] When examining justice as one of the significant conditions of political obligation, Waldron proposes that it is important to understand justice as a moral imperative. For this, it is not enough for us to ensure that the institutions we happen to have are just. Rather the natural duty of justice means that "the demands of justice [ought to] be pursued *period*" and is satisfied only when we do our part to *establish* just institutions.[30] In this light, the demands of the natural duty of justice evoke a sense in which an institution can be just that Waldron considers both to be different from the one adopted by Simmons and Raz in their criticism and to be substantive enough to establish political obligation in terms of such a duty. According to Waldron's understanding, an institution "can be just in the sense that it is doing something that justice requires" and not in the sense that he attributes to Simmons, namely that it is "just in the way it operates."[31] This means that an institution is just not when its internal operations are just without it being important from the point of view of justice that we assist them, but rather when it responds to the demands of justice, that is, when it is a matter of justice that it has its practices realized. And since the demands of justice are overriding, whenever present in an institution they facilitate an explanation of our bonds to that institution *in terms of natural duty*.

This argument does not help to deflect the preceding criticism, however. My argument is that the requirements of justice may be imperative and to this extent affect the evaluation of, and our allegiance to, an institution that satisfies them on purely moral grounds, without any essential reference to its political features. In this way, their importance is asserted through morality, but this does not mean that such requirements entail (or simply are) political obligations. For this, it has to be shown that only a political organization *qua political* is effective and appropriate for realizing these demands, which is what the anarchist doubts. The anarchist conclusions reached above still hold, namely that the moral value of justice might ground the acceptability of an institution, but it does not on its own generate a moral requirement to comply with the institution. Waldron nonetheless prolongs his argument and, as a reply exactly to this objection, provides an account of effectiveness and legitimacy that he sees as tied to the natural-duty theory. I will examine his argument in the discussion of particularity in the next section. For now, the point made is that the value of justice cannot by itself ground a special relationship of obligation to political institutions. This point is reinforced when the natural duty of justice is tested against the particularity condition.

The main upshot of the above considerations on the role of justice in an account of political obligation can now be stated. Justice makes strong moral claims on us. Such demands, however, do not derive from the political status of any institutional organization that may make them. They thus constitute general moral requirements and lead to the approval of the *quality* of any form of social order that reflects respect for them, but they cannot provide a *sufficient* defense of political obligation. Furthermore, the arguments for this conclusion show that anarchism recognizes the importance of the demands of justice in a society. The main anarchist claim, for which the present conclusion provides support, is that the state is not essential to the satisfaction of these demands and that, therefore, the demands of justice neither legitimize the authority of the state nor establish the necessity of its existence.

These claims form the basis of the argument I want to advance in this chapter. Significantly, they reveal the following points. The demands of justice can, in the end, ground the acceptability of certain forms of government, distinguish bad from good governments, and also serve as a criterion for avoiding excesses of power. But this is not enough for settling the problem of obligation to political institutions: good reasons constitute sufficient justification for institutions, if we understand by this that they are legitimate forms of social organization, but not for our obligation to the state. The anarchist view expressed in the present criticism reflects an approach that *goes beyond* a concern with justifying the legitimacy of political constraints, which is a concern with putting limits on political institutions within a background where they are generally accepted as a given. For such an approach, an understanding of the proper role of general moral values in an assessment of political institutions is crucial. And the present demonstration of the lack of connection between one such value and the special political nature of those constraints is the first step in this direction. Political constraints are exclusive and inevitable in nature, and the failure of general moral values to ground political obligation in them as such directs us to a different use of those values in an attempt to evaluate political institutions, one primarily determined by this special nature.

The arguments of the present section can now be completed by stating a final point. On the whole, these arguments reflect the decisive difference between the anarchist approach and the focus of Rawls's account. The anarchist asks the primary question whether there should be any political obligations. Rawls presumes an answer to this question. He presupposes state legitimacy and moves on to concentrate on another normative question, the question about the content of justice, which is: what principles would render a constitution acceptable in terms of justice? Although he remains consistent in his attempt and this fact is recognized in the present discussion, it is crucial to distinguish the two directions. This distinction generates a basic anarchist critique against theories of justice. Most importantly, however, it clarifies the main anarchist argument. The anarchist insists that an account that concentrates on the support of established institutions that embody conventional principles, such as Rawls's liberal theory, leaves behind the most fundamental problem. It presupposes precisely the issue that should concern us most, that is, the very authority about which we should be skeptical.[32]

The argument arising from particularity

Given the above considerations, the most prominent criticism against the Rawlsian natural duty of justice as an account of political obligation concerns its relationship to the *particularity condition* of political obligation. To remind the reader, particularity is the requirement that an account of political obligation should explain the special relationship between persons and the particular government of their country of residence. The criticism focuses on the observation that the duty to support just institutions does not explain the particular relation of each citizen to his or her *own* polity. It rather facilitates support of every system that is just, whenever that is possible.

These points are supported by an extended argument made by Simmons.[33] He asserts, first, that the theory of natural duty lacks a "strong sense of application," namely one that is generated by actions that make an individual "an active participant," when, for example, one explicitly consents. My arguments in Chapter 2 showed that explicit consent constitutes a genuine expression of initiation of and participation in a particular relationship, even though existing polities fail to obtain it. It is also an element that is lacking in natural-duty accounts.

Second, Simmons claims that the natural duty satisfies only a "weak or territorial sense of application," one holding, for example, when we "live in an area in which [the rules of an institution] are enforced," which, not being morally significant, cannot establish "a genuine duty."[34] It is important to note here that this claim is merely that a theory of natural duty can satisfy only this weak sense of application. It is not to be interpreted as a claim that Rawls himself appeals to such a weak notion of application or that it is consistent with his theory as a whole. In fact, he does not appeal to it, since his contractualism is "an idea of reason" (to echo Kant's phrase)[35] rather than an actual recipe for legitimate government. This observation attacks a stronger formulation of the present objection as part of the criticism from particularity. In that formulation the claim is that an appeal to Rawls's phrase "apply to us," as an indication that the duty addresses the inhabitants of a particular community, is *an arbitrary move*: it focuses on "practical considerations," concerning the proximity of each state to the members of the society that it governs, as an important reason for obedience. Such a focus works in defiance of principled considerations, which in fact constitute the proper basis of any attempt to combine particularity with justice. In general, the inclusion of the "application clause" in a natural-duty theory seems illegitimate, mainly because it renders the *justice* of an institution irrelevant to a justification of our political bonds.[36] The position of natural duties within Rawls's theory, especially their relation to his original position as a method of hypothetical contract as specially conceived by Rawls, enables his theory to avoid this problem.[37]

Third, Simmons argues that, while theories of consent and of fair play implement the strong sense of application, their use in order to supplement Rawls's theory of natural duty would condemn the latter to the violation of the generality condition that these theories commit. The anarchist criticism developed in this study shows that neither consent nor the principle of fairness are sufficient to generate political obligation for most of the individuals in existing societies.[38] Also, this supplementation is illegitimate, since it grounds "a quite different sort of moral requirement," obligations rather than duties. According to Simmons, a significant difference between obligations and duties is that the former correlate with "'rights in personam'," namely "rights which are held against a specific person, and are rights to a specific performance or forbearance," while the latter correlate with "'rights in rem'," namely "rights which are held against all other people."[39] The morality of the natural duty of justice secures only the latter and in this creates no connection with the particularistic character of political obligation, to which consent and fairness adhere.

Finally, Simmons argues that only the "strong application," with its "personal transaction" element (which is essentially voluntarist; see the first point of his argument here), can meet the "particularity requirement" as an essential condition of political obligation.[40] Thus, Rawls's idea of natural duty, indeed, any duty-based theory, in violating the particularity condition, fails to ground political obligation. This point is central to the anarchist perspective on political obligation. It expresses the idea that only morally significant features of specific interaction, those involved in transactional evaluation, can establish the particular moral relationship that political obligation requires for its actuality.[41] One of the main aims of my examination of the anarchist criticisms is to see whether this claim is justified. Chapter 2 has given an affirmative answer. The arguments of this chapter (and Chapters 4 and 5) take a more decisive step in this direction. They also help to complete the considerations introduced in the previous chapters with regard to deciding the role of quality for political obligation.

In response to this type of argument, Waldron has proposed a strategy for reconciling the Rawlsian, duty-based view, with the particularity condition. Waldron concludes that "an organization which is just, effective and legitimate ... [establishes] ... the moral requirement that we support and obey such an organization ... not itself based on any promise that we have made."[42] Here I want to examine the steps leading to this conclusion.

A first step is to establish that principles of justice can be "range-limited," namely such that there can be a set of persons who can be distinguished as those whose conduct, claims, and interests it is the point of these principles to deal with, so that they are considered as "insiders" in relation to them.[43] On this basis, principles of justice can be seen to demand special allegiance from the insiders and thus be particularly applied to them as opposed to "outsiders." We need an argument that shows principles of justice to be range-limited such that it avoids a mere appeal to the weak notion of application described above. For this, Waldron appeals to Kant's argument. This argument appears in the prudential reasoning of Hobbes with regard to human nature and the necessity of the state, as well as in Hume's account of justice.[44] But here it takes a special form that draws attention to prudential considerations only as part of the demands of justice, which is more clearly represented by Kant's view.[45] Thus we need to examine whether it provides a solution to the problem.[46] The argument is that the decision to enter political society is not an open question. If individuals are so situated that they are inevitably close to certain others and thus have a claim to the same resources, conflict and violence will be inevitable even if those people are good natured and reasonable. Disputes will arise about the possession of the same resources, and people will still disagree about what seems good and just to each regarding the use of those resources. So in order to avoid conflict and the suffering it entails, people should quickly enter a form of society with those who have interests competing with theirs, namely with their near neighbors. In this way, the principles that are to define their relations are range-limited in the sense that they are the "basis for settling those conflicts which are immediately unavoidable."[47]

It is doubtful, however, whether this is a satisfactory argument. The appeal to immediately unavoidable conflict shows a way of defining a particular application that lies in external circumstances rather than in a principled connection between justice and the generation of particular relations. Thus, in my opinion, it seems to operate the weak notion of application, rather than the strong one that provides a direct principled basis for distinguishing insiders from outsiders. Nevertheless, in order to decide whether the sense in which the argument identifies the demands of justice as range-limited is a strong sense, and whether the argument can establish a demand of special allegiance to political institutions, we need to examine it further.

At this point we can see how the Kantian argument works with regard to the administration of principles by institutions. In the case of political institutions, the claim is that a range-limited application of principles is possible if we apply a specific distinction between insiders and outsiders. If the insiders are those who are constrained to accept a principle of justice and then to accept secondary principles that accompany it—for example, principles that require individuals to accept its supervision by a specific institution that embodies its demands—while the outsiders are those who are constrained only not to interfere with this administration.[48] An institution will be able to administer a range-limited principle of justice if most of the people to whom it applies accept these secondary principles and most of the others accept the principle of noninterference. But for this to work we need to establish that people are *actually bound* to the institutions that claim to have this role.

For Waldron, this can be provided by the satisfaction of a test of legitimacy.[49] According to this test we need to show, first, that the existence of institutions that do justice is significant, second, that it is important for there to be only *one* institution doing justice in a territory and, third, that there are grounds for seeing one particular organization as appropriate for this purpose.

Waldron requires that the first demand be satisfied by Kant's argument analyzed above. Even if this argument were proven to work for the application of principles, however, my counter-argument is that there are reasons for doubting its success with regard to the necessity of political institutions. The discussion of the social contract in Chapter 2 provides the basis for such doubts. The social-contract arguments from the state of nature examined there may show that the state is a good solution to problems of security, peace, and coordination, but they do not establish the state as the only solution. First, they do not provide a proof that the state of nature would make agreement impossible, but they simply assume this. Second, even if it would, there are still proposals in favor of nonauthoritarian decentralized forms of interaction that might also provide the background for resolution of conflicts. It remains an open question as to which alternative will do better, but nonauthoritarian alternatives have been excluded by state-of-nature defenses without proper examination, showing that their appeal to the state as *the* alternative is very quick. So even if principles of justice could be properly range-limited by appeal to the danger of conflict, their application by political institutions is not necessarily entailed, and thus no special relation of obligation to those institutions is justified. The argument does not prove that it is important for the sake of justice that *political* institutions exist.

Nevertheless, it can be argued that political institutions are one important solution to problems of justice, and since we are already within their terrain, this should suffice for their justification. Even if we accept this argument, it remains for us to examine the replies given to the other two demands in order to see if it can ground political obligation. With regard to the second demand of Waldron's test of legitimacy, his argument is that, if we accept that the avoidance of conflict provides a justification for political society, then on this basis we can explain why we should have only *one* such organization. The reasoning here is that if there is more than one organization, there will still be conflict of the same kind in which individuals were involved in the first place: individuals will still support the organization that serves their own reasons as they understand them, and conflict will arise between such organizations as representatives of different claims. This conflict will be even worse, since the fighting will be better organized. Also, given the demands of cooperation, people need an assurance that others follow the same goals as they do so that they know that the others will cooperate with them and achieve these goals. Such an assurance can be provided by the existence of only one system that determines the goals that people are to share, the ways to achieve them, and the cooperation of all. Furthermore, problems of coordination demand a similar solution in order for there to be an assurance that all individuals follow the same one of the various possible ways in which they might be able to coordinate. (For example, although both driving on the left and driving on the right might be equally acceptable solutions, individuals in the same society need to follow only one and the same in order to coordinate.) Both cooperation and coordination are important not only for the avoidance of conflicts, but also for the avoidance of injustice itself.

In response to these arguments, one can claim that when society is organized on a small scale, then the need for a single organization does not seem so urgent. In such alternative societies people communicate more directly and cooperate for smaller goals without the need for centralized supervision and more general goals might be solved through confederation between the smaller groups. Anarchists support exactly these kinds of social solutions. Theorists and activists disagree about their viability, and there might be reasons for doubting that existing societies can afford such a change, but this possibility cannot be excluded on the basis of an assumption that only the state can work. Alternative structures might not be immediately viable, but they are possible. What I think is interesting about this reply is that it resurrects an argument against the state that underlies the defense of alternatives and makes it stronger. The underlying reasoning that I follow here is that the state might seem important because a focus on the necessity of its existence neglects the fact that it might be the very existence and structure of the state that generates the problems that we are then asked to solve. The state is our reality, and it might work well with regard to the problems it is required to solve. Yet it might be that it is the very reality of the state that makes it become the only visible way of solving problems. We find ourselves in it without being asked and without being presented with other possibilities. The problems the state is asked to solve are identified through the experience within it. Alternative structures might not even identify conflict in the same way as it is identified within the state. In the end, the argument from alternatives works primarily as an indication of the uncertainty of the arguments for the necessity of the state. The arguments to follow show this more decisively.

Even if a final solution to the problems of conflict and injustice favored the state, there is still the third demand of the test of legitimacy to be examined. This is quite crucial, because the aim of my argument is to show that granting political obligation seems to be the wrong way to go about justification. According to Waldron's argument, legitimacy demands that an organization be capable of enforcing justice and, for this, that people be *prepared to accept it*: that they can be assured that enough others are disposed to comply with the principles of justice in order to consider a particular institution to be effective, and thus that they are bound to it. The last step for establishing that a particular organization is the appropriate one for exercising justice is to prove its salience. The proposal is that, for proving salience, majority consent, hypothetical consent, or hypothetical majority consent can suffice.[50] Here the idea is that the ground for recognizing a particular scheme as appropriate is justice, namely that it embodies the demands of justice. But a good way of establishing this is to use hypothetical (majority) agreement, as an indication that a given institution "may appropriately embody those demands."[51] This, for Waldron, is not a consent theory of political obligation. We do not try to show the existence of an actual consent as a basis of obligation. Rather we use hypothetical consent as a confirmation of the appropriateness of political institutions in terms of justice. Obligatoriness here becomes a matter of moral background. The natural duty of justice makes justice the ground of obligation, and consent is used to distinguish the institutions that embody it. For this, hypothetical majority consent is all that is needed.

In this argument, we can see an appeal to hypothetical consent similar to the one set out in Chapter 2. The focus is on the qualities of political institutions, on good reasons for accepting them. Consent is used as a thought-experiment for conceiving these reasons, as a moral route through which we discover what the best reasons are for supporting principles and institutions. This, however, helps us understand our moral duties, such as those of justice, but it does not prove an actual relationship to a particular organization. Anarchists agree that justice is an imperative. And Waldron's test of legitimacy might show that certain institutions are just and thus acceptable on general and imperative moral grounds. But hypothetical consent can establish only this. This is what the proof of salience amounts to. Hypothetical consent, or hypothetical popular consent (or even popular consent), does not establish a particular relationship between each person and the institutions that claim his or her allegiance. General political obligation to one society in particular is not proven. Waldron uses legitimacy in a sense different[52] from the one used in the debate on political obligation, where it is seen as the correlate of that obligation.[53] Still, he argues that the satisfaction of his idea of legitimacy is enough as a basis for accounts of obligation, that it establishes the bindingness of institutions. What I argue here, however, is that his ideal of legitimacy generates a demand for the constant evaluation of institutions in terms of justice, rather than a basis for ultimate allegiance to them, which constitutes political obligation.

With regard to Rawls, Waldron himself accepts that his hypothetical consent is "a model-theoretic device for establishing what justice actually amounts to; it has no political or institutional significance, either with regard to obligation or with regard to legitimacy (in the sense [Waldron is] discussing)."[54] Indeed, in Rawls's case it is more obvious how hypothetical consent works as a way of justifying principles for institutions, for discovering the political principles that are supported by the best reasons, rather than as a theory of political obligation. It might still be possible for there to be a connection between his theory of natural duty and particularity on the basis of this understanding of the theory. I will examine this possibility in the following section. The point I argue here is that the connection is not provided by Waldron's account. Still, we can see Waldron's defense of natural duty as a departure from Rawls. Despite his claim on institutional significance, however, the lesson we learn from that defense is that justice matters for legitimacy, and that legitimacy can be understood as a matter of the acceptability of political institutions: of a proof that they can embody and apply justice to a specific society, and of the need to be assessed constantly on this basis. This does not prove that they are the only ones that can do so, nor that their range-limited application derives from their political nature. The questions still remain open whether conflict is the basis for political society and whether a single political authority is justified. Hypothetical consent cannot combine affirmative answers to these questions with its kind of evaluation of political constraints in a way that establishes particularity. The moral importance of justice does not itself make constraints range-limited, and the representation of its demands through hypothetical consent does not provide a salience that generates a special and actual relation binding each individual to his or her own government. Particularity is still not satisfied.

Rawls and particularity

Nevertheless, there are considerations coming from a closer estimation of the relation of Rawls's account of natural duty to particularity that can deal better with the anarchist criticism. In this context Rawls's original position becomes crucially relevant. In the discussion of this framework (in the section "Rawls's theory and the natural duty of justice"), I stressed that Rawls's contractualist methodology is a device used to model what we regard as fair conditions on agreement and acceptable restrictions on reasons for principles of social justice. I also emphasized that his theory of natural duty is more precisely a hypothetical-contract theory of natural duty, since the natural duty of justice to be imposed on individuals is among those principles that would be acknowledged by individuals in his original position.[55] This shows that an appeal to the Rawlsian natural duty of justice as an account of political obligation cannot disregard the role of Rawls's original position and its connection to the issue. Given these features of the theory, we can begin to understand its relation to particularity. According to Rawls, both his two principles of justice and his methodology are designed for a specific form of society: the "formal conditions on principles," the considerations hidden by "the veil of ignorance," and other elements relevant to concerns about social justice involved in the original position[56] include ideas that Rawls believes to be central for citizens who live in societies with a liberal democratic tradition. The original position represents the considered judgments of the citizens of such societies. It is for these societies that Rawls proposes his theory of justice. The construction of the original position amounts to a *deontological* version of the hypothetical contract as a theory explaining what would be considered *good reasons* by reasonable democratic citizens.[57] The natural duty of justice, along with the idea that we need political institutions for a successful implementation of the requirements of social justice, is claimed by Rawls to deserve reasonable acceptance by individuals in his imaginative position. In this way, Rawls's theory seems to satisfy the particularity condition, at least in principle. Through the hypothetical thought-experiment each individual of a democratic society can assert the considerations that reflect his/her reasonable viewpoint as such a citizen, and the principles affirmed on this basis are the result of the best reasons with which he/she identifies. Thus, individuals can be seen to have a particular normative relation to the principles chosen for their societies and to be able to extend this relation to the institutions that embody these principles in these societies. The natural duty of justice is based on the reasonable viewpoint that the citizens of societies with a specific character should have, and it can determine their social relation to the institutions that satisfy this viewpoint. In principle, the strong sense of application is satisfied.

Because this happens only in principle, however, theories focusing on institutional qualities are problematic as accounts of political obligation, even when such theories are based on hypothetical consent with its significant representation of self-governance. The normative force of the original position affects first and foremost the acceptability of principles that can then determine the character of political institutions, not the acceptability of the institutions themselves. Furthermore, such acceptability refers to the character of political institutions rather than the features of a particular relation of authority. Finally, a definition of what counts as the reasonable viewpoint of democratic citizens differs from an identification of their actual viewpoints. The former constitutes a normative standard for assessing their viewpoint, a representation of the idea of political autonomy, but it does not establish any actual authority unless it characterizes their real viewpoint as it actually applies to specific institutions. Rawls's theory might be representative of the general attitude of reasonable democratic citizens of some societies, but this does not prove any application of the specific interaction among individuals and between them and political institutions that is required to establish actual political obligations. Also, in representing what Rawls deems the characteristic reasonable attitude of the democratic citizen in liberal societies, his theory does not examine the considered beliefs of ordinary people who actually live in these societies. So it is not certain that his intuitions reflect accurately those of the public to whom he refers. This observation does not challenge the appropriateness of his abstraction. Rather it suggests that, to be a faithful application of the reasonable that is particular to the culture it addresses, it may be necessary for the abstraction to be more securely connected with the actual reasonable of that culture.[58] A special political relationship can only be created when the reasonableness of accepting a natural duty to our just institutions is asserted in the specific tasks they serve for each and every member of their society and in the corresponding recognition by these members. The general justice of institutions may justify their existence and/or desirability, but not prove that they are actually and continually performing their tasks and are accepted.[59] We will have to examine the specific relations between particular democratic societies and their citizens as governed by the principles of justice in order to see whether in their particular case Rawls's theory can establish special allegiance. As it stands, Rawls's account provides general normative constraints of justice for evaluating political institutions in general and as they already exist. It does not serve the purpose of establishing a particular society and its authority.

Rawls himself clearly concedes this:

[I]n contrast to the various conceptions of the social contract, the several parties do not establish any particular society or practice; they do not covenant to obey a particular sovereign body or to accept a given constitution. Nor do they, as in game theory (in certain respects a marvelously sophisticated development of this tradition), decide on individual strategies adjusted to their respective circumstances in the game. What the parties do is *jointly* acknowledge certain *principles* of appraisal relating to their common *practices* either as already established or merely proposed. They accede to standards of judgement, not to a given practice; they do not make any specific agreement, or bargain, or adopt a particular strategy. The subject of their acknowledgement is, therefore, very general indeed; it is simply the acknowledgement of certain principles of judgement, fulfilling certain general conditions, to be used in criticising the arrangement of their common affairs. The relations of mutual self-respect between the parties who are similarly circumstanced mirror the conditions under which questions of justice arise, and the procedure by which the principles of judgement are proposed and acknowledged reflects the constraints of having a morality. Each aspect, then, of the [Rawlsian] hypothetical account serves the purpose of bringing out a feature of the notion of justice.[60]

Therefore it is concluded that the relation of a Rawlsian theory of political obligation to particularity is this: in principle, Rawls's account of natural duty does not violate the particularity condition. Moreover, when an attempt to base political obligation on the Rawlsian conception of natural duty reflects the centrality and connection of Rawls's original position to the issue, then the attempt preserves the prospect of particularity. But the principled support provided for natural duty within such a framework renders no proof of the actual application in terms of natural duty of the moral relationship between citizens and government that is required for political obligation. The particularity condition for political obligation is not satisfied.

Self-governance, equality, and the role of general moral principles

The above considerations are crucial for the main argument of this study. They shed light on the following observations, with which I end this section. These observations are about a significant connection between the role of general moral principles such as justice in defending political institutions and the affirmation of the importance of self-governance and equality. As argued in Chapter 2, hypothetical consent provides a phenomenology of how individuals can be ruled by themselves, representing a route through which they come to identify with important aspects of their social world even when they do not actually consent. This nevertheless does not itself ground social relations and duties. The preceding discussion of Rawls confirms these points, now as applied with regard to the demands of justice. Furthermore, with respect to the relation of justice to the political aspect of institutions discussed in this chapter, this moral value constitutes a criterion for the acceptability of political institutions and can be used along with other values for moral evaluations of such institutions, values that do not depend on their political nature. In the absence of direct expressions of voluntary submission and a transactional application of the demands of justice, political institutions can be assessed in terms of general values in order for us to recognize aspects of their existence as appropriate. But this does not generate political obligation. And it does not secure individual freedom and social equality unless it is done in light of the defects of political institutions. The results of the debate on political obligation so far show that the exclusive and authoritative nature of political institutions makes them incapable of certain relations and possibilities—such as the kind of interactions that would justify a relationship of political obligation—and this gives us reason to reconsider the way we accept them and let them govern our lives. It indicates the instability of arguments for their necessity. The nature of political institutions is such that within them there is always a point at which self-determination is governed by aspects external to itself. When political obligation is claimed to be defended as a special relationship that gives governments the right to decide the conditions of social life without being challenged in terms of content and degree, and to use coercion to back up this function, then the possibility of re-evaluating those conditions is limited. That is why the basic acts of self-assumed commitment and kinds of social cooperation that involve decentralized, reciprocal, and equal relations do not sit well with such a duty. In order to secure respect for self-governance and equality, the realization of equal-liberty, general moral values can be used as general requirements for institutions that apply constantly and in view of their defects. This goes beyond their use for assessing the acceptability of political institutions and for limiting excesses of institutionalized power.

The implications of the anarchist criticism of natural duty

The implications of the preceding elaboration of the anarchist criticism of the Rawlsian natural duty of justice are as follows.

In many cases, the just character of political institutions is a considerable reason for supporting aspects of them that express this character. It also renders them more suitable and possible candidates of political legitimacy. However, it does not qualify as a ground of political obligation. It fails, despite its moral significance, to be a general basis for obligation that comes to terms with the political character of institutions. Thus, the natural duty of justice is guaranteed a privileged position from the perspective of the general debate on morality and on the desirability of constraints, but not as part of a successful defense of political obligation.

Failure to satisfy the particularity condition does not necessarily condemn Rawls's account of natural duty, since his theory as a whole serves aims quite different from the aim to defend political obligation and since, when accommodated to the latter concern, contrary to first impressions, that account is, at least in principle, compatible with the requirement. But this compatibility does not establish the theory as an account of political obligation. The discussion of Rawls's theory is helpful in that it highlights the significance of the particularity condition as an indispensable part of a theory of political obligation, thus justifying the anarchist insistence upon it. The discussion of particularity confirms the anarchist's demand that we need to focus, as the last court of appeal, on the actual and particular conditions that may generate and characterize the relationship of political obligation. With this demand, our concern with values when assessing political institutions is transformed into a direct and substantive assessment of our social world.

In sum: particularity proves to be a hard test for any account that focuses on the moral qualities of political institutions. Such accounts provide elaborated bases for evaluating political institutions, for understanding the reasons of their existence and the criteria on the basis of which we can explain our relation to them. But they do not provide the ground for an overall justification of political impositions and for their primary determination of the actions of individuals. This can be established only on the basis of the presence of morally important features of the specific interaction between political institutions and individuals, as something that substantially and continually characterizes social reality. At the same time, while justice cannot provide a ground for obeying government, the possibility of attempts to undermine it is restricted by the central role of this idea in morality. This is not to deny that considerations of feasibility and efficiency might require compromise on the part of considerations of justice, to a greater or lesser extent. Justice is not an absolute value, but, just as every other important moral quality of institutions, it remains a strong criterion for their assessment and, as the primary political virtue, perhaps the strongest.

At this point, the role of institutional morality, or quality, within the debate on political obligation becomes clearer. Institutional morality is an indispensable aspect of the evaluation of political constraints, since the latter cannot be taken for granted and as desirable in themselves. In the present case, the justice of institutions plays a central role for morally evaluating our social reality and for imposing principled demands on political structures and practices. Yet for the specific relationship that needs to apply in order for there to be political obligation, this general quality— and any such quality—is insufficient. Instead, it is how such qualities apply to the interaction between existing institutions and each of their citizens and to the relations among those citizens themselves that matters in creating this special political relationship. The failure of defenses of political obligation to combine the moral with the political feature through the four conditions that determine the debate on political authority is indicative of the difficulty of achieving this aim. It is this point that the anarchist criticisms express and that characterizes primarily the perspective involved in the anarchist challenge.

The anarchist proposal itself of an ideal of political legitimacy is guided by these considerations, as the conclusions of this and the preceding chapter declare. According to the conclusions of Chapter 2, a successful attempt to justify political obligation should satisfy the conditions of generality, particularity, bindingness, and content-independence in a way that reflects a recognition of the value of voluntariness, or autonomous choice. This corresponds to the prior anarchist idea of a society that actually involves voluntarist transactions, as a paradigm of legitimacy. The new element to be added as a result of the discussion of this chapter is this: justice is a necessary virtue of political institutions. In order to establish their legitimacy, however, this quality must be proven to be compatible with the main conditions of political obligation, and especially with particularity. At the same time, while justice cannot be secured without at least a minimal level of efficiency, its wholesale sacrifice to the latter deprives an institution of most of its moral character. These considerations reflect another prior vision that determines the anarchist perspective. That is, that a society that would involve the actual distribution of equal rights, opportunities, and other benefits—the actual implementation of just treatment—would be legitimately one where there exists the special relationship between the centralized coercive structures that realize these functions and the citizens who consider them their own.

Thus, the ideal of legitimacy appears in the form of anarchist proposals that vindicate visions of society that represent prior considerations as to what the aim of the debate on political obligation is. It is significant that they stress the importance (and difficulty) of insisting on quality, still in a way reminding us that, for political obligation, this insistence can be meaningful only in relation to actual, particular interaction. The anarchist criticisms bring once more the anarchist perspective and ideals of legitimacy together, thus opening the way to achieve a unified and comprehensive view.

These considerations advance the argument about the problematic character of constraints that distinguishes the anarchist perspective. The demand for a complete absence of constraints might seem an impossible and even undesirable position. We might still have serious reasons for wanting our decisions to be determined by others—a strong need for peace and safety, as well as the demands of important moral duties. But in the case of political constraints, such reasons do not suffice to justify unconditional allegiance to them. Their coercive character takes a permanent, centralist, and exclusive form that undermines not only the opportunity for equal self-government, but also the capacity for self-government itself and all that it mirrors about individuals qua persons, who *as such* need and deserve peace and security. Political domination affects the quality of relations between individuals in a manner and to an extent that it undermines the very basis of equal standing and free participation. It violates the very reasons for which institutions are meant to exist in the first place. In the end, there are no strong arguments for having a duty to the state, unlike in the case of other moral duties. This has significant implications for political institutions themselves.

These points relate to the importance of liberty and equality and to the value of consent, which the preceding anarchist criticisms underline. Self-government matters as the fundamental exercise of our capacity to recreate ourselves as we choose and to control and lead our own lives, without being subjected to arbitrary limitations. As such it preserves and requires relations of a free and equal character, which reflect a respect for human beings. Self-government does involve being ruled. It involves constraints as much as equality does. But it also involves the expression of a desire and demand not to be constrained. This might seem inconsistent. Yet different ways of attending to liberty and equality make a difference, which explains the compatibility of the two demands. Consent has not proven to be an adequate basis of political obligation, but it still points to an obvious way of expressing and exercising personal authority and achieving equal participation. Actual consent is compatible with equal-liberty. It provides an immediate way of realizing self-government, and this to the extent that it is equally realized for other individuals and on the same equal basis as is required for the enjoyment of other advantages. In its absence, it is important that the constraints imposed on us are of a kind that still relates on equal terms to our capacity for critical reflection and decision-making, that they are rooted in *our* decision to be ruled. The unconditional acceptance of political constraints on the basis of their general virtues does not preserve this connection. The failure of quality-based accounts to ground political obligation indicates this problem. It also indicates that such accounts should work as a basis for the regular and regularly re-evaluated assessment of political institutions, which is necessary for ensuring the legitimacy of their functions in light of the instability created by the absence of political obligation. Principles such as justice can be used for assessing the merits of institutions and tracing their legitimate power, in light of their defects and the harm they cause to particular persons. So, in the absence of consent and other features of morally important specific interaction, we need to work very hard to assure that constraints are compatible with self-governance and with proper social relations of equal active participation, that they respect equal-liberty. Proclaiming political obligation is not the right way to go about justification.

The results of the debate on political obligation so far show that it is very difficult for institutions to become legitimate. This cries out for a more demanding approach. The problem of justification goes beyond applying limitations to institutions. It is rather about *how difficult it is for any state to be legitimized* and about *highlighting these difficulties*. This perspective is distinctive of the anarchist position.

Notes

1 The discussion in this and the two following chapters concerns only the most effective deontological accounts of political obligation. In general, I do not discuss antiquated, commonsense, pragmatic, or other more easily dismissed arguments (for these, see McLaughlin, *Anarchism and Authority*, Chapter 4). Also, I do not criticize utilitarianism, although it is a popular theory of good reasons and has serious problems when taken as an account of political obligation. For these problems, mainly the difficulty for utilitarianism to satisfy the particularity and bindingness conditions of political obligation and to be compatible with the demands of morality and justice, see Simmons, *Moral Principles and Political Obligations*, 45–54; Horton, *Political Obligation*, 54–70; Wolff, *Political Philosophy*, 53–60; McLaughlin, *Anarchism and Authority*, 91–92. This limitation does not affect the main argument of the study, since the criticism of natural duty in this chapter renders conclusions about the importance of particularity and justice for theories of political obligation similar to those derived from a criticism of utilitarianism. They are conclusions that centrally affect theories of good reasons, to which utilitarianism belongs, and it is on this matter that I focus this discussion as part of an examination of a different perspective on the problem of the justification of political institutions. Therefore, the present discussion is not affected by the fact that the nature of its argumentation places utilitarianism in the category of instrumental (or teleological), rather than deontological, arguments.

2 For these principles, see Rawls, *A Theory of Justice*, Chapter 6.

3 Although Rawls's normative claim in *A Theory of Justice* could be a basis for attributing such an attempt to him. He writes: "[T]here are several ways in which one may be bound to political institutions. For the most part the natural duty of justice is the more fundamental, since it binds citizens generally and requires no voluntary acts in order to apply" (Rawls, *A Theory of Justice*, 116). And he does include an account of political obligation in his work (in Chapter 6), the one I discuss here. Yet, he makes clear statements that he does not provide a general theory of political obligation in it (e.g., Rawls, "Justice as Fairness," 71, n.22), which is not his main concern anyhow.

4 Rawls, *A Theory of Justice*, 11. For Hobbes's, Locke's, Rousseau's, and Kant's contractualism, see Chapters 1 and 2 here.

5 Rawls, *A Theory of Justice*, Section 3; Rawls, *Justice as Fairness*, 16–17.

6 For these resemblances, see, e.g., Immanuel Kant, "On the Common Saying: 'This May Be True in Theory, but It Does Not Apply in Practice'," in *Kant: Political Writings*, ed. Hans Siegbert Reiss, trans. Hugh Barr Nisbet (Cambridge: Cambridge University Press, 1970, 1991), 79–81; Rawls, *A Theory of Justice*, Section 40 and 251–257; Rawls, *Political Liberalism*, lecture III, Section 2; Rawls, "Kantian Constructivism in Moral Theory"; Rawls, "Justice as Fairness: Political not Metaphysical," esp. 395; Rawls, *Justice as Fairness*, 14–18.

7 For this understanding of contractualism, see Chapter 2 and the discussion below.

8   See, for example, Rawls, *A Theory of Justice*, Section 4, 118–150, 251–257,
      187, and 264; Rawls, *Political Liberalism*, 22–28 and 304–310; Rawls, *Justice
      as Fairness*, 14–18 and part III.
9   See, for example, Rawls, *A Theory of Justice*, Section 11, Section 13,
      Chapter 4; Rawls, *Political Liberalism*, 4–11, 229, 237, 282, lecture VIII:
      Sections 1–2 and 5–9; Rawls, *Justice as Fairness*, part II.
10   Rawls, *Justice as Fairness*, 14–18.
11   Rawls, *Justice as Fairness*, 17.
12   Rawls, *A Theory of Justice*, 579–580.
13   Rawls, *Political Liberalism*, 26. In relation to this, see also on Rawls's idea
      of "reflective equilibrium" (Rawls, *A Theory of Justice*, 19–21, 46–53, and
      578–586; Rawls, *Political Liberalism*, 8, 28, 45, 72, 95–97, 381, 384–385,
      388 and 399; Rawls, *Justice as Fairness*, 26–31, 66–72, 134, and 136), and
      further developments of it (Norman Daniels, "Wide Reflective Equilibrium
      and Theory Acceptance in Ethics," *Journal of Philosophy* 76 (1976): 256–282,
      and George Klosko and David Klein, "Political Obligations: The Empirical
      Dimension" (presented at the Annual Meeting of the American Political
      Science Association, University of Virginia, San Francisco, 2001), Section I).
14   Rawls, *Justice as Fairness*, 17–18. Rawls revises his conception of the original
      position as follows:

> the original position is to be understood as a device of representation.
> As such it *models our considered convictions as reasonable persons* by
> describing the parties (each of whom are responsible for the fundamental
> interests of a free and equal citizen) as *fairly situated* and as *reaching
> agreement subject to appropriate restrictions on reasons* for favoring
> principles of political justice. (ibid., 18, emphases mine)

15   Among other natural duties and the obligations of fairness that Rawls
      acknowledges. See Rawls, *A Theory of Justice*, 114–117 and 333–337.
16   Rawls also refers to the obligations of a limited and well-placed group of
      citizens, those, for example, "who are best able to gain political office and
      to take advantage of the opportunities offered by the constitutional system"
      (Rawls, *A Theory of Justice*, 344). For Rawls, the basis of such obligations is
      voluntarist (and is accounted in terms of the "principle of fairness": Rawls,
      A Theory of Justice, 114, 116, and 344). For an analysis of this principle of
      political obligation, see the following chapter of this study. Yet, for reasons
      such as those examined in that chapter, Rawls does not consider that the
      principle of fairness can be used to explain a general obligation to obey the
      law.
17   Rawls, *A Theory of Justice*, 114–115.
18   Rawls, *A Theory of Justice*, 505–506, n. 30.
19   Rawls, *A Theory of Justice*, 115 (emphasis added). See also 115–117,
      333–337.
20   As Rawls himself stipulates, "just, or as just as it is reasonable to expect"
      (Rawls, *A Theory of Justice*, 115), since no existing institution is perfectly just
      in a stable way. The arguments provided in this chapter apply also to what
      Rawls calls "nearly just" institutions, since he considers his theory of natural

duty to justify both "just" and "nearly just" institutions (Rawls, *A Theory of Justice*, 351, 363). Here I focus only on the just ones, as we should see the effects of the present criticism on the ideal case first in order then to decide those effects on institutions that fall short of the ideal. Presumably, the effects on nearly just institutions will be of the same character as those on just ones, although more severe, and problems with the definition of the former do not play a central role in the present discussion.

21 For some first considerations on the role of quality as an aspect of the evaluation of institutions within the debate on political obligation, see Simmons, "Justification and Legitimacy"; my Chapter 1 and Chapter 2.

22 Raz, *The Authority of Law*, 246–249.

23 Raz, *The Authority of Law*, 246–249.

24 See Raz, *The Authority of Law*, 249.

25 Raz, *The Authority of Law*, 237–241.

26 Raz, *The Authority of Law*, 241. To remind the reader, the generality condition is one essential link between a moral ground and the political character of political obligation. The two are constitutive elements of a satisfactory account of our political bonds. The combination of all the four conditions of political obligation is expressive of the political character of such an obligation. For this, see the sections "The two main aspects of the problem of political obligation" and "The conditions of political obligation" in Chapter 1 of this study.

27 Simmons, *Moral Principles and Political Obligations*, 154.

28 Simmons, *Moral Principles and Political Obligations*, 154.

29 For this analysis, see Waldron, *Liberal Rights*, 27–30.

30 Waldron, *Liberal Rights*, 28–29.

31 Waldron, *Liberal Rights*, 29–30. This latter sense can be derived from Simmons's explanation in Simmons, "Justification and Legitimacy," 754–755. It can also be understood in terms of the elements involved in Raz's discussion of good and just institutions, namely in terms of techniques that constitute a system's substantive functioning and in terms of its containing just laws expressive of its character (Raz, *The Authority of Law*; see the discussion of these elements above).

32 For similar observations, see Pateman, *The Problem of Political Obligation*, 113–129; McLaughlin, *Anarchism and Authority*, 95–96.

33 The quotations together with the components of this argument as presented here are taken, or derived, from Simmons, *Moral Principles and Political Obligations*, 150–156.

34 Simmons, *Moral Principles and Political Obligations*, 150–152.

35 Kant, "On the Common Saying," 79.

36 For these observations, see Simmons, *Moral Principles and Political Obligations*, 153–156; Horton, *Political Obligation*, 104–105.

37 For this, see the discussion of the role of the original position with regard to particularity in the section "Rawls and particularity" below.

38 See Chapters 2 and 4.

39 Simmons, *Moral Principles and Political Obligations*, 15.

40 Simmons, *Moral Principles and Political Obligations*, 155–156.

41 See, e.g., Simmons, "Justification and Legitimacy" (where he formulates this
    position more fully).
42 Jeremy Waldron, "Special Ties and Natural Duties," *Philosophy and Public
    Affairs* 22 (1993): 27.
43 Waldron, "Special Ties and Natural Duties," 13.
44 See Hobbes, *Leviathan*, book I; Hume, *A Treatise of Human Nature*, book III,
    part II, ed. Sir Lewis Amherst Selby-Bigge (Oxford: Oxford University Press,
    1978).
45 See, e.g., Kant, "On the Common Saying," 79–81.
46 For the following analysis of this argument, see Waldron, "Special Ties and
    Natural Duties," 14–15.
47 Waldron, "Special Ties and Natural Duties," 15.
48 See Waldron, "Special Ties and Natural Duties," 15–19.
49 For this and my relevant analysis below, see Waldron, "Special Ties and
    Natural Duties," 20–27.
50 Waldron, "Special Ties and Natural Duties," 26–27.
51 Waldron, "Special Ties and Natural Duties," 26.
52 For this, see also Waldron, *Liberal Rights*, Chapter 2.
53 For this, see my Chapter 1, section "The correlativity thesis."
54 Waldron, "Special Ties and Natural Duties," 26, n. 46.
55 As Rawls himself claims in *A Theory of Justice*, 115.
56 See Rawls, *A Theory of Justice*, 146–147. For "formal conditions on
    principles," see Section 23. For the "veil of ignorance," see Section 24. See
    also Rawls, *Political Liberalism*, 22–28; Rawls, *Justice as Fairness*, 14–18 and
    80–134.
57 To be reasonable is to take the interests of others into consideration, to be
    willing to justify or modify your own reasons according to a basis that they
    can share with you as long as they are similarly motivated. This is reflected
    in Rawls's and Scanlon's formulation of the motivation of the contractors,
    by which they attribute to them "a sense of justice" and a desire to justify
    their claims to others (e.g., Rawls, *A Theory of Justice*, 46, 312, 505; Scanlon,
    "Contractualism and Utilitarianism"; Scanlon, *What We Owe to Each Other*).
58 For this point, see Klosko and Klein, "Political Obligations," Section I. To
    the sets of considered judgments and moral principles that stand in mutual
    support according to Rawls's method of "reflective equilibrium" (Rawls, *A
    Theory of Justice*, 19–21, 46–53, and 578–586; Rawls, *Justice as Fairness*,
    29–32), Klosko adds "the beliefs of ordinary citizens" and calls his own a
    "broad reflective equilibrium" (Klosko and Klein, "Political Obligations," 5).
    This is a further development from Daniels's "wide reflective equilibrium"
    (Daniels, "Wide Reflective Equilibrium"), which itself extends the logic of
    Rawls's account by involving also appeal to "a set of relevant background
    theories," which underlie and serve the evaluation of competing moral
    principles (Daniels, "Wide Reflective Equilibrium," 258). Maybe Klosko's
    appeal to ordinary beliefs should be seen as an "argument from common
    opinion," one resting on the authority of common belief, rather than as one
    "from coherence," of the kind that Rawls's method is (for this point, see Leslie
    Green, "Who Believes in Political Obligation?," in *For and Against the State:
    New Philosophical Readings*, ed. John T. Sanders and Jan Narveson [Lanham,

MD: Rowman and Littlefield, 1996], 2–5). But in the present case, the focus is on the relevance of public opinion for creating particularity, whatever its proper role in a theory might be. To what extent Klosko's and any empirical investigation can deliver true public opinion on complex, normative matters such as political obligation is another issue, which I discuss in Chapter 4 (on this, see Green, "Who Believes in Political Obligation?").

59 For this point, see also Simmons, "Justification and Legitimacy," 754–755.
60 Rawls, "Justice as Fairness," 57.

4

The failure of the principle of fairness as an account of political obligation[1]

In this chapter, I advance an anarchist criticism of fair-play defenses of political obligation. The fair-play, or fairness, approach constitutes perhaps the most prominent of the reciprocity-based theories of political obligation. From the perspective of this study, it is important that the fairness principle exemplifies a condition that makes it a characteristic reciprocal theory, namely "the idea of proportionality."[2] This interprets political obligation as a contribution, or burden, proportional to an individual's received benefits. My aim is to examine the limitations of the principle as an account of our relationship to the state but, at the same time, to explain the value of its role in the debate. The principle of fairness constitutes a further deontological, good reason for political authority, which is, however, different from that involved in the natural duty of justice examined in Chapter 3. It returns to the active aspect of obligation, from which duty-based theories depart. Significantly, it brings us back to the value of voluntariness, which was defended in Chapter 2. The main argument of this chapter is that the element of voluntary acceptance involved in the principle of fairness is of crucial importance to our understanding of political relations, and it is the interpretation of the principle that focuses on this feature that I want to emphasize. I also conclude that the fairness account examined below has a limited application: it can determine the character of the procedures that might apply within political institutions—that is, it can function as the condition that the rules of these procedures are fair—but it cannot justify political obligation.

I begin with a presentation of the main features of the principle of fairness as formulated by H. L. A. Hart and John Rawls. I then go on to discuss certain elements that appear to be heavily involved in the conception of the principle, but that do not seem to me to be integral to its rationale. This will allow for the clarification of their role with regard to the main anarchist arguments against the principle. Finally, I examine those arguments and their implications.

The principle of fairness

Hart explains the principle of fairness in this way:

> When a number of persons conduct any joint enterprise according to rules and thus restrict their liberty, those who have submitted to these restrictions when required have a right to a similar submission from those who have benefited by their submission. The rules may provide that officials should have authority to enforce obedience … but the moral obligation to obey the rules in such circumstances is due to the cooperating members of the society, and they have the correlative moral right to obedience.[3]

As for Rawls, his central formulation runs as follows:

> Suppose there is a mutually beneficial and just scheme of social cooperation, and that the advantages it yields can only be obtained if everyone, or nearly everyone, cooperates. Suppose further that cooperation requires a certain sacrifice from each person, or at least involves a certain restriction of his liberty. Suppose finally that the benefits produced by cooperation are, up to a certain point, free: that is, the scheme of cooperation is unstable in the sense that if any one person knows that all (or nearly all) of the others will continue to do their part, he will still be able to share a gain from the scheme even if he does not do his part. Under these conditions a person who has accepted the benefits of the scheme is bound by a duty of fair play to do his part and not to take advantage of the free benefits by not cooperating.[4]

Comments on these two statements are commonplace within the literature on fairness (of which the bibliography used in this chapter is a representative part). Below I note the aspects of the principle that are most widely regarded as its main features under the two formulations. This will help clarify the formulations themselves. My examination of the arguments for and against the principle of fairness, in the next section, will focus on two central interpretations of it derived from these statements.

The rationale of the principle of fairness is shown by the moral requirement of fair share imposed upon individuals who benefit from the burdensome efforts of their fellow citizens. More precisely, the principle requires reciprocity in the distribution of benefits and burdens; it imposes "a duty not to free-ride on the efforts of others."[5] Thus, it is connected with the problem of social coordination.[6] More evidently, it is connected with the role played in society by public goods and with the problem of restricting people who demonstrate the exploitative motivations of a free-rider with regard to the contribution of others for the provision of such goods.[7]

In its main function, the principle, as formulated by Hart and Rawls, applies within certain contexts characterized by special circumstances. It works within *schemes of social cooperation*, it involves a *restriction of the liberty* of the parties involved in the enterprise, and it concerns the production and preservation of benefits that are *free* in nature.

Rawls's notion of "schemes of social cooperation" (or "joint enterprises," in Hart's formulation) provides a conception of our political communities as "cooperative enterprises on a very large scale,"[8] the members of which share a horizontal relationship of fellow-citizenship and work together for the achievement of common ends. Thus, they owe their political duties, not to the government, but to one another. The "restriction of liberty" condition involves members accepting certain burdens (such as political obligations) corresponding to the benefits distributed by the cooperative scheme in a fair manner.[9] These benefits are "free" in the sense that they have the features of public goods, so they can be enjoyed by any single individual without his or her cooperation, as long as a sufficient number of others contribute.[10] There are three features of public goods, or "open" benefits,[11] that permit this situation: first, indivisibility, namely their equal availability to and consumption by all members (their utility for one person does not affect their utility for others); second, non-excludability, namely the impracticality of their being provided to some members while excluding others from their consumption; and third, the need for the cooperation of large numbers (a public) for their provision.[12]

There is one more feature of the principle of fairness, which is explicit in Rawls's formulation, though not apparent in Hart's, and is closely related to those analyzed above. This is *the voluntary acceptance* of the benefits of cooperation.[13] Although not all theorists of the principle of fairness agree on its importance, this feature exemplifies, in my view, a significant aspect of its rationale: that an important precondition for the operation of the principle is the involvement of some voluntary act on the part of individuals when they receive public benefits. Such an act would qualify the individuals as participants in the cooperative scheme where the requirements of fairness, as stated by the principle, apply.

This feature is contrasted with *mere receipt*, which, however, some theorists of the principle of fairness advocate as part of its proper interpretation. Note that a choice between the two interpretations affects significantly the evaluation of the principle as an account of political obligation. It also creates the most serious difficulties involved in such an evaluation. Yet the notion of acceptance, conceived in its more direct and unqualified sense, clarifies something important with regard to the rationale of the principle. It demonstrates how the principle departs from consent theories of political obligation in an advantageous way while preserving its required moral character: it does not require an act of deliberate undertaking that one performs with the knowledge that one becomes obligated by it. It rather makes the weaker demand that, in the face of benefits provided by a cooperative scheme, one's (voluntary) acceptance of them is enough to bind one to the scheme.[14] It thus gives a clear sign of involvement, which tacit consent fails to provide, without necessarily meaning that it is consent. This seems to increase the possibility of the principle's meeting the generality condition of political obligation, namely the condition that it should apply to most members of a society. At the same time, acceptance preserves the character of a specific and self-assumed act, which is the most obvious application of an actual transactional basis of the relationship of political obligation.[15] In this manner, acceptance also makes the principle of fairness compatible with the particularity condition of political obligation, namely the requirement that the ground of such an obligation should provide a reason for individuals being obligated particularly to their *own* government. More importantly, through acceptance, the core voluntarist aspect that makes consent a significant expression of self-governance is preserved in the principle.

"Triviality," "success," and "justice"

Before embarking on the criticism of the principle of fairness, I want to examine some other elements involved in the discussion of the principle. I discuss them separately because, although they create important conditions for the acceptability of the principle, there is controversy among theorists about their centrality. The three elements that I consider in what follows fall under the following labels: "triviality," "success," and "justice." I discuss each in turn.

(i) *Triviality*. The first element is related to the criticism of the principle of fairness that Robert Nozick provides in his book *Anarchy, State and Utopia*.[16] This criticism consists mainly of a series of examples used to support his claim that the principle is not morally valid and that it fails to create political obligations within social schemes characterized by the main features described above. The main elements of his argument will be considered in the discussion of the most important criticisms of fairness in the section "The anarchist criticism of the principle of fairness." At this point, I focus only on one element, that concerning triviality. It has been pointed out[17] that all of Nozick's examples involve benefits that are of trivial value, benefits such as the broadcasting of entertaining programs,[18] and that this aspect affects substantially the force of his attack on the principle of fairness. These are valid claims. One important condition that should be incorporated within accounts of fairness is that the benefits with regard to which obligations of fairness are created should be *worthy* of the individuals' costs in their efforts to provide them.[19] As we will see later, this condition occupies a central position within Klosko's defense of the principle, and other discussions give it considerable attention as well.[20] The point indicated here is that, while the core of the principle of fairness lies in its demand of a fair share in the benefits and burdens of a cooperative scheme, its application can be properly evaluated only with respect to goods that are important enough to individuals to support this application. That said, the triviality condition remains external to the moral core of the principle of fairness. As "[t]he kind of unfairness condemned by the principle is *taking advantage of* or *exploiting*" "the good-faith sacrifices of others," the basis of obligation is an individual's free enjoyment of a good and not the value or importance of goods.[21] The relevance of the latter lies only in its being more likely to invite the kind of attitude central to the principle and generally to effect its application.

(ii) *Success*. The second element to be considered is success (or, otherwise, the perfection of cooperation within a joint enterprise). Rawls's formulation of the principle of fairness makes precise, as a condition on its application, "that the advantages [a cooperative scheme] yields can only be obtained if everyone, or nearly everyone, cooperates."[22] Following Simmons,[23] I take it that while a need for substantial cooperation in a joint enterprise may render free-riding more objectionable, e.g., for reasons of efficiency, such a condition does *not* elicit the central requirement of the principle of fairness; it is not part of its reciprocal logic. Participants do have an obligation to cooperate, even under circumstances where many others could fail to do so (that is, when their lack of cooperation does not make the provision of the desirable goods impossible). Although the obligations of the beneficiaries are defined relevant to the benefits and burdens allocated to other participants in the scheme, it is not the necessity of compliance that characterizes these obligations. This point is made clearer by an additional observation. In his criticism of the principle of fairness, Smith claims that only the infliction of harm upon the community and/or the deprivation of another individual of benefits proportional (or, according to Smith, "roughly equal") to those we acquire due to his cooperative efforts generates obligations of fairness.[24] However, as Simmons rightly argues, even when the effects of his behavior are not negative on someone else's benefits, it is the fact that the free-rider *takes advantage of others*, who do their part, that makes his attitude objectionable in terms of fairness.[25] As explained in the discussion of the central features of fairness above, the principle defines obligations as part of nonhierarchical relations among cooperative members. This aspect focuses on the quality of the interaction between individuals who are seen as fellow-citizens standing in horizontal relations to each other, thus on whether the behavior of some reciprocates the sacrifices of those others who stand in such relations to them or whether it exploits them. I believe that this point is reflected to an extent in Smith's qualification that the benefits of the affected parties should be proportional. But even if my assumption is mistaken, the main point I make here still stands. While not completely irrelevant, references to the utility of cooperation alone do not capture elements internal to the rationale of the principle of fairness. Thus, success is not an essential condition on this principle.

(iii) *Justice*. The last, and most important, element I want to discuss here is justice. Rawls indicates that the schemes of cooperation where the principle of fairness applies should be *just*.[26] The justice of an institution, however, does not directly determine considerations of fair play. The obligations of fairness concern the reciprocal relationships between the participants of a cooperative scheme. Their bindingness is not derived from the moral character of the scheme, and injustice in it—or the violation of utility or, more generally, a scheme's promotion of immoral ends—need not affect the existence of such obligations. It is not the general character of the scheme, but the fact that fairness-based procedures take place that matters for considerations of fairness. On this basis, the rules of fair play can determine reciprocity and make citizens interact fairly. Also, although the condition of justice may be taken to concern the distribution of benefits and burdens within a cooperative enterprise and, as such, to create a background within which the fairness of the reciprocal relationships of the participants can be secured more easily, the demands of fair play do not necessarily depend on such a background in order to arise. This is because the element that is more directly relevant to considerations of fairness is *proportionality*, not justice.[27] This notion motivates a central point with regard to fairness. It makes more explicit the fact that the principle can apply as long as each of the participants benefits in proportion to the costs (or burdens) each suffers, and that it is this situation that is directly relevant to the principle.[28] But this is a situation that does not arise exclusively in a just system.[29] Of the two notions in play, it is not justice but proportionality (in the distribution of the relevant benefits and burdens) that is integral to the rationale of the principle of fairness.

There is, however, another consideration with regard to justice. The justice of an institution has been accepted in the previous chapter (as a result of the anarchist criticism of the natural duty of justice) as a central feature of an ideal of legitimacy to which visions of society must conform (although not sufficient to ground political obligation). Justice is a significant indication of the bearing and role of considerations about quality, or institutional morality, within the debate on political obligation. The relevance of this point to the present considerations on fairness is this: although justice is not a feature integral to the demands of fair play, the recognition of its significance in an ideal of political legitimacy functions as an *external* condition on the principle of fairness. By this I mean that, although the success of the principle as the foundation of a theory of political obligation should be decided by reference to its internal rationale, its final acceptability as a general basis of legitimate authority is not independent of the satisfaction of central demands of justice. Its establishment as such a basis presupposes recognition of these demands. Thus, a defense of political institutions on the basis of the principle of fairness should also establish the compatibility of the workings of these institutions with the main demands of justice (as distinctive requirements among other moral obligations).

The anarchist criticism of the principle of fairness

Let me turn now to the most important criticism of the principle of fairness as an account of political obligation. This criticism draws upon the problems that the principle faces in meeting the generality condition of political obligation. It is active in two areas. The first concerns the inadequacy of the principle interpreted either in terms of "receipt" or in terms of "acceptance." The account of fairness in this chapter focuses on these two interpretations. The second concerns the conception of community, integral to the rationale of the principle, as "a scheme of social cooperation."

"Receipt" versus "Acceptance"

Objections to understanding fairness obligations in terms of "Receipt"

The formulation of the principle of fairness advanced by Hart legitimates the interpretation under which the central condition for its adequate application as an account of political obligation is claimed to be the mere *receipt* of benefits. So we have this reading of the principle: when individuals *receive benefits* from a political scheme that is sustained by the obedience of other individuals, they are required, in fairness to those who obeyed, to reciprocate by accepting similar obligations as their proportional share of burdens.

A first objection to this claim is provided by the doubt as to whether existing governments actually provide the required benefits. This involves both difficulties related to conflicting beliefs about what these benefits are and the fact that some people, or groups of them, either do not or try not to receive them.[30] The interpretation thus runs into difficulties when faced with the demand for generality. Either the goods provided are not generally regarded as benefits, or the fact that there exists variability in their receipt entails that there is "variability in political obligations."[31] This does not sit easily with the need for the general applicability of the principle of fairness as an account of political obligation. Disparity in the individuals' previous sacrifice and compliance, as well as in the effects of previous disobedience, affects the scope of political obligation in terms of fair play.[32] However, I will pursue this thought no further. We may defuse this objection by accepting that the state succeeds in providing goods such as protection from pollution or the provision of national security, along with other goods deriving from the rule of law,[33] and that such things can be conceived as important benefits and are likely to be received by most citizens.[34] Nonetheless, the most serious criticism of receipt as the proper interpretation of the principle of fairness lies elsewhere.

The most serious criticism relates to a challenging of the *moral validity* of receipt. Nozick's criticism of fairness suggests this objection, demonstrating that it is morally unacceptable to infer obligations from the receipt of goods that are inescapable and thus are forced upon individuals without their consent.[35] The most well known of Nozick's examples reflects this criticism by describing the receipt of possibly desirable yet unsolicited goods. It is the "public address system" example, where a person is required out of fairness to do his part after having benefited from a public broadcast instituted by his neighbors for reasons of public entertainment. According to Nozick, that requirement is morally invalid, since the benefit in question is received independently of the individual's preference and without its having been consensually accepted. This claim is connected essentially with Nozick's view that only requirements created by acts involving consent are morally acceptable.[36] But it can be derived also from Hume's argument against tacit consent discussed in the section "Tacit consent" in Chapter 2, that we cannot assume obligations in terms of consent when the impositions of political institutions are unavoidable.

The objection has, however, taken a more general form. The principle of fairness makes use of the point that the argument from tacit consent failed to make, facing problems with illegitimate inference.[37] This principle indicates our position with regard to important benefits as determinative of our obligation, without basing obligation on the assumption that such a position is a sign of consent. Nevertheless, the present objection in its more general form challenges the applicability of the position required in order to bind us by reference to benefits. The more general form of the objection is represented by the so-called "limiting argument."[38] According to this argument, the principle of fairness cannot apply within schemes that provide benefits with the status of public goods (as described earlier in this chapter), since this status—especially their non-excludability—makes their *voluntary acceptance* impossible. The impossibility of voluntary acceptance of open benefits renders the objection more general, since it is independent of an advocacy of consent as the only proper moral ground. The principle need not be taken to invoke consent. Yet it is not that we have not consented that matters. Rather the inevitable presence of benefits makes any expression of willing acceptance indiscernible. This objection appears in the writings of Rawls. His formulation of the principle makes explicit reference to voluntary acceptance, and his later rejection of it as a ground of political obligation is mainly motivated by the difficulties created by this inapplicability (I discuss these difficulties in the section "Simmons on 'Acceptance' "). The valid applicability of the principle is questioned when the possibility of voluntary acts is threatened.

The main point of the above criticism is that a focus on the receipt of benefits ignores the self-assumed acts that give rise to individual responsibility, while at the same time it assumes such a responsibility. Individuals are considered bound in the absence of their effective participation. But responsibility and obligation may not be derived without the presence and effective expression of free agency and involvement.

The upshot, then, of the two objections above is that the mere receipt of benefits does not give rise to a conception of the principle of fairness upon which it is possible to base its acceptability as a ground of political obligation. First, receipt may not be sufficiently general in existing societies, but second, and more important, even if it is, it has morally unacceptable implications.

Klosko's defense of "Receipt"

The above conclusion, however, has been rebutted by a more sophisticated use of the notion of receipt, found in Klosko's defense of the principle of fairness. Klosko protests that the strength of Nozick's argument lies in the latter's reference to benefits of negligible value,[39] and so Klosko aims at providing moral considerations that give to the receipt of benefits a moral significance that overrides the requirement of voluntary acceptance. In discussing this feature of Nozick's example (namely, triviality), I indicated that the value of goods has some importance for considerations of fairness.[40] So I accept that Klosko's observation provides a plausible motivation for his defense of fairness. That defense depends essentially on three conditions he imposes upon the acceptability of the principle. He claims that the "goods supplied must be (i) worth the recipients' effort in providing them; (ii) presumptively beneficial; and (iii) have benefits and burdens that are fairly distributed."[41] The originality of Klosko's contribution is found in his notion of "presumptively beneficial public goods," which he takes to be those that are reasonably regarded as "*necessary for an acceptable life for all members of the community.*"[42] Examples of such that he gives are "physical security, protection from a hostile environment, and the satisfaction of basic bodily needs."[43] His contention is that in the *indispensability* of such goods we find an importantly relevant and morally overriding feature, sufficient to give rise to obligations through fairness in defiance of the individuals' right to decide for themselves whether to accept them. He completes his defense by providing examples that support his main claim that the members of schemes that provide these goods and also satisfy the other two conditions he imposes are subject to political obligations on the basis of fairness. Finally, he shows how individuals continue to have obligations through fairness in a scheme that meets the three conditions even when it provides "discretionary goods"—that is, goods that "are of less value" or "not essential to people's well-being."[44] Thus, he contends that, according to his view, the principle of fairness can effectively satisfy the generality condition of political obligation.

Klosko's theory provides an improved account of fairness in terms of receipt, which comes as a reply, not only to the limiting argument, but also to Simmons's insistence on voluntary acceptance as an indispensable feature of the principle's application. However, using Simmons's approach, I argue below that Klosko's view and its more effective employment in Arneson, "The Principle of Fairness," and Wolff, "Political Obligation, Fairness and Independence," underestimate the role of acceptance. It is this role that is neglected and that I want to elevate. Nevertheless, I further argue that views that focus on acceptance fail to avoid the violation of the generality condition of political obligation.

Simmons on "Acceptance"

In his discussion of these issues, Simmons concentrates on the notion of "voluntary acceptance" found in Rawls's formulation of the principle of fairness and provides an explanation of "active participation" that makes this notion both meaningful and significant for the principle's applicability.[45] He does this because he believes that the notion is compatible with Hart's formulation as well,[46] and that the principle survives the limiting argument both in its Nozickian and in its Rawlsian conception. That is, it can be defended both against Nozick's view that the principle is unacceptable to the extent that it departs from consent, and against Rawls's view that, in societies where the benefits provided are open in nature, the voluntary acceptance of them is impossible and thus the principle is inapplicable there as an account of political obligation.[47]

The reading of the principle of fairness that concerns us here is the following: individuals who have *willingly accepted the benefits* provided by the state, as sustained by the obedience of other individuals, are bound in fairness to those others to reciprocate by recognizing obligations proportional to their willing enjoyment of the benefits. Because there is a problem that we cannot have obligation in the absence of individual consent, the focus turns on fairness as a principle that shows the individuals' input otherwise. Through acceptance, the principle makes a suitable addition to the theory of tacit consent. By applying on the basis of explicit and operative manifestations of individual involvement, it is offered as a good way of evading illegitimate inferences of such an involvement, like those made in the name of tacit consent. At the same time, it does not involve the strict requirements that make explicit consent unattainable.

Simmons understands acceptance as "active participation."[48] In this he is motivated by an observation about Nozick's criticism of the principle of fairness that differs importantly from that of Klosko (that has already been presented in the section "'Klosko's defense of 'Receipt'"). He observes that, while the value of the benefits must not be arbitrary, as it is in Nozick's examples, the real problem with these examples, as far as fairness is concerned, is that the non-contributors are "outsiders" with respect to the cooperative scheme and so cannot be properly regarded as free-riders.[49] Thus, he concentrates on providing a notion of participation that distinguishes "insiders" from "outsiders" and that is meant to help establish obligations through fairness for the former (in terms of acceptance even in schemes where the benefits provided are open), but that does not obligate the latter at all.[50]

Simmons explains acceptance of a benefit as "either (1) trying to get (and succeeding in getting) the benefit, or (2) taking the benefit willingly and knowingly."[51] The crux of his argument lies in that, in schemes where the benefits are open, acceptance is still possible in *one* of these senses and so can determine who the schemes' proper participants are. He argues that in such schemes it is not clear how individuals would go about trying to get the benefits, since open benefits are received by everyone irrespective of their attitudes.[52] Thus he sees the limiting argument to be effective with regard to the first sense of acceptance, but not with regard to the second. He claims that normally it is in the second sense of acceptance that we can see open benefits being accepted. This sense he analyzes by reference to facts about our attitudes and beliefs such as "[not] regard[ing] the benefits as having been forced upon us against our will, or think[ing] that [they] are not worth the price we must pay for them," and as "an understanding of the status of those benefits relative to the party providing them."[53]

However, generality is still a problem. Although such a notion of acceptance is meaningful and has the status of active participation, it is not the usual attitude of individuals in existing states. It is rare that we consider our political obligations as the correlative burdens of benefits received willingly and knowingly. For example, many citizens hardly notice benefits that they receive and many others do not believe that the benefits received are worth the price imposed on them, as is the case with high taxes, legal restrictions on harmless private pleasures, or compulsory participation in wars of foreign policy.[54] Even though Simmons takes the second sense of acceptance to be applicable within existing societies and thus to allow that at least some individuals could demonstrate it there, he still believes that acceptance cannot meet the generality condition of political obligation within existing societies. This point receives support from the considerations concerning the idea of political communities as schemes of social cooperation, to which I will turn in the section "Fairness, political obligation, and the idea of societies as 'Schemes of Social Cooperation.' "

This argument is also the first step for my disagreement with Klosko as regards the importance he places on the fact that ordinary people think that they have political obligations and tend to conceive these obligations in terms of fairness.[55] Although I concede that the moral beliefs of ordinary people matter, I do not think that the results of Klosko's empirical investigation make any important progress toward establishing political obligation on the basis of fairness. First of all, that the facts are such is itself doubtful: the form of the questions asked in Klosko's investigation and the answers to them do not identify clearly the aspects characteristic of what could be seen as a genuine belief in political obligation, and there are many instances where people's beliefs support the anarchist conclusions.[56] But even if people have the beliefs about political obligation that Klosko's investigation presents them to have, this does not show that they enter the relationship of obligation that they approve of in the actual circumstances applying to them, nor that they demonstrate the attitude of acceptance presented here. Indeed, the previous examples that I gave are characteristic cases where they do not. These overlap with the examples of ordinary belief given by Simmons.[57] Also, even if people do not appear to have any intuitive preference for voluntarist interpretations of the principle, this does not show that such interpretations are not the ones proper and faithful to its rationale. (And I think that Klosko neglects the sense of acceptance explained here in his arguments against the notion.[58]) It is this latter point that I attempt to demonstrate in this chapter. These considerations about the role of Klosko's investigation are closely connected to the idea of schemes of social cooperation involved in the principle, and I develop them further in the context of the discussion of this idea.

The significance of "Acceptance"

Despite the failure of the principle of fairness to meet the generality condition of political obligation when understood in terms of acceptance, I want to argue here that there is a certain significance in Simmons's conception of acceptance. For this I refer to departures from it that form attempts to confirm the interpretation of the principle of fairness in terms of receipt as a basis of political obligation.

Simmons's argument indicates that voluntary acceptance is very important to an evaluation of fairness. This is made explicit by the fact that his conception of the principle involves reference to "subjective" or "psychological facts," that is, to individuals' attitudes to, and beliefs about, the benefits as signs of their conscious and voluntary acceptance of them.[59] This appeal to subjective elements is central to Simmons. It is significant, despite the following objections.

By pointing out that the *magnitude* (or indispensability) of benefits is a feature that obviates the relevance of psychological facts, Klosko, in his defense of fairness, preserves the notion of receipt at the expense of voluntary acceptance.[60] Other theorists find problems with Klosko's notion of presumptive benefits and utilize other elements of his account in order to achieve generality in terms of receipt. Jonathan Wolff, for example, points out that the crux of Klosko's account lies in his two other conditions, namely those of worth and fairness, which in combination with some reference to individuals' "subjective scale of valuation" may establish obligations through fairness in terms of sufficiently general receipt.[61] Richard Arneson provides a more qualified version of the principle along Klosko's lines, which invites obligations in terms of receipt where voluntary acceptance is impossible. He believes that Simmons's reference to subjective requirements licenses "bizarre beliefs" as sources of political obligations.[62]

However, my argument is that the departure of these theorists from subjective elements is problematic. Klosko's reference to indispensable benefits is based on moral principles other than fairness (e.g., on the idea of need and the duty to help persons in such a situation, or on the duty to contribute to projects essential for community life).[63] More importantly, decisions about what is to count, not only as discretionary but also as indispensable benefits, need to be made on the basis of the subjective attitudes of individuals that make active participation possible. If, for example, it is claimed that the environmental protection services of the state oblige individuals to reciprocate, in order to discern the indispensable receipt that invites reciprocation, we need to see: (a) whether those individuals deem such services worthy of the political burdens, (b) whether or not they consider and follow other ways of providing environmental protection as the optimal ones, and (c) whether they continue to enjoy the provision of such governmental services. As Simmons states, "the indispensability of benefits, then, seems … an indication of when the requirement of active participation is most likely to be satisfied."[64]

This argument applies to Arneson and, in my view, to Wolff as well. Arneson appeals, among other things, to the condition that "the benefit [be] uncontroversially a benefit for all."[65] But, as Simmons argues, this requirement avoids being too stringent only if it makes reference to subjective elements.[66] Simmons's qualification of "non-negligence in one's beliefs" also defeats Arneson's objection from reliance on bizarre beliefs. Such a lack of negligence is similar to the conditions of knowledge and rationality that make consent valid (see my Chapter 2, subsection "Actual consent"), although attitudes evaluated on the basis of the principle of fairness need not involve the knowledge that one acquires obligations by one's performance (as involved in the deliberate undertakings that form consent).[67] In the same way, Wolff's condition of a subjective scale of valuation[68] acquires meaning, so as to be used as a test of the generality of the principle's application, only when individuals' beliefs are taken into account as significant criteria for knowing what is, in fact, valuable to each of them. Wolff explains that receipt must be "worthwhile" for each individual, but that this is not the same as trying to see "whether the individual *thinks* it worthwhile," because individuals' own calculations might not be very good.[69] Yet for political obligation it is the attitudes related to these calculations that matter. Wolff himself admits that it is difficult to know how the condition of worth is met for a given individual.[70] It is here that, I argue, the importance of acceptance becomes obvious, as a clear expression of subjective facts. In the case of hypothetical-contract arguments we need to know if ideal rational choice corresponds to actual choice. Similarly in the present case, we need to take into account what individuals actually take as worthwhile in order to build a criterion of worthy receipt that represents their situation fairly and can work for political obligation.

Hence, under the above readings, the principle of fairness says that individuals who receive indispensable benefits (in Klosko's words), or goods that are uncontroversially a benefit to every participant (in Arneson's words), or goods that are fairly distributed and valuable to individuals according to some subjective scale of valuation (in Wolff's words), are obliged to reciprocate. In each of these cases, some explicit element of participation needs to be detected in order to give sense and applicability to valuable receipt. In the end, what does it matter if something has worth if people do not want it? Every time theorists try to specify the convention that the principle involves and that individuals should not violate, they need to articulate some attitude of acceptance that makes it meaningful.

These considerations indicate that acceptance understood by reference to subjective facts cannot be easily dispensed with. No reference to receipt can establish general obligations through fairness without appeal to psychological facts related to the provision, status, and worth of open benefits. Also, this kind of acceptance forms an attitude and activity that provides a realistic example of individuals' social behavior and satisfies a basic and common notion of what could be taken as a sign of active citizenship. It certainly is a clear paradigm of "morally [relevant and] significant features of the specific histories of interaction between individuals and their polities," which compose transactional bases of political obligation.[71] As defended in the previous chapters of this study, such bases seem to be the only ones capturing the particularized and actual nature of social interaction necessary for establishing political obligation. Likewise to be closer to securing the ideal of active participation, the core of the character of social relations to which anarchism aspires. Thus facts of acceptance constitute an appropriate and natural representation of subjective facts. In the end, the point of the argument from active participation is not to decide which one, acceptance or receipt, is superior. Rather, it is to preserve in either notion the features that would establish an actual, specific, and morally significant behavior, which, if sufficiently general in their application within political societies, would ground the relationship of political obligation. The actual and solicited receipt of benefits to most of the citizens of a society would be an appropriate ground of this kind, and this does not clearly differ from acceptance in Simmons's sense.[72] For the main argument here, the distinction between the two is not crucial. What is crucial is that the psychological facts that give applicability and moral significance to the principle (i.e., those constituting Simmons's sense of acceptance, or something similar to it) are rarely demonstrated in the behavior of individuals in existing states. Thus, the principle of fairness is insufficient as the ground of general political obligation.

Quite significantly, such a role of subjective facts brings to the fore the point about the quality, or merits, of institutions elaborated in this study. The present argument is that the most decisive appeals to the principle of fairness as a ground of political obligation need to include a reference to subjective features. This reinforces the following claim: the merits of political institutions—in terms either of positive qualities of their character (such as justice) or of the services that they provide to their subjects conceived as a whole (such as the general provision of benefits)—are an important aspect of their evaluation. By reference to this aspect we can assess and justify their existence. But to decide their relation to the members of their society and, more precisely, their authority as reflected in the generation of political obligation, we must examine the actual and specific functions of these institutions and how they affect each of their citizens through the relevant particular practices, activities, and interactions that would create the relationship of political obligation.

In relation to these points, there is an important aspect about the role of the principle of fairness that underlies appeals to receipt and that the anarchist cannot disregard. There is a specificity of political interaction that makes such an interaction complicated. Social problems involve *interdependence*, the fact that individuals within societies act in ways that affect others. When some individuals act without worrying about how their behavior affects others, their space of free action invades the sphere of other individuals. They act at their expense. This might be selfish and unfair. It is this that the principle of fairness can indicate and correct. Defenders of fairness who focus on political obligation misapply it. It cannot ground political obligation. Yet there is a place for it as a way of putting limits on the free interaction of individuals. On this understanding, fairness in terms of receipt might be a good principle for defining legitimate social interrelations. Being forced to recognize what we have received might designate the limits required for seeing how to live in a society where we are interdependent. The principle explains why there are moral limits to what we can do. It thus can characterize interdependence within political societies in a way that makes them morally justifiable irrespective of voluntary acceptance. The anarchist can concede that this explains why we might have moral obligations from receipt of benefits and why this in turn can make a social system good. But what he asks is why we should assume that the state, even a good state, can enforce such obligations on us. The preceding anarchist argument indicates that, without some expression of individual acceptance, there cannot be any satisfactory specific application of receipt, as required for political obligation. Subjective facts are necessary for us to recognize when valid receipt occurs. However, if we see the principle of fairness as determining the character of social interdependence by generally specifying in terms of receipt that the rules that regulate social procedures are fair, this is a valuable role for it to play, even for the anarchist. This is a limited application of the principle. It defines a background within which obligations can arise and operate properly, but it does not itself generate general political obligation. And it is this that the critical philosophical anarchist presses upon the defender of political institutions.

It is fundamental for the argument of this study that in the notion of acceptance we find a significant way of attending to the kinds of interaction that express self-governance and equality in a society. In Chapter 2 we saw that actual consent, if it existed, would constitute a direct and primary indication of individual self-determination and equal active involvement in social life. A similar indication is found, in the present chapter, in the kind of active participation involved in the fairness principle. The discussion of fairness reveals, through the notion of acceptance, forms of explicit, voluntary involvement on the part of individuals that are indispensable features of certain relations and possibilities of valuable social communication. The willing acceptance of benefits becomes a clear indication of when and how individuals are involved in relations of interdependence with others and of the corresponding obligations. This shows that, for the generation of political obligation as a central characterization of our relation to political institutions, such forms of interaction are necessary. Moreover, whenever they existed, they would primarily manifest the expression of individuality and equal active involvement that makes proper social relations possible. That is, they would create a desired combination of individual authority and social interaction. Yet political institutions, by their very nature, circumscribe such important expressions of self-government and equality. The required forms of participation do not establish an obligation to political institutions, because they are not enabled within societies governed by such institutions. We will see in this study, especially in the final chapters, that the radicalism of the anarchist perspective entails an extension of participation and democracy itself that goes beyond consent and the participatory forms involved in fairness, a "*beyond of democracy*" that involves the questioning of all forms of political power, domination, and hierarchy.[73] I will also show that equal-liberty is a matter of collective autonomy, of an open-endedness and comprehensiveness, which explains that, for instance, political equality cannot exist without economic equality. In turn, political equality gives meaning to civil liberty, which, along with political equality, is necessary for economic equality to be desirable.[74] And this creates endless possibilities for emancipation. Given this framework, the shortcomings of political institutions are even more visible and pressing. At present, however, the participatory character of the relations of fairness that political institutions lack already points in this direction of criticism.

Fairness, political obligation, and the idea of societies as "schemes of social cooperation"

The conclusions of the above discussion lead me to the second area where the principle of fairness faces problems with the generality condition of political obligation. This concerns the conception of political communities as *schemes of social cooperation*. This conception is a significant part and contribution of the principle. It facilitates a different understanding of political societies and relations in terms of their status and worth. The political schemes are understood as "cooperative enterprises on a very large scale" and our obligations are owed to the other participants in such schemes, who work together with us for a common purpose.[75] This idea of political relationships reflects a background that is characterized by a complex web of interactions. This framework gives a more comprehensive picture of the sense of reciprocity involved in the principle of fairness and applied through the kind of active participation discussed in the preceding section. It also departs from the usual picture of political relationships as vertical duties to governmental bodies that monopolize the right to determine the conditions of our social lives. As will be explained in the concluding section below, this departure challenges the established understanding of the political as the sphere where our lives are organized publicly and on a large scale in terms of institutionalized coercion. By "institutionalized coercion," or "institutionalized domination," I mean institutions that work as a body separate from the rest of society and determine the public life of individuals in their territory, by concentrating and monopolizing the authority to define the rights of those individuals and force obligations upon them. In these functions, such institutions are backed by coercion, which they also concentrate and monopolize.[76]

At this point, the significance of the notion of social cooperative schemes for the discussion of fairness as a ground of political obligation is simply stated. Genuine cooperation involves an actual, conscious, and joint attempt to achieve the common good—as evidenced in small-scale, strongly cooperative ventures—rather than the mere "rendering of services" or a rule-imposed or an accidental coordination of activities.[77] It is also this picture that gives rise to our intuitions about fairness. Existing governments do not have the status of cooperative enterprises: they work in large societies, where the sense of sharing a unifying purpose in their everyday social activities and duties is lacking in most individuals. They involve a number of features that make them depart from a genuine picture of a strongly cooperative scheme, features such as the coercive enforcement of rules and the suppression of the independent role of personal morality in sanctioning noncompliance.[78] Present societies incorporate ongoing schemes of social cooperation, those that involve a practice that needs the contribution of a large number of citizens in order to be sustained, and those that create a general obligation that would not be concretized without their existence. Political institutions have a significant instrumental value in maintaining such schemes. Yet these activities do not make political society itself a large and unified scheme of social cooperation. Nor are the moral reasons for acting in ways that sustain such practices based on the fact that political institutions, or the law, facilitate them. So the existence of schemes of this kind within present political societies does not give rise to a general political obligation.[79] Moreover, if we apply to these societies a "loose sense of cooperative scheme," namely as "systems of rules designed to regulate" our activities in ways beneficial to all (or otherwise, as facilitating the provision of services), they cease to provide backgrounds suitable for the application of the principle of fairness.[80] Thus, present societies lack the reciprocity in social relations involved in genuine schemes of social cooperation. In this way they deprive their citizens of a conception of their governments as cooperative schemes characterized by horizontal relationships.

Likewise, the citizens of these societies commonly seem not to regard any benefits provided to them as the fruits of "the cooperative efforts of [others as their] fellow citizens."[81] The attitudes and beliefs of ordinary people lack this reciprocity, conception, and approach even when these people express in general terms a belief in the existence of political obligation, which belief is also generally formulated by the use of elements of the principle of fairness. It is on this ground that, I claim, Klosko's investigation is unsatisfactory.[82] More generally, there is a difference between, on the one hand, people's expressing a belief in political obligation and, on the other, their actually having the belief on the basis of an actual relationship that they have entered; a relationship they thought they should enter, actually believing in every instance in the existence of the elements that create it. Furthermore, and importantly, Klosko's research is conducted within a background of already existing institutions. Thus its results (which are anyway based on a limited group of people) might apply to existing institutions, which might seem to be the only ones that meet general principles, because they are the Establishment and as such they already have an effect on the beliefs investigated. We are not asked whether we can satisfy such principles in other ways, whether we can have other social arrangements and attitudes, whether we can have the benefits in other ways: the assessment of the costs and benefits to be balanced is itself understood differently when we take into consideration the alternative of realistic nonpolitical societies.[83] When people are asked about their obligations, they are not asked on the basis of a more fundamental question regarding all the possibilities of addressing them, other than and beyond the state. In the following chapters of this study, I discuss how the lack of this approach stigmatizes the overall debate on political obligation and how the significance of this phenomenon is indicated by the anarchist criticism.

At the same time, as argued during the examination of the first area of anarchist criticism in this chapter, many of the citizens of existing states seem to lack the attitude of acceptance in further ways: they are likely to be those who "have not taken the benefits (with accompanying burdens) willingly."[84] Not only are people's beliefs schooled out of voluntarist interpretations of the principle of fairness in the same manner in which, as explained above, existing institutions have an effect on people's beliefs at other levels.[85] We can also see in their behavior that they lack the attitudes of active participation that, if it existed, a scheme of social cooperation would cultivate and, most importantly, facilitate. The lack of these elements makes the violation of the generality condition of political obligation explicit. Successful accounts of political obligation that are founded on the principle of fairness would involve the aforementioned elements. Thus, these final considerations on cooperative schemes, regarding the attitudes of citizens, show once more that the principle of fairness fails to establish a general obligation to obey political institutions.

These considerations simply state that existing political institutions fail to incorporate the kinds of interaction that characterize genuine schemes of social cooperation and thus cannot claim political obligation on the basis of fairness. For one thing, they are based on empirical claims that remain the subject of controversy.[86] The main aim of my discussion of the idea of social cooperation, however, is to indicate its value. This idea helps to clarify the character and importance of horizontal relationships. It highlights the way in which forms of interdependence that involve participation, reciprocity, and cooperation stand in opposition to hierarchical relationships. In the former, citizens are seen as equal agents who create, determine, and support their social world in continual interaction with one another. They are equally the legislators and the subjects of the social terms of their interaction. Every claim arises from an individual and is balanced by those arising from the other participants, rather than being dictated from above. The presence, needs, and actions of each participant are themselves part of how social aims and changes are conceived and pursued. And any contribution or achievement on the part of an individual is directed to the other members. Expressions of freedom, obligations, and projects take place by reference to the rest of those who compose the social scheme. All individuals act directly on the basis of proper limits in relation to others.

They do not do something that would undermine others and that would reflect circumstances where others can undermine them. Such a background becomes an explicit reminder that societies are made up of individuals and are characterized by their interrelations. In hierarchical structures, on the other hand, this sense of interdependence is absent. Rights and duties are regulated from above. One group of individuals becomes the exclusive and authoritative designator and coordinator of social aims and interactions, the legislator and the ruler. Individuals understand their relations in terms of hierarchy and their obligations are directed to those who rule, rather than to each and every one of the fellow citizens with whom they inhabit society. The social background becomes one within which relations of inequality are established and encouraged, dismissing the fact that they apply among free and equal human beings. Social relations become a network of domination, subordination, and unequal dependence. It is this framework that the idea of schemes of social cooperation challenges and is meant to replace. As such, it is a valuable idea for existing social organizations to aspire to.

The preceding argument relates to the fact that political institutions have a distinctive character, indicated in Chapter 2. As explained on the basis of Hume's view in that chapter, the inevitable and exclusive character of political institutions does not invite the kinds of attitudes and interactions involved in consent. Nor, as we see in the present chapter, does it do so with regard to fairness. Their assessment should be informed by this special character. Any justification of political institutions should be developed in view of the importance of these elements for political obligation and the fact that the nature of political institutions excludes them. The authority of political institutions cannot be justified in terms either of consent or of the forms of acceptance and cooperation involved in fairness. Those institutions must be evaluated in light of this defect and through a kind of justification that is compatible with their nature. Thus, if their existence is to be justified, we need to search in them for the expression of values that make their dominating, exclusive, and coercive character moral. Since they cannot be social schemes of a cooperative character, political institutions need to be shown to involve in some other way the kinds of values that would make them necessary and acceptable.

The implications of the anarchist criticism of the principle of fairness

The results of the preceding discussion can be summed up in the following points:

(1) While justice is not integral to considerations of fairness, its importance poses a serious constraint on the application of the principle of fairness as an account of political obligation.

(2) The notion of acceptance, conceived properly by appeal to subjective facts, is necessary for an understanding of the principle of fairness and reintroduces the value of voluntariness. It also represents an attitude that clearly satisfies the particularity condition of political obligation. Nevertheless, it involves many theoretical and practical problems, which have to do with the disparity among individuals' attitudes to benefits and the resulting controversial status of their participation within society. Most importantly, it does not save the principle from the difficulties it faces with regard to the generality condition of political obligation.

(3) Existing societies are not schemes of social cooperation and, in this, they fail to provide the sense of reciprocity that the rationale of the principle of fairness requires. Thus, they both lack the desirable features of the idea of political communities as large cooperative schemes and fail to combine satisfactorily accounts of political obligation based on the principle of fairness with the generality condition.

Bearing in mind our concern with the contribution of critical philosophical anarchism to the debate on political obligation, it is necessary to draw out the implications of these results.

First, the justice of an institution continues to be morally relevant for the evaluation of theories of political obligation. This relevance is coherent with the ideal of legitimacy described in the previous chapter on the basis of the anarchist criticisms of the natural duty of justice. In the discussion of fairness, justice preserves the position about the role of institutional morality derived from the previous chapters of this study. That is, considerations regarding quality continue to affect significantly evaluations of political constraints, but they need to take the form of more specific features of social interaction in order to provide grounds suitable to the actuality of political obligation.

Second, through the notion of acceptance and its role in the evaluation of the principle of fairness, the desirability of voluntariness recognized from the perspective of the anarchist ideal in Chapter 2 is confirmed. Although not in the form of deliberate undertaking, a voluntary form of involvement (active participation) retains all of its significance. And this is strong evidence of the central role that specific interaction plays in the creation of political obligation.

Finally, the idea of communities as cooperative schemes becomes an element of great importance for an ideal of political legitimacy. It provides a picture of social life that departs from the dominance and institutionalized coercion of existing states (which they are mainly criticized for, at least from the perspective of anarchism) and that can guide their improvement. It also forms the conception of social relations preferred by the anarchist.

The idea of reciprocal relationships among individuals, reflecting a spirit of cooperation and mutuality in public activities, retains an alternative picture of "the political": a sphere within which social life is organized on a wide scale but, at the same time, within which such regulating efforts are not defined in terms of centralized and monopolized coercion. Social interdependence takes the form of horizontal relations of equal responsibility and benefit. In addition, this picture is a central feature of anarchist social visions, something that inspires theoretical defenses of their possibility as well as empirical efforts toward their realization. The implications of these matters will be discussed in Chapters 6 and 7 of this study.[87] At this point, I restrict myself to two preliminary observations. First, the anarchist proposals for societies composed of free cooperative organizations oppose institutionalized domination, and to this extent they do not face the problems created by the moral elements of the ideal of legitimacy for polities that display an institutionalized coercive structure. Second, the anarchist rejection of political obligations as the core of a conception of our social relationships suggests that anarchist proposals can be defended to meet the required moral demands without having to meet the four traditional conditions that only a theory of political obligation has to satisfy (since, as argued in the previous chapters, these conditions reflect the political nature of that obligation in its traditional conception).

Both acceptance and the idea of schemes of social cooperation provide paradigmatic ways of expressing self-governance and equality on the way to a meaningful realization of equal-liberty. Individuals should be capable of thinking and acting for themselves and in collaboration with others, achieve collective liberty, in order to survive and live complete lives. The two elements distinguished by the discussion of fairness make explicit the value of participation and the form of participation appropriate for this capacity and achievement. The constant and explicit expression within a society of a willing involvement on the part of individuals in its aims and services, which acceptance exemplifies, is a direct application of self-government and the kind of equal active citizenship necessary for it. A sense of horizontal relationships of a reciprocal character, as involved in schemes of social cooperation, cultivates proper social relations, within which self-government and equality are enhanced. Defenders of political constraints need to attend to these elements and to their value for assessing political institutions.

To conclude: in this chapter, the anarchist perspective is made explicit through an insistence, in the language of fairness, on the values of active participation and actual reciprocity as the proper features of the kind of particularized moral relationship that would generate political obligation. This advocacy, on the part of the philosophical anarchist, of the kind of acceptance that would form active participation is also an expression of the fact that this anarchist perspective goes together with an ideal of legitimacy, a prior vision of what an application of proper social relations would be like. This latter is expressed further in the anarchist insistence on the idea of schemes of social cooperation as the defining structures of social life. The failure of the fairness defense of political obligation justifies these claims. In turn, these points suggest the following: first, that political obligation constitutes an actual and particularized relationship that needs to be detected in the specific practices of political institutions and their interaction with individuals. Second, that the fact that it is very difficult for such a relationship to exist in our societies, in this case through the elements of fairness, shows something important about political institutions. They lack an aspect that would justify the claims they make on individuals, and this affects their character and acceptability. In view of the absence of political obligation and the kind of active participation it would reflect, it becomes more crucial to ensure that political constraints have a character that makes them morally justifiable. For this, they need to be justified on the basis of fundamental moral values and in the light of an ideal of legitimacy that they fail to satisfy. The permanent, centralized, monopolistic, and coercive, that is, the dominant character of political constraints creates inappropriate social relations. In order to be justified, political constraints need to be shown to respect constantly the values on the basis of which they are claimed to be defensible in the first place—values such as security and peace, justice and fairness, equality, and even freedom itself. This provides an alternative way of enabling active participation within political societies and the acceptable relations it generates, given the absence of political obligation, one that involves and motivates a more critical and demanding approach to political institutions. The principle of fairness, as one of the above values, can be used as a way of characterizing social interdependence within existing political societies. This principle is suitable for determining some obligations to others and defining the character of social procedures, although it does not establish the state's exclusive enforcement of any duties that we might have.

Notes

1   An early version of this chapter was published in the *Review Journal of Political Philosophy*, vol. 1, University of Sheffield, 2003.
2   Wolff, "Pluralistic Models of Political Obligation," 8–9. Yet, with respect to this idea the principle of fairness is distinguished from other reciprocity based theories such as gratitude in the way they define duties: the former defines the necessary return required from the recipient (as doing his fair share in producing the benefits), while in the latter the recipient decides for himself how to reciprocate (Klosko and Klein, "Political Obligations," 10). And, more generally, fairness involves more complex relationships between the beneficiaries, determined by the idea that they are active participants in a cooperative structure (Simmons, *Moral Principles and Political Obligations*, 172–175; see also Richard Dagger, "Membership, Fair Play and Political Obligation," *Political Studies* 48 [2000]: 112–117). I analyze these features of fairness below.

3   Herbert Lionel Adolphus Hart, "Are There Any Natural Rights?,"
Philosophical Review 64 (1955): 185.
4   John Rawls, "Legal Obligation and the Duty of Fair Play," in *Law and Philosophy*, ed. Sidney Hook (New York: New York University Press, 1964), 9–10.
5   Jonathan Wolff, "Political Obligation, Fairness and Independence," *Ratio* 8 (1995): 92.
6   For a useful introduction to the problem of social coordination, see Raz, "Introduction," 6–11. For Raz coordination, which is a central issue in justifications of political authority, is taken in its ordinary sense, as the problem of

> getting people to act in ways which are sensitive to the way others are guided, or are likely to act, so that benefits can be expected which are less likely if they act without coordinating their efforts, i.e. without basing their own actions on a view as to how others should or are likely to act. Coordination presupposes that people are not trying to foil each other. Rather they are trying to secure goals which are agreed to by all, or perhaps just goals that all should have. But coordination does not presuppose that every participant will improve his position by coordinating. ("Introduction," 7)

In this ordinary sense coordination does not involve subjectivism (and the related exploitative motivations) as it preoccupies game theory, e.g., in the analysis of the Prisoner's Dilemma, and which is applied in traditional approaches to the problem of providing public goods (and, in general, to game-theoretical analyses of coordination; "Introduction," 6–11). Still, it involves the basic features that relate the principle of fairness with the problem of public goods, a problem that is in the focus of this chapter. And the problem of public goods is a kind of coordination problem. For more precision, the problem of public goods is one that can arise as a problem of securing social coordination in its ordinary sense, but also one that usually arises in relation to the free-rider problem of game theory ("Introduction," 8). In this chapter I focus on the latter.
7   For an analysis of this connection and the relevant problems generated, see Richard J. Arneson, "The Principle of Fairness and Free-Rider Problems," *Ethics* 92 (1982): 618–623, and Alan John Simmons, *Justification and Legitimacy: Essays on Rights and Obligations* (Cambridge: Cambridge University Press, 2001), 29–36.
8   Simmons, *Moral Principles and Political Obligations*, 116.
9   Simmons, *Moral Principles and Political Obligations*, 105.
10   On this, see Simmons, *Moral Principles and Political Obligations*, 106; Arneson, "The Principle of Fairness," 621–622; George Klosko, "Presumptive Benefit, Fairness and Political Obligation," *Philosophy and Public Affairs* 16 (1987): 244–245.
11   By "open" benefits I follow Simmons in meaning those usually referred to as public goods. They thus demonstrate all the characteristics of public goods described here, especially their non-excludability, on the basis of which it becomes impossible or very inconvenient to avoid them (Simmons, *Moral*

Principles and Political Obligations, 130). From now on I will use this term interchangeably with the term "public goods."

12   For the explanation of public goods that I follow here, see Rawls, *A Theory of Justice*, 266–270; Arneson, "The Principle of Fairness," 618–619; Taylor, *Community, Anarchy and Liberty*, 40–55, 60–65, and 117–120; Klosko, "Presumptive Benefit," 242–243; Harriott, "Games, Anarchy, and the Nonnecessity of the State," 120.

13   Simmons, *Moral Principles and Political Obligations*, 107–108.

14   Simmons, *Moral Principles and Political Obligations*, 116–117; Horton, *Political Obligation*, 96.

15   For the importance of such a basis, see Simmons, *Moral Principles and Political Obligations*; Simmons, "Justification and Legitimacy"; my previous chapters.

16   Robert Nozick, *Anarchy, State and Utopia* (Oxford: Basil Blackwell, 1974), 90–95.

17   Simmons, *Moral Principles and Political Obligations*, 119; Klosko, "Presumptive Benefit," 246.

18   This benefit appears in Nozick's "public address system" example (Nozick, *Anarchy, State and Utopia*, 93). I will discuss this example in the following section.

19   This point is allowed by a suggestion of Nozick himself (Nozick, *Anarchy, State and Utopia*, 94), and it has been stressed by Simmons (Simmons, *Moral Principles and Political Obligations*, 119).

20   For example, Arneson, "The Principle of Fairness," 617 and 621–623; Wolff, "Political Obligation, Fairness and Independence," 94–96; Dagger, "Membership."

21   Simmons, *Justification and Legitimacy*, 29–36.

22   Rawls, "Legal Obligation," 9–10.

23   Simmons, *Moral Principles and Political Obligations*, 106.

24   Smith, "Is There a Prima Facie Obligation?," 956–957.

25   Simmons, *Moral Principles and Political Obligations*, 106–107.

26   Rawls, "Legal Obligation," 9.

27   For these points, see Simmons, *Moral Principles and Political Obligations*, 110–114.

28   This element expresses a concern with creating and securing proper relations between individuals in a society, which, as indicated in previous chapters, is a central concern of the anarchists and the main source of their challenge to political authority. For more on this point, see the analysis of the anarchist arguments in the present chapter (see the section "The anarchist criticism of the principle of fairness").

29   This point is indicated by Simmons (Simmons, *Moral Principles and Political Obligations*, 112–114), but it is also compatible with Rawls's discussion of the principle (Rawls, "Legal Obligation") and with its defense by Klosko, which is analyzed below (Klosko, "Presumptive Benefit," see, e.g., p. 253 the comments connected with note 32 and, more generally, all his references to the third condition he poses on the application of the principle). See also Dagger, "Membership."

30 For the latter, see, for example, Jonathan Wolff, "What is the Problem of Political Obligation?," *Proceedings of the Aristotelian Society Supplementary* 91 (1990): 166 (his reference to anarchists and to gypsies as such cases).

31 Wolff, "What is the Problem of Political Obligation?," 166–167.

32 Smith, "Is There a Prima Facie Obligation?," 957.

33 Or that it constitutes the best possible way of obtaining the required benefits.

34 Statistical research by Klosko and Klein purports to show that most people think that they benefit from the rule of law and other services of the state (Klosko and Klein, "Political Obligations").

35 Or goods that are avoided only in ways that create great inconvenience or great costs to individuals, conditions that are also undesired (as burdens forced on them).

36 Nozick, *Anarchy, State and Utopia*, 95. For this, see also Simmons, *Moral Principles and Political Obligations*, 118; Klosko, "Presumptive Benefit," 246.

37 For this point and failure, see the section "Tacit consent" of Chapter 2.

38 See Klosko, "Presumptive Benefit," 244.

39 For this, see Klosko, "Presumptive Benefit," 246.

40 This importance also creates a natural combination between this principle as ground of political obligation and considerations about institutional morality. These considerations, as argued in previous chapters, when applied compatibly with the nature of the relationship needed for political obligation, have an important role to play within the debate.

41 George Klosko, *The Principle of Fairness and Political Obligation* (Lanham: Rowman and Littlefield, 1992), 39.

42 Klosko, "Presumptive Benefit," 246 (emphasis added). Klosko derives this explanation from Rawls's notion and conception of "primary goods" (Rawls, *A Theory of Justice*, 62 and 92). Klosko sees his "presumptive public goods" as "the public analogues of Rawls's primary goods": Klosko, "Presumptive Benefit," 246. But this claim should not obscure the understanding that Rawls's primary goods *are* public goods.

43 Klosko, "Presumptive Benefit," 247.

44 For Klosko's whole discussion, see "Presumptive Benefit," 247–259.

45 See Simmons, *Moral Principles and Political Obligations*, chapter 5; Simmons, *Justification and Legitimacy*, chapters 1 and 2.

46 Simmons, *Justification and Legitimacy*, 108.

47 Simmons, *On the Edge of Anarchy*, 251–252.

48 This idea of his is analyzed in Simmons, *Moral Principles and Political Obligations*, Chapter 5; Simmons, "The Anarchist Position"; Simmons, *On the Edge of Anarchy*, 248–260; Simmons, *Justification and Legitimacy*, chapters 1 and 2.

49 This discussion can be found in Simmons, *Moral Principles and Political Obligations*, 119 and 122–123; Simmons, *Justification and Legitimacy*, Chapter 1.

50 This distinction is also active in the problem of securing social coordination understood in its ordinary sense (for the ordinary sense of coordination, see n. 6). It is important both in those situations and in the problem discussed at present that the individuals regarded as participants and whose actions directly affect common enterprises be clearly detected. The distinction between insiders

and outsiders also facilitates the attempt to find and secure proper relations between individuals within a society, which concerns the anarchist most. By understanding whether and how individuals are involved in the generation and operation of social services, we start to explain their interrelations, and thus their obligations, in ways that prevent arbitrary subordination.

51 Simmons, *Moral Principles and Political Obligations*, 132–133.
52 Simmons, *Moral Principles and Political Obligations*, 132.
53 Simmons, *Moral Principles and Political Obligations*, 132.
54 For these examples, see Simmons, *Moral Principles and Political Obligations*, 139.
55 For this position of Klosko that I criticize here, see Klosko and Klein, "Political Obligations."
56 For these kinds of arguments, see also Green, "Who Believes in Political Obligation?"; Simmons, "Philosophical Anarchism," 33.
57 In Simmons, "Philosophical Anarchism," 33. See also Simmons, *Justification and Legitimacy*, 33–35.
58 For these arguments, see Klosko and Klein, "Political Obligations," Sections V and VI.
59 See Simmons, *On the Edge of Anarchy*, 254–257.
60 Klosko, "Presumptive Benefit," 248–249. See the discussion of his argument in the section "Klosko's defense of 'Receipt' " above.
61 Wolff, *Political Philosophy*, 94–96.
62 Arneson, "The Principle of Fairness," 623 and 632. See also Simmons, *On the Edge of Anarchy*, 253–254, n.79.
63 For this argument, see also Simmons, *Justification and Legitimacy*, 35–36.
64 Simmons, "The Anarchist Position," 273.
65 Arneson, "The Principle of Fairness," 633.
66 Simmons, *On the Edge of Anarchy*, 254–255, n.80.
67 And still, while "culpable or negligent ignorance of the source, nature, or value of the benefits one enjoys will not (by itself) excuse one from obligation under the principle of fair play," it is the responsibility of the participants in a cooperative scheme to inform consumers about the "expectations of reciprocation, *not* the responsibility of consumers to pay for what they unavoidably and innocently consume" (Simmons, *Justification and Legitimacy*, 32–33).
68 Or, put differently, of a function of the state that is "worthwhile" for the individuals: Wolff, *Political Philosophy*, 96.
69 Wolff, *Political Philosophy*, 96.
70 Wolff, *Political Philosophy*, 96.
71 Simmons, "Justification and Legitimacy," 764.
72 In his 1999 article, Simmons seems to consider actual receipt as a proper basis of political obligation (e.g., Simmons, "Justification and Legitimacy," 764).
73 See Newman, *The Politics of Postanarchism*, 31–34.
74 Newman, *The Politics of Postanarchism*, 23.
75 Simmons, *Moral Principles and Political Obligations*, 116 and 140.
76 For these, see Wolff, *In Defense of Anarchism*, 3–5; Miller, *Anarchism*, 5; McLaughlin, *Anarchism and Authority*, 74–80. See also my introduction, n. 2.
77 Simmons, *Justification and Legitimacy*, 38–42.

78 Simmons, *Justification and Legitimacy*, 41.
79 For these points, see Raz, *The Authority of Law*, 247–249. These
    considerations are also related to the arguments in Chapter 3 about how
    two main legal techniques, or, more generally, political functions, may make
    political institutions morally worthwhile—more precisely, just—without,
    however, giving rise to a general moral obligation to obey the law.
80 Simmons, *Moral Principles and Political Obligations*, 140–141; Simmons,
    Justification and Legitimacy, 38–42.
81 Simmons, *Moral Principles and Political Obligations*, 139.
82 See Klosko and Klein, "Political Obligations." Such an absence is evident, for
    example, in the fact that the participants in the study did not show a clear
    sense of the relevance of the levels of compliance among the members of a
    cooperative scheme in their views about political obligation; in general, the
    difference between fairness and gratitude was not refined (Klosko and Klein,
    "Political Obligations," 28).
83 Simmons, *Justification and Legitimacy*, 37–38.
84 Simmons, *Moral Principles and Political Obligations*, 139; Simmons,
    Justification and Legitimacy, chapters 1 and 2.
85 See also Simmons, "Philosophical Anarchism," 33–34.
86 Previously (in the sections "Simmons on 'Acceptance'" and "The significance
    of 'Acceptance'") I attempted to give a stronger defense of these claims. Yet,
    this defense invites further discussion in order to convince opposing views.
87 At this moment it suffices to state that this study promotes a position similar
    to that of Saul Newman, that the anti-politics of anarchism involves in fact
    politics: *"a politics that is conceived outside of, and in opposition to, the
    state"* (Newman, *The Politics of Postanarchism*, 4–8).

5

Horton revisited

Let me preface the general conclusions of this book with an examination of the view of an important theorist of political obligation, whose comments and criticisms have been used widely in the preceding discussion. John Horton has developed his own arguments concerning political obligation in his thorough examination of the debate between defenders of the state and philosophical anarchists. He produces a theory of *associative* political obligations.[1] This theory is non-voluntarist. Nor is it offered as a complete and "compelling *moral* justification" of political obligation, and I will not approach it as such here.[2] Nevertheless, it is a quite important and constructive theory, very relevant to the present discussion, the potential of which should be examined. In this chapter, therefore, I attempt to assess its value in the debate, by examining its content and its resistance to central criticisms.

More precisely, I will present Horton's main (three-part) argument for associative political obligation, as anticipated in Part One and as advanced in Part Two of his relevant two-part article, focusing on his response to important arguments of Simmons and those of critical philosophical anarchism in general. I will also discuss Richard Vernon's criticism from moral universalism as derived from, and despite, his support of Horton's endeavor against philosophical anarchism.[3] In the light of these crucial objections, I will attempt to draw conclusions about the value of Horton's theory, although, as I have already mentioned, it is not offered as a theory of general political obligation in the way the debate discussed here demands.

Rather than proving that we *have* political obligations, Horton adopts a "more interpretative or explanatory" approach, which concerns the moral coherence of associative political obligation.[4] His approach is principally phenomenological, yet he recognizes the need for a *positive* account of political obligation.[5] So his aim is to show how intelligible and plausible it is to understand political obligations today through his conception of associative political obligations.

Associative political obligations are the kind of obligations that arise in virtue of our membership in a particular polity that forms a special, nonvoluntary form of association.[6] Their reasonableness and possibility is rooted in the phenomenology of association, the sense that our membership in a polity is morally significant. In a world where the good of order, which we value highly, is provided more by states, we have a reason, subject to certain conditions, to support the state whose territory we happen to inhabit and, as long as it meets those conditions, to value the beliefs and practices that are supportive of its institutions. Political obligation can thus be understood on the basis of this sense and relation of membership that we have toward "our" polities.[7] This is mainly the view that will be evaluated in this chapter.

Horton's preliminary arguments for associative political obligations

Before embarking on his constructive account of associative political obligations, Horton, in Part One of his article, lays the foundations by responding to a number of criticisms against this view. More precisely, he defends associative political obligation against Simmons's criticisms of two argumentative strategies advanced in its favor that the latter identifies. One is a form of "nonvoluntarist contract theory" and the other is the "communitarian approach."[8] In the present section, I will examine Horton's response with regard to the criticisms of both strategies, as well as to Simmons's more direct criticism of associative political obligations. My aim is to distinguish the arguments and the difficulties that will determine his positive defense at a preliminary stage.

About a non-voluntarist contract theory

Regarding the first strategy, which implements a non-voluntarist contract theory, Simmons has four main objections, the nature of which is quite familiar from his previous criticisms, especially in Chapter 4 here. Three are against Margaret Gilbert's representative support of associative political obligations:[9] (a) to feel that we have obligations to our government does not mean that we really have them; (b) only transactional acts or relationships generate political obligations; and (c) reasonable expectations should not be confused with entitlements. The fourth is against Ronald Dworkin:[10] (d) associative obligations do not arise from an equal concern that most citizens show to each other through their political practices.[11]

Horton replies to each in a way that, in my opinion, amounts to a satisfactory response.

In his first objection, Simmons attacks the use of ordinary moral opinion to support political obligations that are not based on voluntary agreement by indicating that such opinion can easily be mistaken and express an oppressed and uncritical thinking, a mass delusion, rather than a valid belief. Horton is right to state that the mere possibility of people being mistaken about the actuality of political obligation does not establish much.[12] It is equally legitimate to use ordinary moral opinion as a starting point and assume that it has some weight without assuming that it is a necessary source of truth, instead of rushing to classify it as false consciousness.

Against the second objection, Horton does not find any conclusive reason why only what Simmons calls "positive, obligation-generating acts or relationships" can give rise to obligations.[13] Horton also detects another category as obligation-generating according to Simmons: certainly not Gilbert's "joint commitments" or any kind of associative obligations,[14] yet surely "general, nonvoluntary duties that bind us simply because we are persons."[15] This denies Simmons's initial claim and gives him no good basis for excluding associative accounts by merely asserting that they must fail. In addition, although throughout this study I have stressed extensively the importance of transactional relations for the generation of political obligation, which can be used here to reinforce Simmons, I concede that we cannot exclude the possibility of associative obligations without examining the theory first. It could be the case that membership in a polity creates a relation to it of a kind that might have the same weight as voluntary acts and relations of the transactional sort. It is one of the aims of this chapter to discover whether this is the case.

Moving to the third objection, it is true that reasonable expectations differ from entitlements, and usually simple reasonable expectations do not generate obligations. Yet some obligations do arise from reasonable expectations that are related to broad and impersonal patterns of behavior rather than close relationships. Horton cites the example of being law-abiding in the case where a farmer has an obligation to respect the right of pedestrians to have access through his land, if he has allowed them to walk across it long enough to make plans based on this expectation.[16] So the difference between expectations and entitlements, and even the possibility of mistakenly confusing the two, does not exclude the possibility of explaining some obligations in terms of reasonable expectations, although it is unlikely that they would generate general political obligation.

As regards the fourth objection, Simmons is right that people in contemporary states do not in general display the attitudes toward others as their fellow citizens that are required for political obligation, certainly not an equal concern toward all of them, which Dworkin contends is what would give rise to associative political obligations. On the other hand, neither are they exclusively concerned with people who are family and friends or members of groups they have voluntarily chosen. Horton is right that expressions such as "it makes me ashamed to be British" are a response to situations and appeals in terms of a common political membership, for example when immigrants in one's country are treated with disrespect and live in shameful conditions.[17] Yet, in my opinion, such expressions show moral considerations and inform obligations that are moral, albeit regarding political issues. We might express them as citizens, but they do not arise necessarily from our identification with and membership of a specific polity. They are acknowledgments of our obligations toward humanity and our fellow human beings expressed in the context of the society we live in. So they are not solely political. In justice to associative accounts, however, they are evidence for the kind of concern that could give rise to political obligations, and their continual expression within political contexts creates the background for this possibility.

In sum, although this study supports the significance of voluntariness for political obligations, it cannot without examination exclude the associative theory merely on the basis of the above inconclusive—I concede to Horton— criticisms against a non-voluntarist theory. Yet the second strategy that Horton wants to defend against Simmons's criticisms faces more serious problems.

On the communitarian approach

The communitarian approach involves two central theses: the "identity argument" and "the normative independence of local practice."[18] The first contends that, since our identities are partly constituted by our role as members of a political community, they include political obligations. The second is the claim that local practices independently determine moral requirements.

Simmons's criticism of the first thesis is that the fact that membership is partly constitutive of our identity and that we understand it to be so (as part of our self-identification) does not entail the moral justification of political obligation. Horton indicates that this in a way repeats the first argument above, mainly that we are socialized into identifying with our polity, and thus our belief in our political membership is a kind of "false consciousness."[19] Moreover, he is right to argue in response that we have as much reason to presume the validity of our beliefs as we have to preclude it, as long as nobody presents a further, more convincing argument against the former. My argument against Horton, however, is that the fact of socialization *is* such an argument. We cannot necessarily assume that socialization leads to false consciousness, yet its unmediated and uncritical effect on us from an early age increases the possibility that our socially constructed belief in political membership is less than an expression of an unquestionable truth. In the same way in which the burden of proof falls on the defender of the state who makes the claim that what we are born into has merit, the burden falls here on the defender of associative political obligation to prove that our identification with polities has ethical significance.

The first thesis is not sufficient to explain political obligation. Since Horton himself considers the second thesis to be more critical and the two theses to be mutually supportive, the decisive move here is to examine the strength of the second thesis, the normative independence thesis.

According to the normative independence thesis, "local social practices (and our roles and places in them) independently determine (some or all) moral requirements."[20] Political obligations can be seen as an example of such normative independence. In support of these claims, Horton wants to deny two main arguments advanced by Simmons against the normative independence thesis: "one obvious fact" and "one broad theoretical disposition."[21] For Simmons, the obvious fact is that the quality of local practices might not be morally acceptable; they "can be unjust, oppressive or pointless." The theoretical disposition is "the belief that universality, or at least a very high degree of generality, is an essential feature of moral judgements."[22]

Beginning from the second argument, Horton argues that Simmons gives no reasons for the theoretical disposition about universality, or generality. But at this point and from the beginning of this work, I believe that generality has been argued for sufficiently. It has been supported as a central condition of political obligation, because, together with the other three, it expresses the political nature of institutions, thus becoming a normative reminder that they should be defended with reference to that nature. Also, it is a reasonable demand itself that the requirement of political obligation should have a universal, or very general, form when it figures in our moral reasoning. Still, Horton claims that the theory of associative political obligation can accommodate universality: "the claim that political obligations are owed to a polity by virtue of people's membership of it can possibly be presented as itself universal in form (or at least very general)."[23] There is no obvious reason to deny this claim, but it is my task here to see if it can be sustained, more precisely, to examine whether membership can combine normative importance with universality and whether this universality can be applied. For this I need to complete the argumentation of this chapter.

The first argument, the obvious fact, questions the quality of local social practices. As I argue throughout this work, the moral quality of institutions is a crucial factor of their evaluation and a precondition of their authority. We cannot begin to discuss further conditions of their acceptance and the possibility of political obligation when institutions are unjust or more generally immoral. So we need independent and more general moral criteria to constrain them, which means that the local practices that could establish the morality of political institutions lack normative independence.

For Horton, the existence of general moral constraints is not so decisive as to eradicate the normative significance of local practices. He believes that these constraints are not "so extensive as to restrict severely the scope of local practices to generate political obligations."[24] Their function is basically to put limits on what can be regarded as acceptable kinds of association according to the morality of the obligations attached to them. So a wide diversity of practices can generate obligations, as long as they do not systematically violate these moral conditions. This might be true. Yet what I think should be stressed here is that the limiting role of moral constraints makes them the last court of appeal. Although they leave a large scope for the obligation-generating function of local social practices, in the end it is those constraints that decide whether the obligations arising from those practices are genuinely moral, and not the practices themselves. This is precisely the function of the criteria established through the anarchist ideal of legitimacy, which constitute serious limitations on the legitimacy of political institutions.

The strong point of this argument, however, is that the moral standing of the social groups that generate associative obligations might be questionable: membership might be attached to involuntary groups that are not morally praiseworthy.[25] As indicated above and as established in previous chapters, therefore, we need an appeal to other values, such as justice, as a precondition determining in which associations membership can generate obligations. In reply, Horton rightly argues that it is unfair to restrict this criticism to associative accounts, since it can equally apply to voluntarist accounts. Since we are considering the quality argument, which defines the existence of political institutions (a precondition for political obligation, although not identical to it), general values apply as criteria to voluntarist and any other accounts of political authority. So as long as their character is acceptable, membership in associations can be seen as a legitimate source of obligations, especially if we focus on the character and value of the relationships included in and created by such membership, which can be of a constitutive rather than solely instrumental character. Nevertheless, I agree with Simmons that the appeal to the value of the character of, or the relationships within, an association as a precondition shows that associative obligations depend on "external justification."[26] Relationships can be meaningful themselves and constitutive of the value of groups such as family or, in the present case, the state. Yet such value is determined by external and more general moral criteria, by values that are already acceptable and determinative of further qualities. Thus membership cannot decide by itself the authority of associations.

Horton insists that Simmons's treatment of the normative independence thesis is too demanding: it requires the *total* independence of local practices, something that the associative account does not necessarily entail. The claim in favor of the thesis is that local practices do make reference to general moral values, their uniqueness lying in that they "give these values a particular substance or content, a particular form, shape and meaning within a specific social or institutional setting or way of life."[27] He gives the example of monogamous marriage, where we can see that the obligations it generates are explained by reference to values such as intimacy and fidelity, without meaning, he believes, that these obligations and the whole institution of monogamous marriage are derived from universal (or general) and externally justified principles.[28] Still, my argument is that although values such as fidelity and intimacy might be operative only within specific practices, their worth can be seen independently of the latter and/or in reference to some external justification. Although practices, relationships, and institutions are constitutive of the way certain values are realized within human society, this does not mean that independent evaluation does not apply constantly. The need remains to affirm such practices by ensuring that they continue to be constitutive of the generally acceptable values and according to externally justified principles. In addition, there is always scope for moral disagreement about the value of a particular association that involves such practices and for the need to weigh its valuable and its negative aspects in relation to each other.

The conclusion that can be drawn from the above considerations is that local social practices that do not involve voluntary undertakings can have moral value and work at some level independently of external justification. This value, however, is not permanently assured, and it ends up being affirmed by reference to externally justified, general moral principles. This does not totally destroy the intuitiveness of the normative independence thesis and the communitarian argument of which it is part, but it certainly weakens their argumentative force. Horton's claim that, as long as polities have some value, they can generate obligations might be legitimate, but this depends on the relevance and primacy of the value we refer to and on the extent it is instantiated within a specific polity.

Against associative political obligations

Horton completes his preliminary arguments with an examination of Simmons's criticism specifically against associative *political* obligations, the kind of associative obligations that the latter considers more vulnerable. Simmons thinks that, even if the normative independence thesis could be vindicated, it still would not support associative political obligations. First, he claims that the content of political obligations is specific, while that of associative obligations is vague and indeterminate.[29] Second, he raises the point that states do not involve something substantial enough to constitute a common life or a shared identity that could entail political obligations.

With regard to the first criticism, Horton proposes that the content of political obligation can be seen as richer and more open-ended than the narrow conception of it as a duty to obey the law.[30] In Chapter 1 of this study, this was already accepted, since political obligation is conceived as the concomitant of a complex right to exclusively and coercively make regulations, impose duties, and demand compliance (i.e., to issue directives).[31] Yet my assertion is that the law is the most widespread expression of the directives of political authority and can be used as the most representative identification of our political obligations without excluding openness. Such openness, however, continues to differ from the indeterminacy of communal, associative obligations. Because of the special character of political society and the centrality of the acknowledgment of a common political authority in the content of political obligation,[32] the latter requires not a narrow but certainly a more determinate content[33] and a distinctive justification, which the normative independence thesis might not be suitable to provide.

With regard to the second criticism, it has already been demonstrated in Chapter 4 that citizens do not have the common life and the attitudes that would entail political obligations in terms of the associative argument or any argument conceiving contemporary states as social cooperative schemes or associations. Horton indicates that, if this is a historical claim about the lack of conditions that would make associative political obligations meaningful, it leaves space for their possibility in case the circumstances change. Philosophical anarchism does not deny this prospect. Still, as Horton himself admits, this possibility is "largely empty."[34] Moreover, Simmons's claim might be empirical and historical, but it involves a conceptual as well as normative aspect: it signifies that the normative implications of the special nature of political institutions might be significantly different from those of other forms of social structure. Horton's more recent and seemingly satisfactory response is that a "reasonably cogent sense of belonging to a single political community, [which] may take many different forms, [is enough] to underpin associative political obligations," and for this all that is required is "an account of a polity as a nonvoluntary association … which has sufficient value to generate obligations."[35] I will examine this response in detail in the following section.

Horton's constructive account of associative political obligations and the anarchist challenge

In the positive account of his theory in Part Two of his article, Horton builds his defense of associative political obligations mainly on three arguments. The first is the argument about *the significance of membership*, or of being a member of a particular group or association (Horton uses the terms "group" and "association" interchangeably[36]) that we do not voluntarily choose to join.[37] The other two arguments concern the polity as a distinctive form of association. One explores its generic value, and I will call it interchangeably the *value* or, following Horton, the *Hobbesian argument*.[38] The other is the *associative argument*, and it explores the relationship we have with the particular polity of which we are members.[39] This argument makes use of the distinctive condition of particularity involved in the debate on political obligation. Horton's aim is to explain the significance of nonvoluntary membership in a polity in creating associative political obligations.

The significance of membership argument

Groups, or associations, are collections of individuals "who either act together, or who cooperate with one another in pursuit of their own goals, or who at least posses common interests."[40] They are real in the sense that "they can act and be the subject of actions."[41] Membership in them or exclusion from them defines the way people understand themselves and one another, and they affect our practical reasoning and deliberation. They also vary across societies, cultures, and periods of time.[42]

The main claim of the argument about the general significance of membership is that membership in associations can give rise to obligations. This is not in itself problematic. Yet the additional aspect of the argument is that groups or associations that are *nonvoluntary* can give rise to obligations. While the voluntariness of membership is usually thought to be crucial for the creation of such obligations, we have seen already that political obligations cannot be self-assumed: most of us do not choose our polity or our membership in it. However, it seems even more difficult to derive political obligations from groups that are nonvoluntary. For this, one must show that membership in nonvoluntary groups can give rise to obligations and that polities are such groups. This is what Horton attempts to do with his three main arguments.

The membership argument covers the first important aspect of this attempt: it concerns the indispensability of nonvoluntary groups or associations as a source of their bindingness. Horton claims that the ethical bindingness of nonvoluntary associations is intelligible and defensible, since some such groups, for example the family, have value for us in the way they are integral to and structure social life.[43] However, it is very plausible to argue that it is not membership that gives rise to obligations within those groups, but rather principles such as gratitude or fairness. In the case of family, for example, it may be gratitude toward our parents that determines our relation to them. Yet Horton is right to point out that the fact that they are "my" parents plays an independent role that is partly constitutive of the relationship and can be enough to explain our obligations within it. Disregard of this aspect could undermine the very nature of the institution and diminish any understanding of it. It is thus justifiable to insist that a relationship that is not based on voluntary commitment, but involves a commonality and a shared concern of which obligations are part, can have its own distinctive moral standing.

Nevertheless, polities might not be among the groups that are morally significant in this way. In order to see if they can be proven to be so, we need to examine the other two arguments that Horton exploits to complete his defense of associative political obligation. These are an argument that shows the value of a polity as a form of association and an argument that demonstrates the existence of a special relationship between us and our polity.

The Hobbesian, or *value*, argument

The second important argument that Horton uses in support of associative political obligations is the Hobbesian, or value, argument. As we have seen in previous chapters, a typical and central argument in defense of the state is that it offers the indispensable good of order (and security). The main realization, established by Hobbes, is that people have differences that, if not regulated, will inevitably lead to conflict. Conflict, and the violence and threat to human life that it entails, can be avoided and human beings can flourish only through the establishment of "order, security and some measure of social stability" by an "effective coercive authority."[44]

Horton claims that, for a polity to have value, this minimum core is enough.[45] Despite people's differences, everybody needs and appreciates the good of order. This good explains and justifies the role of coercion, which is essential to a polity and part of its nature. Nothing more seems to be needed for a polity to be valuable. For Horton, a polity can be unjust, illiberal, or undemocratic and still be considered to have value, as long as it meets this condition. So the provision and maintenance of social order through the use of coercion, which creates a situation of predictability, security, and trust necessary for a common life and social flourishing, suffice for the acceptability of the state and for the possibility of a special relationship with it (if the associative argument works in favor of the latter).

A first response, advanced by theorists such as Leslie Green and Stephen Utz, is that order and security are not a good that all people appreciate and share in the same way, since their differences cannot lead to "the same set of particular obligations" or to "[a] general project by all."[46] Although these theorists might be right about the difficulty of such generalizations, Horton, in my opinion, has a strong point when he says that members of a polity do find security and order important and they have a fair idea of when they lack it.[47] Whatever other values we might have or partly share, this is a good that is usually appreciated as essential for our survival and as a precondition for social interaction.

Yet a second objection is to move further and point out that this minimal condition is not enough. For Dworkin, for example, "*equal* concern for all members" and, more generally, conceptions of fraternity and the integrity of a political community are necessary for associative political obligations.[48] Horton finds these requirements extremely demanding and not essential for the generic good of a polity.[49] Still, that order is a minimal condition for a polity to have value does not mean that it is sufficient to justify it in terms of the value argument. I argued in previous chapters that values such as freedom, equality, justice, and reciprocity are important criteria for the acceptability of a polity and the existence of political obligation. Even if a standard such as the anarchist ideal of legitimacy is deemed very demanding, polities will have to do better than just provide security and order if they are to continue to be the kinds of social structure that people have reason to prefer and support. Horton argues that the realization of this generic value by a polity does not entail its uncritical acceptance on the part of its members.[50] He might be right that the acceptance of a polity on this basis is not incompatible with social criticism and proposals for radical social and political change, and that the provision of order creates an ethical basis for obligations. Nevertheless, I believe that such a minimal demand facilitates the lack of flexibility in political thinking and the dominating role of exactly the kinds of establishment that have created repeatedly problematic and immoral relations among human beings.

The latter point above takes us to a final objection to the Hobbesian argument. Even if we accept that the minimal conditions of order and security are sufficient for a polity to be considered as a form of association valuable enough to create obligations, this does not exclude other possibilities. Anarchists support different forms of social order and offer their own proposals as alternatives to the state, which have not yet been fully evaluated. This argument has already appeared in previous chapters and will be further examined in the following ones. Horton himself admits that he does not address the question whether the polity is unique in providing the generic good or whether other ways of providing it are "equally viable or even better."[51] Throughout this study I have advanced an alternative idea of what can be seen as "political" and I have pointed out that part of the anarchist contribution is to remove the prejudice in favor of the state. Beginning to think that the state is not the only or the most effective way of providing even the basic good of order might lead us to see that the generation of associative or any other form of political obligations is not as inevitable and indispensable to social relations and life as it has been thought to be.

The associative argument

The most crucial part of Horton's defense of associative political obligations is the associative argument. This argument is used to explain "why we have a special relationship to the *particular* polity of which we are members."[52] The previous arguments explain membership and the value that a polity must have in order to merit obligations. Thus, they prepare the way for the associative argument, although, as we have seen above, not without problems. But this final argument is decisive for establishing the intelligibility and plausibility of associative political obligations, which Horton sees as his aim. This is the argument that, if successful, meets the particularity condition of political obligation in a way that is also comprehensive with regard to the other three conditions that define the nature of the political.

The philosophical foundation of the associative argument is that membership in particular groups or associations, such as polities, is one of the social practices and contexts that shape and constrain in fundamental respects our self-understanding. Horton gives an excellent example, using Jim Jarmusch's film *Ghost Dog*: the hero in the film tries to live according to the code of "The way of the Samurai," and the main reason he cannot *be* a Samurai is that the social context in which he lives—late twentieth-century, urban America—does not provide the background that would make such a life a meaningful option. The point is that having our identity shaped by the social elements "which constitute the fabric of our lives" is a very natural thing. Even if we want to reject or escape our identity, it already affects our self-understanding and lives. Our identity does not have to be chosen voluntarily, but our actions that accept or renounce it are proof that it is part of the way things are. Here we can see that a simple phenomenology offers the required elements. We all start from somewhere, and the different roles, expectations, debts, and obligations that we inherit from our families, tribes, or cities in their history are the given of our lives.[53] This can be acknowledged and inform the way we understand our relationship to a polity as it does the way we understand our selves.

So, in the case of political obligation, we can say that it is the relationship we acknowledge to the institutions of a particular polity we are born into and the membership in them that is part of our identity. If membership is transformed, a dimension of our lives changes and this affects both our self-understanding and our understanding of and relations to others. Horton gives some reminders of the myriad ways in which this relationship is manifest in our lives:

> we speak of *our* government,...we distinguish members from non-members of our polity, we see our government, at least in many contexts, as acting in our name,...we recognise that our government is entitled to make claims on us and we may have legitimate expectations of it,...we pay taxes [and we recognise the legitimacy of its threat of punishment if we do not],...we [have feelings of] pride or shame in relation to the actions of our polity and fellow members...and much of [all this] is true for a great many of us.[54]

This is a phenomenology of political membership that Horton contends has the ethical material necessary for political obligation. The philosophical anarchist thinks that these are exactly the kinds of uncritical behavior that have to be questioned and filtered out if any sort of political structure is to be justified. The challenge here is to see if Horton's attempt to use these elements as legitimate aspects of such a justification, which is the exact opposite of the anarchist approach, is somehow convincing.

The associative argument has two aspects, the "objective" and the "subjective."[55] The objective concerns the fact that political identity as derived from nonvoluntary membership is an ascribed status. Citizenship is simply assumed within the polity where we are born and, in the vast majority of cases, nothing special needs to be done to acquire it. Horton calls this the objective side, because it does not depend on the members' point of view, on their sentiments, attitudes, or emotions. The subjective aspect draws attention to an understanding of membership shared by both the polity and the member. This involves a sense of belonging to, or *identification with*, the polity, "an acknowledgement of membership by the member," and relates to emotions, attitudes, and moral sentiments, to a self-understanding.[56]

This latter sense of identification plays a crucial role in the associative argument and in the whole defense of associative political obligation. Horton points out that identification is different from endorsement in the sense that someone might be critical of a group and its practices, yet see himself as part of it and be devoted to it, while endorsement of the practices of a polity is likely, and naturally so, to be partial.[57] He also points out, correctly in my opinion, that central to identification with a polity is "the acknowledgement of a common political authority [and that] this is the core content of political obligation."[58] The correlativity between political authority, or the state's right to rule, and political obligation has been granted and stressed already in Chapter 1 of this study.[59] Here we concentrate on the normative side of this statement, which is involved in an argument that is built on notions of group, membership, identity, and identification and works on the basis of their interconnection.

Thus, identification with a polity is acknowledgment of its common authority, which plays a central role in our self-understanding and relation to others. Such identification is embedded in a shared narrative in which the fate of a polity is connected with that of a member. Our sense of political membership is constructed through the "various narratives of identity,"[60] or "ethically constitutive stories": "Such stories proclaim that members' culture, religion, language, race, ethnicity, ancestry or history, or other such factors are constitutive of their very identities as persons in ways that both affirm their worth and delineate their obligations."[61] So our sense of political identity is articulated by this variety of stories insofar as they relate to political membership. It is one of many identities and can be more or less important to different people.

With the associative argument and the ideas of identity and identification that it involves, the general proposal in support of associative political obligation is complete. It states that when both the objective and the subjective aspects of political identity occur for a polity that also manifests its generic value, then all conditions for political obligation are met. This is a very comprehensive and attractive proposal, carefully constructed and argued. If, according to the above defense, the elements of the associative argument are as decisive as they seem, and assuming that the problems with the value and membership arguments do not arise, then we have a persuasive and promising account of political obligation (meeting Horton's ambitions and even transcending them). It is here, however, that the anarchist challenge begins.

The anarchist challenge

Horton himself recognizes that the two aspects of the associative argument, the objective and the subjective, might come apart: people might alienate themselves from the polity they are objectively considered to be members of, which would make their membership contestable and political obligations problematic for them; or identification with their polity might be very weak, where obedient behavior might come out of habit and conformism but in fact reflect and result in apathy and political alienation.[62]

Philosophical anarchists detect both cases, even without reference to the two aspects of the associative argument. The general anarchist challenge has been that people tend to act as if they have political obligations and to believe they do because they find themselves in a social world functioning in these terms. Moreover, many people, like anarchists or immigrants, may reject their polity or citizenship and so separate themselves openly from what their particular status is expected to be. In terms of associative political obligations, membership, particularity, and identification come apart in these cases, and the anarchist argues that they do so in the case of most people within contemporary societies.

There is also another problem I want to indicate, preceding these difficulties. We saw that, being a reflection of the way the quality of institutions is a precondition for political obligation, the provision of order and security, the generic good of a polity, *should always be confirmed* as a precondition for the associative argument to work. We might accept that this good is enough to justify political authority and put aside the more demanding criteria of justice, fairness, freedom, and equality. Still, it might be the case that particular polities do not provide it and, more importantly, that alternative ways of securing this good have not been evaluated properly.

Returning to the associative part of Horton's defense, he himself finishes his argument by recognizing that, without reference to particular polities and their specificities, only very general features of membership and political obligation can be discussed and articulated. So the precise content and extent of political obligations cannot be decided at this level of generality in his theory. He is indeed right to insist that political authority is a normative concept and that its coercive aspect defines the content of political obligations, admitting further that speaking in terms of obedience to the law is not mistaken, even if he finds it limited.[63] Yet it is these factors that give ground to the critical philosophical anarchist to say that, empirically speaking, nothing can be proven as final for political obligation. Coercion, centralization, and exclusion, the whole spectrum of domination itself, cannot meet the ethical: the very nature of political authority is the obstacle to normative justification. Even if the phenomenology of association proves suitable for the latter, it is probably very unlikely that people will generally demonstrate all the attitudes necessary for the associative justification to succeed.

Horton accuses philosophical anarchists of bad faith: they criticize political obligation, belief in which is what sustains political societies, but still do not distance themselves from the reality of the state and the benefits it provides.[64] It is understandable that, within a world where the state is prominent, it is corrosive to deny the functionality of people's belief in political obligations—that they might have such obligations and that they matter. Nevertheless, a general moral justification of the existence of political obligation has not been given, and it does not seem possible. Until this changes, there is no good reason why a world where alternative social structures are cultivated should be undesired and unviable, and why, in such a world (or even in this world), moral criteria and moral obligations cannot play the role attributed to political ones, avoiding instability and chaos. Philosophical anarchists do not free themselves from participation in our political world and the responsibility this entails. Rather they remind us that the fact that we cannot easily do without the state should not discourage us from criticizing it and from the effort to try other possibilities. And this fact certainly should not encourage its sanctification.

The challenge from moral universalism

The belief in the existence and sharing of a general morality the criteria of which justify and define all action (personal, social, and political), or in the existence of a general moral perspective, is called "moral universalism."

In his 2007 article "Obligation by Association? A reply to John Horton," Richard Vernon argues that, in his effort to defend associative political obligations against philosophical anarchism, and rightly so, Horton risks handing them over to the camp of moral universalism. In the end, the latter is a more comprehensive view and can accommodate the phenomenology of associative obligation.[65]

In this section, I want to argue that moral universalism can indeed accommodate aspects of political morality more fully than Horton's associative theory and can facilitate the associative argument. Despite the philosophical anarchist claim that moral universalism does not support political obligation, however, critical philosophical anarchism is not incompatible with it. On the contrary, this anarchist view advocates a general morality that imposes more demanding criteria on theories of political obligation. As long as these theories do not meet the relevant criteria, any obedience is actually convergence with independent moral demands rather than deference to (morally justified) political authority. For anarchists this is not a problem, but for the defenders of political obligation it definitely is.

The first difficulty that Horton's theory faces, according to Vernon, is with the irreducibility claim.[66] According to this claim, associative political obligations are based on the importance of political membership and the particular relations that it involves, so they cannot be reduced to principles of general morality. Different ways of explaining this claim can be intelligible and acceptable, but they do not say much about the independent moral force of associative obligations. For example, it can be admitted that particular obligations do not contain only elements that can be understood in terms of, or derived from, general morality. Also, the "phenomenological jewel" of the associative thesis, as Vernon calls it, that "associative obligations do not require prior subjective acknowledgement of general principles by which they might be supposed to be supported," is true.[67] But these positions are compatible with the view that principles of general morality still underlie the existence and function of such obligations, constituting the criteria by reference to which these obligations are justified as particular standards representing those principles in different locales and conditions. Political acts are of the kind that needs to respond to justifiable principles. The real question, as Vernon puts it, is whether justification in terms of general moral principles and the phenomenology of the experienced obligations have to coincide. In reference to this central issue, Vernon goes on to examine two different situations that raise different questions. Where associative obligations coincide with universal ones, the redundancy issue arises against the latter, and where they do not, there is an issue about the independent force of associative obligations.

In the case of coincidence, the "independence" claim is used to support redundancy: it is the view that associative obligations might be consistent with principles of general morality, but the latter are not necessary for the strength of the former.[68] As Vernon points out, it is difficult to separate the cases and see exactly whether there is real independence and where it lies. The contexts of life are complex, multiple, and varied and could probably be captured better by the phenomenology of the associative account.

Nevertheless, there is something to be said about the power of general moral principles. Vernon describes the historical process through which local practices have come to converge with general principles as a slow, long, and rigorous process of election, a screening through which local practices have been approved by those principles and have come in later years to be applied without further appeal to them. He also refers to the conceptual reason of convergence, which has to do with the fact that local practices and general principles respond to similar considerations. This latter indicates the importance of principles in reducing the vulnerability of human beings to suffering, which is the principal consideration that guides judgments about locally valued practices. But the historical reason is even more crucial here. Pointing to the fact that local practices have acquired independence through a screening process selecting them according to the demands of civil equality validates even more the significance of general morality. Once more it verifies the anarchist approach: the importance of the anarchist insistence on the moral aspect of the problem of political obligation and on the necessity of filtering the institutions and practices of political authority. Particular practices and relations are central to political life, and the local nature of associative obligations is suitable for capturing this. Yet my point is that this latter observation offers no proof that general principles are not necessary to those obligations and that they cease to underlie independently applied practices. On the contrary, considerations concerning the reduction of suffering and the egalitarian constraints on partial concerns confirm the "triumph of public morality."[69]

In the case of conflict with principles of general morality, the issue is whether associative obligations can have any independent moral force. If the conflict leads to their cancellation, then these obligations are "subordinate, derivative or conditional" in character.[70] Horton's argument against this criticism is that, in the same way that principles of general morality might be cancelled by overriding considerations, yet without losing their moral weight, associative obligations can retain their moral force when cancelled by such principles.[71] In reply, Vernon wants to examine whether a parallel between the example of honor among thieves that Horton uses and the indicative example of the cancellation of promises can be successful. In the case where someone promises to perform a murder, the principle against taking a life voids the principle of promise-keeping, but this does not mean that the latter loses its moral weight. A thief who keeps faith with the arrangement he has made with his co-robbers is praiseworthy in this respect, despite the fact that morality rejects theft.[72] So particular obligations within such a group do not lose their value, even though the moral principle against theft cancels the value of the group. Vernon does not believe that this example establishes local obligation, however. The case of the promise-keeping murderer is one of "undermining" rather than of "overriding": the promise is no longer regarded as having moral weight; it is voided by the wrongful purpose of murder.[73] The parallel ends up having negative consequences for membership obligations, because in the same way that the weight of promises depends on the legitimacy of the purpose to which they are put, the weight of such obligations depends on how justifiable they are within general morality. In defense of associative obligations, the reply could be that the activity of promising does not lose its general moral force just because it is undermined in particular cases. The same goes for associative obligations: although they have no force in particular cases, they do not lose their general moral force. Yet Vernon is right to argue that such a response would lead to the opposite of the associative account. It would require a categorization that puts each of the associative obligations we wish to rescue as morally valuable within a general and morally sanctioned class analogous to that of promising. This would bring us back to the terrain of general morality. Thus, the last court of appeal seems once more to be the values of general morality, rather than the obligations of associative membership.

Equally important to the present discussion is an examination of the prospect of resolving conflicts between local obligations and general principles.[74] Associativism claims that when conflicts occur, neither local morality nor general principle decides the matter, but rather the two views stay separate. Then again, from the perspective of moral universalism, or of the view advocating the importance of general morality adopted here, and in the case of coincidence examined above, the local and the general may share common aims. One way of seeing how conflicts might be resolved is to recognize the importance of *grasping the general in the particular*. One attack on general morality would use partiality to present it as detached and inhuman when special obligations to particular people arise. When, for example, people shelter fugitives in a period of war, or protect their guilty children from the police, morality seems to require them to choose to not lie over saving those involved with them in that particular relationship. Thus it seems to discard and betray the importance of certain ties or the affective tone of special relations. Still, we can see that in those cases it is a sense of shared humanity or general compassion that moves the agents, and so what matters is the "humanity-in-proximity," not the particularity of the victim.[75] So the generalization involved within morality seems necessary to the local and particular, rather than opposed to it. It is through the capacity to generalize that we can capture the importance of specific acts and relations. Professional ethics are a good example: although there are special professional duties that define professional contact, we cannot separate ourselves as professionals from ourselves as whole persons. Professional obligations might be decisive in many certain cases, but, in the end, to play this role, they are "mediated by a process of [more general moral] reflection."[76] Such mediation can be transferred from professional to other relations, such as familial ones, and any special characteristic of such relationships can be integrated within morality. In the end, through generalization, mediation, and transference, we can see that conflicts can be resolved and answers given that include both the general and the particular, or better the particular as situated within the general.

The special strength of associative obligation theory, however, might be its ability to explain our special relationship to a particular polity. All the above might explain the content of obligation, that associative obligations are mediations of general morality. In order to account for political relationships, however, morality should be shown to establish local objects. The phenomenology of associativism seems to provide immediately the necessary element: associative political obligations are immediately attached to particular institutions. So the importance of particularizing obligations might still be a powerful tool in the hands of the defender of associativism.

Even in this respect, though, we have seen above that Horton's theory might face problems: the subjective and the objective aspect of the associative argument might come apart, it might prove difficult for that kind of phenomenology to account for the precise content and extent of political relationships, and, in the end, the theory does not bring particularity, membership, and identification together to form a complete justification (see the discussion of Horton's positive arguments in the section "Horton's constructive account of associative political obligations and the anarchist challenge", especially the subsections "The associative argument" and "The anarchist challenge").

The final argument that can be added here regarding the problems of associative theory arises when we examine both the locality and the obligation aspect of local obligation. Locality is important and it is necessary for any theory of political obligation to provide ways of accounting for it. This study shows that no theory has succeeded in this respect so far. Horton's theory might not be based on the ambition for a complete justification, but Vernon is right that the establishment of its reasonableness is not enough for obligation: the middle ground this theory occupies by advocating that we should give way to the demands of our associations—instead of our personal judgment that philosophical anarchism insists on or the universalist claims of a general morality—is only conditional.[77] This is the conclusion of all the above arguments in this section. The other aspect of establishing local obligation, the obligation aspect, is even more indicative of these shortcomings. Horton's theory bases obligation on the fact of shared convictions about its existence. That others endorse certain beliefs might be a consideration to take into account, but it is not a reason good enough for one's own belief and for any moral obligation attached to it. As we have seen above, such considerations have moral weight only by reference to an underlying general morality that provides the final justification.

According to Vernon, Horton's theory cannot provide the ground for avoiding the critical philosophical anarchist demand for independent personal evaluation. Only a theory based on moral universalism has such hope. The examination of the above arguments leads us to the conclusion that he is right. Specifically, associative obligations can be accommodated by a universalist moral theory, which can deal better with the problems that associativism is proposed to solve. Yet Vernon sees philosophical anarchism as the complete opposite of moral universalism and as a view to be avoided. In completing this section, it is this part of his argument that I want to oppose. Critical philosophical anarchism is not inconsistent with moral universalism. To insist on personal evaluation does not exclude the existence and adoption of a general morality to which one can appeal when applying personal judgment. Critical philosophical anarchism argues that, so far, moral universalism does not entail political obligation, and this is the main reason why the latter lacks justification. The task that Vernon believes defenders of the state have is the same task demanded by the anarchist. At this point we can agree that Horton's theory does no better in meeting this demand than the previous theories examined in this study.

Concluding remarks: The value of Horton's associative theory

The preceding presentation of Horton's associative theory of political obligation leads to certain conclusions about its value.

Horton's arguments establish the reasonableness of his associative theory. It is plausible and acceptable that we conceive, understand, and explain political obligations in terms of our membership in a particular polity. The merit of this account is that it is a very direct and pragmatic proposal. It starts, in a classical manner, by indicating the danger of conflict and the importance of security and order. It simply says that, as far as they provide this good, we are obligated to our polities in *so many* ways, those that the phenomenology concerning our observed political behavior and our beliefs shows. So instead of moving toward more holistic, metaphysical, or demanding explanations, we should take that as a sign of the existence of political obligation and explain it on the relevant grounds. It is more than enough to appreciate the value of our existing political experience and try to make it more intelligible to ourselves and others.

This picture is quite appealing. It represents a philosophy that is connected to everyday life and respects the history and values of our political experience. It is a form of empirical philosophy that makes use of and provides practice for the qualities, roles, attitudes, relations, and interrelations appearing and characterizing the political canvas of most contemporary societies. It also recognizes the demand to satisfy the argument about the quality of political institutions, which is a precondition for any account of political obligation.

Nevertheless, as demonstrated through the preceding arguments, it is not a complete and compelling theory of political obligation. The phenomenology of membership and identification alone does not have the normative significance that the debate of political obligation requires and Horton himself recognizes.[78] It is necessary for the general moral values that provide the criteria for filtering political institutions and relations to underlie this and every similar account. Moreover, the strongest element of the associative argument, its ability to satisfy the demand for particularity, does not prove so effective. Even this explanation of political relationships, with its descriptive and empirical as well as normative character, lacks the specificity necessary to determine the content of political obligations. Much depends on the traditions, values, and institutions of each particular polity, which philosophy cannot say anything about in detail to a very great extent. However, the generalization that characterizes philosophical thinking does not lose its significance here, since it provides the critical distance necessary for an appropriate evaluation of our political practices, relations, and lives, a generalization that the account examined at present does not seem qualified to provide.

Nonetheless, Horton's associative theory can be appreciated in another important way. At this point we can see its relation to the anarchist ideal of legitimacy, which comes hand in hand with the anarchist demand for a moral evaluation of the normativity of political institutions and provides the horizon for such an evaluation. Along with the values of freedom, equality, justice, and fairness, we can consider now the values of membership and identification. In examining the principle of fairness, participation was appreciated as a central value and practice within social and political life. This kind of involvement is also demonstrated within the theory of associative political obligation. The additional elements of belonging and a sense of identification with our polity as well as of the importance of our role as citizens in the construction of our personal identity supplement this picture. They give us a better idea of what it is to build a personality and different roles within the social world we inhabit and of what responsibilities this generates. Horton's reminders of the different ways we are obligated to our states constitute a useful picture of the ways our citizenship can be realized, corrected, and developed, whether there is a general political obligation or not. Our existing attitudes and beliefs and our existing relation to a particular polity cannot alone ground a theory of political obligation. Still, the associative account includes a description of political experience, relations, and responsibilities that any standard for the evaluation of political reality must take into consideration. Thus, it provides valuable elements for the anarchist ideal of legitimacy and, more generally, for the perspective on political institutions and the new outlook on what is "political" that the anarchist criticism urges us to adopt.

Notes

1 See Horton, *Political Obligation*, Chapter 6; John Horton, "In Defence of Associative Political Obligations: Part One," *Political Studies* 54 (2006); John Horton, "In Defence of Associative Political Obligations: Part Two"; John Horton, "Plural Subjects and Political Obligations," *Jurisprudence: AnInternational Journal of Legal and Political Thought* 4(2), (2013): 280–286; John Horton, "Political Legitimacy, Justice and Consent," *Critical Review of International Social and Political Philosophy* 15(2) (2012): 129–148.

2 See Horton, "In Defence of Associative Political Obligations: Part One," 428; Horton, "In Defence of Associative Political Obligations: Part Two," 2. He offers his theory as a justification "only in the weak sense" of showing such obligations not to be morally and philosophically objectionable in certain ways, of "showing the general intelligibility, moral reasonableness and plausibility of thinking in such terms" (Horton, "In Defence of Associative Political Obligations: Part One," 428). Yet, in his largely phenomenological approach, Horton recognizes the need for a positive account of political obligations (see Horton, "In Defence of Associative Political Obligations: Part Two," 17, n. 3). So, reformulated, his "principal aim is simply to show how the conception of associative political obligations [that he develops] provides an intelligible and plausible way of understanding political obligations within a modern state" (Horton, "In Defence of Associative Political Obligations: Part Two," 2).

3 See Richard Vernon, "Obligation by Association? A Reply to John Horton," *Political Studies* 55 (2007): 865–879.

4 Horton, "In Defence of Associative Political Obligations: Part One," 428.

5 See Horton, "In Defence of Associative Political Obligations: Part Two," 17, n.3. See also n. 2 above.

6 See Horton, "In Defence of Associative Political Obligations: Part One," 429; Horton, "In Defence of Associative Political Obligations: Part Two," 3, 5, and 10; Simmons, "Philosophical Anarchism," 249–252; Vernon, "Obligation by Association?," 865; Christopher Heath Wellman, "Associative Allegiances and Political Obligations," *Social Theory and Practice* 23 (1997): 181–204: they "obtain only among special associations" and "are neither explicitly agreed upon nor consented to" (Wellman, "Associative Allegiances and Political Obligations," 182).

7 This description is based on Vernon's summary of the associative view (see Vernon, "Obligation by Association?," 865).

8 Or the "communitarian theory" (Simmons, "Philosophical Anarchism," 261). For Horton's first reference to the two strategies, see Horton, "In Defence of Associative Political Obligations: Part One," 430. For his discussion concerning the first, see Horton, "In Defence of Associative Political Obligations: Part One," 430–433. For his discussion concerning the second, see Horton, "In Defence of Associative Political Obligations: Part One," 433–441.

9 See Margaret Gilbert, "Group Membership and Political Obligation," *The Monist* 76 (1993): 119–131.

10 See Ronald M. Dworkin, *Law's Empire* (Cambridge: Harvard University Press, 1986), Chapter 6.

11 For these criticisms, see Simmons, "Philosophical Anarchism," 256–260; for Horton's presentation of these criticisms, see Horton, "In Defence of Associative Political Obligations: Part One," 430–433.

12 See Horton, "In Defence of Associative Political Obligations: Part One," 431.

13 Simmons, "Philosophical Anarchism," 257.

14 Gilbert, "Group Membership," 126.

15 Simmons, *Justification and Legitimacy*, 95.

16 Horton, "In Defence of Associative Political Obligations: Part One," 432.

17 Horton, "In Defence of Associative Political Obligations: Part One," 433.

18 Simmons, "Philosophical Anarchism," 261–262.

19 Simmons, "Philosophical Anarchism," 264. For Horton's reply, see Horton, "In Defence of Associative Political Obligations: Part One," 434.

20 Simmons, "Philosophical Anarchism," 262.

21 Simmons, "Philosophical Anarchism," 266.

22 For these, see Simmons, "Philosophical Anarchism," 266; Horton, "In Defence of Associative Political Obligations: Part One," 435.

23 See Horton, "In Defence of Associative Political Obligations: Part One," 435.

24 Horton, "In Defence of Associative Political Obligations: Part One," 436.

25 See Dagger, "Membership," 110.

26 Simmons, *Justification and Legitimacy*, Chapter 5.

27 Horton, "In Defence of Associative Political Obligations: Part One," 438.

28 Horton, "In Defence of Associative Political Obligations: Part One," 438.

29 Simmons, "Philosophical Anarchism," 271.

30 See Horton, "In Defence of Associative Political Obligations: Part Two," 15.

31 See the section "The correlativity thesis" (on the correlativity thesis). See also, e.g., Raz, "Introduction," 2; McLaughlin, *Anarchism and Authority*, 54.

32 This point is stressed by Horton himself. See Horton, "In Defence of Associative Political Obligations: Part Two," 13.

33 For this, see also George Klosko, "Fixed Content of Political Obligations," *Political Studies* 46 (1998): 53–67.

34 Horton, "In Defence of Associative Political Obligations: Part One," 440.

35 Horton, "In Defence of Associative Political Obligations: Part One," 440.

36 See Horton, "In Defence of Associative Political Obligations: Part Two," 5.

37 Horton, "In Defence of Associative Political Obligations: Part Two," 5–7.

38 Horton, "In Defence of Associative Political Obligations: Part Two," 7.

39 Horton, "In Defence of Associative Political Obligations: Part Two," 5, 10–15.

40 Andrew Mason, *Community, Solidarity and Belonging: Levels of Community and Their Normative* (Cambridge: Cambridge University Press, 2000), 21.

41 Horton, "In Defence of Associative Political Obligations: Part Two," 5.

42 I draw these aspects of the definition of groups or associations from Keith Graham, "The Moral Significance of Collective Entities," *Inquiry* 44 (2001): 21–42.

43 Horton, "In Defence of Associative Political Obligations: Part Two," 6.

44 Horton, "In Defence of Associative Political Obligations: Part Two," 8. For a more detailed and extensive discussion of the Hobbesian argument, see Chapters 1 and 2 here.

45   Horton, "In Defence of Associative Political Obligations: Part Two," 8.
46   See correspondingly Green, *The Authority of the State*, 233; Stephen Utz,
     "Associative Obligations and Law's Authority," *Ratio Juris* 17 (2004): 304.
47   Horton, "In Defence of Associative Political Obligations: Part Two," 18, n.16.
48   Dworkin, *Law's Empire*, 200.
49   Horton, "In Defence of Associative Political Obligations: Part Two," 8–9.
50   Horton, "In Defence of Associative Political Obligations: Part Two," 9.
51   Horton, "In Defence of Associative Political Obligations: Part Two," 18, n.16.
52   Horton, "In Defence of Associative Political Obligations: Part Two," 10.
53   For these, see Alasdair C. MacIntyre, *After Virtue. A Study in Moral Theory*
     (London: Duckworth, 1981; second edition, with postscript 1985), 204–5;
     Horton, "In Defence of Associative Political Obligations: Part Two," 11–12.
54   Horton, "In Defence of Associative Political Obligations: Part Two," 4.
55   Horton, "In Defence of Associative Political Obligations: Part Two," 12.
56   Horton, "In Defence of Associative Political Obligations: Part Two," 12.
57   Horton, "In Defence of Associative Political Obligations: Part Two," 13.
58   Horton, "In Defence of Associative Political Obligations: Part Two," 13.
59   See the section "The correlativity thesis."
60   Horton, "In Defence of Associative Political Obligations: Part Two," 13.
61   For this, see Rogers M. Smith, *Stories of Peoplehood. The Politics and Morals
     of Political Membership* (Cambridge: Cambridge University Press, 2003),
     64–65.
62   Horton, "In Defence of Associative Political Obligations: Part Two," 14.
63   Horton, "In Defence of Associative Political Obligations: Part Two," 15. His
     criticism against the identification of political obligations with obedience to
     the law was discussed in the first part of this chapter (in the section "Against
     associative political obligations"), where Klosko's (and Raz's) view was
     supported in reply to this criticism. See also Horton, "Peter Whinch and
     Political Authority," for his understanding of political authority.
64   Horton, "In Defence of Associative Political Obligations: Part Two," 15–16.
65   Vernon, "Obligation by Association?," 866.
66   For this, see Vernon, "Obligation by Association?," 867–869.
67   Vernon, "Obligation by Association?," 868.
68   See Vernon, "Obligation by Association?," 870–872.
69   Vernon, "Obligation by Association?," 872.
70   For this issue, see Vernon, "Obligation by Association?," 872–874.
71   Horton, *Political Obligation*, 156–157; Horton, "In Defence of Associative
     Political Obligations: Part One," 437.
72   Horton, "In Defence of Associative Political Obligations: Part One," 438.
73   Vernon, "Obligation by Association?," 873.
74   Vernon, "Obligation by Association?," 874–876.
75   Vernon, "Obligation by Association?," 874.
76   Vernon, "Obligation by Association?," 875.
77   Vernon, "Obligation by Association?," 866–867, 877–878.
78   Horton, "Peter Whinch and Political Authority"; Horton, "In Defence of
     Associative Political Obligations: Part One," 429 and 437–438; Horton, "In
     Defence of Associative Political Obligations: Part Two," 3 and 15.

6

Where friends of political institutions and anarchists are in the same boat

In this chapter I collect together and elaborate on the results of the preceding discussion and demonstrate the value of critical philosophical anarchism within the debate on political authority. The aim of the chapter is to show the contribution that critical philosophical anarchism makes to evaluations of political institutions, arguing that, whether or not one is an anarchist, there is a distinctive and indispensable insight within this anarchist position. This insight should affect the framework of the debate on political obligation and be taken into consideration by other perspectives on the justification of political institutions.

In the first part of this chapter, I begin with a summary of the *negative points* of the anarchist criticisms of theories of political obligation found in each of the previous chapters. Then, I describe and analyze the *positive points* of these criticisms. I also anticipate the program of work that awaits political thought as a result of the challenge of critical philosophical anarchism. In the second part of the chapter, I provide the main analysis of the *contribution of critical philosophical anarchism*, especially as it is involved in the positive points of this position elaborated in the chapter.

Negative and positive points resulting from the anarchist criticisms

The negative conclusions

The *negative* conclusions as derived from the anarchist criticisms of different theories of political obligation above are as follows.

In Chapter 2, the anarchist critique showed that the voluntary undertakings of individuals, which constitute the core of consent and contract theories of political obligation, cannot be satisfactorily combined with the generality condition in a way that preserves the political nature of that obligation. The problem of agreement remains unsolved, and no version of voluntarism establishes a form of undertaking that actually binds individuals to the state to a sufficiently general extent. Thus, voluntarist theories fail to meet the basic conditions of a comprehensive account of political obligation. This failure is explained on the basis of their most central commitment.

The conclusion of Chapter 3 maintains that, while the Rawlsian natural duty of justice does not in principle violate the particularity condition of political obligation, it does not establish actual political obligation. The just character of an institution does not provide sufficient ground for such an obligation. While the demands of justice form moral criteria for the acceptability of institutional organizations, they are not derived from the essentially political nature of those organizations. But an acceptable moral defense of the authority of the state demands that political obligations derive from precisely that feature of public institutions.

The principle of fairness discussed in Chapter 4 fails to satisfy the generality condition of political obligation. This inadequacy is related both to the notion of active participation necessary to capture the essential rationale of the principle and to the idea of society as a scheme of social cooperation that the principle involves. Both these elements form distinctive proposals of the fairness account and make the principle theoretically attractive. Yet their detachment from real political circumstances disqualifies the principle of fairness as a general ground of authority.

Horton's associative account of political obligations is examined in Chapter 5 as an alternative view, which does not exactly fall into the category of complete theories of obligation. It is thus evaluated by different standards. Still, its examination confirms the continual failure to establish a complete justification of political obligation.

These conclusions show that there is no general political obligation and that critical philosophical anarchism provides a perspective from which the limitations of defenses of political obligation can be seen clearly. This viewpoint allows for an accurate exposition of the aspects in which each theory would have to be refined in order to account satisfactorily for political obligation. It also informs the theorist about deeper difficulties that such a demand for refinement designates, which are discussed in the rest of this chapter.

The positive conclusions

The *positive* upshot of the critical philosophical anarchist critique is reflected in its incorporation of *ideals of legitimacy* and, more importantly, in the *perspective* it proposes on approaches to political institutions and on our conception of political relations and lives.

As I claimed in the previous chapters, the anarchist ideals of legitimacy indicate what political societies must *not* be like, by corresponding to accounts of what a successful attempt to justify political authority would look like and by representing paradigms of political legitimacy that existing states must exemplify. They thus relate to both features of what Simmons offers as a more comprehensive part of philosophical anarchism.[1] The first feature is found in the different anarchist ideals themselves, which are offered as prior visions of the appropriate social relations that existing societies must realize in order to be legitimate. The collection of the moral ideas that have been derived from the anarchist criticism and shown to be indispensable criteria for morally acceptable authority, or social organization more generally, is already incorporated into ideal accounts of their actual and specific application within societies. The role of these standards in evaluating political institutions constitutes the best possibility for assessing their legitimacy. The second feature of the comprehensive theory of critical philosophical anarchism is found in the demand for a combination of the moral ground proposed by each theory with the four formal "conditions of political obligation" adopted in this study—namely generality, particularity, bindingness, and content-independence, which together express the nature of the political as presented in the four "theses on the political."[2] The debate on political obligation concludes that attempts at this combination are unsuccessful.

The arguments examined in this study provide three moral forms of the anarchist ideal of legitimacy. The first is *"the ideal of voluntariness."* It involves a recognition of the substantial role of voluntariness. That is, the ideal focuses on the conditions of free deliberation and choice as vital features of participation in the public sphere, which would establish a morally significant relation between political institutions and each of their subjects if they actually applied; it expresses in this sphere the political analogue of self-assumed obligation and free agreement (Chapter 2). The second is *"the ideal of justice."* It concentrates on the centrality of justice as a necessary feature of public institutions, which, in order to ground political obligation, must be represented in the specific practices of such institutions and characterize their particular interaction with their citizens; it must also be compatible with a degree of efficiency in order for these practices to be feasible and meaningful (Chapter 3). A third anarchist proposal of an ideal of legitimacy is found in *"the ideal of social co-operation."* This ideal depicts, as the most suitable implementation of actual and morally significant social relationships, a political community that exemplifies purely and effectively the characteristics and the spirit of a scheme of social cooperation. Such a scheme gives rise to a more fruitful conception of "the political," found especially in the horizontal relationships and the ethos of reciprocity, cooperation, and mutual aid among individuals that are its central features. Fundamentally, it reflects the value of voluntary participation (Chapter 4). This view of social relationships is enhanced by the (non-voluntarist, yet important) *"ideas of identification, membership, and association"* advocated in Horton's theory (Chapter 5). Meanwhile, in terms of the traditional defenses of the state, all these versions of the ideal preserve the demand that any defense of that kind should make clear that the four conditions of political obligation are satisfied.

The function of the anarchist ideals of legitimacy just described corresponds to two main aspects of the philosophical anarchist perspective itself, as reflected in the results of the anarchist critique presented above. This perspective imposes the satisfaction of the conditions of political obligation as a precondition for any theoretical defense of the legitimacy of political authority. This test concerns only the attempts to justify political authority and the existence of political obligation. Furthermore, in the moral requirements that it demands to be met by both defenses of the state and anarchist visions of stateless societies, the anarchist perspective finds moral principles that must be embodied in the actual and specific interactions that most characterize these social structures in order for them to be legitimate.

Voluntariness remains a desirable feature of a valid justification of authority. Most importantly, it is a valuable expression of the capacity for self-governance, that is, the ability, responsibility, and right of individuals to determine their own lives and act accordingly. The anarchist arguments in Chapter 2 indicate that the problem with theories that appeal to voluntariness is what these theories try to justify and their use of voluntariness for this justification: the desirability of voluntariness verified by the anarchist highlights the problematic nature of the notion and existence of political obligation. This, in turn, suggests that voluntariness be seen as part of an understanding of our public lives that calls into question appeals to a principled defense of authority, rather than as part of such a defense.

The recognition of the value of justice in Chapter 3 provides another part of a proper idea of what a satisfactory organization of public life might involve, one that also enhances equality. It thus accepts the appropriateness of the theoretical appeal to this ideal, yet highlights the shortcomings of accounts that make the justification of political authority the focus of social organization. Once more, the appeal to a desirable moral value results in the failure of defenses of political obligation and, in this, suggests a revision of our understanding of political relationships and lives. Significantly, the discussion of the principle of justice indicates more clearly difficulties that arise from the very nature of political constraints.

Finally, the idea of societies as schemes of social cooperation in Chapter 4 supplements the proposed revision of our view of the political with a comprehensive example of what political life understood in opposition to a principled appeal to authority would be like. Again, since existing institutions do not exemplify such schemes, a defense of their authority in terms of the principle of fairness becomes problematic. The idea of reconstructing social relations along these new lines, however, remains attractive, since it can perhaps be implemented *without* appeal to authority and the centralized functions of the state. This approach can be further enhanced by important elements of the membership and the associative argument examined in Chapter 5. Together all these aspects of the anarchist ideal represent and protect equal-liberty.

The question remains, however, whether anarchist social visions have better prospects as forms of public organization. This question is motivated by the thought that such visions are not offered as representations of legitimate political authorities, but rather of alternative forms of social life. Their legitimacy, then, might be established only on the basis of the suggested moral ideas and without satisfying the four traditional conditions that only an account of *legitimate political* authority needs to satisfy. It is interesting to examine whether anarchist social structures substantiate schemes of social cooperation of the kind that anarchist ideals of legitimacy exemplify, to examine, that is, whether anarchists can meet their own standards in defense of an alternative view of social life.

The value of the anarchist perspective and ideal of legitimacy is affirmed in that the moral ideas that they highlight as criteria of acceptable forms of social organization are derived from the anarchist criticism itself and constitute its positive features. They are the result of the arguments preceding the conclusions of each previous chapter, which were presented in order to be open to critical evaluation. The acceptability of these conclusions and the moral conditions they sustained as criteria then explains the acceptability of the anarchist perspective and ideal of legitimacy. The fact that the anarchist criticism is based on general intuitions about freedom, equality, justice, community, and the value of cooperation, and that the anarchist challenge reflects an insistence on the importance of these values, shows that this challenge aspires to moral reasons that everybody can accept. (Everybody except those who have extreme and dangerous views, like fascists.) In articulating acceptable moral beliefs, the substantial moral standards preserved by the anarchist perspective open the way for expressing suitably and perhaps addressing the motivations that underlie the problem of political obligation. These motivations constitute a worry on our part about suffering an unquestioned, unqualified, and unlimited imposition of political requirements and their consequences upon us, a worry that, in turn, gives rise to doubts about the very idea of being obliged in the first place and to a demand for an explanation and justification of such requirements.[3]

The point just stated depends on another central feature of the anarchist perspective. This is the position that, within the debate on political obligation, the relevant moral values cannot generate this obligation when they are offered in an abstract, theoretical form, nor when they are translated into general moral qualities and accomplishments of political institutions. Their respect within an account of appropriate social relationships can be shown only in a direct and particular application of them in our political reality. To the extent that this demand is not satisfied, defenses of political obligation fail. But such a position about the role of moral values within the debate on political obligation retains a further function. It suggests that, nevertheless, in their more general applications, these values continue to provide indispensable criteria for the acceptability of political notions, doctrines, and institutions. This observation redefines the tasks of political theorists. It provides the basis for a more informed, far-reaching, and comprehensive evaluation of constraints, one that transcends the boundaries of the debate on political obligation, although it is still motivated by it. For all these reasons, the anarchist insistence on a moral grounding of authority and on the seriousness of the failure of philosophical defenses of state authority becomes theoretically relevant and, perhaps, indispensable. These points provide the core of the evaluation of the contribution of critical philosophical anarchism advanced in this study and will be developed in the second part of this chapter.

The critical philosophical anarchist perspective and its adherence to certain ideals of legitimacy, as well as the new light under which they promote the relevant moral values, show that the accounts of the state examined earlier fail to prove that existing states respect the relevant moral ideas in the way the problem of political obligation demands. The anarchist criticism of the state rests primarily upon the following claim: all human beings must be treated as free and equal such that no one has, in principle, the right to decide for and command others. Therefore, only a form of ruling that satisfies the four conditions of political obligation, or that actualizes within particular interactions principles that express the recognition of the above moral ideas as generally acceptable moral reasons, would be legitimate.[4] Defenses of political institutions fail to meet these requirements. This presents a strong reason for questioning the possibility of their legitimacy.

The above claim expresses two central and related anarchist concerns, which give rise to the anarchist challenge. First, the anarchist focuses on freedom as an ideal and a characteristic of the status of human beings that cannot be compromised easily. In view of this ideal, political constraints remain a problem, even when they are necessary. If they are claimed to be necessary and legitimate, political institutions must prove to be so in terms of that very idea. They must provide a form of freedom that, even if different from the freedom belonging to human beings outside political structures, is equally substantive and valuable, a form that involves the capacity for self-preservation and a direct assertion of morality as responsibility and successful decision, which is freedom in its most basic form.[5] And they should apply it constantly in their practices and in their interactions with each and every one of their subjects. Furthermore, they should aspire to the kind of equal-liberty that makes freedom possible only if enjoyed equally by all.[6] Alternatively, political institutions must respect and concretize other values that are important enough to express a concern with compensating losses of freedom and equality, or the implementation of which can itself be seen as a promotion of equal-liberty, or compatible with it. Justice and community are such values, and they are stressed by the anarchist perspective and its ideals of legitimacy. But then the state must show steadily that it actually applies and preserves such values, in order to justify the constraints that it imposes. The problem of political obligation concerns one area where political institutions are shown not to do so. The anarchist stresses this failure and its importance. Still, such a demand on political institutions concerns wider justifications of constraints. The anarchist position within the debate on political obligation motivates a focus on more careful attempts in that direction.

Second, the anarchist concern with liberty, equality and other values is related to the fundamental anarchist concern with achieving appropriate social relations and highlights its importance. This fundamental concern can be expressed otherwise as a claim that anarchism is "about the quality of relations between people."[7] Anarchists do not worry merely about the problem of subjecting individuals to the interests or the will of other individuals. Rather, they see the "problem of subjugation," or *domination*, namely the problem of the subjection of one person to another, as primarily one "of the relations between one person and another," which, to be proper, should involve equal power, mutual respect, reciprocity, and fair cooperation.[8] In social reality this would be expressed properly only in the attainment of active, substantial participation, such that all members of a society see social affairs as their own and are in control of them.

The aspects of the anarchist perspective just analyzed incorporate and reflect a commitment to two fundamental anarchist arguments against political authority. The first concerns *self-government* and *participation*. The anarchist critique developed in Chapters 2 and 4 indicated that the voluntarism involved in consent and other attitudes of willing participation is a substantial expression of self-government. Self-government creates the proper conditions for individual self-realization and for proper relations between persons as free and equal agents. The enhancement of this capacity within social life is achieved by the cultivation and establishment of equal active participation, and this is why social structures must enable such forms of interaction. The voluntary commitment to and participation in social life becomes an actual and effective way for individuals to express their freedom and equality, to determine their own lives and social world on an equal basis, and to act on these determinations. Ideal, participatory ways of social interaction form a reminder of the kinds of demands that individuals have the responsibility to themselves and to one another to impose on their social world.

This argument relates to the second central argument involved in the anarchist position, the argument about the *undesirability of political constraints.* The philosophical anarchist criticism of political obligation indicates one aspect in which political institutions are defective: they do not function on the basis of a morally justified relationship with individuals. Indeed, this defect is rooted in the very nature of political constraints and draws attention to it. Although self-government might involve and indeed need constraints, it involves constraints that one puts on oneself—through the careful consideration, choice, and implementation of commitments that individuals themselves decide that can help build their personality and should determine their life—not external constraints. But political constraints have an exclusive and authoritative character. They establish a framework within which some are ruled by others. This opposes self-government and equality and constitutes inappropriate personal and social relations. The failure to ground political obligation on the basis of voluntary participation and ideal schemes of social cooperation that enhance individual responsibility and equal interaction highlights this defect. In turn, this defect initiates a different approach to political institutions. The fundamental moral values affirmed within the debate on political obligation have a central role to play here. They function as the criteria on the basis of which we can develop a new way of evaluating institutions. The general idea here is that political constraints need to be evaluated in view of their special character and its defects. This character makes them unable to meet the conditions of the relationship of political obligation. But it is compatible with an evaluation on the basis of the fundamental moral principles that their defenders claim that political institutions incorporate. This provides an alternative way of ensuring meaningful participation, given the absence of political obligation. It also initiates a more demanding kind of institutional evaluation. Significantly, it reflects the central claim of the anarchist position: *that it is very difficult for any state to be legitimate.* These points were already suggested in the previous chapters and will be fully elaborated in the second part of the present chapter.

  The negative and positive aspects of the anarchist critique are expressed more directly in the subversive campaign of philosophical anarchists.[9] That campaign's work is to demonstrate, through the criticism of the state, that the nonexistence of a general political obligation affects in general our thinking and acting in the public sphere. This is the immediate role of the anarchist criticism. Such criticism exposes the difficulties involved in attempts to defend political obligation, challenges our attitudes of obedience, and thus changes our view of our position in political society. At the same time, the anarchist perspective and ideals of legitimacy insist on a set of generally acceptable moral standards for us to adopt in order to conceive and apply adequately political ideals in an attempt to construct political institutions. Thus, they function as a principled reflection of the seriousness and the implications of an attempt to justify political authority. The anarchist position already cultivates the critical attitude suggested by its subversive campaign. This is the different attitude toward the activities, demands, and position of political institutions that the removal of a presumption in favor of obedience generates.[10] In addition, it already constitutes a strong basis for a deeper understanding and improved conception of our political relationships and lives. Yet to understand the ultimate strength of these aspects of the anarchist position, in fact the real extent of the effects of the anarchist enlightening campaign itself, we need to examine and understand the fundamental demands underlying them. This is the central rationale of my discussion of the contribution of the anarchist position over the course of this study.

We may conclude from the discussion of the negative and the positive points of the anarchist challenge that, within the debate on political authority, anarchism provides a constant awareness of the limitations of arguments for political authority, which entails the need for their refinement and, possibly, their complete abandonment, as well as a change in our attitude toward political society. In turn, this affects further justifications of constraints, and it must have an effect on *real* institutions.

The implications of the anarchist challenge for political thought and practice

In the next few paragraphs, I discuss the tasks of future approaches to political institutions, as these are suggested by the preceding discussion.

The anarchist perspective and its *ideals of legitimacy* must function as a shared normative horizon for both the defender of political institutions and the anarchist. The two opponents can then continue their dialogue on a better basis. They can challenge one another and criticize their own beliefs in a non-question-begging way. They will have to respect the conditions of political obligation that an account of political authority needs to satisfy. More importantly, they will have to respect the appropriate moral requirements as expressed in the relationships suggested by the ideals of legitimacy, moral requirements that are provided as the ultimate criteria for morally acceptable forms of social order.

Regarding *friends of the state*, the main effect of the argument from the anarchist perspective is that their victory against philosophical anarchism is not assured. It has been argued in their favor that the standpoint from which the state is criticized by the anarchist is unfairly biased.[11] Anarchists fail to shoulder any part of the burden of proof, demanding that friends of the state defend it against the anarchist critique while not demonstrating that they can solve more effectively the problems of social order and cooperation that worry those defenders. However, in the light of the results of the debate on political obligation, anarchists do not seem to occupy a privileged position unjustifiably. They can say in response that, by failing to take seriously some of the problems that form the core worry for anarchist theorists, defenders of the state have won an unstable victory. If they *did* take these criticisms seriously, they would have to do more by way of argument. The anarchist perspective involves an insight that every political theorist needs to share. It is this claim that I will elaborate in the rest of this chapter.

Thus, the anarchist position now at hand provides the philosophical claims that need to be taken more seriously by friends of the state and that determine how their efforts must be directed in the future as regards the problem of political obligation. It indicates how each theory of the state fails significantly to satisfy one or more of the four conditions of political obligation and how this violates the demands of central moral principles for a plausible account of political legitimacy. The arguments for political authority, then, need to be refined on the basis of the negative and positive conclusions of the anarchist criticisms applied to each. The defenders of the state might win a more stable victory, if they manage to reconstruct these arguments to meet the indicated demands. But the greatest value of these instructions lies in their more far-reaching implications for attempts to justify constraints, especially in what they tell us about the very status of political authority, which, in turn, may affect other areas where such defenses apply.

For *political anarchists* and with regard to *any political agenda espoused by philosophical anarchism*, on the other hand, the work to be done is to address the challenge advanced on the part of the defenders of the state. They should show that the social vision of political anarchism lives up to an ideal of legitimacy in a way that proves not only its desirability, but also its feasibility. This is the route for them to follow in order to show that they can refine their own accounts in accordance with the demands that they themselves raise. But this is not my task in this study. However, I will make attempts in this direction in the next chapter.

In both directions, the tasks of the theorist reflect an approach that is also the responsibility of every individual to adopt, affecting directly our position and behavior within social reality. The dialogue between defenders and anarchists is one that can be entered by the wider population, and its results will affect social life for us all.

The discussion of this study is based mainly on the first of the two directions in which the anarchist contribution can be demonstrated, to wit, on the significance that the position of critical philosophical anarchism might have for the evaluation and improvement of defenses of political institutions. The role of the discussion so far has been to provide a clearer view of the nature of the anarchist critique in order to derive the elements that characterize it most and that can be used for a more comprehensive evaluation of the anarchist contribution. These elements are (1) the anarchist perspective, especially as represented in the arguments about self-government, equality, and the evil of political constraints, and (2) the provision of ideals of legitimacy.

The contribution of critical philosophical anarchism

In the rest of this chapter, I provide an argument that elaborates on aspects of the positive side of critical philosophical anarchism as presented above (in the section "The positive conclusions"). This argument shows the steps through which the criticism of political obligation leads to a different and more radical approach to political institutions, and the way in which the anarchist arguments about self-governance, equal relations, and the undesirability of political constraints are combined with and underlie this process. My aim is to give a clearer demonstration of the implications of the critical philosophical anarchist perspective and thus of the positive role of the anarchist position and its contribution to evaluations of political institutions.

The anarchist perspective

The preceding arguments lead the critical philosophical anarchist to certain claims about the approach characterizing the debate on political obligation on the whole. The anarchist criticism I developed reveals that the moral principles that are offered as bases of political obligation are valid requirements. When they express general qualities that characterize political institutions, they provide important reasons for seeing these institutions as acceptable social structures (and this should be acknowledged by anarchists on the basis of the criticism, even if it runs counter to anarchist common sense). For political obligation to be established, however, such qualities need to be actually incorporated into the specific instances of interaction between individuals and their political institutions. This latter demand is shown not to be satisfied so far, and the results of the examination of defenses of political obligation express exactly this fact. This conclusion, in turn, affects our attitude toward political institutions.[12] Furthermore, and correspondingly, the critical philosophical anarchist offers ideal accounts of what social structures that incorporated the required relationships would be like, which can be used as standards for existing institutions to aspire to. The arguments from self-governance, equality, and the defects of political constraints play a central role in this discussion. My claim is that these aspects of the anarchist view comprise a unified position, which has been missed by approaches to the role of anarchism in the philosophical debate. I argue that this position reflects a very valuable perspective. It is this perspective that I attempt to defend in the rest of this chapter.

The aforementioned aspects of the anarchist criticism are the most important, because they reveal a deeper problem regarding the approach to the issue of political obligation characteristic of its defenders.[13] Take, for example, the approach of consent theorists.[14] As a representative defender of political institutions, the social-contract theorist focuses on the idea that justification should proceed from individuals, that political authority should be voluntarily accepted if it is to be binding. With this in mind, he concentrates on the need for political institutions and asks the question: which form of government would merit a duty to obey it? The idea of the contract is used to produce answers to this question. On the basis of an actual contract, the theorist aspires to say that, "because you *have agreed* to a certain form of government, it is therefore legitimate and you should obey it." On the basis of a hypothetical contract, the theorist wants to show that, "because from a position of equality (a 'state of nature' in the absence of government) and after careful deliberation you *would agree* to a certain form of government, it is thereby legitimate and any instances of this form should be obeyed."

The anarchist follows step by step the arguments in terms of different forms of consent and contract.[15] Actual consent would be a satisfactory justification of political authority, because it represents an actual connection of individual will with the conditions of political obligation. But it is hardly proven that this combination has ever been the case. That is, this form of consent has never taken place to a sufficiently general extent, either in a historical or in a personal form: there has very seldom been an original contract, the conditions of valid choice rarely take place in real life, and most of us have never had the experience of such a choice with regard to our relation to our governments. Moreover, when instances of tacit consent are offered as implicit though actual signs of consent, they either require detailed disclosure and specific application at the empirical level, which can hardly be generalized so as to acquire normative significance, or they are products of illegitimate inference. The implications for the commitment of future generations of the difficulties with all these forms of actual consent are quite obvious.

As an alternative, hypothetical consent constitutes a thought experiment. If it is taken to detect the possible results of our deliberations and perceive them as having literal implications regarding our obligations, this needs to be asserted as positively as the actuality of personal consent. It thus faces difficulties similar to those confronting the latter, as just explained above. If, on the other hand, it is taken as a heuristic device for detecting principled demands on reason, then it is hardly relevant to the concern with the actual, self-assumed acquisition of obligations characteristic of the voluntarist tradition. Such a heuristic device works as a moral route of conception of what ought to be a subject of agreement, and agreement ceases to work as a literal expression of voluntary undertaking. The result is that it can be valuable when used as a framework for testing the legitimacy of principles for existing institutions on the basis of individuals' capacity for self-governance, but not as a way of motivating political obligations in the first place. According to this understanding, the idea of reasonable agreement as the subject matter of contractualism functions as a heuristic device for the formulation of legitimate moral principles. The latter might next apply to existing political institutions, as they actually function and develop, and determine their acceptability.

The perspective of hypothetical contractualism gives a new direction to the role of the social contract in relation to political institutions. The aim is not to prove a general obligation to obey the law, but to find and justify principles. This form of contractualism does not see its role as arguing for actual obligations. Actual obligation could only result in the (improbable) case of absolute coincidence between actual institutions and ideal principles. In general, it is a matter of practice: of whether the form and activities of actual institutions provide a proper application of legitimate principles, which requires these institutions to interact with their citizens, who are able to change them if they do not satisfy their demands. Therefore, contractualists who make this use of the hypothetical contract,[16] in contrast to those who use it as a basis for obligation, are immune to the anarchist accusation that their starting point is illegitimate. Instead of saying that we need political institutions to escape a state of war, as the voluntarist defenders of political obligation argue,[17] they say that we have institutions anyway and must decide what to do with them. A hypothetical reasonable contract is, in their hands, a form of reasoning applied when we examine the legitimacy of the activities of political institutions from within and apart from an establishment of their bindingness. It functions only within the scope of the *content* of legitimacy. This approach presupposes the fundamental question about the *existence* of legitimacy that concerns the anarchist. Still, this question is a neglected yet distinct (although not totally independent) and legitimate philosophical concern to be examined on its own merit.

Hence, the overall result of the above considerations is that voluntarism establishes no general political obligation. These conclusions lead us to the deeper problem with the defenders' accounts. Take the hypothetical-contract theorists: the problem lies in that their use of the idea of the hypothetical contract connects directly the existence of coercive structures with their bindingness in one and the same move. Acceptability and obligation become through contract two inseparable parts of such methods of defense. For theories of actual consent, this is not a real problem. Due to its actuality (and as characterized by the conditions of validity presented in Chapter 2), this form of consent would succeed in connecting existence, legitimacy, and obligation in one move if and whenever it took place: regular actual consent to governments would make them both acceptable and obligatory. Yet actual consent theorists might be taken to join other defenders of political obligation in missing the point that, as I explain below, anarchism tries to stress. For they too start from the idea of consenting to *already existing*

forms of political institutions, failing to take seriously the *constant* demand
for their justification.

Returning to the problematic method of defense of hypothetical-
contract theorists, their argument goes like this: defenders take it that, if
one can show that from a position of equality (depicted in the procedure of
reasoning represented by the contractualist device of agreement) we would
choose (contract to) a certain form of government, which therefore *merits
existence*, then we should *obey* a government that takes this form. They start
from the idea that we need institutions in order to escape an undesirable
state of endless conflict, instability, and danger. They aim to demonstrate
how we can get out of this situation as quickly as possible, in order to show
that what are good reasons for escaping it provide a basis for considering
the alternative state of political organization necessary and thus obligatory.
Good ideas about how to avoid a state of war are provided as good reasons
for obligation to the political alternative.

This approach conflates two separate questions. The first question is this:
*what principles should a government be bound by in order for its existence
to be morally justifiable?* This is a question about *acceptability*. The second
question is this: *do we have a duty to obey such forms of government?* This
is a question about *obligation*. The perspective of these political theorists is
one that conflates these two different questions and deduces an answer to
the second from an answer to the first. That is, good reasons for abandoning
the state of nature become in their eyes principles of acceptability that also
bind individuals to the form of government that satisfies these reasons.
Thus they take it that, by giving some answer to the question of justifiable
existence, they also prove the existence of political obligation. The issue
thus becomes an explanation of the acquisition of political obligation, not
of "the very possibility of obligations."[18]

But should this be so? Does not collapsing two distinct questions obscure
the significance of each of them? The importance of the anarchist arguments
and their results is primarily that they reveal the effects of this conflation and
of the obscurity it creates for the debate on political institutions. The results
of the anarchist criticism of voluntarist theories of political obligation reflect
exactly what is missing in their approach: the failure of all forms of contract
to ground political obligation on the very idea that they adopt shows that
in fact they have taken too much for granted. From the anarchist point of
view, defenders of political institutions proceed from *an inadequate starting
point. They assume what they should seek to prove.*

The anarchist instead separates the two questions and gives proper
attention to the way a fundamental question underlies each of them. The
question to be asked is not whether from a position of equality we would
or would not contract to a form of political institution, in order to show
it to be acceptable and on this basis obligatory. Rather, the fundamental
question is whether we should have institutions at all: what contract would

we make regarding the existence *or not* of political institutions if we started from a position of equality?[19] This question lies at the heart of the anarchist position. In the case of political obligation, it can be translated as a question about the very possibility of such an obligation. It is this question that the anarchist criticism of theories of political authority vindicates. Hence, the anarchist enters the political debate with a *unique perspective*. In the following two sections I analyze the process that grounds these claims.[20]

To an extent, this argument coincides with Simmons's view that the task of justification of the existence of political institutions, which is also challenged by the anarchist, is different from the task of justifying political obligation and that the defenders usually commit the mistake of collapsing the two.[21] But my argument does not advance this distinction and my aim is to transcend it and show that the anarchist aims are unified. In fact the challenge to the very existence of political institutions is the most characteristic anarchist position, although not the one obviously shared by all forms of anarchism. As explained in the introduction of this study, it is the challenge to the authority of the state, namely to political obligation, that is shared directly by all anarchists. In echoing Simmons's distinction at this point of the argument, I want to specify the different aspects of the evaluation of political institutions that philosophical anarchism helps notice and clarify (it is the distinction between different kinds of evaluation that I share with Simmons, as becomes obvious in my arguments in Chapters 1–5). But my final position is that the anarchist challenge to the acceptability of political institutions and the anarchist challenge to political obligation are linked in such a way that they show the anarchist position to involve a consistent and unified perspective, and that the distinctions observed by the anarchist are part of, rather than an obstacle to, this effect.

The significance of the question of obligation

The anarchist criticism shows that by focusing, through the device of the hypothetical contract, on good reasons for creating political institutions—qualities, such as justice, or their accomplishments, such as the provision of valuable goods—the defender does not prove the relationship needed for political obligation. He does not create a moral basis that characterizes the particular interaction between each and every individual and the institutions that govern the society where these individuals live. He merely provides reasons for wanting them when these institutions have these qualities. This would generate political obligation only if such qualities were constantly proven to be translated into the specific practices of institutions and their interactions with each and every citizen. So the defender fails to prove general political obligation. This is reflected in the way each theory, other than contractualism, fails to meet the four conditions characteristic of the nature of the organizations they are offered to support. Once he enters the debate on political obligation, the defender needs to understand this criticism and adopt this perspective on the problem, in order to address it properly. These considerations, as explored in Chapters 2–5, provide a detailed way of advancing the anarchist complaint that the arguments of the defender of political obligation are based on previous, unproven assumptions about our basic moral duties and the best way to discharge them.[22]

This problem is related to the special nature of political constraints, as indicated by the anarchist argument about their undesirability. They are permanent, exclusive, and authoritative. They involve the kind of domination, centralization, and hierarchy that are characteristic of a situation where some are ruled by others. They *are* the external constraints that define relationships of unequal power and subordination. That they can be evaluated on the basis of moral virtues that they display shows their existence to be defensible. But it shows only this. It does not show that they stand in a legitimate relationship with their citizens. And it does not show that they can be justified once and for all. Rather, the limited defense that their very nature allows reveals the defects of political institutions and the difficulty their defects create for their justification. It is the character of justification appropriate to them and the limitations of their justification that the anarchist criticism indicates.

The result of the defenders' failure to ground political obligation is that institutions lack a very central feature of their existence, namely the special relationship that should characterize their coexistence with individual citizens. This result has an immediate influence in changing our attitude to our position in political reality, and thus it already affects significantly political institutions, an influence indicated mostly by the anarchist subversive campaign, as explained by philosophical anarchists themselves.[23] But through this influence it also motivates a further question: how can institutions, even if we still need them, exist and function when they lack any special relationship that characterizes them as political? Because to *issue directives*, *coerce*, and *be obeyed*, which the justification of political obligation would give them the right to do, *is* to be political. This question becomes the first sign of how the challenge to political obligation might translate into a more general challenge to political institutions. If political institutions lack the relationship of political obligation, why are they not seen as perhaps desirable yet optional social organizations? And if their political nature (especially their permanent, monopolistic, and centralist character) does not allow them to be so, why have them at all? These considerations throw light on an argument about how the question of political obligation generates a challenge to the existence of political institutions. The anarchist criticism presses the defender to account for the very possibility of political obligation, and the results of this perspective vindicate a doubt about the very possibility of political institutions themselves. The question we begin to ask is *whether there is anything at all about political institutions that merits our support*. Below I explain this argument.

In attempting to justify the existence of political institutions, the defender is on the same terrain as the anarchist: he accepts that the necessity of political institutions needs to be proven and sets out to provide arguments for exactly this. In the way in which he develops his arguments, however, he does not address what he means to address. Through the arguments from the state of nature, for example, the defender demonstrates merits of the institutions that make them desirable, but he does not depict their defects too. We can already observe this in the case of classical contractualists: Hobbes argues that the state solves the problems of conflict and coordination that the state of nature creates. For Locke, people in the state of nature fail to know what the moral laws demand, and when they know it they fail to enforce it, so they need the state. For Rousseau, they come to a situation where natural freedom cannot be secured anymore and where a higher kind of freedom is needed, which can be established only in civil society.[24]

Thus the defender does not account for the fact that in themselves constraints are undesirable—they take away freedom and create relations of unequal power—and thus the merits that might motivate them need to be considered in the light of this defect. They need to be considered in the light of situations that lack constraints and to be constantly asserted. Characteristically, in his approach, the defender fails to present what a genuine pre-social situation would be like. Nor does he present fairly in the state of nature the nonpolitical, social alternatives in terms of equally important merits that they might involve, nor compare political institutions to them in view of such merits. Ultimately, there is no proof, no conclusive explanation on the part of the defender that the state of nature ends up in a state of war. The anarchist is justifiably invited to prove whether social order and cooperation would be possible in the absence of coercive structures. Yet, it is indicative that the arguments of the defender of the state, characteristically in game theory, preclude this possibility, rather than explain the failure by taking into account both the difficulties and the advantages involved. Defenders have not yet provided a convincing explanation for why political institutions are the only viable and desirable solutions. For example, the descriptions of the problem of scarcity and of human motivation in the imaginative state of nature are presuppositions of the theorist that favor the state, rather than explanations of universal facts or universally accepted beliefs about the human situation. Descriptions that are favorable to nonpolitical solutions are excluded for no decisive reason.[25] Quite importantly, this is rooted in traditional theories (for example, in how Hobbes failed to use his methodology of the hypothetical contract correctly) in a very basic way (although Hobbes attempted to avoid this failure and did better than others on this): these theories depicted in the state of nature aspects of human behavior that are more the effects of socialization, of institutions as we experience them, and of what becomes "natural" within them, than a pre-social situation; they added to it more facts about human nature than they should have.[26] Only a clear view of what a pre-social situation would be like could lead to valid conclusions about political institutions. Such a view would throw light on both their merits and their defects. Even if anarchists might also make their own assumptions under the influence of socialization, their views are by their own character more likely to facilitate a proper description of a neutral situation.[27]

The defender addresses only those who have learned to need and desire political institutions anyway. To ask accurately how things would be *without* institutions entails going beyond the hypotheses we make about political institutions when we are already affected by them and trying to see what is really natural. The assumptions of the defenders fall short of this. The fact that they focus only on the merits of institutions and not also on their defects reflects this weakness. These failures are already represented within the debate on political obligation itself, by the failure of theories of this obligation to transform general qualities into specific interactions. In the end, what the defender's argument really achieves is to show that, once we are convinced that we need them, political institutions can sustain this conviction, and it presumes that they merit it once and for all. Instead, the anarchist demands that the defender do all that is required from him once he enters the terrain of the justification of political institutions. In this respect the anarchist perspective must be shared by every theorist. In the debate on political obligation this demand becomes explicit, and, I argue, this helps redirect the defender to the proper approach.

Political obligation is a relationship that is normative, enduring, and exacting. An adequate defense of it overrides ideas merely about what we have and what it would be good for us to do. It concerns the difficulty of particularizing the relationship of government through an actual relation to political practices on the part of the individuals affected by them. This process extends beyond a demonstration of the merits that certain forms of political order might initially have.[28] Some defenses of political institutions, which are central to political philosophy, move on too quickly. It is to these that I am concerned to apply the anarchist perspective. We should see the role of the anarchist not in a tendency to refute each and every evaluation of the state, not as adopting the position of the skeptic and waiting for offers to reject. There are evaluations of governments, those that do not examine the problem of political obligation and do not attempt to motivate their existence in the first place, that might preserve the possibility of a satisfactory account. But the role of the anarchist is significant in his addressing only those who engage with the fundamental worry represented by the anarchist skepticism and in his saying that the relevant theorists have not confronted the implications of such an endeavor.

When the defender claims that we need the state as an exit from a state of war, he enters a territory that involves a very demanding approach. He invites the question of the very possibility of institutions, thus embarking on the anarchist boat. Once he embarks on the anarchist boat, he cannot leave it easily. When the theorist claims to defend political obligation, he undertakes the task of establishing whether or not there can be such a bond. But the form that his claims take shows that he has dismissed in one impatient move a worry that does not go away. *Rather than adopt the assumption that we need political institutions, and then try to assert their merits and derive our obligation from them, he needs to deal with the prior question of what it is that institutions demand of us and whether these demands can themselves be justified.*

By showing that the theories of political obligation do not establish the particularity that would guarantee the ideal of active participation, the anarchist criticism indicates that political institutions lack, in one fundamental way, the ability to generate and protect this important practice. This is already a defect and, in turn, it reveals and advances a fundamental demand: the real challenge is to show whether political institutions are any answer at all to the concern with proper relations within social life. For this purpose, moreover, it is not satisfactory to show them to be good enough as the most directly available social possibilities. Theorists are invited to realize that they should start to view political institutions as minor evils, as possible solutions to social problems that nevertheless create their own problems and thus remain disputable.

The anarchist argument about the importance of self-governance and equality plays a crucial role in supporting this approach. The capacity to determine their life on equal terms and to act on self-imposed constraints is indispensable for the survival of and proper relations between individuals. Within social life, it can be realized and expressed through equal active participation on the basis of full political, social, and economic equality. The absence of political obligation under any comprehensive account of it indicates the absence of such participation within existing political societies. The main defect of political institutions is that their dominative character establishes and cultivates exactly the kind of relations that make self-government and the presupposed equal active participation impossible: those who rule participate actively and determine the constraints imposed on them and on others (along with the exclusive enjoyment of other benefits). Those who are ruled do not participate and suffer external constraints. That institutions do not function on the basis of morally justified political obligations opens the way for us to see what they seriously lack: the kind of participation that activates self-governance and equality and the relations of equal power that this presupposes. This is a pressing problem to take into consideration when we try to evaluate them.

The anarchist perspective applies to the other theories of political obligation, of which theories of hypothetical consent have been used here as a representative example. Defenders of the state who implement the criterion of justice and the idea of reciprocity involved in the principle of fairness, as well as the idea of membership in an association, take the existence of institutions for granted and rush to base the legitimacy of certain forms of them on their preferred moral ground, whether justice, fairness, or association.[29] Theorists infer a perspective of legitimacy by asking what are the principles for institutions that are just or fair or protective of our identity. They deduce obedience from the justice- or fairness- or association-based general character of the forms institutions might take. But anarchist arguments against these theories show that success is far from secure, and that this does not lie in the falsity of the criteria chosen, but in the very thing that is supposed to be defended on the basis of them, to wit, in political obligation. First, general ideas about the character of political institutions cannot base a special relationship to them. Second, even when such arguments base certain claims about the desirability of political institutions, the results of the debate on political obligation show that, in the way these claims are promoted, they cannot decide the existence of political institutions and motivate their acceptability once and for all. In contrast with the perspective of such defenses of political institutions, the anarchist makes the question whether we need institutions at all a persistent demand and appeals to consent, justice, fairness, or membership to solve *this* problem.

Justification as an endless process

The anarchist insistence on the question of obligation shows that, even if a theory proves the state to be justified once, the task of justification does not end here. This is a crucial feature of the anarchist perspective, concomitant with the primacy of the question of obligation that this perspective suggests. It is in this respect that, under the influence of the anarchist position, the debate on political obligation puts *any* justification of political constraints on a new basis. This is a point already involved in the preceding argument. My aim here is to highlight its special force within that argument.

The anarchist may grant that the defender has given a good reason for creating political institutions, that they help us avoid serious social problems (for example, by bringing criminals to justice or by providing healthy environments and stimuli to poor and/or abandoned children), and this can outweigh their defects. But this justification is limited by the very fact that it is given only once. Since the defender grounds the state on the basis of certain values—such as peace and security, justice and fairness, and ultimately equality and freedom itself—he should also be able to render an account of it whenever it violates these values. The moment when institutions threaten the values with regard to which they are first proved to be acceptable, their validity ceases. It is this possibility of *illegitimate constraints* that concerns anarchism most. It is their presence that undermines the quality of relations between people, which is the focus of the anarchist challenge in the first place. This means that *the demand for justification is constant.*

The way in which the anarchist attention to illegitimate constraints is advanced through the question of political obligation helps vindicate this demand. Political obligation requires an actual relationship the particular aspects of which need to be constantly affirmed, applied, and renewed. The question of obligation is distinctive and valuable in that it arises at every point. This throws light on the fact that, in a similar manner, the anarchist attention to illegitimate constraints makes the need for justification persistent more generally. Constraints are not desirable in themselves. They always take something away. External constraints suppress our ability to determine our own lives. They remove our autonomy. So they need to be continually defended in terms of the values they are held to be protecting, to counterbalance what they take away, and thus to respect our status as reflective human beings. In this way, they become compatible with the situation appropriate to persons, namely as beings determined by self-imposed constraints. This is an alternative way of ensuring active participation. Political institutions must always be viewed as evils, even minor ones: they might help us to avoid certain social problems, but they continue to create their own, the unaccountable imposition of which needs to be guarded against. The moment they cease to fulfill their duties, they are no longer wanted. They simply limit our ability to determine our own lives, and thus they exist on the basis of inappropriate interpersonal relations. The defender of political institutions might say that there are mechanisms for testing their activities. But it is here that the anarchist has the privilege of pressing the interrogation further, of insisting that the theorist should bear this in mind and apply the test regularly. It is then that all theorists must realize that they have not engaged sufficiently with the process of justification and that the work that awaits them is not easy. Once you embark on the anarchist boat and you want to complete the journey, you have to remain in it as long as the destination requires.

At this point, it might be helpful to summarize the process through which anarchism contributes to the debate on political obligation and raises a new demand with regard to the justification of political constraints. In the process of providing arguments against accounts of political obligation, the anarchist establishes a context within which opposing claims about our relation to political institutions are weighed against each other. The result of this dialogue, as derived from the anarchist criticism, is that no defensible principle of political obligation can be reasonably accepted, and thus so far there is no general political obligation. This alerts the defender of the state, not only concerning the failure of his account, but also to the very instability of the aim to establish constraints in terms of political obligation. The failure of any general principle of political obligation to heed the moral criteria that the defenders of the state use and that anarchists themselves stress is alarming. The instability of defenses of political obligation that this failure reveals highlights the importance of confronting the fundamental question whether we should have political obligation at all: the result of anarchist criticism reveals the difficulty of defending political obligation and shows that "[o]bedience remains as much in need of justification as disobedience."[30] This, in turn, redirects us to the fundamental question that motivates the anarchist in the first place. Thus the anarchists' demand, implicit in their criticism at the outset, to understand the real implications of this question for political institutions and to ask it properly comes to the fore. The arguments of the defenders of political obligation and the counter-arguments of anarchists need to be assessed in this light. Having in mind the fundamental question about the very possibility of political institutions, the philosophical anarchist does not neglect, but rather concedes, the demand that anarchists provide and defend their own ideas and social alternatives. The prior picture of ideals of legitimacy is offered in interaction with (political) anarchist replies to this demand.

Also, the anarchist criticism confirms that the moral criteria used in accounts of political obligation are not themselves flawed. Voluntariness, justice, fair participation, and association survive the failure of these accounts. This motivates the idea that they can continue to be used in further attempts to decide the nature of our social relationships. These criteria are demands that *cannot be reasonably rejected* by, and thus are appealing to, the rest of us. They thus retain their validity as standards within the very process of argumentation, during which different reasons interact toward a delivery of a common basis of justification with regard to the problem of political obligation. In other words, they can be seen as general principled conditions within the framework of the debate. As I explain in the first part and in the following paragraphs of this chapter, these criteria constitute central elements of ideals of legitimacy that are implicit in the anarchist perspective and motivate the anarchist criticism from the beginning. The anarchist enters the debate with a positive and comprehensive view of the demands it involves (and this remains the anarchist's own proposal, whether or not the rest of us would agree to adopt these criteria). Furthermore, and importantly, the anarchist criteria can apply as tests in any further justification of constraints, still in the light of the implications of the debate on political obligation. Even if it is proven that the existence of political institutions is necessary, which does not mean that the question of obligation is answered, this necessity is not firm and such moral requirements may still be applied in deciding the forms of imposition that are enough to motivate it. As argued here, theorists cannot build their defenses on the basis of a presupposition that we need political institutions, because the relationship of political obligation overrides demonstrations of institutional merits. Thus a proof that we need institutions does not establish that the relationship of government is justified (i.e., that we have general political obligation), nor that we need them once and for all. It rather raises the demand that, in the absence of such justification, every form of institutional constraint needs to be motivated regularly in terms of legitimate principles or other applications of moral conditions. The demand for justification remains constant. In the face of the importance of the question of obligation and the failure to answer it, which the anarchist challenge establishes, as well as of what this shows about the character of political constraints, it becomes more pressing and more difficult for the defenders of any operative forms of imposition—institutions, laws, and policies—to address this demand.

Hence, there is a way in which everyone should start from the anarchist question: what is the point of having political institutions and what is it that they demand of us? From this we should pressingly ask on a regular basis whether our institutions are justified in terms of certain values.

In the direction of anarchism itself, contemporary endorsements of anarchist political action involve this realization: the anarchist attempt to accomplish social reconstruction is an *endless struggle*. The creation of alternatives to dominative, hierarchical, and exploitative social relations does not exclude the possibility of the re-emergence of dominative patterns within these very sites of social reconstruction. Since there is no guarantee that the will to possess power and all human tendencies for domination and exploitation can be eradicated even within favorable social conditions, the resistance needs to be restless and constant. As Uri Gordon indicates, "the inherently diverse and voluntary nature of the anarchist project leaves it necessarily open to change and challenge from within."[31] However, this very nature is genuinely liberating, so its continual proliferation is in itself the answer for overcoming these entrenched behaviors and anarchists commit themselves to the task.

The anarchist ideal of legitimacy

The anarchists always focus on what institutions *take away* and not only on what they have and give. This focus is necessary for every theorist who wishes to obtain justification. And it is what makes the task of justification harder. By asking whether there is any point in having constraints at all, the anarchist advances the question whether there is any constraint that it is unreasonable to reject. This makes the question of justification a persistent process of interrogation. The anarchist perspective then represents an indispensable and unified position that reintroduces a very pressing demand. In the following paragraphs I attempt to make the implications of this challenge clearer.

The anarchist position discourages people from inventing political institutions. The anarchist's twofold aim is, first, to show the illegitimacy of political institutions (which is exemplified in the philosophical anarchist arguments against accounts of political obligation and in the political anarchist additional detection of the evils of political institutions) and, second, to work for their removal (which is distinctive of political anarchist action). I remain agnostic as to whether this latter is an achievable aim. This is a substantial question to put to anarchism itself, and I will discuss it in the next chapter of this study. But even if anarchists do not succeed in sustaining their contention against political institutions, even if, that is, we conclude that we need some form of political power, the role of the anarchist challenge does not disappear.

I explained in the preceding sections that the need to prove the existence of an actual obligation arises constantly, and that by stressing the question of obligation, the anarchist alerts us to the demand that the need for the justification of forms of imposition is continual. That we might need to have institutions does not mean that any form of constraint is enough to motivate them. What we need, then, is a proper test for deciding what forms of imposition are legitimate. This aspect of the contribution of the anarchist challenge establishes the demand that *every constraint is in need of justification and thus any new form of institution should pass a test of legitimacy in order to be accepted*.[32] The question of legitimacy thus becomes more pressing when the defender of political institutions returns to it via the anarchist challenge. In this context, "legitimacy" continues to designate the aspect that is correlative to political obligation and thus to determine assessments of this problem.

More importantly here, however, it acquires an additional use: it applies according to the idea that, even when we accept the existence of institutions, in the absence of political obligation we need to show that any new forms of coercion are not arbitrarily imposed on us, but are rather *compatible with acceptable moral values*. This idea was analyzed in the preceding paragraphs and it is explained further in this final part of Chapter 6. This latter sense of legitimacy functions among its various senses used in political debates that are distinguished from the problem of political obligation. Such senses are, for example, that the government is legitimate because of its good qualities, or when "it has acquired its political power in the proper way (e.g., by free election...)" or, in an international context, "if it is recognized as legitimate by other governments."[33] Legitimacy in the sense analyzed here can be effected through, or be identified with, some of these other senses.

The anarchist provides the required test of legitimacy. Throughout my account of the anarchist criticism of theories of political obligation, I explained how anarchist ideals of what a legitimate state would look like are involved in it. I explained how the moral criteria that define the relations that these ideals describe are characteristic of the very concern that initiated the anarchist challenge in the first place. That criticism, far from being merely negative, involves attention to these requirements. The anarchist perspective itself—the questions it raises, the process of argumentation it offers, and the results it delivers from the dialogue about political obligation—inherently involves these criteria. In its development the anarchist criticism clarifies that the values used in theories of political obligation, if successfully combined with the conditions of political obligation, would offer acceptably complete accounts of this obligation. Such accounts are translated by the anarchist into ideal pictures of proper social relations between institutions and individuals and among citizens themselves. Voluntariness, justice, and fairness as well as the value of association are strong and generally acceptable requirements. They have been used in the form of general principles for evaluating the character of political institutions. The anarchist indicates that they need to continue to be used in such a way with regard to every function of institutions, and that they can be used to determine social relationships if transformed into actual features of the specific interactions they are meant to characterize.

Thus the anarchist *ideal of legitimacy* lies at the center of the positive character of the anarchist argument. It is the normative horizon established by the debate on political obligation as defined by the anarchist criticism. That is, it functions in the form of ideal accounts of social interaction that constitute normative standards determining the considerations we put forward when we seek to justify forms of social organization as a common basis of our responsibilities and actions.

As explained at the beginning of this chapter (in the section "The positive conclusions"), this involves that the test apply to anarchist social visions as well. Although they do not have the nature of political institutions and do not involve the relationship of political obligation, they still need to be assessed in terms of the relevant moral values that the social interactions characteristic of them are meant to exemplify. More generally, they need to be proven to be morally acceptable social forms. Such visions are, for example, those analyzed by Samuel Clark and Benjamin Franks.

Samuel Clark defends the possibility of an anarchist utopia along certain lines, or, as he puts it, his book *Living without Domination* (2007) is "an exercise in practical utopianism."[34] He characterizes utopianism as "the creation and use of utopias" and utopia as "a text which makes use of a historically developed and developing vocabulary of tropes, story-fragments, and rhetorical and argumentative tactics."[35] Describing an ideal way of life can be used for a variety of purposes and with a number of consequences. A typical task to which utopias have been put, and the primary one for our purposes, is as "political interventions."[36] Utopian political interventions have two pairs of opposing features: storytelling and construction; criticism and the expansion of political imagination.[37] Clark focuses on the latter pair, which I find to be an extremely important function of the utopian texts and the one most relevant here. The description of utopias serves as a criticism of the unsatisfactory existing structures and social relations. The expansion of political imagination serves as a demonstration of the possibilities of improvement, of the potential to escape the disappointing here, which is not inescapable, and to defend and create better alternatives.

Within this framework, Clark develops a theory of society that makes external shared meaning and criticism possible. This comes as a response to Michael Walzer's objection that the meaning and ways of life of others in other societies, distinct from ours, are unavailable to us and so only internal criticism on the basis of shared social meanings is possible.[38] Clark rejects social totalities, unilinealism, and evolutionary approaches to society. According to these views, societies are discrete and mutually exclusive units, with their boundaries and internal subsystems and perhaps their own internal evolutionary dynamic.[39] And they pass through the same sequence of stages of social types over time, developing from lower to higher forms.[40] Against this perspective, Clark adopts a theory of society that works as "a mapping of the landscape of human sociability"[41] and suggests that social organizations "are networks of humans interacting in various ways."[42] Human beings create and assign capacities of domination and resistance within the framework of overlapping and interpenetrating social networks. These networks have various features: they create and assign capacities; they incorporate mechanisms for their own preservation, the tendency of human beings to institutionalize; they face the challenge of creating new networks and capacities, overturning the existing level of institutionalization;[43] and they are "functionally promiscuous," tending to perform other actions and be used for purposes other than those for which they were deliberately created.[44] The capacities of domination and resistance that human beings create and assign within social networks are cooperatively, rather than individually, created.[45] This means (following Hobbes) that the equal vulnerability of human beings, their equal chances of getting harmed or killed, makes the cooperative support of others necessary for these capacities to be created. They also frequently cooperate to create them. These capacities have and appear in various facets and are related to two contested concepts, those of power and freedom. "Domination is distributed power" and freedom is the opposite of this,[46] so any dimensions of domination have their corresponding unfreedoms.[47] Three historically common forms of domination and resistance to it involve violence, authority, and property. States involve all three ways of enacting domination, and anarchists have been critical of all of them, although in the case of authority they have not been indiscriminately skeptical of all its forms.[48]

On the basis of this account, Clark discusses the possibility of anarchic alternatives, the elements of a possible anarchist utopia, which are real examples of human sociability. Through an examination of the Nuer social form[49] and the kinds of organization created during the Spanish Civil War,[50] he provides respectively indicative examples of the ability of human beings to develop systems of conflict resolution and to maintain egalitarian and relatively peaceful social forms in high-technology, industrial situations. Together these examples show how conflict resolution through alternative tactics such as mediation, networking, production, and distribution as well as federalization are available features of a utopia drawing on human social experience, features that can expand political imagination and inform an alternative perspective on social problems.

Within the same logic and in continuation of their political program, anarchists can focus on more recent forms of prefiguration. In *Rebel Alliances: The Means and Ends of Contemporary British Anarchisms* (2006), Benjamin Franks examines a variety of anarchist organizational structures and tactics.[51]

Franks bases his approach on a prefigurative ideal, the criteria of which are used to evaluate the quality of each kind of structure and tactic. This ideal is compatible with the ideal of legitimacy of critical philosophical anarchism. While referring to different criteria, they involve the values supported by the latter. The general criteria of Franks's ideal are four: "a complete rejection of capitalism and the market economy," "an egalitarian concern for the interests and freedoms of others as part of creating non-hierarchical social relations," "a complete rejection of state-power and other quasi-state mediating forces," and, more basically, "a recognition that means have to prefigure ends."[52] Franks's ideal reflects a focus on freedom, equality, justice, and cooperation against the menace of domination and hierarchy similar to that of critical philosophical anarchism's ideal of legitimacy. So its application to anarchist organizations and tactics reflects a criticism parallel to that based on the ideal of critical philosophical anarchism. I enhance my claim with a few examples from contemporary anarchist structures and tactics.

The structures are basically divided into workplace and non-workplace ("community") organization.[53] Although he follows this distinction for methodological reasons, Franks concludes that the division "has been superseded," since the two types have shared interests, can use similar practices, and constitute similar responses to domination.[54]

Among contemporary anarchist structures, workplace organization has been given strategic supremacy and has a great tradition and a close relation to anarcho-syndicalism. Yet the prefigurative ethic supports a multiplicity and diversity of organizational forms and is against elevating one organization to a universal form. So anarcho-syndicalism can be appreciated for its advantages, and some of its elements can be incorporated into other structures, but it should not be considered as the primary organization. Within class-struggle anarchism there has been a great schism between anarcho-syndicalism and the support of community organization by libertarian communists, hence Murray Bookchin's different understanding of worker control and the related criticism of anarcho-syndicalism (see my Chapter 7, the sections "The tasks of political anarchists" and "Bookchin revisited"). Anarcho-syndicalism considers industrial organization and its tactics to be the basis of revolutionary activity and the desired future society, seeing a union of production, economy, and administration under the control of the workers. Political action is epiphenomenal. Still, the two traditions can be mutually consistent. The attraction of syndicalism for anarchists lies in its general organizational aim of uniting the workers into a federalization of industrial bodies and its role as a site of direct action, with its distinctive simple revolutionary tactic, the general strike, applied along with other effective tactics, such as sabotage and boycotts (some of which will be presented below, in my discussion of tactics).[55] In contrast to trade unions, workers' associations do not have mediators and try to escape representation and participation in the machinery of the state. Anarchist syndicates have different aims and organizational tactics, are organized on the basis of industry instead of trade, and concentrate on creating networks of workers within the industry, moving in the direction of using manifold methods and tactics against oppression. Historically syndicalism is regarded as arising from the failures of cell-based movements, as a reaction to the elitism and hierarchy resulting from the activity of small groups of individuals exercising propaganda by deed. Workplace organization is consistent with the multiplicity supported by the anarchist archetype, however, and it can run in parallel with the propaganda by deed of smaller cells and largely promote direct action.[56]

Community organization is as diverse and flexible as workplace structures. It includes groups, campaigns, and movements ranging from squatting to the support of community facilities, and a preoccupation with unemployment and environmental issues.[57] It varies in structures and participants and tends toward informal networks of solidarity based on localized activity. One important structure included within community organization consists in the environmental groups: communities and tribes.[58] In Chapter 7 I will evaluate Bookchin's theory on the basis of the anarchist ideal. A vital aspect of it is his social ecology: a central ecological dimension of its analysis motivated by the homonymous concerns.[59] In parallel with this and other relevant philosophies advanced[60]—which move the focus of concern and analysis from political and economic structures and relations to our relation with the environment as the one indicative of the dominative authoritarian tendencies of human society—the action of environmental groups takes place as an important strand of contemporary anarchism. By adapting more and more sophisticated methods and reasserting their relationship with the local residents of each site of their action, these activists reclaim the preservation of our planet through protests, the destruction of harmful arrangements and developments, the support of ecological constructions and forms of energy, as well as educational campaigns.

Another important anarchist community structure is the Global Community of the Internet. The internet creates alternative and expanding avenues of communication and solidarity that are central to anarchism. It becomes a great source of information and coordination among activists and encourages free expression, dialogue, and participation.[61] However, its place within anarchist (anti-)politics in line with the anarchist ideal is ambiguous. On the one hand, the flow of information makes it difficult to locate useful sources, access to the internet throughout the world is comparatively small and unequal, and personal traits within mainstream society, such as arrogance, absolutism, and racism, can be reinforced in cyberspace.[62] In addition, as Uri Gordon indicates, technology is "political" and can involve and encourage the dominative patterns and relationships of existing society: as a part of technological progress, the infrastructures enabling the internet can be highly centralizing, involving "authoritative coordination for production, maintenance and further development" and "one of the most resource-costly, polluting and exploitative industries."[63] On the other hand, international solidarity, decentralization, and flexibility remain important features and results of the internet that can attract anarchists. One of its indicative effects is that it creates new structures and tactics, such as the tactic of hacktivism. Hacktivists counteract established venues of propaganda and interaction by coordinating through "independent web-based radios and news periodicals" and subverting governmental websites (for example, by sabotaging ebusiness operation through spamming).[64] Consequently, the internet includes both negative and positive structural and tactical characteristics as part of an anarchist politics. Beginning from our mention of the latter characteristics, we can move on to examine further existing anarchist tactics, other than those involved in computer communication, to which Franks's work draws attention.

Anarchist organizational tactics are numerous. They vary from the revolution, which is considered "the accumulation of ever-expanding and growing incidents of prefigurative anarchist actions" rather than "a single phenomenon," the rebellion and the resurrection, which are "less frequent, more geographically contained incidents of libertarian resistance," as well as the Temporary Autonomous Zone (TAZ), which encompasses "immediate insurrectionary moments" of a nonhierarchical, inventive, and inspiring character;[65] to industrial activity, such as the strike, sabotage, and industrial boycott; methods of propaganda, for example propaganda by deed, propaganda by word, and situations; community sabotage, e.g., squatting, theft, and boycott; and anarchist atypical tactics, such as overproduction, hyperpassivity, and disengagement.[66] Below, I will analyze briefly three representative examples from the above areas.

A propagating tactic mentioned frequently in this study is propaganda by deed. It is compatible with the logic of combining different tactics, thus being interdependent with the activity of the syndicates and of the community, but it is usually associated with individual terror (mostly assassination). When insisting on indiscriminate violence and seeing their actions and targets as the central revolutionary strategy, propagandists by deed can recreate divisions within prefigurative action between the activist and the subjugated groups, thus entailing the hierarchies, and they also provoke a manipulated interpretation of their acts by dominative powers. Yet propaganda by deed refers to a wide variety of actions, becoming almost synonymous with direct action, engaging the oppressed subjects themselves and avoiding elitism and hierarchy. An indicative example is the attacks on the Apartheid African Embassy during the Poll Tax riots of 1990.[67]

A different form of propaganda is Situations (SI).[68] Situations are constructed moments of life, functioning as organized games of events with the purpose of subverting—through ridicule, interruption, or deconstruction—different forms of oppression. Situations give quality and meaning to momentary interventions and create temporary moments of autonomy. Despite their fleeting existence, their playful and temporary character reflects the flexibility, variety, and non-authoritarianism of anarchist prefiguration. They are a form of TAZ.

Squatting, a final example of anarchist tactics, is a form of community sabotage. As a rent-boycott it attacks homelessness and offers possibilities for new uses of spaces. But further, it serves new links of solidarity and wider forms of struggle. Whether seen as the aim itself or as more radically enabling new modes of protest, "[s]quatting is a useful multiple tactic": compatible with direct action, it involves in the process those affected and thus avoids elitist separations between activists and residents, but it also develops and engages other types of protestors; it challenges private property and the capitalist consumer society as well as its social arrangements on the whole; it makes spaces available not only to cover needs, but also for creative and innovative use; and, by directly forming alternative ways of living, it reveals how means can prefigure ends according to the anarchist vision.[69] For example, the London Squatters Campaign (formed in 1968) moved from symbolic demonstrations against the statist housing system to practical direct action that assisted the homeless, created affinity with the local community, and spread all over the country, providing an arena for wider resistance.[70]

The general perspective of Franks's work is that anarchism involves "fluid, polymorphous movements,"[71] that it concerns a variety of networks, types of relationships, forms of struggle, and prefigurative acts, with their related agents and aims. The struggle is multifaceted and should begin from the oppressed subjects themselves, from the groups of people that have direct reasons to react to dominative power.[72] "The revolution is an amalgamation of prefigurative rebellious acts whose frequency and intensity creates a critical mass that fundamentally alters a multitude of interdependent repressive practices and powers."[73] This position, adopted not only by Franks but also by Clark, Gordon, and other anarchist thinkers, is representative of the contemporary political anarchist perspective. Each expression of it, in the form of prefigurative networks, needs to be tested by the ideal of legitimacy of critical philosophical anarchism. For the purposes of this study, I will apply the test only to one exemplary case. So, the prefigurative project just outlined provides the background in view of which, in the next chapter, I will apply the demands of the anarchist ideal to Bookchin's municipalist vision.

In the opposite direction, which has been the focus of this study, the ideal standards of critical philosophical anarchism are applied in the light of the failure to justify political obligation. They help further evaluations of institutions by imposing the relevant moral criteria as principled conditions on existing and newly arising forms of domination. Two possible ways of ensuring that political constraints attend to these values are that such conditions function either as legitimate general principles with which constraints should be proven to be compatible, or as "*enabling* conditions... for the legal institutionalization of... discursive processes of opinion- and will-formation through which" we can authorize constraints.[74] The extent to which these models become appropriate ways of heeding the demands of the ideal of legitimacy and the idea of active participation it represents depends on the implementation, structure, regularity, and efficiency of the mechanisms we establish for their realization.

Hence by stressing the question of obligation, anarchism ends up effecting a more general approach to political institutions. It offers a proper test to be applied to and determine any defense of constraints. Even if political institutions are proven to be desired, the criteria of legitimacy that anarchism supplies provide a standard by reference to which defenders of those institutions can attempt to maintain their desirability: we examine what demands are put on political institutions and what is needed to motivate them in every instance, in view of what is owed to particular individuals. The anarchist versions of an ideal of legitimacy provide a new horizon for political argumentation and make legitimacy exigent, because it is difficult to see how institutions can meet their requirements. The anarchist ideals are probably unattainable, and even if existing institutions were at some point entirely guided by them, the continual need to verify this application would make justification unstable. Still, this allows another difficult task to remain meaningful: the task of ensuring that institutions are constantly assessed by, and tend to approximate, these ideals. Through this, the ideal of legitimacy reaffirms the force of the question of obligation: the more difficult it is for existing institutions to satisfy this standard, the more the anarchist concern with the possibility of obligations is strengthened.

The anarchist perspective is once more vindicated: political institutions cease to be viewed as lovable, and they need to be tested on the basis of the problems they create. Furthermore, the anarchist ideal explains the link between philosophical and political anarchism: it reminds us of the enduring deficiency of the state as a position that is initially shared by both forms of anarchism; and the moral conditions involved in it as part of philosophical anarchism are intended to be inherent in the society that political anarchism seeks to realize.

Finally, the anarchist perspective brings together Raz's argument about how political institutions can be compatible with freedom, on the one hand, and an insistence on the special role of choice in sustaining self-imposed constraints as the only ones appropriate to human freedom, on the other. In Chapter 1 I explained the difference between two distinctive views for respecting autonomy in political societies. One was that freedom can be allowed in a government that serves good reasons even when this government is not autonomously chosen. The other was that individual choice is indispensable for freedom. Raz's position that autonomy is respected when government serves reasons that apply to individuals themselves represents the first view. And the way of assessing political institutions defended by the anarchist results in Raz's view. Nevertheless, as I also argued in the first chapter, this view does not alone address the concern with freedom that underlies the demand for justification. For this, the role of choice needs to be asserted: it is important that through government we *remain* free. Through the anarchist criticism of theories of political obligation, we understand that this demand involves recognizing the importance of the question of political obligation and of the difficulty of addressing it. This is a way of asserting the importance of choice for securing self-government, and it directs us to an alternative way of respecting choice. Recognizing, in light of the absence of political obligation, that constraints need to be assessed and justified on the basis of the values of the ideal of legitimacy, as it traces harm to particular individuals, is a way of affirming choice without facing the difficulty that accounts of political obligation based on choice face—a difficulty that Raz himself has pointed out correctly. It thus is a way of returning to Raz while sustaining the fundamental role of individual choice for political justification. Such justification is based on the idea of self-imposed constraints, which removes the appearance of a paradox in the relation between constraints and freedom.[75]

Conclusion

The distinctive perspective of critical philosophical anarchism is that it revives the question whether we should have political institutions by questioning our obligation to them. The criticism of accounts of political obligation that it provides and the results of that criticism raise this question, which has been overlooked for too long in discussions of political authority. Rather than promoting a duty to justify constraints, anarchism *makes compelling a duty not to accept illegitimate constraints*: it focuses on what constraints take away and thus on the need to account for the point of their very existence. Critical philosophical anarchism makes us think about what freedom and equality and their loss imply for the way we want to defend political institutions, helping us reestablish our methods of justification. It presents an indispensable outlook: it reassesses the very approach to political authority that has been used incorrectly hitherto as a starting point for the debate, offering a clear view of the character, possibilities, and problems of political constraints that points out and corrects this approach. It thus establishes a new horizon of argumentation, where the possibility of political obligation and the need for justification remain a persistent concern and are harder to obtain. This perspective constitutes the core of the anarchist contribution to the philosophical debate on political obligation. It is in this respect, namely in adopting this perspective, that, I claim, political theorists need to acknowledge the terrain they share with anarchists. At the same time, the anarchist position preserves its authenticity. It is not about putting limits on political institutions out of a concern to preserve them. It does not put emphasis on the justification of the legitimacy of the state. The anarchist is motivated by the problem of domination, or subjugation, how improper relations among people are demeaning. The defect of political institutions detected through the anarchist criticism of political obligation is that political constraints, by their very nature, tend to accept, cultivate, and establish that subjugation. In the end, the anarchist position is rather about *how difficult it is to substantiate political legitimacy*. This is the beginning of the political anarchist struggle for social change.

Notes

1   See Simmons, "Philosophical Anarchism," 36, n.9. For a presentation of these features, see the section "The variety of anarchisms. Defining critical philosophical anarchism within the current debate on anarchism" of my Introduction.
2   See Chapter 1, the section "The problem of political obligation."
3   These motivations are explained in Chapter 2, the section "Dismissing the conceptual argument for political obligation."
4   This is also a reaction to pluralist, or supplementary, accounts of political obligation, such as those suggested by Gans and Wolff (in Gans, *Philosophical Anarchism*, and Wolff, "Pluralistic Models of Political Obligation," respectively).

5   For this, see the final section of Chapter 2, inspired by Rousseau's position
    in 1762 (Rousseau, "On Social Contract"), Book 1, chapters 6 and 7. In the
    end, the state must be proven to be a *self-imposed constraint* on the part of
    individuals—or that within it they *remain* free—in order for it to be justified
    to them (for this fundamental demand, see the discussion in Chapter 1, the
    sections "The paradox of authority," "Dissolving the paradox. Rousseau as a
    paradigm of state justification," and "The argument for critical philosophical
    anarchism," and in the section "The contribution of critical philosophical
    anarchism" of the present chapter).
6   Newman, *The Politics of Postanarchism*, 20–25. See also Chapter 2 here, the
    section "The implications of the anarchist criticism of consent".
7   Taylor, *Community, Anarchy and Liberty*, 3. See also May, *The Political
    Philosophy of Poststructuralist Anarchism*; Alan Carter, *A Radical Green
    Political Theory* (London: Routledge, 1999); Franks, *Rebel Alliances*; Gordon,
    Anarchy Alive; Newman, *The Politics of Postanarchism*.
8   See Raz, "Introduction," 16–17, and the discussion of his theory in Chapter 1,
    the section "Raz's theory as an illustration."
9   Miller, *Anarchism*, 18. For a fuller presentation of this campaign, see
    my Introduction, the section "The main parts and underlying ideas of
    my argument," and Chapter 1, the subsection "Simmons's theory." For
    representative bibliography, see Wolff, *In Defense of Anarchism*, 11 and
    18–19; Smith, "Is There a Prima Facie Obligation?," 969–973; Simmons,
    Moral Principles and Political Obligations, 191–201; Simmons, "The
    Anarchist Position," 275–279; Simmons, *On the Edge of Anarchy*, 263–269.
10 For more on the anarchist campaign, the attitude it cultivates, and its
    radicalism, see Chapter 1, the sections "Simmons's theory" and "A more
    general departure from Simmons's approach."
11 Wolff, "Pluralistic Models of Political Obligation"; Wolff, "Anarchism and
    Skepticism."
12 This effect is typically claimed to be what is involved in the subversive
    campaign of philosophical anarchism. In the present part of Chapter 6 I
    attempt to provide a deeper explanation of the importance of this campaign,
    as well as of the importance of the rest of the anarchist claims presented in this
    paragraph.
13 To remind the reader, the debate on political obligation involves two main
    features: (a) the distinctively "*political*" character of such obligations and the
    institutions to which they are owed, and (b) the requirement for a *moral* basis
    of these obligations that is necessarily linked with their political character
    (see Chapter 1, the section "The two main aspects of the problem of political
    obligation"). Voluntariness, justice, fairness, and association are such bases.
    The main elements used to demonstrate and determine this important link
    between the political and the moral feature are the four conditions imposed by
    the anarchist and used traditionally in the debate (see Chapter 1, the section
    "The conditions of political obligation"), to wit, "generality" (Raz, *The
    Authority of Law*, Chapter 12), "particularity" (Green, *The Authority of the
    State*, 84 and 227–228; Simmons, *Moral Principles and Political Obligations*,
    34–35), "bindingness," and "content-independence" (Green, *The Authority
    of the State*, 225–226). The main difficulty for theories of political obligation

is to connect these conditions with the moral ground provided by every such theory. Particularity constitutes the crucial obstacle to this effect, especially because it is the element most indicative of the need for political obligations to be actual and specifically related to all affected parties. The particularity condition is also central to the distinctiveness of the anarchist approach. For these points, see Chapters 1–5.

14 In the following paragraphs, I will use voluntarism as representative of the defenders with whom the anarchist enters a dialogue. As shown in the previous discussion, the anarchist criticism and its results about political obligation as well as the present anarchist claims apply with regard to the other theories of political obligation that are the object of this criticism. Thus these claims concern the debate as a whole. And a demonstration of their importance affects all the relevant theoretical accounts, as it will be further explained later in this chapter.

15 For a detailed analysis of the following points, see Chapter 2.

16 For example, Scanlon, "Contractualism and Utilitarianism"; Scanlon, *What We Owe to Each Other*.

17 For the anarchist criticism of this illegitimate move, see the following paragraphs.

18 Ripstein, "The General Will," 219. Ripstein attributes this latter approach to Rousseau. So Rousseau is presented as being concerned with exactly this question, while the above outlook is more prominent in Hobbes and, on certain readings, in Locke. On the other hand, Rousseau might be interpreted as not accounting for the problem of political obligation at all. And in a preceding paragraph on the hypothetical contract, I refer to a contemporary development of that form of social contract influenced by Rousseau's idea of the "general will" that is a promising improvement within this tradition and yet the task of which is distinguished from the problem of political obligation. Nevertheless, within the context of the debate on political obligation, it remains possible that a development of Rousseau's own use of the general will could establish the possibility of political obligation and do so as part of a justification of the existence of political institutions, because his main outlook seems to connect the two in a way that addresses the anarchist challenge (see Habermas, "Human Rights and Popular Sovereignty," Section III; Ripstein, "The General Will").

19 This question relates to what would be an accurate account of *how things would be without institutions*, which is what the hypothetical contractualists' representation of the state of nature lacks. For this point, see my analysis below.

20 The following analysis has been introduced in Chapter 1. The role of the present chapter is to give a detailed and complete examination of these arguments in order to establish the position of this study as outlined in Chapter 1 and defended in Chapters 2–5.

21 Simmons, "Justification and Legitimacy."

22 For this complaint, see Simmons, "Justification and Legitimacy," 766–769.

23 For example, Simmons, *Moral Principles and Political Obligations*, 200–201.

24 The way Rousseau sets out to develop his arguments for civil society, however, tends to remain valid, because he conceives from the beginning and remains

faithful to the demand that political institutions can be justified only in terms of a very valuable thing that we lose in abandoning the state of nature, namely freedom, and that they should be shown to be doing very well in this respect. That constraints take freedom away might never be justified unless they offer something that corrects this loss. This approach does take into account the demand that we attend to the defects of political institutions and not only to their merits. This also comes from the fact that Rousseau guards against socially affected readings of the state of nature, and he sees the pre-social attitudes that create war as the features of a situation that is an intermediate stage between the state of nature and political society (see, e.g., Rousseau, "On Social Contract," Book 1, chapters 1–6). Nevertheless, it is more likely that Rousseau's project concerns a conceptual analysis of the form of justification that would legitimize institutions as they already exist rather than a justification of their existence.

25   For relevant arguments, see Gregory S. Kavka, "Hobbes's War of All against All," *Ethics* 93 (1983): 291–310, and Sanders, "The State of Statelessness," 264–265.

26   For such an argument, see Rousseau, "On Social Contract," Book 1, Chapter 2.

27   The present argument removes a very important burden to an assessment of their views that also applies to this assessment equally. Most importantly, the fundamental question that the anarchist perspective reveals already reflects the significance of this argument and shows the anarchist to concede to it in a way that the defender does not. For this latter point, see the rest of my analysis in the present chapter.

28   These states might "merit our support" but this "is not at all the same as saying that they have a right to direct and coerce us, which we are bound to honor" (Simmons, "Justification and Legitimacy," 70). And, as we will stress below, they are not guaranteed to merit support once and for all.

29   Although, in fairness to Horton, he does not see his theory as such an attempt. Still, his approach is criticized here to the extent that it can be, and has been, used in the relevant way.

30   Simmons, *Moral Principles and Political Obligations*, 200; Simmons, "Philosophical Anarchism," 38–39, n. 30.

31   Gordon, *Anarchy Alive*, 46.

32   For Uri Gordon, for example, the criterion for legitimacy is non-domination (see the section "The Gordonian 'Anarchy Alive!'" in my next chapter).

33   Simmons, *Moral Principles and Political Obligations*, 40–41, 197.

34   Clark, *Living without Domination*, 1.

35   Clark, *Living without Domination*, 12. For the information included in this paragraph, see the whole of Clark's introduction.

36   Clark, *Living without Domination*, 13.

37   For these, see Clark, *Living without Domination*, 16–23.

38   Michael Walzer, *Spheres of Justice: A Defense of Pluralism and Equality* (New York: Basic Books, 1983), 9.

39   Clark, *Living without Domination*, 51–58.

40   Clark, *Living without Domination*, 53. For unilinealism, see Ernest Gellner, "Soviets against Wittfogel: Or, the Anthropological Preconditions of Mature Marxism," in *States in History*, ed. John A. Hall (Oxford: Basil Blackwell, 1986).

41 Clark, *Living without Domination*, 49.
42 Clark, *Living without Domination*, 60.
43 Michael Mann, *Sources of Social Power* (Cambridge: Cambridge University Press, 1986–93), 1: 15. For these features, see also Clark, *Living without Domination*, 59–60.
44 Mann, *Sources of Social Power*, 1: 17.
45 For this account, see Clark, *Living without Domination*, 65–73.
46 Clark, *Living without Domination*, 67. For domination, see also my account in "The Gordonian 'Anarchy Alive!' " based on Gordon, *Anarchy Alive*, 29–34.
47 For three such dimensions, see Steven Lukes, *Power: A Radical View* (London: Macmillan, 1974).
48 For this see, Clark, *Living without Domination*, 69–70; McLaughlin, *Anarchism and Authority*, 29–36. For a detailed analysis of the three common forms of domination and resistance, see Clark, *Living without Domination*, 69–73.
49 For characteristic studies of the Nuer, see Edward Evan Evans-Pritchard, *The Nuer: A Description of the Modes of Livelihood and Political Institutions of a Nilotic People* (Oxford: Clarendon Press, 1940) (who lived with them in the 1930s); Sharon E. Hutchinson, *Nuer Dilemmas: Coping with Money, War, and the State* (Berkeley: University of California Press, 1996) (who lived with them in the 1980s and 1990s). For Clark's account, see *Living without Domination*, 110–120. The elements discussed are based on accounts of the past, but I use present tense because the Nuer are not extinct today.
50 For such a presentation, see *Living without Domination*, 128–138; Burnett Bolloten, *The Grand Camouflage: The Spanish Civil War and Revolution, 1936–39* (London: Pall Mall, 1968), 216–217; George Orwell, "Homage to Catalonia," in *Orwell in Spain: The Full Text of Homage to Catalonia with Associated Articles, Reviews and Letters from The Complete Works of George Orwell*, ed. Peter Hobley Davidson (London: Penguin, 2001), 50–51; Robert J. Alexander, *The Anarchists in the Spanish Civil War*, 2 vols. (London: Janus, 1999), 1: 248.
51 Franks, *Rebel Alliances*, chapters 4 and 5, respectively.
52 Franks, *Rebel Alliances*, 12–13. This ideal is referred to and applied throughout Franks's book. For the anarchist groups and organizations that are examined in his book under the heading of "class struggle anarchism" as those meeting these four criteria, see Franks, *Rebel Alliances*, 12: organizations such as the Anarchist Black Cross (ABC), Anarchist Federation (AF), Anarchist Youth Network (AYN), Anarchist Workers Group (AWG), Solidarity, Solidarity Federation (SolFed), Direct Action Movement (DAM), Earth First! (EF!), and many others.
53 Franks, *Rebel Alliances*, 196. See also the main part of Franks's Chapter 4.
54 Franks, *Rebel Alliances*, 257–258.
55 Pierre Monatte, "Syndicalism: An Advocacy," in *The Anarchist Reader*, ed. George Woodcock (Glasgow: Fontana/Collins, 1980), 217. For these and the following points, see Franks, *Rebel Alliances*, 234–239. For direct action, see my Chapter 7, especially the sections "The tasks of political anarchists" and "The Gordonian 'Anarchy Alive!'."

56 Franks, *Rebel Alliances*, 234–246. See also Barbara Mitchell, "French Syndicalism: An Experiment in Practical Anarchism," in *Revolutionary Syndicalism: An International Perspective*, ed. Marcel van der Linden and Wayne Thorpe (Aldershot: Scolar Press, 1990), 27.

57 See, e.g., Anarchist Communist Federation (ACF, now AF), *Beyond Resistance: A Revolutionary Manifesto for the Millennium*, 2nd ed. (London: Anarchist Communist Editions, 1997), 23–24.

58 Franks, *Rebel Alliances*, 250–253.

59 See, e.g., Bookchin, *Toward an Ecological Society*; Bookchin, "Libertarian Municipalism"; Bookchin, "A Politics for the 21st Century."

60 For example, Carter, *A Radical Green Political Theory*; John Zerzan, *Future Primitive: And Other Essays* (New York: Autonomedia, 1994).

61 See the example of the Zapatistas and the way their use of technological developments altered methods of struggle (through computer communication networks): Franks, *Rebel Alliances*, 254–255.

62 For such problems with computer activism, see Harry Cleaver, "The Zapatistas and the International Circulation of Struggle: Lessons Suggested and Problems Raised," (1998) (accessed May 7, 2013. http://www.eco.utexas.edu/faculty/ Cleaver/lessons.html); Franks, *Rebel Alliances*, 255–257.

63 Gordon, *Anarchy Alive*, 114–127, 130–135 (quotes from pages 118 and 134, respectively).

64 Franks, *Rebel Alliances*, 254.

65 Franks, *Rebel Alliances*, 261, 266.

66 For all these groups of tactics, see Franks, *Rebel Alliances*, Chapter 5.

67 Franks, *Rebel Alliances*, 297–300.

68 See Franks, *Rebel Alliances*, 314–315; Situationist International (a), "Preliminary Problems in Constructing a Situation," in *Situationist International Anthology*, ed. and trans. Ken Knabb (Berkeley: Bureau of Public Secrets, 1989); Situationist International (b), "Definitions."

69 For these, see Franks, *Rebel Alliances*, 332–335.

70 For further important tactics, see Jean Baudrillard, *In the Shadow of the Silent Minorities … or, The End of the Social, and Other Essays*, trans. Paul Foss, Paul Patton, and John Johnston (New York: Semiotext(e) Foreign Agents, 1983), and *The Ecstasy of Communication*, trans. Bernard Schütze and Caroline Schutze (New York: Semiotext(e) Foreign Agents, 1987).

71 Franks, *Rebel Alliances*, 196. This position is expressed and stressed throughout chapters 4 and 5 of his book.

72 See, e.g., Franks, *Rebel Alliances*, 210–211. Also, for the importance of the relevant political recommendation to release subjugated discourses, see May, *The Political Philosophy of Poststructuralist Anarchism*, 116–118.

73 Franks, *Rebel Alliances*, 268.

74 For the latter idea, see Habermas, "Human Rights and Popular Sovereignty," 12–13.

75 For this seeming paradox, as well as for the role of Raz's theory, see Chapter 1, the sections "The paradox of authority" and "Raz's theory as an illustration."

7

Anarchism: Philosophical and political

Critical philosophical anarchism constitutes a very comprehensive position, which represents an indispensable outlook on approaches to political institutions. But what about the other direction that the anarchist contribution can take? What about its implications for political anarchism itself? How does the critical stand with regard to political authority that the philosophical anarchist position shares with political anarchism relate to the tasks of the advocates of the latter?

There are three main parts to this examination. In the first and second part, I provide some considerations regarding the proposals and tasks of political anarchism in relation to the contribution of critical philosophical anarchism. This project is facilitated through a discussion and criticism of Bookchin's anarchist program against the background of other recent anarchist prefigurative politics. In the final part, I discuss what the view of critical philosophical anarchism proposes for addressing concrete dilemmas within existing societies governed by the state.

The tasks of political anarchists

As already indicated in Chapter 6, in the light of the framework established with the help of philosophical anarchism and the normative horizon of the anarchist ideal of legitimacy, anarchists themselves have to undertake their own tasks. In order to address concerns of the defenders of the state and in order for their proposals for social organization to be taken seriously, political anarchists have to show that their own social visions live up to the moral criteria of the ideal of legitimacy in a way that proves both their desirability and their feasibility and viability. This will also weaken the force of arguments to the effect that we need the state, and it will make the call of political anarchism to demolish the state more understandable and intuitive.

As stated in the Introduction, anarchists focus on the social character of human life and on the ethos of voluntary cooperation, which is represented fairly by communal (or social) anarchism. So this anarchist position qualifies as a political position paradigmatic of what anarchism proposes as a social alternative. However, this form of anarchism has difficulties in providing an answer to the question of how to achieve and sustain stable, harmonious, social cooperation without coercion. This problem with political anarchism lies in the fact that, in its commitment to social cooperation, it is bound to recognize the necessity of forms of social order, social conventions, and obligations, which are difficult to define without "an element of coercion."[1] Social criticism and pressure, especially in small communities, can have strikingly coercive effects on individuals, not to mention their inefficiency in large cities.[2] Given that communal anarchists accept a degree of coercion in forms of social order necessary for the survival of anarchic communities, it follows that, for those anarchists, the issue of political obligation becomes problematic: they either "reintroduce" political obligation or appeal to proposals that are open to objections similar to those that anarchists themselves make against institutionalized coercion.[3] What becomes crucial, then, is to find a consistent way to incorporate within the political anarchist view the explicit arguments against political obligation provided by philosophical anarchists. A demonstration of the compatibility of political anarchist social visions with the perspective and ideals of legitimacy shown in this study to be provided by philosophical anarchists, and their proximity to them, would achieve this and establish continuity within the anarchist ideology. It would provide a combination of a diagnostic of what goes wrong with coercion with an explicit positive horizon of harmonious social relations without the state.

It is on this terrain, then, that political social anarchism, and any other positive proposal that is characterized by its advantages and disadvantages, needs to be tested under the auspices of an ideal of legitimacy. Anarchism must prove that the social visions it proposes can deal effectively with the problem of achieving cooperation, order, and safety without coercion. This demonstration could best be effected through the elements already implemented within the anarchist tradition, that is, by a more complete development of the theoretical anarchist arguments concerning the Prisoner's Dilemma, public goods, and morality, and by the empirical observation and cultivation of its manifestations within real societies. Further, although anarchist visions do not have to meet the conditions of political obligation, since they reject it, this demonstration must proceed in ways compatible with the moral criteria that the anarchist position sustains.

There is a continued development of theoretical arguments in defense of anarchy, which are customarily advanced in the political debate and stand in interaction with the anarchist work on social structures. Anarchists advance solutions to the Prisoner's Dilemma and to the argument from public goods in order to address the problems of coordination of activities, cooperation, and social order without appeal to institutionalized coercion and formal law.[4] For example, in the case of the Prisoner's Dilemma, they focus on iterated forms of the game: depicting the game in a number of times to allow repeated interaction among the parties provides great potential for the emergence of strategies that result in cooperation.[5] Another solution involves "experimental arguments," which support these theoretical possibilities by providing examples of cooperative behavior and of support of voluntary associations evidenced in real life.[6] Along these lines, the most important anarchist claim is that, by realizing the highly abstract and unrealistic construction of the dilemma as far as its various features are concerned and by relaxing some of them, the possibility of cooperation on a voluntary basis becomes more and more obvious.[7] A successful application of the anarchist structures and practices plays a primary role to this effect.

Additionally, anarchists argue for the possibility of relying on generally accepted moral reasons, in order to show that anarchism need not lead to widespread unrest, and thus to counteract criticisms that appeal to the impossibility of a unifying moral view. Along the lines of these criticisms, it has been claimed that the difficulty of making everybody share a common set of moral principles generates infinite disagreement, making anarchism unattractive.[8] The anarchist practices for social order and a reflection of central anarchist principles in them (principles such as decentralization, participatory democracy, egalitarianism, self-sufficiency, and ecology), as well as of the ultimate ideals of freedom, equality, and solidarity that underlie those principles, constitute the most essential elements for replies to this criticism.[9] Indeed, the position of critical philosophical anarchism has already been shown to involve, and to redirect us toward, generally acceptable moral reasons. This is not incompatible with the fact that, as I will confirm in the following section, critical philosophical anarchism embraces certain poststructuralist elements. The rejection of essentialism and holistic perspectives on the part of poststructuralist political theory does not entail a denial of the possibility of common ethical principles.[10]

Furthermore, many anarchists aspire to a gradual and stable reconstruction of social life envisaged as a social scheme of cooperation, one end of the spectrum of views that has, at its opposite extreme, the institutionalized coercion of states.[11] A central tenet of anarchism is that, through the implementation of prefigurative social structures and experience within them, individuals will cultivate the attitudes and abilities of trust and cooperation that are required for an alternative construction of social life, and that life in states has made us lose.[12] Such a structural preparation applies a characteristic anarchist belief, namely that the means toward social change should be the same as, or compatible with, the ends forming this change.[13] Although these ideas propose immediate changes, they do not contradict the proposal for gradual social reconstruction. Rather, they reflect the anarchist position that the application of this reconstruction should be directly and consistently of the kind that the anarchist envisages and explain the forms that comprise it.

Anarchists present us with a picture of non-dominative, noncoercive, and equal social relations. These are reflected in the anarchist work on social structures, in a social background constituted by a multiplicity of decentralized, voluntary associations, which are realized by a variety of groups, organized on a human scale, are of all forms and degrees, and involve many important practices, tactics, and goals (social units such as local communes, different kinds of cooperatives, and contemporary movements, all serving a variety of causes regarding various areas of life); these are confederated with each other in order to apply, coordinate, improve, and expand the relations among them as well as between them and the surrounding system.[14] These features, as actual implementations of the ideals of freedom, equality, cooperation, and solidarity, should be tested by the moral standards provided, and by experience.

This study does not undertake the tasks of political anarchism. But an initial application of the ideal of critical philosophical anarchism to at least one political anarchist proposal might provide illumination and be a first step in this direction. This is the attempt of this chapter.

"Whole communities"[15]—such as the traditional communes constructed around the world, especially in the form of the "secular family commune" they took in the 1960s[16] and its more contemporary development in the 1980s[17]—might acquire a very valuable character if developed in accordance with Murray Bookchin's political program of "Libertarian Municipalism."[18] Bookchin characterizes Libertarian Municipalism as "an explicit attempt to update the traditional social anarchist ideal of the Federation of Communes or 'Commune of communes,' that is, the confederal linking of libertarian communist municipalities in the form of directly democratic popular assemblies as well as the collective control or 'ownership' of socially important property."[19] He argues that, for a promising alternative social framework, there should be an immediate sphere of popular self-management where cooperation and commitment to community come to the fore. This is the *democratic municipality*. He sees the municipality as the "authentic unit of political life ... as a whole, if it is humanly scaled, or in its various subdivisions, notably the neighborhood."[20] The neighborhood becomes the vital space for discussions of political, cultural, and economic issues. His claim is that the immediate spheres for learning to be familiar with "the political process" and units of an alternative culture should be "the villages, towns, neighborhoods, and cities in which people live on the most intimate level of political interdependence beyond private life."[21] Bookchin's vision is one of a society where people are actively involved in public matters through interaction within municipal assemblies whose members meet constantly for direct discussion and decision-making on every matter of their lives. These assemblies are further coordinated by delegates who represent them in "local confederal councils" and "who are rotable, recallable, and above all, rigorously instructed in written form" about their position on the issues discussed in the councils.[22] This process extends to every level, creating thus a confederal network that interlinks municipal assemblies through local councils, all organized from the bottom up.[23]

There are four recurrent themes running through Bookchin's vision that are extremely important for the organization of social life in anarchist terms and in line with the anarchist commitment to equal, active participation and its new view of the political. The first is Bookchin's concern to revive citizenship through appeal to municipal politics, where he conceives politics in its Greek meaning, namely as the self-management of the community, or "popular ways of managing the city," as evidenced in and inspired by the Greek *polis* and other cities of the past.[24] With this idea, Bookchin highlights an alternative to what has been conceived as political so far. This may be constituted upon anarchist lines both as a replacement of the practices characteristic of the state and for the cultivation of a new kind of collective action that may socialize us into, and help us arrive at, social change. The second interesting theme is Bookchin's distinction between policy-making and administration, according to which he considers the former to be the practice of individuals as citizens within the assemblies, their main political function, while the latter he sees as the job of those appointed and working in each specific area of society, which frees citizens from time-consuming preoccupation with administrative details. This distinction applies also at the federal level with regard to assemblies and councils: the former involve policy-making, while the task of the latter is coordination and administration.[25] This idea helps anarchist organizations preserve participation while achieving the required coordination of activities that would make them viable and effective as well as able to extend to the larger society. Another theme characteristic of Bookchin's project is "the municipalization of the economy," according to which property should be in the custody of the community and the economy arranged on the basis of the decisions of citizens in the municipal assemblies with regard to both production and distribution.[26] In this way individuals control the economy as citizens within the assemblies and in their decisions they are guided by the needs of the community, while as workers they concentrate on specific tasks without concern for the management of the particular economic units in which they work. Bookchin thinks that this idea is essentially liberating for the workers and provides an improved conception of the notion of "worker control" (which within anarchosyndicalism has been connected to the direct management as well as ownership of the economic units by workers, see the section "The anarchist ideal of legitimacy" above): he thinks that it helps workers "escape the tyranny of the factory, rationalized labour, and planned production," thus giving them free time and freedom from an abuse of labor; at the same time, it avoids the privatization of the economy and the competitiveness it entails, which he sees to be involved in the anarchosyndicalist idea of "collectivized enterprises."[27] This idea can be updated according to the achievements and needs of current working

conditions and apply to any profession within contemporary societies, as a
new way of organizing the work environment. A final theme in Bookchin's
politics is the interaction between, and independence of, communities
through confederation, as a way of avoiding inefficiency, isolation, and
a narrow parochial outlook. This is a way of arriving at his "ultimate
agenda," that is, his vision of a world in which the state is replaced by "a
confederal network of municipal assemblies," with the future task that we
"radicalize the democracy we create [namely the democratic municipalities
within which we are to preserve and expand freedoms], imparting an even
more creative content to the democratic institutions we have rescued and
tried to develop."[28] With confederation Bookchin aspires to carry the ideas
of decentralization and small scale to their ultimate expansion.

All these central ideas can apply also to the form of "partial community,"
namely "a wide variety of cooperatives, collectives, neighbourhood
associations, and other practices and projects of direct action, mutual aid,
and self-management."[29] *Direct action* was originally applied as a political
tactic adopted by anarchists and other radicals for creating an immediate
effect on situations and on the range of choices of the individuals affected,
e.g., involving actions such as sabotage and strikes. Today it is conceived
and used in a more sophisticated and inclusive way, as a social practice,
or a multiplicity of tactics, through which individuals directly intervene
in, participate in, and manage social affairs.[30] It covers a wide range of
activities: it encompasses nonviolent resistance to authority through various
campaigns, movements, and affinity groups as well as the organization of,
and work within, cooperatives and other prefigurative forms.[31] The specific
practices included within the social structures of the counterculture—
practices such as reciprocity, democratic participation, distributive justice,
public pressure, socialization, and ecology—are of central importance for
testing its acceptability and viability.[32]

Although promising, these aspects of the anarchist project are still
incomplete, and to this extent the difficulty with coercion that anarchism
faces remains. We will see how this affects Bookchin's project in the following
section. A preliminary overview of the problems faced by whole communities
prepares the way for applying the critical philosophical anarchist test more
specifically and in view of these difficulties. David Pepper discusses four
serious problems that anarchist structures face and that their development
aims to solve, for them to qualify as core units of social change.[33] First,
these structures suffer a gap between principle and practice. This means
that their members fail to live up to the principles they profess to adopt.
In traditional communes this is mainly due to the communards having
compromised original ends in a pragmatist concern with efficiency. Second,
there is a lack of ideological clarity, namely of a clear and shared vision
of principled perspective and purposes. This is because there is nowadays
less talk about principles and more about direct practical issues concerning

day-to-day survival and comfort, which helps avoid conflicts among the participants, but also facilitates the gap between principle and practice. Third, communards lack contact with a wider audience through effective outreach. That is, with their ideas and practices they fail to reach the larger population by keeping connections with other social movements and with the rest of society. This is both due to the lack of ideological clarity and person power within the communes and because of the concentration on personal relations at the expense of organized collective action and outside political activity. Fourth and finally, communes suffer a tension between "the private" and "the public." Their members see their personal lives to be detached from more general and common concerns that would help cultivate solidarity and a union between individual freedom and communal reciprocity. My focus on Bookchin's and other, alternative, contemporary proposals (in the next section) points in a direction that deals with these problems. Federation and an initial adoption of a clear view of how to oppose the system play a central role to this effect, at the same time using the system in a way that addresses the social reality within which both it and the counterculture work. But these are still proposals that need actual and patient implementation and expansion.

The difficulty that anarchism faces with regard to coercion can be expressed in a more challenging form in light of the framework that, as this study shows, the anarchist position establishes. Anarchism wants a society where there is the imposition of no imposition, where the imposition of some on others is prevented. But here the concern arises with how there can be an imposition of no imposition such that the former differs from the latter. If anarchists promise us a land of no constraints, how are they to sustain this land with no use of constraints? The anarchist proposals for social organization do not seem yet to qualify to solve this problem. Even if people desire a noncoercive world, they will still disagree with anarchists and among themselves about how to sustain a noncoercive order. Not everyone accepts the anarchist plan of socializing people to structures that do not involve institutionalized coercion, and this itself creates a ground for further conflicts and the need for their resolution, which in turn reintroduces an appeal to constraints. Ultimately, anarchists have to think of institutions that prevent the emergence of constraints in a way that makes this prevention both sustainable and characteristically anarchic. Sustaining constraints under inexplicit criteria is not anarchism. Sustainability without constraints has not yet been proven successful. This is a serious dilemma for anarchism, a very challenging conception of the central philosophical and political problem that it faces. In view of this difficulty, the anarchist claims that we should abolish the state and we can live without it remain weak. And the challenge that anarchism entails chaos gains ground.

Yet the perspective of critical philosophical anarchism argued for in this study has something very valuable to offer in the direction of political anarchism. It provides the latter with a general proposal for how to look at social life and set out to organize it that both constitutes a fresh outlook and may guide the specific proposals of political anarchism to more fruitful directions in view of the specific problems that their defenses face. More importantly, in view of the main dilemma that haunts anarchism, critical philosophical anarchism has been shown to represent a view that does not start from a duty to justify constraints, but rather expresses *an aversion to illegitimate constraints and defines a duty not to harm others*. This, I argued, is the core feature of the anarchist perspective imposed on defenses of political institutions, and now it is the key to understanding the tasks of political anarchism. In light of this challenge, when anarchists are asked to provide an account of constraints to no constraints, they can begin to build their reply on this basis: *we need some constraints, but only those that prevent the emergence of illegitimate constraints. Such are those that it would be unreasonable for us to reject.*

This position gives every value to the anarchist's initial concern with the question whether we should have institutions at all. If no constraint can be reasonable, then the anarchist is justifiably pretty unconvinced. If there can be reasonable constraints, then we need to prove in each case that it is only those that apply. The distinctive focus on the *quality* of constraints, involved in the perspective proposed by critical philosophical anarchism, is central to this idea. The anarchist attack on the state becomes grounded and acquires new force. This position also throws light on the acceptable moral criteria that the anarchist test on legitimacy imposes: these values may be seen as the reasonable constraints that anarchism itself can adopt consistently and the basis of any constraint that is deemed reasonable. Finally, and importantly, it is a view that, when applied to anarchism's own proposals, neither repeats the traditional method of designing utopias and then struggling to prove them to be possible nor is a defense of "minimal state."[34] Rather, the defenses of alternative social structures such as those discussed above must first be guided by the newly established and more realistic demand that we prevent the imposition of illegitimate constraints, and anarchists must apply the relevant practices as part of an effort to redeem this demand.

With respect to the anarchist attack on the minimal state, there is a rather salient yet significant connection between anarchism and socialism. As Carter argues, economic equality is an aspect regarding which anarchism, as a theory of "no state," is closer to "more state" than to "less state." To the extent that equality is highly valued in anarchy (something that my study supports), versions of less state such as the "minimal state" are opposed. This is because the minimal state, in being confined to "providing security, enforcing contracts and preserving property," fails to provide welfare with its egalitarian implications; and "[i]n failing to provide welfare, it would most likely require a massive coercive apparatus to protect the inequalities that would inevitably arise," something that makes it "more coercive" and thus "all the more objectionable to anarchists" in general.[35] Hence, although anarchism is distinguished by its critique of the state and although it involves an attack on the institutionalization of welfare,[36] functions of the state that are not rooted in the ultimate causes of it as a paradigm of institutionalized domination and coercion (these causes being the real object of the anarchist attack) are not necessarily rejected. Among such functions is egalitarian distribution, the institutionalization of which may be preferred by anarchists if less state or monarchy are the only alternatives. Thus the characterization of theorists who support the minimal state, such as Nozick, as anarchists is refuted, a refutation about which I am in agreement with Carter.[37] Most importantly, the present explanation of the anarchist opposition to the minimal state highlights more specific aspects that make the perspective of critical philosophical anarchism incompatible with such a structure.

Thus the main, classical anarchist ideas and propositions remain promising and proper ways of completing the anarchist project. But to ensure that anarchists take a sustainable course in dealing with the problems that these propositions involve and in providing them as social solutions, and that they work consistently in this direction and compatibly with their attack on the existing social reality, they need *always* to be guided by the proposal offered by critical philosophical anarchism. In this way, their propositions are newly motivated. On the whole—in a way that philosophical and political anarchism are united—the anarchist project continues to be the characteristic anarchist position against the state. Its demanding approach to justification retains the radicalism appropriate to the anarchist outlook while, at the same time, it maintains a perspective that all sides must share and that is first and foremost applied to its own terrain.

In these terms, my suggestion is that, if it can combine its positive view of society with a description of how cooperation without coercion can obtain, all within the boundaries of the ideal of legitimacy, anarchism looks like the most appealing position. For this to be achieved, however, there is work to be done. The theoretical discussion conducted in this study is only a first motivating step in this direction. In the next section, I will provide a demonstration of the anarchist contribution in this direction by applying the ideal of critical philosophical anarchism to Bookchin's program. I will facilitate this critique by denoting certain ideas and proposals offered by other contemporary anarchist writers.

A critical philosophical anarchist critique of Bookchin's anarchist political program

Critical philosophical anarchists can develop their own micropolitics of power: their own discourses, practices, institutions, and identities. The conclusions of this study support a different point of departure, creating a basis for examining how the perspective of critical philosophical anarchism can relate to and motivate political anarchism. It is thus important to look further into the most promising contemporary implementations of anarchist networks, which are rooted in a concern with free and equal social relationships. Although it is not necessarily the most acceptable among the proposals of political anarchism, Bookchin's theory is quite promising and serves as a representative example. Once I have examined a significant part of it, and David Pepper's related references to anarchist practices, I will conclude my analysis here by applying the anarchist critique to his concrete anarchist political program. Bookchin's libertarianism, like any other proposal of political anarchism, should be tested according to the standards of the philosophical anarchist ideal of legitimacy. This section applies the test as an illustration of the critical philosophical anarchist contribution in the direction of anarchism itself. For this, it evaluates Bookchin's municipalism on the basis of the values that constitute the ideal and with reference to elements that the contemporary anarchist studies of Uri Gordon and the advocates of poststructuralist anarchism offer.

Bookchin revisited

Despite the merits of Bookchin's theory, it faces a variety of problems, most notably the problem of coercion, which, as indicated above, troubles political anarchism more generally. In Bookchin's case, I think his theory is open to criticism from both directions of the problem: on the one hand, his proposal suffers from the ineffectiveness of noncoercive practices and, on the other, it is prone to the emergence of dominative patterns, which anarchists hate most of all. In view of these shortcomings, there is a different current within anarchism, followed by a disparate group of theorists, such as Samuel Clark and Benjamin Franks (whose views were discussed in Chapter 6, the section "The anarchist Ideal of legitimacy"), John Clark, Uri Gordon, David Harvey, and the poststructuralist anarchists Saul Newman and Todd May. These thinkers focus on more flexible views of human nature, sociability, and society and on more fluid and open approaches of anarchism and anarchy (and utopia). I will criticize Bookchin along these lines, with a view to improving anarchist political theory and expanding its horizons in the directions that critical philosophical anarchism aspires to, facilitates, and legitimates.

Under the auspices of the anarchist ideal, Bookchin's libertarian municipalism should pass the test of voluntariness and equal participation, as indications of self-determination and active choice, and also the test of justice and association, as indications of the quality of social relations and arrangements. The different problems that Bookchin's theory faces should thus be dealt with by reference to the values of the anarchist ideal. These problems form a considerably long list. I will discuss the most serious and representative ones on the basis of the anarchist values.

The main themes of Bookchin's program are quite fixed, and syndicalism does not have sufficient advantages to be the dominant trend in successful anarchist politics. Nor is the rationalism of the Enlightenment—adopted by classical anarchism and, through the incorporation of its basic ideas, in Bookchin's theory—liberating enough to accommodate the continual reassessment and recreation of anarchist objectives. More generally, his central concepts, such as the idea that the libertarian municipality is the principal political unit, are not in complete harmony with the moral values of the anarchist ideal. More precisely, Bookchin's political program faces the following difficulties:

(1) it involves dominative patterns that repeat the dominative and coercive apparatus of the state, which are contrary to voluntariness and equality and, more important, betray the anarchist perspective.

(2) The kind of democratic participation that Bookchin envisages entails both practical and theoretical problems: the possibility of its implementation is meager and the relevant concepts and conceptions are not thoroughly developed. In this respect, his theory does not meet the criteria for participation and/or association.

(3) His theory shows elements of dogmatism, sectarianism, and abstraction, and it is vague and short-sighted, in contrast to the anarchist perspective.

Already Bookchin's first theme (see the section "The tasks of political anarchists" in this chapter), which suggests municipal politics as the proper activity of libertarian citizens, despite its innovative and inspiring character, lacks clarity, flexibility, and acceptability.[38] His view of the political places municipality at the center of democratic activity. As John Clark correctly points out, however, the exclusion of the neighborhood and other foci of anarchist networking from the center of anarchist politics is unjustifiable.[39] The municipality takes over the management of the community in every social area, from education to economics. Social interaction is determined primarily, almost uniquely, by assemblies and local officials. This limits the possibility of direct and active participation in the way the anarchist ideal demands. In relation to this ideal, we will see in the following subsections the importance of open-endedness and variety for anarchist practice. Moreover, the exclusion of other social and political subdivisions, such as the family or the affinity group, or larger contexts, such as nature and society, will most probably be accompanied by the related dominative attitudes on the part of the municipal members. Clark indicates "competitiveness, egotism, theatrics, demagogy, charismatic leadership, factionalism, aggressiveness, obsession with procedural details, domination of discussion by manipulative minorities, and passivity of the majority."[40] These limitations on social action and their effects on social behavior constitute an attack on self-realization through meaningful participation, in opposition to the ideal of equal-liberty.

Difficulties with the implementation of Bookchin's program make things worse. The kind of democratic participation proposed on the basis of assemblies, local councils, and their confederation lacks practicality and applicability. The size of the assemblies within contemporary societies is too large for people to exercise the kind of deliberation required for the radical democracy that anarchists and Bookchin himself envisage. As Clark claims, "the term 'face-to-face democracy' that Bookchin often uses in reference to these assemblies seems rather bizarre when applied to these thousands of faces (assuming that most of them face up to their civic responsibilities and attend)."[41] Nor is the creative thought of the citizens likely to thrive without a multiplicity of networks. Regarding, for example, the judicial realm, Bookchin ignores alternatives such as "popular juries" or "citizens' committees" for performing judicial functions, leaving there a complete void.[42] In the end, it is more likely that transparency and lack of mediation will give way to manipulation and dominating behaviors, which are antithetical to anarchism both in principle and in practice.

Bookchin's separation of political participation from administration in his second theme involves similar problems. Administrators would have greater involvement in policy-making than he believes: they would play a significant role in the formulation of specific directives on complex matters. Furthermore, there is some distance between theory and practice in terms of a disparity between immediate proposals and long-term goals. Sometimes Bookchin supports changes that do not place the assembly at the center of policy-making, such as the neighborhood planning assemblies in Burlington, Vermont, and yet, on the whole, he rejects any proposal or movement that departs from his municipalist program.[43] The first problem that entire communities face, according to Pepper's account (see the section "The tasks of political anarchists" above), indicates the dismal prospects of this disparity. The members of such communities fail to live up to the principles they profess to hold, as would the members of Bookchin's municipality, since his view does not take into account the historical circumstances and cultural influences that determine these members, as well as the related alternative anarchist proposals, something that the separation he proposes in his second theme also confirms. Thus, they will not pass the test of the anarchist ideal: theory and practice in such communities are unlikely to meet the demands of voluntariness, equality, and justice.

Ultimately, the whole idea of a municipal anarchist democracy, which has the municipality and its assemblies at its core, goes against the anarchist ideal of legitimacy:

One might imagine a "power to the people's assemblies" that would result in harsh anti-immigrant regulations, extension of capital punishment, institution of corporal punishment, expanded restrictions on freedom of speech, imposition of religious practices, repressive enforcement of morality, and punitive measures against the poor, to cite some proposals that have widespread public support in perhaps a considerable majority of municipalities of the United States. It is no accident that localism has appealed much more to the right wing in the United States, than to the Left or the general population, and that reactionary localism is becoming both more extremist and more popular. The far right has worked diligently for decades at the grassroots level in many areas to create the cultural preconditions for local reactionary democracy.[44]

Bookchin's scheme, therefore, does not guarantee the realization of democratic participation. The same goes for equality, since all the above issues reflect major inequalities within this scheme, which would probably grow. David Harvey believes that Bookhin's solution looks "suspiciously like a state, sounds like a state system, and will almost surely act like a state system no matter what the intent of its proponents might be."[45] Besides this worry, Harvey thinks that libertarian municipalism would require and in the end develop forms of hierarchical organization above the community level: "not only public and private, but collective and associational, nested, hierarchical and horizontal, exclusionary and open—will all have a key role to play in finding ways to organize production, distribution, exchange and non-consumption in order to meet human wants and needs on an anti-capitalist basis."[46] This agrees with the concerns expressed here, that is, the need for multiplicity and open-endedness in Bookchin's vision and the worry about its applicability, both with reference to the principled demands of the anarchist ideal.

Bookchin's third theme, regarding the municipalization of production, introduces further complications. His proposal does not seem practical or fair. Bookchin's conception of the political is problematic. Among other things, he conceives the political as an autonomous realm that absorbs any other social sphere, production being one such sphere. The municipalized economy is primary in Bookchin's vision, although it is not clear why it is not seen as one alternative among other enterprises. Again, multiplicity and open-endedness are central to anarchist networking, and this should affect the economic spectrum as well. Moreover, it is unrealistic to disregard other structures and practices that have historical and cultural significance, some of which entail that independent citizens as such might be involved in production, management, and contribution as well as policy-making, for example, the individual producers and small partnerships that could form part of "a growing economic cooperative sector that would incorporate social ecological values."[47] Bookchin's view becomes non-dialectical, dogmatic, and abstract here.

In addition, his view creates a basis for conflict between the perspective of the workers and that of the members of the assembly, as citizens of the municipality, given the disparity between the focus on the needs and responsibilities related to production and on those related to the local community, respectively. That his system is unviable is also apparent in the absence of realistic answers to basic questions, such as those concerning the realization of a consistent and pragmatic municipal economic plan within municipalities of thousands or millions of people. Nor does Bookchin give precise account of how the Marxist economic principle, "from each according to his abilities, to each according to his needs," which he adopts, can function within his libertarian municipality. How does the municipalization of the economy meet the demands of this principle? How does it measure abilities and needs? How exactly does it apply these measurements? In parallel with the need to try solutions in practice through real experiments, by real people, in actual communities, and because of the need, Bookchin's theory should provide the required theoretical basis for such efforts, toward a feasible future. In the section "The Gordonian 'Anarchy Alive!'" below, I will show that Bookchin's fourth theme, which is about confederation, has similar drawbacks.

All the above problems originate in the way Bookchin conceptualizes citizenship, participation, and the political itself (as already suggested here). Bookchin privileges the libertarian municipality and the political as the fundamental units of our social lives. In this way, our political role, that of a citizen, is conceived as determinative of our personal identity, citizenship of the municipality becomes the central form of participation, and the political takes precedence over the social. The first excludes other dimensions of selfhood, which are equally constitutive of one's identity and have political implications on their own. The second, Bookchin's focus on municipal participation, does not represent the common understanding of actual people, who usually understand their citizenship in relation to the state rather than to the municipality. In the same manner, it underestimates the importance of our membership in smaller or larger units, which range from the family and neighborhood to nature and the Earth. Additionally, his analysis lacks precision and articulation. As Clark indicates, these concepts are "mere abstractions" and can only "gain concrete content...through their embodiment in the history of society, or, more precisely in the practice of a community—in its institutions, its ethos, and its images," which constitute the background within which individuals can recognize, engage with, and transform their social reality.[48] The same observations go for his related conception of the political. Bookchin believes that "the People" are the primary historical agent,[49] thus disregarding many other levels of social being, such as the person, the parent, or the member of an economic class.[50]

All these limitations render Bookchin's view divisive, dogmatic, and impractical. Being the cause of the problems that his theory faces more generally, as examined in the above paragraphs, they account for the distance between his vision and the ideal of critical philosophical anarchism. Its lack of broad, open, and rich conceptions of participation and citizenship leads to the failure of his system to apply freedom as a natural, social, and political expression and expansion of personhood, and to view participation as an active involvement and interaction within a variety of possibilities, encompassing equal treatment, just and fair distribution of responsibilities and rewards, as well as meaningful membership. From the centrality Bookchin bestows on the assemblies and the municipality, as criticized in relation to his first, second, and third themes, to the primacy he gives more generally to the concepts related directly and exclusively to his libertarian municipalism, his theory exhibits a rigidity that fails to encompass the *reasonable legitimate constraints* demanded by the anarchist perspective and ideal.

In the light of these difficulties, Bookchin, like any anarchist theorist, is responsible for the second problem that communes face, according to Pepper, namely, the lack of ideological clarity—of a clear and shared vision of principled perspective and purposes—that might characterize activists. The fact that until now there has been less talk about principles and more about direct practical issues is exacerbated by the vagueness and contradictions of a theory that is expected to provide a proper ideological background. Both of these weaknesses create a gap between principle and practice, vision and realization.

Bookchin's view of "the People," as just criticized, leads to another problem. The idea of voluntariness that he adopts differs from the way critical philosophical anarchists discuss and prioritize this value. Bookchin's view displays a Bakuninist "voluntarist overemphasis on the power of revolutionary will,"[51] which is the exact opposite of self-realization and the anarchist focus on equal-liberty for the individual and with regard to social relations. The values of voluntariness and equal participation are abandoned, and with them all the concrete and complex aspects of freedom and equality involved in the formation of personhood that the anarchist idea of equal-liberty encapsulates. Social and ecological interconnectedness, moreover, conceived as "concrete unity-in-diversity," determines our understanding of social practice in a way that contrasts with the priority that Bookchin gives to ideology and the way he places consciousness at its service.[52] Similarly, Bookchin's distance from "bioregionalism," which is based on a commitment that involves "giving oneself over to the other" in the deepest recognition of the other's claims, deprives his view of a full understanding of freedom and choice in another sense.[53] The relation to other individuals and to the community that together they create becomes an extension of one's selfhood that transcends his individualist conception of choice within the libertarian municipal community, which involves merely choosing and doing what one likes. In all these respects, Bookchin's perspective opposes the anarchist ideal of legitimacy once more.

A poststructuralist intervention

Various anarchist views are subject to the aforementioned criticism, which should be used to pursue anarchist aspirations further. However, various anarchist views also adopt this standpoint. This is apparent in a critique that targets Bookchin's perspective more generally.

According to a criticism that Bookchin initiated on the basis of his division between "social" and "lifestyle" anarchism, the latter type of anarchism, and with it a related perspective of poststructuralist anarchism, must be rejected. Benjamin Franks agrees with this criticism. Class struggle anarchists, those who belong to groups and organizations that meet Franks's ideal and have his support, share Bookchin's view in discarding what they see in "lifestyle anarchism" as an individualist rebellion that neglects social relations and solutions in favor of a more atomized form of revolt.[54] In contrast, the poststructuralist anarchist Saul Newman discusses and refuses this distinction and defends personal liberation in a way that I find persuasive and quite significant for the present analysis.

Bookchin's criticism is basically that "lifestyle" anarchism favors what he terms "individual autonomy" at the expense of "social freedom," the former conceived as a hedonistic, narcissistic, and apolitical personal rebellion that rejects any concern for social responsibility and equality and the collectivist legacy of anarchism.[55] Newman marshals many responses against this claim, such as the moral Puritanism and the hopeless nostalgia for an authentic anarchism of the past that it exhibits,[56] but the most convincing reply lies, in my opinion, in his discussion of freedom and anarchist anti-politics. As we have seen earlier in this study, Newman's Stirnerite and Foucaultian notion of the self follows from a rejection of the ontological foundations and epistemological categories of classical anarchism, its belief in a fixed human essence and in a rational development of social forces. This leads to a defense of the principle of equal-liberty, which is adopted in this study. In its unification of freedom and equality, this principle negates any opposition between them as well as a supposed primacy of social freedom and the collective interest of society over individual autonomy. I agree with Newman that the anarchist idea of freedom embodies individual liberty and consists in a more encompassing view of human emancipation, which goes hand in hand with equality (overriding both the liberal and the socialist understanding).[57] This invites us to see the practices of young activists who do not belong to a social movement as expressions of responsibility and solidarity, rather than of egoistic and nihilistic individualism.

The anti-politics following from this view of freedom and anarchist action and supported by poststructuralist anarchism is not "an avoidance or withdrawal from political struggles, but rather the revolutionary abolition of formal politics of power (particularly in its statist form), and this is also obviously a *political* gesture."[58] The political is positioned between society and the state and has two functions: first, to achieve a "moment of 'dis-identification'," of a break with existing social identities, roles, and relations, and, second, to indicate that radical politics have tasks much deeper and wider than the attack on state power.[59] The "*politics of anti-politics*," or "*anti-political politics*," involve an an-archic dislodgment, an "aporetic moment," a project of radicalism and renewal, which, at the same time, is an engagement with the here and now starting from the local, a micro-politics affecting our attitudes, practices, relationships, and modes of living.[60] The political pole of these politics imposes limits by indicating and struggling against the reality of the dangers regarding society, dangers such as domination and subjugation at numerous levels. The anti-political pole "invokes an outside, a movement beyond limits," "the moment of utopia," or "the moment of ethics," which is external to the existing order and points toward an alternative.[61] Newman also agrees with Franks that anarchist (political) ethics must be "a situated ethics: an understanding of ethics as situated within, and contingent upon, specific social practices, communities and organisations," which, as he recognizes, involves autonomy and pluralism.[62] Yet he adds that this needs to be further supplemented with "an understanding of *ethical subjectivation*," of "the processes by which a subject becomes an ethical (and indeed political) subject," which can be found in theories such as Foucault's "ethics of the care of the self" discussed in Chapter 2 of this study.[63]

In the end, this poststructuralist perspective of freedom and politics is compatible with the contemporary network approach of anarchism, favoring the multiplicity that leads to the constant recreation of the self and of social arrangements. This perspective and the above criticism highlight the shortcomings of the ontology that underlies Bookchin's vision, with its dogmatic attitude toward social development along anarchist lines. Given his theory's problems with domination and with meeting the anarchist values, as discussed above, these shortcomings make it all the more necessary for it to satisfy the philosophical anarchist ideal.

The Gordonian "Anarchy Alive!"

Uri Gordon's work completes the above picture. His critical account of domination and his support of prefigurative politics in terms of decentralization, diversity, open-endedness, and, more generally, direct action are offered as part of a project for the revival of anarchist practice and theory. This account and project are quite crucial both for confronting the problems arising in Bookchin's proposal and for confirming the demands of critical philosophical anarchism.

For Gordon, "[t]he term 'domination' in its anarchist sense serves as a generic concept for the various systematic features of society whereby groups and persons are controlled, coerced, exploited, humiliated, discriminated against, etc.—the dynamics of which anarchists seek to uncover, challenge and erode."[64] Because domination includes innumerable articulations of forms of oppression, exclusion, and control, it gives rise to countless sites of resistance on the part of those subjugated. Regimes of domination are compulsory and overarching in conditioning individuals and their socialization, to the extent that people's patterns of behavior and their expectations themselves reflect and perpetuate dominating relations. The mere attempt to live outside such regimes and relations is an act of resistance. Thus, for anarchists, acts of resistance range from "*naming* domination" to any "particular actualization of a more systematic opposition to" it.[65] As the exact opposite of domination, the anarchist places the commitment to decentralization, on the basis of which networks of resistance work as an everyday reproduction and cultivation of social life that is completely antithetical to the mechanisms and relations that reproduce domination.

Before moving to decentralization and its centrality within anarchist political action, however, it is important to examine the concept of *power-with*, which is operative within anarchist structures and is related to both domination and decentralization. This discussion turns to real questions on issues concerning perspectives, dilemmas, and controversies that arise from within the anarchist struggle. Gordon discusses three kinds of power, suggested by the eco-feminist writer Starhawk, by reference to which we can see the anarchist struggle develop: *power-over*, which is domination in hierarchical and coercive settings and constitutes the kind of power that anarchism mainly opposes; *power-to*, which is the capacity to affect reality—a capacity to achieve results, alter physical reality, or cause an effect—and is the source and basis of the other two kinds of power; and *power-with*, a power among people who view themselves as equals, which is exercised as noncoercive influence and initiative.[66] The latter is crucial for anarchists, because it is equally imperative to their opposition to domination to deal with forms of unequal exercise of power and its effects that appear in anarchist networks themselves. Power-with is expressed in the form of suggestions rather than commands, but, as a power to influence the group of equals to which one belongs, it usually results in obedience.

Power-with is acceptable persuasion on the basis of rational argument, yet there is more to it. Among activists this power can become abused and abusive, because it involves resources that are difficult or impossible to transfer, such as the personality traits of articulate speech and self-confidence, something that creates problems for the redistribution of the sources of power and their use within the movement.[67] This problem becomes more serious given that who they are and how they "play the game in the anarchist arena of power" depends a lot on whom they know, which relates to the problems of invisibility and the lack of accountability generated by the so-called "tyranny of structurelessness" (TToS).[68] Theorists like Bookchin and Jo Freeman insist on more formal group structures within anarchist prefiguration, in order to avoid the problem of structurelessness that they see as central within anarchism. The tendency toward diversity and multiplicity supported by contemporary anarchism seems to generate this problem. The criticism is that structurelessness becomes a dogma and allows the emergence of informal hierarchical structures, generating difficulties such as the lack of organization, the invisibility of power, and the unaccountability of those exercising it. Power-with is used invisibly behind the scenes, so that those it is exercised upon cannot even know it, and responsibility is not clearly delegated, mandated, overseen, and revocable.[69]

These issues relate to the key discussion of enforcement. Enforcement is coercion with two additional features: it is "rationalized and institutionalized" and "it is coercion where the threat is permanent."[70] As explained in this chapter, anarchists have a problem with coercion: how to justify its existence within their own structures in order to avoid instability and chaos. The solution resulting from the perspective of the present study lies in the acceptability of reasonable constraints. Here Gordon helps us go further and understand that the problem anarchist networks face is not so much with coercion in general as it is with the forms of coercion involved in enforcement. Enforcement involves precisely those illegitimate forms of coercion that anarchists reject, but the lack of it, and the unaccountability and invisibility of power that this entails, create further issues for anarchists, apart from those arising from instability and disorganization.

Yet visibility might be impossible. Indeed, its opposite could be elevated to a positive value within anarchist structures, since, for example, public forums for influence might be more restricting and oppressive to those who cannot exercise influence within large, formal groups.[71] Invisibility can actually become politically meaningful, if we see that within the movement what matters is not strict accountability, but rather a cultivation of a spirit of solidarity in the use of power-with, intersecting with resource-sharing through the habit of redistributing political resources. This is related to the role of democracy in anarchy. In anarchy enforceability and bindingness are replaced with individual initiative, reasonable influence, and active participation, so outcomes cannot be mandatory. People do not arrive at collectively binding decisions of the classical democratic nature. Instead, what anarchism represents is "an altogether different paradigm of collective action," the process of *consensus decision-making*—and, with it, the power of veto on the part of the minority, the lack of any obligation for them to comply, and a climate where decision is more a matter of consultation and arrangement, of influence and free persuasion.[72] The likelihood of carrying out decisions depends on and increases with the cultivation of equal and voluntary participation, again, a spirit of solidarity and freedom arising from the fact that, through consensus, individuals feel ready to implement decisions because they have actually made them. This culture of solidarity regarding influence, resource distribution, and decision-making can thrive within prefigurative politics exactly because the latter is based on decentralization, diversity, and open-endedness, ultimately coming out as direct action. This setting is quite different from Bookchin's vision. The problems that his view of democratic participation faces, as we saw above (in the section "Bookchin revisited"), originate precisely from the formality and inflexibility of the structures and practices that he proposes. These structures and practices support and cultivate tendencies and attitudes that give rise to a political culture almost in opposition to the kind of collective action presently described, action that encourages the kind of initiative and participation that are consistent with the anarchist ideal.

Decentralization is an anarchist commitment related to the central anarchist tenets, indicated throughout the study, that liberation must come from those who suffer themselves the different kinds of domination, that it is primarily *self-liberation*, and that it should be exercised in the process of resistance, within the very practices and structures that form both the alternative and the challenge to the oppressive ones. Thus, decentralization becomes an end in itself, and prefigurative politics "represents a broadening of the idea of direct action, resulting in a commitment to define and realize anarchist social relations within the activities and collective structures of the revolutionary movement."[73] A different conception of politics, the devotion to non-dominating social relations, and the prefiguration of the desired society constitute anarchist positions and goals that are interwoven in a unified view and a direct activism. Direct action, in the form of attitudes and ways of living, propagating tactics, practices, structures, and networks of all kinds, is the necessary strategy in the struggle against domination that actualizes the commitment to resist the separation between processes and results. As Gustav Landauer famously stated:

> The state is a condition, a certain relationship among human beings, a mode of behaviour between men; we destroy it by contracting other relationships, by behaving differently toward one another...We are the state, and we shall continue to be the state until we have created the institutions that form a real community and society of men[74]

Thus, as Gordon points out, "the nurturing spaces created by activists" constitute sites of individual self-realization for overcoming "entrenched oppressive behaviours," an actual practice that works alongside the attack on the state to uproot the state within us. Both domination and liberation, both confrontation and constructive direct action "are each seen to supply each other's motivation" and to revive anarchist individualism "articulated as a present tense demand rather than merely a principle for some future society."[75]

Bookchin's confederal theme aims to expand decentralization and direct action, but falls short of its commitment. The impracticality of separating policy-making from administration, which was discussed in relation to Bookchin's three other themes in the section "Bookchin revisited," reappears at the federal level, since the role of the members of councils on which confederation depends cannot be limited to administration and coordination. How can those councils, which are meant to carry out the will of the assemblies, deal with any disagreement among the assemblies? And how is policy-making to be avoided at the confederal level if the assemblies rely only on majority rule, without some application of the method of consensus? Aside from these issues, impracticality becomes impossibility when we try to understand how the chain of responsibility works in Bookchin's confederalism. The problem is that the appointment of strictly instructed and revocable members to the confederal councils is unworkable within contemporary cities of thousands or millions of people, with hundreds or thousands of neighborhood assemblies and councils that should form further confederations.[76]

The real point, however, is that the problem is more than practical. A scheme that is unable to deal with conflict, responsibility, and coordination on any level will fail on every level to realize direct action and decentralization, the core features of the proposed alternative to centralized power. By reference to fundamental anarchist demands, Bookchin's system is unsuccessful. David Harvey's criticism of Bookchin's confederation further highlights this problem, and in more direct relation to justice and equality as values of the anarchist ideal:

> This is what Murray Bookchin's confederal system of autonomous municipalities would almost certainly be unable to achieve [namely, to prevent large-scale inequalities and injustices from developing in between poorer and richer communities and to equalize opportunities and outcomes], to the degree that this level of governance is barred from making policy and firmly restricted to the administration and governance of things, and effectively barred from the governance of people. The only way that general rules of, say, redistribution of wealth between municipalities can be established is either by democratic consensus (which, we know from historical experience, is unlikely to be voluntarily and informally arrived at) or by citizens as democratic subjects at different levels within a structure of hierarchical governance. To be sure, there is no reason why all power should flow downwards in such a hierarchy, and mechanisms can surely be devised to prevent dictatorship

or authoritarianism. But the plain fact is that certain problems of, for example, the common wealth, only become visible at particular scales, and it is only appropriate that democratic decisions be made at those scales.[77]

Another central aspect of the revolutionary demand is the focus on the here and now, which connects to diversity and open-endedness.[78] Contemporary anarchist approaches are characterized by pluralism and heterogeneity. Instead of endorsing a unique and all-inclusive revolutionary event and talking about future utopias, anarchists today see in the diverse and multiple structures, practices, and tactics of prefigurative politics the core realization of anarchy. The imperfect, developing, and open experiments of the present are viewed as the primary proposal of the movement. Diverse and fleeting moments of unconventional, cooperative, and egalitarian activities, various temporary autonomous zones and spontaneous happenings, manifold campaigns and modes of interaction constitute an innovative expression of collective action, the playful "here and now" application of a contemporary idea of utopia.[79] Gordon points out that this orientation toward creativity, open-endedness, and diversity has affinities with poststructuralist thinking, especially in the formation of new critiques and theories.[80] We have seen an example of this contribution in the previous subsection. It is crucial that this proclivity for change and rejection of absolutes has become, against Bookchin's rigidity and dogmatism, the permanent anarchist practice. John Clark's criticism of Bookchin's non-dialectical focus on the primacy of the assemblies expresses exactly this viewpoint:

> The mind of society—its reason, passion, and imagination—is always widely dispersed throughout all social realms. And the more that this is the case, the better it is for the community. Not only is it not *necessary* that most creative thought take place in popular assemblies, it is *inconceivable* that most of it should occur there. In a community that encourages creative thinking and imagination, the "mind" of society would operate through the intelligent, engaged reflection of individuals, through a diverse, thriving network of small groups and local institutions in which these individuals would express and embody their hopes and ideals for the community, and through vibrant democratic media of communication in which citizens would exchange ideas and shape the values of their community.[81]

This process is necessarily and crucially an *everlasting struggle* against the re-emergence of dominative patterns.

In conclusion, Bookchin's contribution is unquestionable, yet his approach needs substantial improvement. As a representative example of a contemporary political anarchist proposal, and as a way to realize the implications of the anarchist demands, Bookchin's view is open to critique from the perspective of critical philosophical anarchism. These implications are profound. All the main aspects of Bookchin's theory invite criticisms that challenge both the viability and the morality of his vision. As Clark himself concludes:

> Bookchin has made a notable contribution...insofar as his work has helped inspire many participants in ecological, communitarian, and participatory democratic projects. However, to the extent that he has increasingly reduced ecological politics to his own narrow, sectarian program of libertarian municipalism, he has become a divisive, debilitating force in the ecology movement, and an obstacle to the attainment of many of the ideals he has himself proclaimed.[82]

Anarchist approaches to concrete dilemmas

The previous discussion concentrated on the prospects of concrete anarchist proposals for preparing and developing a world with functioning and viable anarchist structures and tactics. But it must be completed with an examination of another aspect of the responsibility involved in adopting the position of critical philosophical anarchism. As long as the perspective of critical philosophical anarchism is offered in a world where there is a state, what is such an anarchist committed to in such a world, parallel to, alongside with, and aside from preparing a different one? This is the final important question to put to the anarchist. How does the anarchist ideal of legitimacy help address *concrete dilemmas*? How does the anarchist help us meet the claims that others make on us within the framework of contemporary states? More precisely, what is the anarchist position on police? On health-care and education? On international relations and the duty to help strangers in need? On our relation to the environment? If we do not want the minimal state, and if the anarchist ideal supports our demands on the state in terms of shared ethical concerns on the basis of which we judge the quality of its institutions, how is this translated into answers with regard to the issues just mentioned?

I believe we can answer these questions along the lines of the solutions outlined and proposed in the above arguments in defense of political anarchism. The anarchist subversive campaign represented in the criticism of political obligation encourages a critical attitude toward political institutions. This means that we attend to the fact that the state is not itself a source of ethical concerns, and so any claim by the state that its functions are for our own good needs to be tested, to be traced with reference to concrete harm done to individuals. So, for example, when the state claims that it needs the support of the army and the police in order to protect us, we should determine whether on the basis of acceptable moral reasons these functions of the state are appropriate. Since we have no political obligation, we need to examine both whether these services are acceptable on their own and whether there are acceptable alternatives to them. This means that, as long as we live within the state apparatus and it is very difficult to replace its institutions suddenly, we need to see which state apparatus functions properly.

The police is a typical and immediate way of providing civil protection. Thus we cannot suddenly make this institution disappear. But it is also a central aspect of state machinery: a form of political repression and a source of violent assault in the name of law enforcement and the suppression of crime.[83] So we can demand that the police exercise its duties in a legitimate way, namely that officers interfere without excessive use of intimidation, insults, physical force, or weapons, and only where and when necessary. The right to restrict or punish on the basis of ethical duties that we owe to each other belongs to all of us, but we need to agree on acceptable and common ways of discharging these duties, and an administration that already exists might be an efficient means for that. Again, it is not that we should be against even strong elements of the state, but they have to be balanced with their justification in terms of the ideal of legitimacy and the way it traces harm done to particular persons. At the same time, given that we know that the police is not an institution based on distinctive moral demands, but can function compatibly with independent moral demands that must be respected, we can work toward establishing alternative ways of providing protection, which gradually might replace the police. Political anarchists talk about civil militia. Furthermore, any method of resolving conflict and resisting domination and violence, such as mediation and propaganda by deed (discussed in the previous chapter, in the section "The anarchist ideal of legitimacy"), is relevant here. These and other forms of group-based, nonhierarchical administration might not be accepted by all citizens, and my claim is not that the anarchist should impose such a task on us. Nevertheless, given the anarchist view on domination and enforcement that the lack of political obligation justifies, such attempts are to be expected and thus appear now as totally acceptable and available alternatives that we can learn to apply within the state.

The same applies to health care and education. The state can be seen to justifiably provide (where it does) for these on the basis of legitimate ethical concerns. That is, it is a good way of helping discharge our relevant obligations toward one another in a fair manner. The anarchist perspective, therefore, does not lead immediately to a demand for the withdrawal of these functions of the state. Still, education can be seen as part of the state's method of civilizing,[84] and health care, being indispensable, can become an instrument of dependence and maltreatment. So anarchism makes it more critical for us to test the specific rationale and justification of the relevant state functions. It is critical to check and criticize specific laws and practices on education and health, to demand replacement of illegitimate and inefficient ones, which create harm, and to resist efficiency if it is exploited in the name of arrangements that represent interests other than the ones that should be served in these areas. For example, we should consider what the real motivations are, and if there is real need, for gradual replacement of state functions by private companies in cooperation with the state—the privatization of public institutions. At the same time, the anarchist perspective motivates, for those who want to try them, attempts at the replacement of the state institutions in these areas by non-centralized organizations. The visions of partial community that anarchists suggest—in the form of groups functioning at the level of the neighborhood, deciding within assemblies, coordinating by confederation, and administrating by rotation, for various purposes (from organizing alternative educational schemes to campaigning for the rights of children and old people and against the institutionalization of mentally ill individuals)—are available alternatives that can gradually develop and expand with considerable force.

Finally, states have external relations to and duties toward other states and the world as a whole. They need to protect themselves from foreign attack, support distant peoples who are treated unjustly, and in general cooperate with other states for just purposes. What is the position of the anarchist in relation to these issues? The lack of legitimacy shows that we have no obligation to help the state preserve itself or see its provisions for helping other people as the only ones that are applicable and justifiable. This does not mean eliminating the army suddenly, but it does mean that the anarchist perspective considers its maintenance optional and supports its eventual removal. The army is a very characteristic means through which state (and state related) agents serve their own interests and through which relations of domination and exploitation are cultivated and expanded. A striking example is the so-called "war on terror," which, in the name of protection and the support of ideals, involves moral, social, and political discrimination, propaganda, and the degradation of the very status, conscience, and perception of the general population. In the end, it itself perpetuates terror.[85] Anarchists are in complete opposition to these phenomena. Their attack on the legitimacy of political power is primarily motivated by them. We have no reason to help the state serve the purposes of its preservation and supremacy (no reason to support domination, coercion, hierarchy, and exploitation in themselves). Yet we have reason to accept international institutions for cooperation among the states, since they exist, to the extent that such organizations provide ways of reciprocal checking on the part of the states in international affairs. Indeed, we should evaluate the states at the international level in the same way we evaluate them separately and by reference to their domestic affairs. Thus, all the above demands apply to and within the framework of contemporary multistate organizations as well (e.g., the European Union). More importantly, we want to help other people in need. In this case, anarchism encourages participation in international organizations (especially independent ones) for peace and the support of the needy and the constant creation, cooperation, and expansion of affinity groups all over the world for these purposes. We can thus discharge our duties to others as individuals and as citizens of the world. (For anarchist groupings with international action, see the discussion (by Franks) in the section "The anarchist ideal of legitimacy" and in the previous section.) So an anarchist will not join the army, will not go to war, and will not contribute to the preservation of violent and exploitative means of supporting policies, practices, and aims. This is an area where the critical outlook toward the state finds a very direct expression.

A similar approach applies with regard to the environment and the environmental crisis the Earth faces. Every aspect of irresponsible behavior, dominative tendencies, and unequal, exploitative, and oppressive relations and structures is reflected in the way we treat life surrounding human beings and human societies. The ecological crisis is an ethical, social, and political crisis, threatening the health of the planet itself. It will have dire effects if we do not face our responsibilities and correct our mistakes. Recognizing and reacting to this problem, we can assist the multiple action of many contemporary environmental groups spread all over the world, with a wide range of philosophies and various effective organizational methods.[86]

Thus, the basis for answering the questions relating to the above problems *is* the outlook supported by critical philosophical anarchists. But it needs to be stressed that this does not extend only to claims for privacy and independence against the state when it interferes with harmless private behavior and demands high taxes. It applies to every area and it is accompanied by responsibilities and demands for work on our part. As long as taxes are for the purpose of public services, of helping the poor and funding health and education, they are a legitimate sacrifice we should make until we find alternative ways of helping people. Those among us who claim they are anarchists, cannot, as such, insist that they are free to escape that within the state which frustrates their individual pleasures, but also to enjoy in it what they find pleasant. They must take the bad with the good. They must, like everyone else, have responsibility as well as freedom. As has been argued in this study, these are two sides of the same coin. Again, the inquiring approach on the basis of shared ethical concerns that the ideal of legitimacy represents is applied: in the light of the knowledge that the state is no necessary or exclusive source of ethical concerns, at every instance all of us have the responsibility to consider carefully whether and why what the state requires, or does, is acceptable, or whether it creates harm. This is the way of tracing harm done to individuals and distinguishing reasonable from illegitimate constraints. Those accepted are those that have been tested and deemed appropriate. Thus, in the hands of critical philosophical anarchism, the challenge to political obligation has more pressing implications than the advocates of this anarchist position have thought. In this case, it becomes a positive and widely applied position about our attitudes and moral responsibilities.

Notes

1 Horton, *Political Obligation*, 120–123.
2 For similar points, see Miller, *Anarchism*, 174–177.
3 Horton, *Political Obligation*, 122–123.
4 For an explanation of the Prisoner's Dilemma and the argument from public goods, along with representative bibliography on these issues, see my discussion of the social contract in Chapter 2. For public goods, see also Chapter 4.
5 See Axelrod, *The Emergence of Cooperation*; Taylor, *Anarchy and Cooperation*; Taylor, *The Possibility of Cooperation*.
6 See Harriott, "Games, Anarchy, and the Nonnecessity of the State," 131–134.
7 See, for example, Sanders, "The State of Statelessness," 264–265.
8 For this, see Wolff, *Political Philosophy*, 52–53. See also Gregory S. Kavka, "Why Even Morally Perfect People Would Need Government," in *For and Against the State: New Philosophical Readings*, ed. John T. Sanders and Jan Narveson (Lanham, MD: Rowman and Littlefield, 1996), 41–61, where the writer offers a variety of reasons for proving that even perfect moral agents (angels) would need the state as the most effective solution to moral disputes.
9 See, for example, Taylor, *Community, Anarchy and Liberty*; Ward, *Anarchy in Action* (London: Freedom Press, 1982); Pepper, *Communes and the Green Vision: Counterculture, Lifestyle and the New Age* (London: Green Print, 1991); Bookchin, *Toward an Ecological Society*; Bookchin, *From Urbanization to Cities* (London: Cassell, 1995); Bookchin, "Libertarian Municipalism"; Carter, *A Radical Green Political Theory*; Clark, *Living Without Domination*; Franks, *Rebel Alliances*; Gordon, *Anarchy Alive*; Newman, *The Politics of Postanarchism*.
10 For a related examination of questions of ethics arising for poststructuralists, see May, *The Political Philosophy of Poststructuralist Anarchism*, ch. 6.
11 For a reply to the criticism that "instant anarchism" has adverse effects, see Sanders, "The State of Statelessness," 271–274. See also Colin Ward, *Anarchy in Action*, 131–133.
12 The anarchist idea of "a 'prefigurative' model of revolution": see Tom Cahill, "Co-operatives and Anarchism: A Contemporary Perspective," in *For Anarchism: History, Theory, and Practice*, ed. David Goodway (London and New York: Routledge, 1989), 235–236; Carter, *A Radical Green Political Theory*, 266–276.

13 See Cahill, "Co-operatives and Anarchism," 235–236; Joll, *The Anarchists*, Chapter 4.

14 On the whole, these schemes and their federation constitute a culture of "pre-figurative forms" or of "cooperative autonomy" (Carter, *A Radical Green Political Theory*, 266–276. See also Bookchin, *Toward an Ecological Society*; Bookchin, "Libertarian Municipalism"; Murray Bookchin, "A Politics for the 21st Century" [presented in The Lisbon Conference on Libertarian Municipalism, Lisbon, Portugal, 1998]). For more complete accounts, see also the section "The anarchist ideal of legitimacy" in Chapter 6 and the rest of Chapter 7 here.

15 Taylor, *Community, Anarchy and Liberty*, 169.

16 For an excellent survey of these social units, see Philip Abrams and Andrew McCulloch, *Communes, Sociology and Society* (Cambridge: Cambridge University Press, 1976).

17 For this, see David Pepper, *Communes and the Green Vision*.

18 For this, see Bookchin, "Libertarian Municipalism"; Bookchin, "A Politics for the 21st Century."

19 Bookchin, "A Politics for the 21st Century," 1.

20 Bookchin, "Libertarian Municipalism," 175.

21 Bookchin, "Libertarian Municipalism," 175.

22 Bookchin, "Libertarian Municipalism," 177.

23 Bookchin, "Libertarian Municipalism," 178–179.

24 Bookchin, "A Politics for the 21st Century," 5. As more recent examples of the form of institutions to which he aspires, Bookchin indicates the town meetings of the colonial New England (Murray Bookchin, "New Social Movements: the Anarchic Dimension," in *For Anarchism: History, Theory, and Practice*, ed. David Goodway [London and New York: Routledge, 1989], 268), the assemblies of revolutionary Paris, and the community life during the Spanish revolution (Murray Bookchin, *From Urbanization to Cities*, 189–192).

25 For these, see Bookchin, *From Urbanization to Cities*, 177–179.

26 Bookchin, *From Urbanization to Cities*, 184–186.

27 Bookchin, *From Urbanization to Cities*, 185–186.

28 Bookchin, *From Urbanization to Cities*, 194–195.

29 Taylor, *Community, Anarchy and Liberty*, 169. For forms of "partial community," see Ward, *Anarchy in Action*; Cahill, "Co-operatives and Anarchism"; Carter, *A Radical Green Political Theory*, 274–275.

30 See, for example, Franks, *Rebel Alliances*, Chapter 5.

31 For an account of forms of direct action, see Carter, *A Radical Green Political Theory*, 229–230, 233, 241, 268–260, 281, 316. See also the ideas presented and the bibliography used in the section "The anarchist ideal of legitimacy" (in Chapter 6) and in the section "A critical philosophical anarchist critique of Bookchin's anarchist political program" here. For an extensive development of the idea of "mutual aid" and an exemplary vision of society as a unit organized on that basis, see Kropotkin, *Mutual Aid*.

32 For anarchist practices for social control and equality, see Taylor, *Community, Anarchy and Liberty*; Ward, *Anarchy in Action*; Bookchin, "New Social Movements"; Pepper, *Communes and the Green Vision*; Carter, *A Radical Green Political Theory*; Franks, *Rebel Alliances*, Chapter 5. For a virtue-based

conception of "practices," see MacIntyre, *After Virtue*, chapters 14–17. Although MacIntyre is not an anarchist, his theory might help for an improved understanding and application of the "internal" values, rationale, and workings of social practices adopted by anarchists.

33 For the following analysis, see Pepper, *Communes and the Green Vision*, 59–62 and 200–203.

34 For such a defense, see Nozick, *Anarchy, State and Utopia*.

35 For these, see Carter, *A Radical Green Political Theory*, 258–260, 259, n. 10.

36 For this, see, e.g., Ward, *Anarchy in Action*, Chapter 12.

37 Carter, *A Radical Green Political Theory*, 259.

38 See the bibliography referring to Bookchin in the section "The tasks of political anarchists" above. See also Murray Bookchin, *Remaking Society. Pathways to a Green Future* (Montreal: Black Rose Books, 1989).

39 John Clark, "Municipal Dreams: A Social Ecological Critique of Bookchin's Politics," in *Social Ecology After Bookchin*, ed. Andrew Light (New York: The Guilford Press, 1998), 169.

40 Clark, "Municipal Dreams: A Social Ecological Critique of Bookchin's Politics."

41 Clark, "Municipal Dreams: A Social Ecological Critique of Bookchin's Politics."

42 Clark, "Municipal Dreams: A Social Ecological Critique of Bookchin's Politics," 165.

43 Clark, "Municipal Dreams: A Social Ecological Critique of Bookchin's Politics," 160.

44 Clark, "Municipal Dreams: A Social Ecological Critique of Bookchin's Politics," 159.

45 David Harvey, *Rebel Cities: From the Right to the City to the Urban Revolution* (New York: Verso Books, 2012), 152.

46 Harvey, *Rebel Cities: From the Right to the City to the Urban Revolution*, 87.

47 See, Clark, "Municipal Dreams," 170.

48 Clark, "Municipal Dreams," 147.

49 See, for example, Murray Bookchin, *The Last Chance: An Appeal for Social and Ecological Sanity* (Burlington, VT: Comment, 1983); Bookchin, *Remaking Society*, 159–207 ("From Here to There").

50 Clark, "Municipal Dreams," 149–152.

51 Clark, "Municipal Dreams," 141.

52 Clark, "Municipal Dreams," 142.

53 Clark, "Municipal Dreams," 180.

54 See, Franks, *Rebel Alliances*, 269, 404. See also my analysis of Franks's support of anarchist structures and tactics in Chapter 6, in the section "The anarchist ideal of legitimacy."

55 Murray Bookchin, *Social Anarchism or Lifestyle Anarchism: An Unbridgeable Chasm* (San Francisco: AK Press, 1995).

56 Newman, *The Politics of Postanarchism*, 143.

57 For Newman's response to Bookchin, see Newman, *The Politics of Postanarchism*, 142–147.

58 Newman, *The Politics of Postanarchism*, 146. For anti-politics and a new understanding of the political and of politics, similar to that promoted in

this study, as well as their relation to utopia and to a more radical notion of democracy, see also Newman, *The Politics of Postanarchism*, 4–11, 31–34, 68–70, 113–116, 127–130, 149–153, 161–163, Chapter 6. For more relevant points on poststructuralist anarchist political theory, see also May, *The Political Philosophy of Poststructuralist Anarchism*, Chapter 5.

59   Newman, *The Politics of Postanarchism*, 169.
60   Newman, *The Politics of Postanarchism*, 4–11, Chapter 6.
61   Newman, *The Politics of Postanarchism*, 7.
62   Newman, *The Politics of Postanarchism*, 160–161.
63   Newman, *The Politics of Postanarchism*, 160–161. See the section "The implications of the anarchist criticism of consent" of Chapter 2 here.
64   Gordon, *Anarchy Alive*, 32.
65   Gordon, *Anarchy Alive*, 33 and 34, respectively. For the whole discussion of domination here, see Gordon, *Anarchy Alive*, 29–34.
66   Starhawk, *Truth or Dare: Encounters with Power, Authority and Mystery* (San Francisco: HarperCollins, 1987). For a discussion of this threefold understanding of power, see Gordon, *Anarchy Alive*, 48–55.
67   See Gordon, *Anarchy Alive* 55–61.
68   Gordon, *Anarchy Alive* 61–62. For TToS, see Jo Freeman, "The Tyranny of Structurelessness," *Black Rose* 1 (1970) (accessed May 7, 2013: http://flag.blackened.net/revolt/hist_texts/structurelessness.html).
69   See Freeman, "The Tyranny of Structurelessness"; Murray Bookchin, *Social Anarchism or Lifestyle Anarchism*, and "The Communalist Project," *Harbinger, A Journal of Social Ecology* 3(1) (2003) (accessed May 7, 2013: http://www.social-ecology.org/2002/09/harbinger-vol-3-no-1-the-communalist-project/); the discussion of his anarchist proposals in the section "The tasks of political anarchists" here; Gordon, *Anarchy Alive*, 62–65.
70   Gordon, *Anarchy Alive*, 67–68.
71   Gordon, *Anarchy Alive*, 71–77, especially the related feminist critique.
72   Gordon, *Anarchy Alive*, 69–71.
73   Gordon, *Anarchy Alive*, 35.
74   Gustav Landauer, "Schwache Stattsmänner, Schwacheres Volk!" *Der Sozialist*, June, 1910, trans. in Eugene Lunn, *Prophet of Community: The Romantic Socialism of Gustav Landauer* (Berkley: University of California Press, 1973), 226.
75   Gordon, *Anarchy Alive*, 38 and 40, respectively.
76   For these criticisms, see John Clark, "Municipal Dreams," 178.
77   Harvey, *Rebel Cities*, 152–153.
78   For these, see Gordon, *Anarchy Alive*, 40–46.
79   See also Newman, *The Politics of Postanarchism*, on "the event," 6, 13, 47, 108, 127–130, 132, 138, 170, 178.
80   Gordon, *Anarchy Alive*, 42–43. See, e.g., Todd May, *The Political Philosophy of Poststructuralist Anarchism*; Saul Newman, *From Bakunin to Lacan: Anti-authoritarianism and the Dislocation of Power* (Lanham, MD: Lexington Books, 2001), and *The Politics of Postanarchism*; Lewis Call, *Postmodern Anarchism* (Lanham: Lexington Books, 2002).
81   See Clark, "Municipal Dreams," 164.
82   Clark, "Municipal Dreams," 182.

83 For the role of the police within the state, see Carter, *The Political Theory of Anarchism*, 38–41. See also Alex Comfort, *Authority and Delinquency in the Modern State* (London: Routledge and Kegan Paul, 1950); Hannah Arendt, *The Origins of Totalitarianism* (London: Allen and Unwin, 1958).

84 See Max Stirner, *The False Principle of Our Education*, ed. James J.Martin (Colorado Springs: Ralph Myles, 1967), e.g., 95–97.

85 For the importance of avoiding the financial and political dependence of smaller states and weaker peoples on bigger and stronger ones, see Kant's excellent essay on the way toward perpetual international peace (Immanuel Kant, "Perpetual Peace: A Philosophical Sketch," in *Kant: Political Writings*, ed. Hans Siegbert Reiss, trans. Hugh Barr Nisbet [Cambridge: Cambridge University Press, 1970, 1991:93–130.]). For characteristic literature on international relations, propaganda, and the war on terror, see, e.g., Chomsky, *For Reasons of State*; Chomsky and Herman, *Manufacturing Consent*; Chomsky, *The New Military Humanism*; Carter, "The Nation-State and Underdevelopment"; McLaughlin, *Anarchism and Authority*, 175–177.

86 From Greenpeace to Earth Liberation Front (ELF) and Friends of the Earth (FoE). For an examination of British environmental movements, see Franks, *Rebel Alliances*, 250–253. See also all of Murray Bookchin's relevant work (including the part of it used in this study), and a criticism from the perspective of social ecology of his approach to ecological concerns, in John Clark, "Municipal Dreams: A Social Ecological Critique of Bookchin's Politics," 39–42. For the activities of environmental movements, see my discussion based on Franks in the section "The anarchist ideal of legitimacy".

Epilogue

At this point I provide concluding remarks in terms of an overview of the preceding discussion that further demonstrates the distinctive contribution that critical philosophical anarchism advances in the debate on political obligation. I also indicate the wider implications of this contribution, for anarchists and for people in general.

Overview of the results of the study

The examination of theories of political obligation from the anarchist perspective has resulted in the following key conclusions.

None of the most comprehensive theories of political obligation, nor their combination, provides a persuasive account of such a relationship. Thus there is no general political obligation as a special political bond that determines the relationship between individuals and the governments of their countries of residence. This in turn frees our view of political institutions from a presumption in favor of obedience and encourages a critical approach to their construction and specific demands, which represents a different outlook to political reality and our position in it.

Part of the above outcomes is an emphasis, through the anarchist criticism, on the importance of establishing morally important features of actual, specific interaction between governments and each of their citizens as the only proper and satisfactory basis of political obligation, as well as on the difficulty of such an endeavor. These are the aspects that the accounts examined fail to account for, something that is reflected at the theoretical level by their failure to meet one or more of the conditions of political obligation, which together are expressive of the political nature of such bonds. But the character itself of the relationship required indicates the inevitable instability of such accounts: the resulting failure reflects and highlights the endlessness of a process aiming to discover and maintain particular and morally acceptable interactions that establish authority within a world of nation- and multination-states with extensive government over huge and variable populations. This in turn suggests that support for political institutions should probably move in a different direction.

Another part of the anarchist criticism and its results, concomitant with the preceding one, is that they verify and maintain the importance and desirability of the moral standards that are offered as bases of political obligation. These uncontroversial grounds are the central elements of ideals of legitimacy that constitute paradigmatic demonstrations of the relations that would characterize a legitimate society and its active citizenship, which existing societies do not have. But these values also work as general moral criteria that the ideals of legitimacy force on the assessment of political constraints as they exist and arise in the absence of political obligation.

Chapters 1–5 provided a detailed discussion of the anarchist criticism against leading positions within the debate on political obligation. This discussion reformulated their central claims and offered the elements that may be used as the defining features of a more comprehensive and positive position involved in the challenge of critical philosophical anarchists. My discussion sought to challenge the view that the theoretical project of critical philosophical anarchism is merely a negative and academic position. The discussion in Chapters 2–5 anticipated a more complete reply to this accusation, not only by supplying the main elements of such a reply, but also in being a genuine representation of the deepest anarchist concerns. Its revelation of the particular character of the relationship under discussion, as well as of the difficulties that this creates, represents and justifies the primary commitment to freedom and equality and the hostility to domination that are at the heart of anarchism. Also it verifies the latter's corresponding attention to the creation and protection of proper relations among persons within social reality. Finally, the discussion established a new horizon for the continuation of political dialogue, one involving a fresh starting point and carefully specified demands both in the direction of the defender of political institutions and in the direction of anarchism itself.

Chapter 6 followed with a direct demonstration of the significance and value of the above framework. This demonstration concentrates on the distinctive contribution of critical philosophical anarchism in the direction of defenses of political constraints. The central elements of this contribution are found in the special perspective that characterizes anarchism and the ideal of legitimacy that it involves as already detected in the discussion of the previous chapters. In Chapter 7 the contribution of critical philosophical anarchism was examined with regard to the direction of anarchism itself. Its perspective applied to political anarchism and the two were brought together to comprise a unified and more complete picture of anarchism. All these elements of Chapters 6 and 7 were elaborated as follows:

(1) The anarchist approach to political obligation reveals the mistake made by traditional theorists of attempting to derive it from general positive qualities of political institutions that may be used to account for their existence and desirability. Anarchism reveals that theorists begin from the wrong starting point and make very quick moves toward the justification of political obligation: they are guided by an assumption of the necessity of the state and focus on its possible merits in a way that neglects its defects and reflects an inaccurate depiction of what life without political institutions

would be like. They then attempt to derive political obligations from these merits. But they pay no attention to the particularized and enduring character of political obligation, which, being at the heart of their failures, itself shows that they have not asked properly the fundamental question that needs to be asked: whether we should have political institutions at all. Thus they rush to defend political obligation in a way that leaves behind the prior and essential basis of any possible defense. The failure of their accounts and the specific aspects of this failure, which the anarchist criticism reveals, redirect the defenders to the root of the weakness of their theories and to a perspective that they all need to share.

(2) This approach is carried to wider evaluations of constraints. The attention given to the question of political obligation and the accompanying clarification of the demands and difficulties that it involves shake the foundations of other supports of political institutions. First, the view of political relations that the results of the debate on political obligation force on us already changes our approach to political institutions. Second, the absence of political obligation itself constitutes a serious gap in the status and function of these institutions and thus, by itself, makes us question their validity and viability. But third, and most importantly, the attention given to the issue of political obligation shows it to reveal a demand that underlies more generally our view of political constraints. Through the question of political obligation the fundamental question whether or not institutions should exist and the initial view of political institutions as enduring evils that it represents become the starting point and determining basis of any attempt to evaluate them. Thus we can try to show the desirability of political institutions in terms of general qualities and accomplishments or to justify their particular activities. But the only way to understand the real force of these aspects is to apply them within a background defined by the fundamental question. In this respect the demand for their justification becomes harder.

(3) The anarchist is concerned with the imposition of illegitimate constraints. Political institutions exist, and there might be no point in attempting their removal. Indeed, philosophical anarchists need not be, and are often not, committed to overthrowing institutions. But the fundamental question that the anarchist reminds us to ask throws light on this fact: even when political institutions remain necessary, despite the absence of political obligation, the defects of political coercion can be counterbalanced only if instances of coercion are shown to serve the values that they are claimed to serve in the first place. For this to happen, however, every existing and every new form of constraint needs to be shown to actually respect these values and to continue to do so in every instance of its social function. Political obligation is a relationship that is enduring and exacting because of its actual, particularized, and normative character, which reflects the implications of the fundamental political question. This is what makes its

justification an endless and probably unattainable task. This fact might not condemn political institutions to nonexistence, but, in light of the failure it involves, their assessment itself becomes a more difficult and a persistent process. Hence the demand that we pay attention to the defects of political institutions represents the central concern with preventing illegitimate constraints. It thus carries with it the demand that we assess these institutions regularly in terms of the merits on the basis of which they can be acceptable forms of social organization. The general anarchist message that it is very difficult to justify political institutions is now evident and pressing.

(4) Given the reasserted demand for justification, the anarchist ideal of legitimacy acquires a newly formulated and important role. In its function as a paradigmatic depiction of the form of societies where political obligation would exist, it works now also as a reminder of what it is that the defenses of political institutions need to do as long as societies fail to assimilate this picture. It becomes a test on political constraints in terms of the central values of voluntariness, justice, fairness, and association that it provides as criteria for their assessment. Thus, in addition to the reformulation of the demand that it establishes with regard to justification, anarchism provides a proposal for how to apply this demand. And this proposal is one that applies to the anarchist too: despite their lack of institutionalized domination and of political obligation as the bond that characterizes their social relations, the general character of the visions of political anarchism and the social interactions that they involve should reflect the moral values of the anarchist ideal. This relates to the problems with enforcement, coercion, and stability that anarchism itself faces and that I discuss again in the final part of this Epilogue.

(5) The appearance of the paradox that we are ruled because we do not want to be ruled, with which the anarchist challenge to defenses of political institutions began, disappears, since the new test of legitimacy shows a way in which political constraints become constraints that individuals put on themselves and are expressive of their own participation. As anticipated in Chapter 1 and explained in Chapter 6, the anarchist insistence on self-government results in the view defended by Raz—which asserts the realization of autonomy through the state's application of reasons applying to individuals themselves—yet via the establishment of the important role of choice as affirmation of self-government. Such choice need not have the form of actual particular consent (and the failure of defenses of political obligation shows that this cannot be achieved). But it needs to be affirmed in the existence of constraints that are of such a quality that reflects an authentic and equal participation on the part of individuals in the workings of government. In this way, the approach of political theorists ceases to look paradoxical, because they can show that the political constraints that (they claim) we (should) accept are part and indications of our very willingness

not to be externally and arbitrarily constrained. This view is also compatible with the demands of equality.

(6) Thus every theorist needs to share the anarchist perspective. The anarchist versions of an ideal of legitimacy must become a general testing ground for every evaluation of constraints. This sheds new light on the subversive campaign that advocates of philosophical anarchism are committed to. The different perspective of our position within political society that this campaign establishes and the corresponding removal of the habit of compliance that it strives for become an expression of an innovative position. As philosophical anarchists themselves argue, these changes do not lead to widespread disobedience and chaos, since the absence of political obligation does not destroy other assessments of institutions and since it does not eliminate the existence of other important moral reasons for supporting them. Moreover, any change of political reality that they encourage is gradual and part of a large series of careful (even if sometimes spontaneous), well-organized, and patiently applied efforts. Yet the perspective and demands that critical philosophical anarchism is shown to involve imbue the anarchist campaign with a *radicalism* that has not been detected by its advocates. The fundamental question that the anarchist critique of political obligation advances and the process of justification this question entails show that the presumption removed by the anarchist enlightening campaign and the critical attitude it cultivates are indications of a more drastic challenge to political institutions. They also reveal that this challenge and attitude function within a framework that makes appropriate the support of government only to the extent it does enough to protect us. In turn, this question and process are themselves expressions of a constant reminder of the enduring defects of the state, of the unacceptability of illegitimate constraints, and of a project toward actual social changes. The demand for the limitation of political power to aspects that reflect moral *quality*, the insistence on the importance of equal-liberty, and a view of political constraints as acceptable only to the extent that they are compatible with these ideas join together into an insurgent perspective.

(7) All the above are further demonstrated through a discussion (in Chapter 7) of political anarchism with reference to the perspective of critical philosophical anarchism. The project of political anarchism is a difficult one. It should be compatible with the demands of philosophical anarchism. It should also deal with the problems that the implementation of an anarchist society faces. Still, anarchist thought and practice are constantly renovated and there are various elaborate and inspiring proposals on the part of contemporary anarchist thinkers. These proposals should be taken into serious consideration, since they contribute significant elements to a fresh view of our political world.

In the end, critical philosophical anarchism meets political anarchism. It follows the latter in becoming a constant guardian against the corrupting tendencies of the state, which political anarchists stress as part of their more general attack on domination. See, for example, the famous exclamation by Proudhon:

> To be GOVERNED is to be at every operation, at every transaction, noted, registered, enrolled, taxed, stamped, measured, numbered, assessed, licensed, authorized, admonished, forbidden, reformed, corrected, punished. It is, under the pretext of public utility, and in the name of the general interest, to be placed under contribution, trained, ransomed, exploited, monopolized,...robbed; then, at the slightest resistance, the first word of complaint, to be repressed, fined, despised, harassed,...sacrificed, sold, betrayed; and, to crown all, mocked, ridiculed, outraged, dishonoured. That is government; that is its justice; that is its morality.[1]

This is a crucial part of the political anarchist criticism of the state, which goes beyond the detection of the failures of justifications of it. For a more recent example of this line of criticism, in addition to those contemporary lines of criticism discussed in the previous chapter, Colin Ward's comment is characteristic. It indicates that the state stands in a reverse relation with the rest of society, occupying and formalizing at the expense of the latter any space unused by social participation:

> There is an inverse correlation between the two [namely, the libertarian and the authoritarian tradition]: the strength of one is the weakness of the other. If we want to strengthen society we must weaken the state. Totalitarians of all kinds realise this, which is why they invariably seek to destroy those institutions which they cannot dominate. *So do the dominant interest groups in the state*....[2]

In addition to its support of this stand, critical philosophical anarchism gives attention to, and facilitates the construction and support of, the social proposals involved in political anarchism. More generally, it expresses the so-called "'anarchist invariant': the recurring desire for life without government that haunts the political imagination."[3] Critical philosophical anarchism is representative of a position that characterizes anarchism on the whole.

Conclusion

The anarchist position issues a fundamental demand. And by issuing it, everything changes. Even if we cannot abandon political institutions or escape their constant determination, we are still inspired by and committed to a different perspective. We assert anew an old and unjustifiably forgotten position: we demand without cease that institutions become better and we participate in this endeavor. Even when the state is good, its very existence is morally problematic. We should not put excessive trust in it, but rather exercise critical caution. Our arguments are fragile and present a temporary victory. No one wins. We need to help each other. We have to apply this position. In the end, everybody has to ask the anarchist question actually and persistently. When we complain that we have been harmed, we should remember that it is we who have the primary responsibility for the elimination of this evil. We must do this, because it is the best affirmation of our free and equal involvement in the social world that we have created, that we inhabit, that we are truly able to maintain and improve. We owe this to ourselves, if we want to be active and responsible citizens, independent and fulfilled human beings.

Notes

1 Proudhon, *General Idea of the Revolution*, 294. See also, e.g., Bakunin, "Power Corrupts the Best."
2 Ward, *Anarchy in Action*, 24 (emphasis mine). For a very recent philosophical criticism of the state in terms of political social anarchism, see Carter, *A Radical Green Political Theory*, and Chapter 7 here.
3 See Newman, *The Politics of Postanarchism*, 1. The term was coined by Benjamin Noys in Benjamin Noys, "Anarchy-without-Anarchism," No Useless Leniency blog, accessed June 5, 2009, http://leniency.blogspot.com/2009/06/anarchywithoutanarchism.html. Originally published as Editorial 11, Sans-Philosophie.net (October 2006).

BIBLIOGRAPHY

Abrams, Philip and Andrew McCulloch. *Communes, Sociology and Society*. Cambridge: Cambridge University Press, 1976.

Alexander, Robert J. *The Anarchists in the Spanish Civil War*, 2 vols. London: Janus, 1999.

Anarchist Communist Federation. *Beyond Resistance: A Revolutionary Manifesto for the Millennium*, 2nd edition. London: Anarchist Communist Editions, 1997.

Anscombe, Gertrude Elizabeth Margaret. "On the Source of the Authority of the State." In *Authority*, edited by Joseph Raz, 142–173. Oxford: Basil Blackwell, 1990.

Arendt, Hannah. *The Origins of Totalitarianism*. London: Allen and Unwin, 1958.

Arneson, Richard J. "The Principle of Fairness and Free-Rider Problems." *Ethics* 92 (1982): 616–633.

Axelrod, Robert. *The Emergence of Cooperation*. New York: Basic Books, 1984.

Bakunin, Mikhail Aleksandrovich. "Power Corrupts the Best." In *Idem, Marxism, Freedom, and the State*, edited by Kenneth Joseph Kenafick. London: Freedom Press, 1950.

———. *Statism and Anarchy*, edited by Shatz S. Marshall. Cambridge: Cambridge University Press, 2005.

Barker, Rodney. *Political Legitimacy and the State*. Oxford: Clarendon Press, 1990.

Barsky, Robert F. *Noam Chomsky: A Life of Dissent*. Cambridge, MA: MIT Press, 1997.

Baudrillard, Jean. *In the Shadow of the Silent Minorities ... or, The End of the Social, and Other Essays*, translated by Paul Foss, Paul Patton, and John Johnston. New York: Semiotext(e) Foreign Agents, 1983.

———. *The Ecstasy of Communication*, translated by Bernard Schütze and Caroline Schutze. New York: Semiotext(e) Foreign Agents, 1987.

Bolloten, Burnett. *The Grand Camouflage: The Spanish Civil War and Revolution, 1936–39*. London: Pall Mall, 1968.

Bookchin, Murray. *Toward an Ecological Society*. Montreal: Black Rose Books, 1980.

———. *The Last Chance: An Appeal for Social and Ecological Sanity*. Burlington, VT: Comment, 1983.

———. *From Urbanization to Cities*. London: Cassell, 1987(new edition 1995).

———. *Remaking Society. Pathways to a Green Future*. Montreal: Black Rose Books, 1989.

———. "New Social Movements: The Anarchic Dimension." In *For Anarchism: History, Theory, and Practice*, edited by David Goodway, 259–274. London and New York: Routledge, 1989.

———. *Social Anarchism or Lifestyle Anarchism: An Unbridgeable Chasm*. San Francisco: AK Press, 1995.

———. "Libertarian Municipalism." In *The Murray Bookchin Reader*, edited by Janet Biehl, 172–196. London and Washington: Cassell, 1997.

———. "A Politics for the 21st Century." Presented in The Lisbon Conference on Libertarian Municipalism, Lisbon, Portugal, 1998.

———. "The Communalist Project." *Harbinger, A Journal of Social Ecology* 3.1 (2003), Accessed May 7, 2013. http://www.social-ecology.org/2002/09/harbinger-vol-3-no-1-the-communalist-project/.

Cahill, Tom. "Co-operatives and Anarchism: A Contemporary Perspective." In *For Anarchism: History, Theory, and Practice*, edited by David Goodway, 235–258. London and New York: Routledge, 1989.

Call, Lewis. *Postmodern Anarchism*. Lanham: Lexington Books, 2002.

Carter, Alan. "Outline of an Anarchist Theory of History." In *For Anarchism. History, Theory, and Practice*, edited by David Goodway, 176–197. London and New York: Routledge, 1989.

———. "Towards a Green Political Theory." In *The Politics of Nature*, edited by Andrew Dobson and Paul Lucardie, 39–62. London and New York: Routledge, 1993.

———. "The Nation-State and Underdevelopment." *Third World Quarterly* 16 (1995): 595–618.

———. *A Radical Green Political Theory*. London: Routledge, 1999.

———. "Analytical Anarchism: Some Conceptual Foundations." *Political Theory* 28.2 (2000): 230–253.

Carter, April. *The Political Theory of Anarchism*. London: Routledge and Kegan Paul, 1971 (new edition 2010).

Chomsky, Noam. *For Reasons of State*. London: Fontana, 1973.

———. *The New Military Humanism: Lessons from Kosovo*. London: Pluto Press, 1999.

——— and Edward S. Herman. *Manufacturing Consent: The Political Economy of the Mass Media*. New York: Pantheon Books, 1988.

Clark, John. "Municipal Dreams: A Social Ecological Critique of Bookchin's Politics." In *Social Ecology after Bookchin*, edited by Andrew Light, 137–191. New York: The Guilford Press, 1998.

Clark, Samuel. *Living Without Domination: The Possibility of an Anarchist Utopia*. Aldershot: Ashgate, 2007.

Cleaver, Harry. "The Zapatistas and the International Circulation of Struggle: Lessons Suggested and Problems Raised." 1998. Accessed May 7, 2013. http://www.eco.utexas.edu/faculty/Cleaver/lessons.html.

Cohen, Gerald Allan. "Reason, Humanity and the Moral Law." In *The Sources of Normativity*, edited by Christine Marion Korsgaard, 167–188. Cambridge: Cambridge University Press, 1996.

Comfort, Alex. *Authority and Delinquency in the Modern State*. London: Routledge and Kegan Paul, 1950.

Dagger, Richard. "Membership, Fair Play and Political Obligation." *Political Studies* 48 (2000): 104–117.

Daniels, Norman. "Wide Reflective Equilibrium and Theory Acceptance in Ethics." *Journal of Philosophy* 76 (1979): 256–282.

De George, Richard T. *The Nature and Limits of Authority*. Lawrence: University Press of Kansas, 1985.

De Jasay, Anthony. "Self-Contradictory Contractarianism." In *For and Against the State: New Philosophical Readings*, edited by John T. Sanders and Jan Narveson, 137–169. Lanham, MD: Rowman and Littlefield, 1996.

Dworkin, Ronald M. "The Original Position." In *Reading Rawls: Critical Studies on Rawls*, edited by Norman Daniels, 16–52. Oxford: Basil Blackwell, 1975.

———. *Law's Empire*. Cambridge, MA: Harvard University Press, 1986.

Evans-Pritchard, Edward Evan. *The Nuer: A Description of the Modes of Livelihood and Political Institutions of a Nilotic People*. Oxford: Clarendon Press, 1940.

Flood, Merrill Meeks. "Some Experimental Games." *Management Science* 5 (1958): 5–26

Foucault, Michel. *Discipline and Punish: The Birth of Prison*, translated by Alan Sheridan. London: Penguin, 1991.

———. *The Essential Works of Foucault 1954–1984, Volume 1: Ethics. Subjectivity and Truth*, edited by Paul Rabinow, translated by Robert Harley. London: Penguin, 2002.

———. *The Essential Works of Foucault 1954–1984, Volume 3: Power*, Edited by James Faubion, translated by Robert Harley. London: Penguin, 2002.

Franks, Benjamin. *Rebel Alliances: The Means and Ends of Contemporary British Anarchisms*. Edinburgh: AK Press, 2006.

Freeman, Jo. "The Tyranny of Structurelessness." *Black Rose* 1 (1970). Accessed May 7, 2013. http://flag.blackened.net/revolt/hist_texts/structurelessness.html.

Friedman, Richard B. "On the Concept of Authority in Political Philosophy." In *Authority*, edited by John Raz, 56–91. Oxford: Basil Blackwell, 1990.

Gans, Chaim. *Philosophical Anarchism and Political Disobedience*. Cambridge: Cambridge University Press, 1992.

Gauthier, David. *Morals by Agreement*. Oxford: Clarendon Press, 1986.

Gellner, Ernest. "Soviets against Wittfogel: Or, the Anthropological Preconditions of Mature Marxism." In *States in History*, edited by John A.Hall, 78–108. Oxford: Basil Blackwell, 1986.

Gilbert, Margaret. "Group Membership and Political Obligation." *The Monist* 76 (1993): 119–131.

Godwin, William. *An Enquiry Concerning Political Justice and Its Influence on General Virtue and Happiness*. London: G.G. J. and J. Robinson, 1793.

Goldman, Emma. *Anarchism and Other Essays*. New York: Dover, 1969.

Gordon, Uri. *Anarchy Alive: Anti-Authoritarian Politics from Practice to Theory*. London: Pluto Press, 2008.

Graham, Keith. "The Moral Significance of Collective Entities." *Inquiry* 44 (2001): 21–42.

Graham, Robert. "The Role of Contract in Anarchist Ideology." In *For Anarchism: History, Theory, and Practice*, edited by David Goodway, 150–175. London and New York: Routledge, 1989.

Green, Leslie. *The Authority of the State*. Oxford: Clarendon Press, 1988.

———. "Who Believes in Political Obligation?" In *For and Against the State: New Philosophical Readings*, edited by John T. Sanders and Jan Narveson, 1–18. Lanham, MD: Rowman and Littlefield, 1996.

Habermas, Jürgen. "Human Rights and Popular Sovereignty: The Liberal and Republican Versions." *Ratio Juris* 7 (1994): 1–13.

Hampton, Jean. *Hobbes and the Social Contract Tradition.* Cambridge: Cambridge University Press, 1986.

———. *Political Philosophy.* Boulder: Westview Press, 1997.

Harriott, Howard H. "Games, Anarchy, and the Nonnecessity of the State." In *For and Against the State: New Philosophical Readings*, edited by John T. Sanders and Jan Narveson, 119–136. Lanham, MD: Rowman and Littlefield, 1996.

Hart, Herbert Lionel Adolphus. "Are there any Natural Rights?" *Philosophical Review* 64 (1955): 175–191.

———. "Commands and Authoritative Legal Reasons." In *Authority*, edited by John Raz, 92–114. Oxford: Basil Blackwell, 1990.

Harvey, David. *Rebel Cities: From the Right to the City to the Urban Revolution.* New York: Verso Books, 2012.

Hill, Thomas E. *Autonomy and Self-Respect.* Cambridge: Cambridge University Press, 1991.

Hobbes, Thomas. *Leviathan*, edited by Crawford Brough MacPherson. Harmondsworth: Penguin, 1968.

Horton, John. *Political Obligation.* London: Macmillan, 1992 (revised 2nd edition in 2010).

———. "Peter Winch and Political Authority." *Philosophical Investigations* 28 (2005): 235–252.

———. "In Defence of Associative Political Obligations: Part One." *Political Studies* 54 (2006): 427–443.

———. "In Defence of Associative Political Obligations: Part Two." *Political Studies* 55 (2007): 1–19.

———. "Plural Subjects and Political Obligations." *Jurisprudence: An International Journal of Legal and Political Thought* 4.2 (2013): 280–286.

———. "Political Legitimacy, Justice and Consent." *Critical Review of International Social and Political Philosophy* 15.2 (2012): 129–148.

Hume, David. *A Treatise of Human Nature*, edited by Sir Lewis Amherst Selby-Bigge. Oxford: Oxford University Press, 1978.

———. "Of the Original Contract." In *Hume: Political Essays*, edited by Knud Haakonssen, 186–201. Cambridge: Cambridge University Press, 1994.

Hutchinson, Sharon E. *Nuer Dilemmas: Coping with Money, War, and the State.* Berkeley: University of California Press, 1996.

Joll, James. *The Anarchists.* London: Methuen, 1964.

Kant, Immanuel. *Groundwork of the Metaphysics of Morals*, edited by Mary Gregor. Cambridge: Cambridge University Press, 1998.

———. *Critique of Practical Reason*, edited by Mary Gregor. Cambridge: Cambridge University Press, 1999.

———. "On the Common Saying 'This May Be True in Theory, But It Does Not Apply in Practice'." In *Kant: Political Writings*, edited by Hans Siegbert Reiss, translated by Hugh Barr Nisbet, 61–92. Cambridge: Cambridge University Press, 1970, 1991.

———. "Perpetual Peace: A Philosophical Sketch." In *Kant: Political Writings*, edited by Hans Siegbert Reiss, translated by Hugh Barr Nisbet. Cambridge: Cambridge University Press, 1970, 1991.

————. *The Metaphysics of Morals*, edited by Mary Gregor. Cambridge: Cambridge University Press, 2001.

Kavka, Gregory S. "Hobbes's War of All against All." *Ethics* 93 (1983): 291–310.

————. "Why Even Morally Perfect People Would Need Government." In *For and Against the State: New Philosophical Readings*, edited by John T. Sanders and Jan Narveson, 41–61. Lanham, MD: Rowman and Littlefield, 1996.

Klosko, George. "Presumptive Benefit, Fairness and Political Obligation." *Philosophy and Public Affairs* 16.3 (1987): 241–259.

————. *The Principle of Fairness and Political Obligation*. Lanham, MD: Rowman and Littlefield, 1992.

————. "Political Obligation and the Natural Duties of Justice." *Philosophy and Public Affairs* 23 (1994): 251–270.

————. "Fixed Content of Political Obligations." *Political Studies* 46 (1998): 53–67.

———— and David Klein. "Political Obligations: The Empirical Dimension." Paper presented at the annual meeting of the American Political Science Association, San Francisco (2001): 1–38.

Korsgaard, Christine Marion. "The Authority of Reflection." In *The Sources of Normativity*, edited by Christine Marion Korsgaard, 90–130. Cambridge: Cambridge University Press, 1996.

Kropotkin, Petr Alekseevich. *Mutual Aid: A Factor of Evolution*. Boston: Extending Horizons Books, 1955.

————. *Kropotkin's Revolutionary Pamphlets*, edited by Roger Nash Baldwin. New York: Dover, 1970.

————. *Fields, Factories and Workshops Tomorrow*. London: George Allen and Unwin, 1974.

————. *The Conquest of Bread and Other Writings*, edited by Shatz Marshall, Cambridge: Cambridge University Press, 1995 (reprint of 1913 revised edition).

Ladenson, Robert. "In Defense of a Hobbesian Conception of Law." In *Authority*, edited by John Raz, 32–55. Oxford: Basil Blackwell, 1990.

Landauer, Gustav. "Schwache Stattsmänner, Schwacheres Volk!" *Der Sozialist*, June, 1910, translated by Eugene Lunn *Prophet of Community: The Romantic Socialism of Gustav Landauer*. Berkley: University of California Press, 1973.

Lewis, Thomas J. "On Using the Concept of Hypothetical Consent." *Canadian Journal of Political Science* 22 (1989): 793–808.

Lloyd Thomas, David A. *Locke on Government*. London and New York: Routledge, 1995.

Locke, John. *Two Treatises of Government*, edited by Peter Laslett. Cambridge: Cambridge University Press, 1988.

Lukes, Steven. *Power: A Radical View*. London: Macmillan, 1974.

Luxemburg, Rosa. *The Mass Strike*. London: Bookmarks, 1986.

Lyons, David. "Need, Necessity, and Political Obligation." *Virginia Law Review* 67 (1981): 63–77.

MacIntyre, Alasdair C. *After Virtue. A Study in Moral Theory*. London: Duckworth, 1981. second edition, with postscript 1985.

Malatesta, Errico. *Errico Malatesta: His Life and Ideas*, edited by Vernon Richards. London: Freedom Press, 1965.

————. *Anarchy*, translated by Vernon Richards. London: Freedom Press, 1984.

Mann, Michael. *Sources of Social Power*, 2 vols. Cambridge: Cambridge University Press, 1986–93.

Marshall, Peter. "Human Nature and Anarchism." In *For Anarchism: History, Theory, and Practice*, edited by David Goodway, 127–149. London and New York: Routledge, 1989.

———. *Demanding the Impossible: A History of Anarchism*, Revised edition. London: Fontana, 1993.

Martin, Rex. "Anarchism and Scepticism." In *Anarchism*, edited by James Roland Pennock and John William Chapman, 114–127. New York: New York University Press, 1978.

Marx, Karl. "On the Jewish Question." In *Karl Marx: Selected Writings*, edited by David McLellan, 39–62. Oxford: Oxford University Press, 1977.

———. "Economic and Political Manuscripts." In *Karl Marx: Selected Writings*, edited by David McLellan, 75–112. Oxford: Oxford University Press, 1977.

Mason, Andrew. *Community, Solidarity and Belonging*. Cambridge: Cambridge University Press, 2000.

May, Todd. *The Political Philosophy of Poststructuralist Anarchism*. Pennsylvania: Pennsylvania State University Press, 1994.

McGilvray, James, ed. *The Cambridge Companion to Chomsky*. Cambridge: Cambridge University Press, 2005.

McLaughlin, Paul. *Anarchism and Authority: A Philosophical Introduction to Classical Anarchism*. Farnham: Ashgate, 2007.

McPherson, Thomas. *Political Obligation*. London: Routledge and Kegal Paul, 1967.

Meckled-Garcia, Saladin. *Membership, Obligation and Legitimacy: An Expressivist Account*. Unpublished PhD dissertation, University College London, 1998.

Miller, David. *Anarchism*. London: Dent, 1984.

Mitchell, Barbara. "French Syndicalism: An Experiment in Practical Anarchism." In *Revolutionary Syndicalism: An International Perspective*, edited by Marcel van der Linden and Wayne Thorpe, 25–43. Aldershot: Scolar Press, 1990.

Monatte, Pierre. "Syndicalism: An Advocacy." In *The Anarchist Reader*, edited by George Woodcock, 213–220. Glasgow: Fontana/Collins, 1980.

Munoz-Darde, Véronique. "Decision under Plurality: Rousseau's General Will." Paper presented at the 2001–2002 Centre for Politics Law and Society Seminars, University College London, London, December, 2001.

Newman, Saul. *From Bakunin to Lacan: Anti-authoritarianism and the Dislocation of Power*. Lanham, MD: Lexington Books, 2001.

———. *The Politics of Postanarchism*. Edinburgh: Edinburgh University Press, 2011.

Noys, Benjamin. "Anarchy-without-Anarchism." Formerly No Useless Leniency blog, Accessed June 5, 2009. http://leniency.blogspot.com/2009/06/anarchywithoutanarchism.html. Originally published as Editorial 11, Sans-Philosophie.net (October 2006).

Nozick, Robert. *Anarchy, State and Utopia*. Oxford: Basil Blackwell, 1974.

Olson, Mancur. *The Logic of Collective Action: Public Goods and the Theory of Groups*. Cambridge, MA: Harvard University Press, 1965.

Orwell, George. "Homage to Catalonia." In *Orwell in Spain: The Full Text of Homage to Catalonia with Associated Articles, Reviews and Letters from The*

Complete Works of George Orwell, edited by Peter Hobley Davidson, 28–215. London: Penguin, 2001.

Pateman, Carole. *The Problem of Political Obligation: A Critique of Liberal Theory*, 2nd ed. Oxford: Polity Press, 1985.

Pepper, David. *Communes and the Green Vision: Counterculture, Lifestyle and the New Age*. London: Green Print, 1991.

Pitkin, Hanna. "Obligation and Consent." In *Philosophy, Politics and Society, 4th series*, edited by Peter Laslett, Walter Garrison Runciman, and Quentin Skinner, 45–85. Oxford: Basil Blackwell, 1972.

Plamenatz, John Petrov. *Consent, Freedom and Political Obligation*. Oxford: Oxford University Press, 1968.

Proudhon, Pierre-Joseph. *General Idea of the Revolution in the Nineteenth Century*, translated by John Beverly Robinson. London: Freedom Press, 1923.

Raphael, David Daiches. *Problems of Political Philosophy*. London: Macmillan, 1976.

Rawls, John. "Legal Obligation and the Duty of Fair Play." In *Law and Philosophy*, edited by Sidney Hook, 3–18. New York: New York University Press, 1964.

———. *A Theory of Justice*. Oxford: Oxford University Press, 1971.

———. *Political Liberalism*. New York: Columbia University Press, 1993.

———. "Justice as Fairness." In *John Rawls: Collected Papers*, edited by Samuel Richard Freedman, 47–72. Cambridge, MA: Harvard University Press, 1999.

———. "Kantian Constructivism in Moral Theory." In *John Rawls: Collected Papers*, edited by Samuel Richard Freedman, 303–358. Cambridge, MA: Harvard University Press, 1999.

———. "Justice as Fairness: Political not Metaphysical." In *John Rawls: Collected Papers*, edited by Samuel Richard Freedman, 388–414. Cambridge, MA: Harvard University Press, 1999.

———. *Justice as Fairness: A Restatement*, edited by Erin Kelly. Cambridge, MA: Harvard University Press, 2001.

Raz, Joseph. *The Authority of Law*. Oxford: Oxford University Press, 1979.

———. *The Morality of Freedom*. Oxford: Oxford University Press, 1986.

———. "Introduction." In *Authority*, edited by Joseph Raz, 1–19. Oxford: Basil Blackwell, 1990.

———. "Authority and Justification." In *Authority*, edited by Joseph Raz, 115–141. Oxford: Basil Blackwell, 1990.

Read, Herbert. *The Philosophy of Anarchism*. London: Freedom Press, 1940.

———. *Anarchy and Order: Essays in Politics*. London: Souvenir Press, 1974.

Ripstein, Arthur. "The General Will." In *The Social Contract Theorists: Critical Essays on Hobbes, Locke and Rousseau*, edited by Christopher W. Morris, 219–237. Maryland: Rowman and Littlefield, 1999.

Rousseau, Jean-Jacques. "On Social Contract or Principles of Political Right." In *The Social Contract and Discourses*, edited by George Douglas Howard Cole, John Henry Brumfitt, and John C. Hall. London: Everyman, 1973.

Ryan, Cheyney. "The State and War Making." In *For and Against the State: New Philosophical Readings*, edited by John T. Sanders and Jan Narveson, 217–234. Lanham, MD: Rowman and Littlefield, 1996.

Sanders, John T. "The State of Statelessness." In *For and Against the State: New Philosophical Readings*, edited by John T. Sanders and Jan Narveson, 255–288. Lanham, MD: Rowman and Littlefield, 1996.

Sartwell, Crispin. *Against the State: An Introduction to Anarchist Political Theory*. Albany: State University of New York Press, 2008.

Scanlon, Thomas Michael. "Contractualism and Utilitarianism." In *Utilitarianism and Beyond*, edited by Amartya Sen and Bernard Arthur Owen Williams, 103–128. Cambridge: Cambridge University Press, 1982.

———. *What We Owe to Each Other*. Cambridge, MA, and London: The Belknap Press of Harvard University Press, 1998.

Schmidtz, David. "Justifying the State." In *For and Against the State: New Philosophical Readings*, edited by John T. Sanders and Jan Narveson, 81–97. Lanham, MD: Rowman and Littlefield, 1996.

Senor, Thomas D. "What If There Are No Political Obligations? A Reply to A. J. Simmons." *Philosophy and Public Affairs* 16 (1987): 260–268.

Simmons, Alan John. *Moral Principles and Political Obligations*. Princeton: Princeton University Press, 1979.

———. "The Anarchist Position: A Reply to Klosko and Senor." *Philosophy and Public Affairs* 16 (1987): 269–279.

———. *On the Edge of Anarchy*. Princeton: Princeton University Press, 1993.

———. "Philosophical Anarchism." In *For and Against the State: New Philosophical Readings*, edited by John T. Sanders and Jan Narveson, 19–39. Lanham, MD: Rowman and Littlefield, 1996.

———. "Justification and Legitimacy." *Ethics* 109 (1999): 739–771.

———. "Locke's State of Nature." In *The Social Contract Theorists: Critical Essays on Hobbes, Locke and Rousseau*, edited by Christopher W. Morris, 97–120. Lanham, MD: Rowman and Littlefield, 1999.

———. "Political Consent." In *The Social Contract Theorists: Critical Essays on Hobbes, Locke and Rousseau*, edited by Christopher W. Morris, 121–141. Lanham, MD: Rowman and Littlefield, 1999.

———. *Justification and Legitimacy: Essays on Rights and Obligations*. Cambridge: Cambridge University Press, 2001.

Situationist International (a). "Preliminary Problems in Constructing a Situation." In *Situationist International Anthology*, edited and translated by Ken Knabb. Berkeley: Bureau of Public Secrets, 1989.

Situationist International (b). "Definitions." In *Situationist International Anthology*, edited by Ken Knabb. Berkeley: Bureau of Public Secrets, 1989.

Skinner, Quentin. *The Foundations of Modern Political Thought*. Cambridge: Cambridge University Press, 1978.

Smith, M. B. E. "Is There a Prima Facie Obligation to Obey the Law?" *Yale Law Journal* 82 (1973): 950–976.

Smith, Rogers M. *Stories of Peoplehood. The Politics and Morals of Political Membership*. Cambridge: Cambridge University Press, 2003.

Starhawk. *Truth or Dare: Encounters with Power, Authority and Mystery*. San Francisco: HarperCollins, 1987.

Stirner, Max. *The False Principle of Our Education*, edited by James J. Martin. Colorado Springs: Ralph Myles, 1967.

———. *The Ego and Its Own*, edited by David Leopold. Cambridge: Cambridge University Press, 1995.

Taylor, Michael. *Anarchy and Cooperation*. London: John Wiley and Son, 1976.

———. *Community, Anarchy and Liberty*. Cambridge: Cambridge University Press, 1982.

———. *The Possibility of Cooperation*. Cambridge: Cambridge University Press, 1987.

Utz, Stephen. "Associative Obligations and Law's Authority." *Ratio Juris* 17 (2004): 285–314.

Vernon, Richard. "Obligation by Association? A Reply to John Horton." *Political Studies* 55 (2007): 865–879.

Waldron, Jeremy. "Special Ties and Natural Duties." *Philosophy and Public Affairs* 22 (1993): 3–30.

———. *Liberal Rights: Collected Papers, 1981–1991*. Cambridge and New York: Cambridge University Press, 1993.

Walzer, Michael. *Spheres of Justice: A Defence of Pluralism and Equality*. New York: Basic Books, 1983.

Ward, Colin. *Anarchy in Action*. London: Freedom Press, 1982.

Weber, Max. *The Theory of Social and Economic Organization*. London: William Hodge, 1947.

Wellman, Christopher Heath. "Liberalism, Samaritanism and Political Legitimacy." *Philosophy and Public Affairs* 25 (1996): 211–237.

———. "Associative Allegiances and Political Obligations." *Social Theory and Practice* 23 (1997): 181–204.

Wilkin, Peter. *Noam Chomsky: On Power, Knowledge and Human Nature*. New York: Saint Martin's Press, 1997.

Williams, Sir Bernard Arthur Owen and John Jamieson Carswell Smart. *Utilitarianism: For and Against*. Cambridge: Cambridge University Press, 1973.

Wolff, Jonathan. "What is the Problem of Political Obligation?" *Proceedings of the Aristotelian Society Supplementary* 91 (1990): 153–169.

———. "Review of Chaim Gans, Philosophical Anarchism and Political Disobedience, and George Klosko, Political Obligation and the Theory of Fairness." *Mind* 102 (1993): 500–504.

———. "Political Obligation, Fairness and Independence." *Ratio* 8 (1995): 87–99.

———. "Pluralistic Models of Political Obligation." *Philosophica* 56 (1995): 7–27.

———. *Political Philosophy: An Introduction*. Oxford: Oxford University Press, 1996.

———. "Anarchism and Skepticism." In *For and Against the State: New Philosophical Readings*, edited by John T. Sanders and Jan Narveson, 99–118. Lanham, MD: Rowman and Littlefield, 1996.

Wolff, Robert Paul. *In Defense of Anarchism*. London and New York: Harper and Row, 1970.

Woodcock, George. *Anarchism: A History of Libertarian Ideas and Movements*. Harmondsworth: Penguin, 1975.

Zerzan, John. *Future Primitive: And Other Essays*. New York: Autonomedia, 1994.

Zimmerman, David. "The Force of Hypothetical Commitment." *Ethics* 93 (1983): 467–483.

INDEX

Note: The letter 'n' followed by locators refers to notes.